PRACTICING COGNITIVE THERAPY

NEW DIRECTIONS IN COGNITIVE-BEHAVIOR THERAPY

A Series of Books Edited By

Robert L. Leahy

Cognitive Therapy
Basic Principles and Applications
Robert L. Leahy

Practicing Cognitive Therapy
A Guide to Interventions
Robert L. Leahy, Editor

☙

PRACTICING COGNITIVE THERAPY

A Guide to Interventions

edited by
Robert L. Leahy, Ph.D.

JASON ARONSON INC.
Northvale, New Jersey
London

Production Editor: Elaine Lindenblatt

This book was set in 11 pt. Cheltenham by Alabama Book Composition of Deatsville, Alabama, and printed and bound by Book-mart Press, Inc. of North Bergen, New Jersey.

Library of Congress Cataloging-in-Publication Data

Practicing cognitive therapy : a guide to interventions / edited by
  Robert L. Leahy.
      p.   cm.
  Includes bibliographical references and index.
  ISBN 1-56821-824-9 (hardcover : alk. paper)
  1. Cognitive therapy.   2. Cognitive therapy—Case studies.
I. Leahy, Robert L.
RC489.C63P73   1997
616.89′142–dc21   97-5689

Printed in the United States of America on acid-free paper. For information and catalog write to Jason Aronson Inc., 230 Livingston Street, Northvale, New Jersey 07647-1731. Or visit our website: http://www.aronson.com

to Aaron Beck

CONTENTS

Foreword
Aaron T. Beck   xi

Acknowledgments   xv

Contributors   xix

PART I   TECHNIQUES AND CONCEPTUALIZATION

1. Cognitive Therapy Interventions
    Robert L. Leahy   3

2. The Use of Hypnosis in Cognitive-Developmental
    Therapy
    E. Thomas Dowd   21

3. Case Formulation in Cognitive-Behavioral
    Therapy
    Michael A. Tompkins   37

4. Resistance and Self-Limitation
    Robert L. Leahy   61

PART II   APPLICATIONS TO PSYCHIATRIC DISORDERS

5. Depression
    Ruth L. Greenberg   87

6. Panic Disorder
    Mary Ann Mercier   107

7. Generalized Anxiety Disorder
    John H. Riskind   123

8. Obsessive-Compulsive Disorder
    Stephen J. Holland   151

9. Hypochondriasis
    Mark Sisti   169

10. Post-Traumatic Stress Disorder
    Mervin R. Smucker   193

11. Substance Abuse
    Cory F. Newman   221

PART III   SPECIAL POPULATIONS AND ISSUES

12. Marital Conflict
    Norman Epstein   249

13. Sexual Dysfunction
    Jerry M. Friedman   277

14. Borderline Personality Disorder
     Mary Anne Layden   295

15. Psychotic Disorders
     Rhonda S. Karg and Brad A. Alford   315

16. HIV Risk Behavior
     Scott A. Cohen   341

17. Physical Disability
     Cynthia L. Radnitz and Dennis D. Tirch   373

18. Integrative Cognitive Therapy
     Stephen J. Holland   391

19. Family Therapy
     Frank M. Dattilio   409

20. Reflections on Cognitive Therapy
     Robert L. Leahy   451

Index   467

FOREWORD

Since its development thirty-five years ago, the practice of cognitive therapy has been extended beyond the treatment of depression. It is now effectively used with panic disorder, post-traumatic stress, substance abuse, paranoid delusional disorder, marital conflict, sexual dysfunction, and a range of affective, anxiety, and personality disorders. The present volume marks a significant advance for the application of cognitive therapy, representing state-of-the-art treatment by some of the leading practitioners in the country.

During the early years of the development of cognitive therapy at the University of Pennsylvania, my colleagues and I recognized that depression could often be alleviated by helping the patient identify and test his or her negative interpretations. Initially, we felt both encouraged and cautious in generalizing this approach, realizing that what may work for us may not work for others. In an attempt to provide clinicians with a guide to the treatment of depression, we published *The Cognitive Therapy of Depression* in 1979, a treatment manual

that could be used in outcome studies of the efficacy of
cognitive therapy. Empirical studies of cognitive therapy indicated that depression could be significantly reduced in a
relatively short-term period without medication by the use of
this new therapeutic approach. Consequently, we were encouraged in exploring how this approach might be extended to
other problems. The contributors to this important collection
have advanced the field to these new areas.

Today cognitive therapy has proved to be an effective
treatment for a range of psychiatric disorders that I did not
initially anticipate would be treated with this method. The
creative and productive trainees who initially worked with us
at the Center for Cognitive Therapy are represented in this
current volume. They have taken the approach of cognitive
therapy to new frontiers, analyzing and treating a range of
difficult problems that many have viewed as intractable to
therapeutic interventions.

This volume is a significant and unique contribution that
will be invaluable to clinicians interested in applying cognitive
therapy to a wide range of psychiatric problems. Each chapter
is written by a leading clinician in the field of cognitive therapy
with clear, concise, and effective treatment descriptions and
interventions. The reader will find in each chapter rich clinical
detail that will be valuable to the practitioner interested in
why the method works and how to apply it in the realities of
clinical practice. Clinicians from different orientations will be
especially interested in how some cognitive therapists are able
to utilize other theoretical orientations when working within a
cognitive framework.

Chapter 1, by Robert Leahy, "Cognitive Therapy Interventions," provides a good beginning to understanding the basics
of this approach and can be supplemented by reading Leahy's
Cognitive Therapy: Basic Principles and Applications and Judith
Beck's *Cognitive Therapy: Basics and Beyond*. The current
volume is divided into three important parts: "Techniques and

Conceptualization," "Applications to Psychiatric Disorders," and "Special Populations and Issues." Part I provides the reader with fundamentals, clear descriptions of the techniques used for a variety of disorders, and detailed and creative approaches to case conceptualization and the treatment of resistance. Part II covers most of the affective and anxiety disorders as well as substance abuse. Here the reader will find excellent guides to the treatment of most of the adult disorders seen in clinical practice. Finally, Part III provides excellent descriptions of how cognitive therapy is used with marital conflict, sexual dysfunction, patients with paranoid delusions, individuals with disability, HIV-risk behavior, borderline personality, and other important groups. The range and depth of information contained in this important collection of papers is remarkable.

One cannot help but be impressed with the ability of these clinicians to adapt the cognitive therapy model to the needs of individual patients, recognizing the importance of conceptualizing each individual and to be flexible in the application of technique. By focusing on individuals rather than simply generalizations about groups of people, each author provides the reader with an invaluable understanding of how therapy is individualized.

My hope is that the interested reader will be motivated beyond the reading about cognitive therapy to obtain supervision and training in this approach. There are now numerous excellent workshops offered throughout the world and most major metropolitan areas now have centers or institutes offering supervised instruction in cognitive therapy. The contributors to this volume have provided an important resource for those who wish to learn how to use cognitive therapy.

Finally, it is a personal pleasure for me to see that many of those whom I have trained and worked with have made this approach "their own." They have brought to their work intelligence, humanity, creativity, and insight that make each of them a unique therapist and person. Although all are cognitive therapists, they approach their patients in their own individualized manner, reflecting the fact that this approach is not reducible to a cookbook of techniques, but requires the ability to integrate the work into the individuality of both therapist and patient.

Aaron T. Beck

ACKNOWLEDGMENTS

The idea for this book began as I was working on the text of *Cognitive Therapy: Basic Principles and Applications*. My friend and colleague, Carol Spero, of Cornell University Medical College, suggested that it would be useful to provide lots of concrete case examples so that readers unfamiliar with cognitive therapy could gain some insight into how the therapist actually works. I would like to thank Carol for making this important suggestion.

It is also my distinct pleasure and good fortune to have worked with both Aaron "Tim" Beck, the founder of cognitive therapy, and David D. Burns, the author of the popular books *Feeling Good: The New Mood Therapy* and *The Feeling Good Handbook*. For those of us fortunate enough to have worked closely with Tim, it is fascinating to observe his analytical and penetrating Socratic approach to clinical issues. His contribution to the field of psychopathology is legendary, but it is the result of his continued inquisitiveness, his tendency to take nothing for granted and to recognize that it is our patients who teach us if we are fortunate enough to ask them the right questions. It is not an overstatement to claim that in the last half of the twentieth century the name of Aaron Beck stands preeminent in the field of psychiatry. Indeed, he is the proverbial bridge to the next century.

All of the contributors to this volume have been directly trained by Beck or by his students, so it is with gratitude that we dedicate this book to him.

My colleague and friend David Burns has had an immense effect on my thinking and style of conducting therapy. Millions of readers of his valuable books have been assisted with their problems through David's informative, practical, and good-humored approach to therapy. I was fortunate to have obtained supervision with David, who demonstrated why many of us view him as the master of the techniques of cognitive therapy. David's style is one of energy, enthusiasm, and optimism, and the thousands of people who have attended his workshops in cognitive therapy can attest to the excellent role model he provides.

I would like to thank my colleagues at the American Institute for Cognitive Therapy in New York City. The advantage of working within an institute structure is that we have been able to learn from each other by challenging our own preconceived ideas. Several contributors to this volume are current or past members of the Institute staff. Our weekly case conferences and didactics meetings, and the classes and workshops we offer, have been mutually stimulating. I wish to thank (in alphabetical order) Mudita Bahudar, Scott Cohen, Jerry Friedman, Steve Holland, Lynn Marcinko, Mary Ann Mercier, Laura Oliff, and Mark Sisti for the excellent collegiality that they have provided. In addition, Marge Beddow, our intake coordinator, has been invaluable in helping us bring our theories down to earth.

I know that all the contributors believe, as I do, that our patients teach us about therapy and, if we are smart enough, we will use their ideas and claim them as our own. So often I have sat in sessions and listened to patients describe theories of depression and anxiety and rational responses that I could only wish originated with me. Perhaps every theory deserves an acknowledgement to the unnamed patients—our true collaborators—who help guide us to helping them. I wish to say to all of the people that I have helped: "Thank you for helping me."

To my friends Bill Talmadge and Dave Wolf I owe considerable personal gratitude for their positive encouragement in all of my endeavors. I would also like to thank my wife, Helen, for her support and understanding throughout this project. Her insight, creativity, kindness, and experience have provided me with an invaluable resource—indeed, my greatest resource.

CONTRIBUTORS

Brad A. Alford, Ph.D., ABPP, is associate professor of psychology, University of Scranton. A frequent contributor to the literature on cognitive therapy, Dr. Alford coauthored, with Beck, *The Integrative Power of Cognitive Therapy.*

Aaron T. Beck, M.D., is university professor of psychiatry emeritus at the University of Pennsylvania and president of the Beck Institute for Cognitive Therapy. He is the author of *Cognitive Therapy of Depression* (with Rush, Shaw, and Emery), *Anxiety Disorders and Phobias* (with Emery and Greenberg), and *The Integrative Power of Cognitive Therapy* (with Alford).

Scott A. Cohen, M.A., C.A.C., is in the doctoral program in clinical psychology at New York University, a project coordinator in the HIV Clinical Research Program at Cornell University Medical Center, and a staff therapist at the American Institute for Cognitive Therapy. He is currently researching the psychological impact of body-image changes on people with HIV.

Frank M. Dattilio, Ph.D., ABPP, is clinical associate professor in psychiatry at the Center for Cognitive Therapy at the University of Pennsylvania School of Medicine. His publications include *Cognitive-Behavioral Strategies in Crisis Intervention, Cognitive Therapy with Children and Adolescents: A Casebook for Clinical Practice,* and *Integrative Cases in Marriage and Family Therapy: A Cognitive-Behavioral Perspective.*

E. Thomas Dowd, Ph.D., ABPP, is the president-elect of the International Association for Cognitive Psychotherapy and the editor of the *Journal of Cognitive Psychotherapy.* Dr. Dowd is the coauthor (with Golden and Friedberg) of *Hypnotherapy: A Modern Approach* and *Case Studies in Hypnotherapy.* He is professor and director of counseling psychology at Kent State University.

Norman Epstein, Ph.D., is a professor in the Department of Family Studies at the University of Maryland, College Park. His extensive publications include *Cognitive-Behavioral Marital Therapy* (with Baucom) and *Cognitive-Behavioral Therapy with Families.*

Jerry M. Friedman, Ph.D., is adjunct assistant professor, Department of Psychiatry, SUNY-Stony Brook, a diplomate of the American Board of Sexology, and director of clinical training at the American Institute for Cognitive Therapy in New York City.

Ruth L. Greenberg, Ph.D., is lecturer, Department of Psychiatry, University of Pennsylvania School of Medicine, and for many years has been associated with the Center for Cognitive Therapy. She is the coauthor of *Anxiety Disorders and Phobias.*

Stephen J. Holland, Psy.D., is on the staff of the Columbia Counseling Center in Columbia, Maryland, and has been an adjunct faculty member in the graduate program in clinical psychology at Teachers College, Columbia University. He is currently working on a book on integrative psychotherapy.

Rhonda S. Karg, M.A., is in the doctoral program at Auburn University, Alabama. Her areas of interest include severe and chronic psychopathology, substance abuse, and addiction.

Mary Anne Layden, Ph.D., is Director of Education at the Center for Cognitive Therapy, Department of Psychiatry, University of Pennsylvania School of Medicine. She coauthored *Cognitive Therapy of Borderline Personality* with Newman, Freeman, and Morse.

Robert L. Leahy, Ph.D., is clinical associate professor of psychology, Department of Psychiatry, Cornell University Medical College, and founder and director of the American Institute for Cognitive Therapy in New York City. Dr. Leahy's previous books include *Cognitive Therapy: Basic Principles and Applications, The Child's Construction of Social Inequality,* and *The Development of the Self.* He is Editor-elect of the *Journal of Cognitive Psychotherapy.*

Mary Ann Mercier, Ph.D., has served on the faculty of the Department of Psychiatry of Columbia University. She is a supervising psychologist at the American Institute for Cognitive Therapy in New York City.

Cory F. Newman, Ph.D., is the clinical director, Center for Cognitive Therapy, and assistant professor of psychology, Department of Psychiatry, University of Pennsylvania School of Medicine. He is the coauthor of *Cognitive Therapy of Borderline Personality* (with Layden, Freeman, and Morse) and *Cognitive Therapy of Substance Abuse* (with Beck, Liese, and Wright).

Cynthia L. Radnitz, Ph.D., is an assistant professor of psychology at Fairleigh Dickinson University, Rutherford, New Jersey, and a staff psychologist at the Bronx Veterans Affairs Medical

Center. She is currently working on a book on cognitive-behavioral therapy with persons with disabilities.

John H. Riskind, Ph.D., is professor of psychology at George Mason University; director of training, Greater Washington Institute for Cognitive Therapy; and director of the Center for Cognitive Therapy of Northern Virginia. He recently published *Looming and Loss: Cognitive Mechanisms in Emotion Dysfunction.* Dr. Riskind's research interests include the specific cognitive content of anxiety and depression.

Mark Sisti, Ph.D., has been a staff therapist at Freedom from Fear/Department of Psychiatry, Columbia University, and the American Institute for Cognitive Therapy. He is the director of the Center for Cognitive Therapy in Brooklyn, New York.

Mervin R. Smucker, Ph.D., is the director of the Cognitive Therapy Institute of Milwaukee and clinical associate professor in the Department of Psychiatry of the Medical College of Wisconsin. He is completing a book on imagery rescripting with victims of childhood sexual abuse.

Dennis D. Tirch is a doctoral candidate in the Department of Psychology at Fairleigh Dickinson University.

Michael A. Tompkins, Ph.D., is associate and director of professional training at the Center for Cognitive Therapy, Oakland, California. Dr. Tompkins is writing a book on fear of commitment.

I

TECHNIQUES AND CONCEPTUALIZATION

1

COGNITIVE THERAPY INTERVENTIONS

Robert L. Leahy

Twenty years ago cognitive therapy was identified with the treatment of depression. Aaron Beck's seminal work in the 1970s (*Cognitive Therapy and the Emotional Disorders*, 1976) proposed that depression is the consequence of the conscious negative thoughts of the depressive who viewed self, experience, and the future as bleak and empty. Beck proposed that specific cognitive content characterized each psychiatric disorder and that the goal of therapy was to identify and modify the patient's distortions or biases in thinking and the patient's idiosyncratic cognitive schemata. The cognitive model suggested that neurotic functioning was maintained and aggravated by the self-fulfilling negative information processing of the patient.

In a similar orientation, Abramson and colleagues (1978) advanced the attributional model of depression, which proposed that depression is the consequence of negative explanatory style. Depressive pessimism and low self-esteem were seen as the consequence of attributing negative events to lasting personality traits of the self that led the depressive to generalize failure to other tasks and to future events. Similar to Beck's cognitive model, the attributional model stressed the conscious thought processes of depressed individuals, but focused on the patient's attributions of causality for failure and success and the patient's disposition to generalize negatives across situations and over time.

Beck and colleagues (1979) published the treatment manual *Cognitive Therapy of Depression*, which not only provided clinicians with detailed guidelines for the treatment of patients, but also provided researchers with a standardized treatment protocol for outcome studies of cognitive therapy of depression. Since the publication of the treatment manual, an overwhelming number of outcome studies have demonstrated that cognitive therapy is as effective as medication in the treatment of depression and may have long-term preventative advantages. In addition to the substantial empirical support for the treatment model, the cognitive model of depression has also received wide empirical support, demonstrating that depression is characterized by the distortions in information processing that Beck and his colleagues had first proposed (Dobson 1989, Hollon et al. 1996).

Beck's cognitive model of psychopathology was never limited to a specific diagnostic category. Rather, the cognitive model posits that different psychopathological conditions are characterized by specific cognitive schemata. Thus depression is associated with negative schemata of failure, loss, and emptiness; anxiety is characterized by threat, imminence, and danger; and paranoia is marked by themes of distrust and the fear of domination and manipulation. The schematic model of affective and anxiety disorders has been extended by Beck and Freeman (1990) to the investigation of personality disorders, with each personality disorder characterized by specific schematic content and specific styles of coping.

The implication to draw from this is that there is no *one* cognitive therapy for all psychiatric disorders. For example, the cognitive therapy model and treatment of depression is significantly different from the model and treatment of panic disorder (see the chapters by Greenberg and Mercier, this volume). Similarly, the cognitive therapy of paranoid delusional disorder is different from the cognitive therapy of narcissistic personality disorder (see Alford 1986, Karg and Alford this volume, and Leahy 1995). Cognitive therapy is not a simplistic, reductionistic approach with one size fitting all. Rather, as will become apparent in this book, there are many versions of cognitive therapy for the wide variety of disorders that are treated.

In the "early days" of cognitive therapy—that is, the 1970s— Beck was cautious in generalizing his model to disorders other than depression. In a systematic and intellectually rigorous and honest manner, Beck would limit his claims to demonstrated results. Today, even to Beck's own surprise, I believe, the cognitive therapy approach has been successfully applied to a wide range of problems. Not only have the anxiety disorders been treated effectively with cognitive therapy, but also substance abuse, borderline personality, paranoid delusional disorder, marital conflict, and anger.

BASIC PRINCIPLES OF COGNITIVE THERAPY

The cognitive model emphasizes a number of commonalities. Cognitive therapists generally emphasize current behaviors and thoughts and conscious processing of information. However, we attempt to uncover the patient's underlying assumptions—that is, the patient's rules or values—that predispose him to depression, anxiety, or anger. Typical rules are "I should be perfect," "I should be liked by everyone," "My worth depends on others' approval," "I need to be certain," and "My partner should understand and meet my needs without my having to tell him." It is important for the therapist to recognize that each individual has his or her own idiosyncratic rules or assumptions. The process of inquiry and questioning employed by cognitive therapists is useful in uncovering the underlying assumptions of the patient. For example, I was quite surprised to learn that a severely depressed woman believed that if she could make herself physically still, she could be closer to her father (who had suffered chronic paralysis before he died). We should never assume that we know more than the patient about his underlying beliefs. We only know how to ask the questions that lead to their answers.

Cognitive therapists also focus on the patient's "automatic thoughts" or "cognitive distortions"—that is, the conscious, spontaneous thoughts that are associated with negative affect. It is customary for us to categorize these distortions into their typical bias or illogic. Examples are the following: "She thinks I'm an idiot" (mind reading), "I'll fail the test" (fortune-telling), "I'm a loser" (labeling), "I can't stand it—it's awful" (catastrophizing), "My successes are trivial" (discounting positives), "I fail at everything" (all-or-nothing thinking), "If I fail at this, I'll fail at other things too" (overgeneralizing), and "The divorce was all my fault" (personalizing). It is important to realize that "automatic thoughts" are sometimes true or partly true—maybe that person at the party really does think I'm a loser. Perhaps the use of the word "distortion" is inaccurate—perhaps we should speak of "biases" in thinking. After all, depressed and anxious people are often correct—bad things do happen. Examples of automatic thought distortions are shown in Table 1–1.

But it is the underlying assumptions and the personal schemas (the patient's vulnerabilities) that lead the individual to become depressed. For example, if I have the automatic thought that Susan does not like me, I probably will not become depressed unless I believe that I need Susan's approval

Table 1–1. Cognitive Distortions*

1. **Mind reading:**   You assume that you know what people think without having sufficient evidence of their thoughts. "He thinks I'm a loser."
2. **Fortune-telling:**   You predict the future—that things will get worse or that there is danger ahead. "I'll fail that exam" and "I won't get the job."
3. **Catastrophizing:**   You believe that what has happened or will happen will be so awful and unbearable that you won't be able to stand it. "It would be terrible if I failed."
4. **Labeling:**   You assign global negative traits to yourself and others. "I'm undesirable" or "He's a rotten person."
5. **Discounting positives:**   You claim that the positives that you or others attain are trivial."That's what wives are supposed to do, so it doesn't count when she's nice to me." "Those successes were easy, so they don't matter."
6. **Negative filter:**   You focus almost exclusively on the negatives and seldom notice the positives."Look at all the people who don't like me."
7. **Overgeneralizing:**   You perceive a global pattern of negatives on the basis of a single incident. "This generally happens to me. I seem to fail at a lot of things."
8. **Dichotomous thinking:**   You view events, or people, in all-or-nothing terms. "I get rejected by everyone" or "It was a waste of time."
9. **Shoulds:**   You interpret events in terms of how things should be rather than simply focusing on what is. "I should do well. If I don't, then I'm a failure."
10. **Personalizing:**   You attribute a disproportionate amount of the blame to yourself for negative events and fail to see that certain events are also caused by others. "The marriage ended because I failed."

11. **Blaming:**   You focus on the other person as the source of your negative feelings and you refuse to take responsibility for changing yourself. "She's to blame for the way I feel now" or "My parents caused all my problems."

12. **Unfair comparisons:**   You interpret events in terms of standards that are unrealistic—for example, you focus primarily on others who do better than you and find yourself inferior in the comparison. "She's more successful than I am" or "Others did better than I did on the test."

13. **Regret orientation:**   You focus on the idea that you could have done better in the past rather than on what you can do better now. "I could have had a better job if I had tried" or "I shouldn't have said that."

14. **What if?**   You keep asking a series of questions about "What if" something happens, and fail to be satisfied with any of the answers. "Yeah, but what if I get anxious? Or what if I can't catch my breath?"

15. **Emotional reasoning:**   You let your feelings guide your interpretation of reality—for example, "I feel depressed, therefore my marriage is not working out."

16. **Inability to disconfirm:**   You reject any evidence or arguments that might contradict your negative thoughts. For example, when you have the thought "I'm unlovable," you reject as irrelevant any evidence that people like you. Consequently, your thought cannot be refuted. "That's not the real issue. There are deeper problems. There are other factors."

17. **Judgment focus:**   You view yourself, others, and events in terms of evaluations of good-bad or superior-inferior, rather than simply describing, accepting, or understanding. You are continually measuring yourself and others according to arbitrary standards, finding that you and others fall short. You are focused on the judgments of others as well as your own judgments of

yourself. "I didn't perform well in college" or "If I take up tennis, I won't do well," or "Look how successful she is. I'm not successful."

*From Leahy 1996. Copyright © 1996 by Jason Aronson Inc., and reprinted by permission.

---

or unless it activates my underlying schema (or belief) that I am a loser and unlovable. The cognitive therapist differs from the behavioral therapist in the sense that the cognitive therapist is interested in "why" negative events have such profound meanings for the patient. For example, although the breakup in a relationship often results in sadness for many people, we differ in the meaning we attach to it. The patient's schemas (or themes of vulnerability) might lead him or her to ascribe any number of meanings to a breakup, such as abandonment, unworthiness, helplessness, emptiness, or unlovability. It might even activate positive schemas, such as liberation or autonomy. The relationship between schemas, assumptions, and automatic thoughts is illustrated in Table 1–2.

Throughout this book you will notice that a variety of therapists use similar techniques. Cognitive therapists draw on behavioral therapy, using exposure to feared stimuli, modeling and behavioral rehearsal, relaxation training, activity scheduling, graded task assignments, assertiveness training, communication and listening skills, and self-reinforcement. The cognitive therapist has a set of powerful techniques drawn from the cognitive model, including thought monitoring, categorizing the negative thoughts, vertical descent, identifying the underlying assumptions and schemas, the double standard technique, examining the costs and benefits of a belief, role-playing with the therapist, acting in opposition to the thought, and developing coping statements and new adaptive assumptions. Examples of these behavioral and cognitive techniques are shown in Table 1–3 below.

Table 1–2. Relationships Among Schemas, Assumptions, and Automatic Thoughts

Schema	Assumption	Automatic Thoughts
Unlovable	If I impress people, they will like me. If people get to know me, they'll think I'm a loser.	He doesn't like me. I'll be rejected. I'm boring.
Helpless	If I don't have someone to help me, then I won't survive. I won't be able to support myself.	I can't do anything right. If I make a mistake, things will fall apart.
Abandonment	If I don't get constant reassurance, then I'll be abandoned. It's not possible to be happy on my own.	He's going to leave me. It's awful to be alone. I'll always be alone. I must be a loser.

Table 1–3. Behavioral and Cognitive Techniques

Behavioral Techniques	Examples
Behavioral targets	Specific behaviors that the patient wishes to modify. Examples: the number of minutes of exercise, checking, hand washing, homework done.
Exposure	Confronting a feared stimulus. Example: The obsessive-compulsive patient is asked to

	refrain from washing his hands after he places them in dirty water.
Response/stimulus hierarchy	A list of most to least feared responses or situations to be used in exposure. Example: The patient and therapist make a list of situations or behaviors that the patient fears, ranking them from least to most feared. The patient afraid of elevators ranks "thinking of an elevator" as least feared and "riding on the elevator to the top of the World Trade Center" as most feared.
Modeling	Therapist demonstrates the desired response. Example: The therapist demonstrates in session an appropriate assertive response that the patient then imitates.
Imitation	Patient copies the therapist's response. Example: The patient "copies" and enacts the behavior that he observes in another person.
Behavioral rehearsal	Patient enacts the behavior that he plans to conduct outside of therapy. Example: The patient demonstrates in session how he would assert himself with his boss.
Relaxation training	Relaxing different muscle groups in sequence; imagining relaxing images; practicing slow breathing. Example: The therapist guides the patient through progressively

	tensing and relaxing different muscle groups, finishing with an image of a relaxing scene.
Activity scheduling	Tracking activities throughout the day and rating them for pleasure, mastery, anxiety, sadness, fear, or other feelings or sensations. Example: The patient uses an hourly schedule to track his moods and activities.
Graded task assignments	Planning and enacting behaviors that are expected to produce pleasure or mastery. Often these behaviors are chosen from a reward menu that the patient and therapist construct. Example: The patient lists behaviors that he used to engage in before he was depressed and agrees to assign these activities to himself beginning with the least difficult and progressing to the more difficult.
Assertiveness training	Instruction in how to make legitimate requests that will enhance one's pleasure or self-esteem. Example: The therapist instructs the patient in how to make responsible requests for changes in the behavior in someone else. The patient then practices assertive responses outside of sessions.
Communication training	Instruction in how to use editing and clear "I statements" when speaking to others. Example: The therapist

	instructs the patient in non-aggressive communication, with the emphasis on editing, non-accusatory speech, "I statements," and statements of preferences that the patient has.
Active listening training	Instruction in how to use inquiry, rephrasing, empathizing, and validating. Example: The patient learns how to ask others for more information about their feelings and thoughts (inquiry), the patient paraphrases what he hears ("You are saying that . . . "), the patient indicates the feeling the other person has ("You're feeling angry . . . "), and the patient tries to find some truth in what the other person is saying ("I can see why you would say that because . . .").
Self-reward	Using self-praise or concrete reinforcements to the self to increase desirable behaviors. Example: The patient may reward himself by tangible positive consequences (food, a movie, a present, or a pleasant behavior) or by positive self-statements ("I'm proud of myself for trying").

Cognitive Techniques

Identify the negative thoughts.	The patient monitors the thoughts that are associated with

	depression, anxiety, and anger. Example: The patient self-monitors what he is thinking when he feels worse. "When I felt anxious I was thinking that I was going to fail."
Rate the degree of belief in the thought and the degree of emotion associated with the thought.	After the patient identifies his negative feelings (e.g., sad, angry, frustrated), he indicates which thoughts are associated with each feeling. He then rates (from zero to 100) how "sad" he feels and how much he believes his negative thought. Example: "I felt 85% sad when I thought 'I'll never find someone who will love me.' I believed that thought 90%."
Categorize the negative thought.	The patient classifies the thought according to the thinking (cognitive) distortion exemplified by the thought. Examples of these distortions are fortune-telling, mind reading, mislabeling, catastrophizing, personalizing, all-or-nothing thinking, discounting the positives, and overgeneralizing.
What would it mean if the thought were true? (Vertical descent)	The therapist asks, "If [your thought] is true, what would that mean to you? Why would that be a problem? What would happen?" These questions are asked for each answer given. For example, "If you got rejected at the party, you

said that would mean you're not attractive. What would happen if you were not attractive?"

What is the underlying assumption?	The therapist examines the patient's underlying rules. For example, the patient's "if-then" or "should" statements. For example, "If someone doesn't like me, then it means I'm unlovable."
What are the costs and benefits of the thought?	The therapist asks the patient to list all the advantages and disadvantages to himself (herself) of the thought and to divide 100 points between the advantages and disadvantages. This addresses the patient's motivation to change the thought.
What is the evidence?	The patient lists the evidence supporting and refuting his thought. How does the evidence weigh out? What is the quality of the evidence?
Place the event in perspective.	The patient is asked to examine the event along a continuum, from zero to 100. What will actually happen if the event does occur? What could be worse, better, the same in consequence? What would you still be able to do even if the event does occur?
Double-standard	The therapist asks the patient, "Would you apply the same standard to others? Why (why not)?"

Argue back at the thought.	The therapist and the patient take roles in which the patient is asked to argue against his negative thinking. Roles can be switched.
Logical analysis	Is the patient drawing conclusions that are unwarranted? For example, "If I fail on the exam, then I'm a failure"?
Lack of information	Does the patient have all the information necessary to draw the conclusions? For example, the patient notices a lump in her breast and concludes it is cancer. Can a doctor provide her with more (accurate) information?
Is there an alternative explanation?	The patient is asked to examine as many alternative causes and consequences as possible, especially less negative alternatives.
Is there a problem to be solved?	Can the patient approach his thought as a problem solver? What is the problem; what would the goal be; what resources, information, skills, and actions are relevant? What plans can the patient think of to carry out to solve the problem?
Acceptance	Is there a reality that the patient can learn to accept, rather than trying to fix or struggle with it?

Although most of the chapters in this book are based on derivations of Beck's work, the authors draw from other cognitive and behavioral models as well as "theoretically integrative" work. Behavioral models include the work of Foa, Lazarus, Lewinsohn, Bandura, O'Leary, Jacobson, and Rehm. Cognitive and cognitive-behavioral models include the work of Ellis, Burns, Barlow, Linehan, Mahoney, and Meichenbaum. Theoretical integration is reflected in the chapter by Holland on the cognitive and psychoanalytic interface and my chapter on resistance in which I attempt to integrate cognitive theory with social psychology, microeconomic theory, and Piagetian structuralism.

The experienced cognitive therapist does not approach every patient with the same bag of tricks. The therapist attempts to develop a case conceptualization, considering the patient's idiosyncratic cognitive schemata, coping style, and interpersonal reality (see Tompkins, this volume; Persons 1989). The early criticisms of cognitive therapy as lacking a model of resistance have been addressed by several authors in evaluating personality disorders (Beck and Freeman 1990) and in examining strategies of self-limitation (Leahy 1996; also, this volume). Moreover, cognitive therapists integrate behavioral techniques, hypnosis, and imagery induction and restructuring in order to activate cognitive schemata and modify thinking and affect (see Dowd, Mercier, Riskind, and Smucker, this volume). In fact, it is difficult to imagine conducting cognitive therapy without employing behavioral techniques, whether to activate the depressed patient (Greenberg), utilize exposure techniques for panic or obsessive-compulsive disorder (Mercier and Holland), or modify interaction, sexual, or communication patterns in couples (Epstein and Friedman).

Cognitive therapy is not an easy therapy to employ. The therapist must be active, engaging, informed, and effective. I am often struck by the surprise that some trainees exhibit when they observe me engaging in a cognitive-therapy dialogue. From my own experience receiving excellent supervision from David Burns, I recall wondering how I would ever know what questions to ask the patient. Obviously, there is no substitute for extensive supervision and training, but the therapist new to cognitive therapy can quickly learn some of the basic techniques and questions and develop from there. I know that in the first few months when I was doing cognitive therapy, I used Beck's treatment manual on depression as a roadmap for every session. Therapists develop their own style of conducting therapy. I know that the contributors to this volume have different styles and conceptualizations of the therapeutic process. They are all effective and all different. The new therapist will find a style and method that fits his or her personality. I tell trainees that "this is the way that I do it, but there may be other ways that fit you better."

It would be too narrow to think that there is only one cognitive therapy. All of us are indebted—and most of us use—the substantial contributions of other cognitive-behavioral therapists, such as Albert Ellis, David Barlow, Peter Lewinsohn, Arnold Lazarus, and Neil Jacobson. Moreover, many cognitive therapists integrate the work of other psychological models into their work. For example, Guidanno and Liotti have enriched all of our work with difficult patients by helping us understand how Bowlby's work on attachment is so central to understanding the patient's schemata and resistance to change. Cognitive-behavioral therapy advances itself, not through intellectual territoriality or elitism, but by integrating the important work of other theoretical and treatment models. But it is also interesting to note that when psychologists are asked which model they try to integrate into their approach, the cognitive model is the most frequently mentioned (Alford and Beck 1997, Alford and Norcross 1991).

The contributors to this casebook are some of the leading cognitive therapists in the country. Many of them have been trained directly by Beck or by Beck's students. When I attended a dinner in honor of Beck, I was struck by the fact that Beck has had such a lasting influence on the many people who worked with him. Many of us have been scattered across a variety of continents, yet we have managed to maintain and broaden our contacts with each other over the years.

Many of us are involved in training therapists in the cognitive model. Today most major cities in the United States and many major cities in the world (e.g., London, Tokyo, Rome) have centers or institutes where people can obtain training. Several authors of this casebook are actively working at either the Center for Cognitive Therapy at the University of Pennsylvania or the American Institute for Cognitive Therapy in New York City. We hope that this book, as well as my text *Cognitive Therapy: Basic Principles and Applications*, will motivate the reader to integrate cognitive therapy into his or her practice.

REFERENCES

Abramson, L. Y., Seligman, M. E. P., and Teasdale, J. D. (1978). Learned helplessness in humans: critique and reformulation. *Journal of Abnormal Psychology* 87:102–109.

Alford, B. A. (1986). Behavioral treatment of schizophrenic delusions: a single-case experimental analysis. *Behavior Therapy* 17:637–644.

Alford, B. A., and Beck, A. T. (1997). *Cognitive Therapy: An Integration of Current Theory and Therapy*. New York: Guilford.

Alford, B. A., and Norcross, J. C. (1991). Cognitive therapy as integrative therapy. *Journal of Psychotherapy Integration* 1(3):175–190.

Beck, A. T. (1976). *Cognitive Therapy and the Emotional Disorders*. New York: International Universities Press.

Beck, A. T., and Freeman, A. (1990). *Cognitive Therapy of Personality Disorders*. New York: Guilford.

Beck, A.T., Rush, A. J., Shaw, B. F., and Emery, G. (1979). *Cognitive Therapy of Depression*. New York: Guilford.

Dobson, K. S. (1989). A meta-analysis of the efficacy of cognitive therapy of depression. *Journal of Consulting and Clinical Psychology* 57:414–419.

Hollon, S. D., DeRubeis, R. J., and Evans, M. D. (1996) Cognitive therapy in the treatment and prevention of depression. In *Frontiers of Cognitive Therapy*, ed. P. M. Salkovskis, pp. 293–317. New York: Guilford.

Leahy, R. L. (1995). Cognitive development and cognitive therapy. *Journal of Cognitive Psychotherapy: An International Quarterly* 9:173–184.

—————— (1996). *Cognitive Therapy: Basic Principles and Applications.* Northvale, NJ: Jason Aronson.

Persons, J. (1989). *Cognitive Therapy in Practice: A Case Formulation Approach.* New York: Norton.

2

THE USE OF HYPNOSIS IN COGNITIVE-DEVELOPMENTAL THERAPY

E. Thomas Dowd

Cognitive therapy, although relatively new, has already undergone significant development. Originally developed independently by Albert Ellis, Aaron Beck, and Donald Meichenbaum as a way of identifying and changing distorted thinking patterns that were thought to underlie psychological disorders, it has evolved into a highly flexible and multifaceted collection of treatment procedures. While Ellis, Beck, and Meichenbaum each had their own idiosyncratic methods, probably based on their own personality style as much as on their respective theories, their approaches share four underlying assumptions. First, they assumed that psychological disorders were associated with a set of negative cognitions regarding abilities, self-worth, or behavior. These cognitions, while not always present, would be activated under stress-producing situations (Beck 1987). Second, these negative cognitions were assumed to be relatively *ahistorical* in nature. It was considered more important what individuals thought or said to themselves now, rather than in the past. Likewise, little or no attention was paid to *why* these negative cognitions were present; it was enough to concentrate on changing them at this time. If that were done, emotional relief would be obtained. Third, while each system emphasized somewhat different procedures, there was an underlying emphasis on counteracting the negative cognitions. Each theorist used a somewhat different counteracting process, again likely based as much on personality style as theory, with Ellis relying on direct disputation, Beck using the presentation of contradictory evidence, and Meichenbaum developing new coping strategies. Fourth, there was an assumption that the negative cognitions were accessible to consciousness, at least with help from the therapist. The concept of inaccessible cognitions (i.e., repression) had earlier been discarded by the behavior therapy precursors to cognitive therapy. It can be seen that some of these assumptions represent a reaction against psychoanalytic thinking.

Dowd (in press) has recently described the evolution of the cognitive therapies and noted the return of certain psychodynamic concepts that had hitherto been banished from the cognitive and behavior therapy literature. These include the continued influence of past events, the important role in human development played by primary caregivers (e.g., parents), the structural nature of human knowledge in the development of core schemata, and the role of tacit knowledge in human cognition. Dowd and Courchaine (1996) have described the operation of tacit knowledge and implicit learning and their implications for the practice of cognitive therapy. Taken together, these phenomena suggest the importance, previously ignored, of the progressive structural development of human cognition and knowing processes—the cognitive-developmental model.

In the cognitive-developmental approach, cognitive activity is seen as progressively elaborated and differentiated by the repeated interaction of individuals with their environment over time. These interactions result in the formation of organized knowledge structures, called schemata or schemas, tacit rules that organize and provide meaning and a sense of consistency to ongoing experience (Dowd and Pace 1989). Schemata are formed by initial interactions with important people and events early in life. Once formed, they are arranged in a hierarchical order from the highly concrete to the highly abstract and generally act to constrain and channel incoming sensory data in a manner consistent with the preexisting schema. Occasionally, however, the incoming data are so powerful and so schema-discrepant that schema modification is virtually forced, resulting in profound psychological change and occasionally disorganization. It should be noted that these concepts are quite consistent with the assimilation–accommodation concept of Jean Piaget (Rosen 1989) as well as the personal cognitive organization (PC Org) of Vittorio Guidano (1987).

It can be seen that schemata or organizing cognitive rules are powerful governing agents of human activity. As they become progressively more organized and structurally differentiated, they increasingly constrain the interpretation of new sensory data in consonance with preexisting cognitive categories (Dowd and Courchaine 1996), thus resulting in the truism that people tend to interpret new events in light of what they already know and believe. Indeed, they may not even notice schema-disconfirming events at all! In reciprocal fashion, these interpretations provide new data supporting the existing schema. Only with repeated and massive disconfirmations can the existing cognitive structure be successfully challenged, and then often at the cost of significant psychological disruption. Thus schemata act as conservative cognitive structures, preserving an ongoing sense of meaning and personal identity.

Much, perhaps most, cognitive activity is tacit or implicit in nature (Dowd and Courchaine 1996) rather than explicit, and the former is often richer and more elaborate. As a result, it cannot be readily accessed, even with the help of a therapist, by verbal means. Verbal psychotherapies were developed largely for use with explicit knowledge and it is with that kind of knowledge they work best. Tacit knowledge, by contrast, being less accessible, is also less easily modified. These two knowing processes should not be seen as polarities, however, but as complementary processes in constant interaction. Both are elaborated and differentiated over the life span.

Several implications result from the above discussion. First, modification of tacit knowledge and implicit learning may best be accomplished by other than verbal means. Nonverbal therapies include imagery work, emotional processing, body therapies, and hypnotic (counter)conditioning. Such tacit knowledge may actually be richer and more elaborated than explicit knowledge, as well as less accessible. It follows that these nonverbal techniques may be especially important in cognitive-developmental therapy.

Second, resistance, far from being an annoying by-product of human psychological activity, may represent a necessary aspect of cognitive functioning. Dowd (1993a) has discussed evidence indicating that reactance, a form of resistance, is an individual-difference variable-mediating therapeutic process and outcome. Reactant individuals are more likely to be autonomous, independent, and dominant and therefore more difficult to engage in therapy. They may resist following therapist directives. They may miss more sessions and terminate therapy earlier. Resistance, however, may be necessary to protect the cognitive system from too-rapid change, resulting in psychological disorganization and loss of core identity and self-concept structures. The therapeutic truism that advocated a slow and measured approach to significant psychological change was likely well founded. Because of this cognitive resistance, small and repetitive steps may be more efficacious than large interventions delivered once. The Erick-

sonian hypnotherapists, especially, have argued that hypnotherapeutic methods are particularly useful in bypassing,
discharging, or displacing resistance (Dowd 1993b).

Third, interventions that directly address core schemata of
identity, self-concept, and tacit rules may be more effective
than those that address more peripheral behaviors and attitudes. There are two problems here, however: identifying the
core schemata and developing interventions to modify them.
This chapter focuses on hypnotherapeutic methods for addressing both issues.

THE IDENTIFICATION OF CORE COGNITIVE SCHEMATA

Schemata by their very definition are tacit cognitive constructs and therefore not easily accessible to consciousness,
even with therapist assistance. Indeed, client resistance to
significant schema modification, in order to protect core
identity structures, generally prevents their easy detection.
Nevertheless, with persistence and client cooperation schemata can be identified. One particularly useful tool is the
Schema Questionnaire developed by Jeffrey Young (1990).
Young has identified fifteen "Early Maladaptive Schemas" in
four domains: autonomy, connectedness, worthiness, and limits and standards. Furthermore, Young has identified three
schema processes: schema maintenance, schema avoidance,
and schema compensation. For example, a borderline client
might have a schema of abandonment/loss (the fear that one
will lose significant others and be emotionally isolated), which
is part of the connectedness domain. This schema might be
maintained by selecting friends who are likely to abandon her,
may be *avoided* by carefully limiting her friendship circle, and
compensated for by placing excessive relationship demands on
her existing friends.

In addition to the Schema Questionnaire, there are other

methods that the cognitive developmental hypnotherapist might use to detect tacit schemata. One is the use of guided imagery while in a hypnotic trance. For example, a client who seems to possess a social undesirability schema (in the worthiness domain) may be asked to imagine himself at a social gathering and attempting to engage in conversations with strangers. Generally, the higher level of affect that is generated, the more likely it is that a core schema has been tapped (Young 1990). Thus, schemas may be arranged in a hierarchical order by the amount of affect observed during hypnotic imagery.

Golden and Friedberg (1986) have described the use of a related technique, called *evocative imagery*, in hypnotherapy. The client is asked to visualize a personally stressful situation and to focus on the thoughts and feelings associated with it. For example, the visualization of a stressful business situation might trigger thoughts and feelings of an incompetence/failure schema (in the worthiness domain). Unlike guided imagery, evocative imagery is not directed by the therapist.

Another hypnotic technique to identify and validate early maladaptive schemas is age regression. Because age regression is most useful with more hypnotizable clients, it may not be appropriate for everyone. However, clients who are not highly hypnotizable may benefit from a spontaneous reviewal of past memories while in a trance. For example, a client who appears to have a vulnerability to harm and illness schema (in the autonomy domain) may be progressively age-regressed to a time when she felt especially vulnerable and then asked to describe the situation in detail, thus generating material to validate the therapist's hypothesis. In a review of past events, the therapist may simply ask the client, while in a trance, to describe certain past events or people that the therapist thinks have played an important role in the client's life. The similarity to free association should be obvious. Often, the identification of these early events may be sufficient to begin a spontaneous schema-reevaluation process. Most commonly, however, the modification of these early schemas will require repeated comparison with current reality as the client examines the evidence for and against the schema.

THE MODIFICATION OF CORE COGNITIVE SCHEMATA

Both Freeman and colleagues (1990) and Young (1990) have described several interventions for changing underlying assumptions and core schemata. Hypnotherapeutic methods may be especially useful for some of them. One important class of methods is mental imagery techniques (Freeman et al. 1990). These, along with their hypnotherapeutic adaptations, are discussed below.

Replacement and Coping Imagery

Many distressed clients experience automatic dysfunctional images in problematic situations. Often these images are so fleeting that clients are hardly aware of them. Hypnosis is an ideal vehicle for eliciting and replacing these images. For example, a client with a fear of public speaking could be asked, while in a trance, to imagine herself speaking before an assembly along with the accompanying fear and then asked to replace that image with one in which she is speaking slowly and clearly and with the fear gradually diminishing. Replacement and coping imagery may be even more tightly structured by the technique known as age progression. Whereas age regression brings the client to a past event, age progression brings the client to a future hypothesized or actual event. The client may be instructed while in a trance to project herself into a public speaking situation that she knows will occur in the near future and to imagine herself feeling confident, speaking clearly, and being effective. The hypnotherapist can guide the coping image for the client, in this manner:

> I'd like you to imagine yourself walking slowly to the podium, feeling confident and in charge. You know that you know the material, don't you? And you can see the audience's eagerness to hear you. As you begin to speak, you feel a momentary anxiety—but you remind yourself that you know the topic. You also remind yourself to speak unusually slowly and pause frequently, knowing that the audience will understand you better that way. And the more you speak, the more confident you feel—and the more confident you feel, the better you speak and you can feel your anxiety slowly diminish.

Desensitization and Flooding Imagery

Systematic desensitization and flooding are in many ways hypnotic techniques. Not only is the client relaxed, in many instances actually in a trance, but the hierarchies designed and implemented by the therapist are very similar to hypnotic routines. They differ mainly in the rationales used and in the more limited goals of desensitization and flooding. To adapt these techniques to hypnosis, it is only necessary to redefine the procedure as hypnotic and suggest anxiety reduction in a more deliberate fashion.

Cognitive Rehearsal

Here the client imagines himself behaving in a different, more adaptive, manner of his choosing. For example, he may wish to be more direct in asking a woman for a date. After identifying the new behavior he wishes to exhibit, the client, in a hypnotic trance, can imagine himself behaving that way in asking for a date. Furthermore, he can be asked by the hypnotherapist to observe and identify the feelings that accompany this new behavior and to compare it to usual feelings in dating situations. The hypnotic routine might be structured like this:

> Imagine yourself walking up to Karen, standing up straight and looking her in the eye, and asking her to go to a dance Saturday night. Observe her reaction and notice how you feel. Now replay that situation in your mind, with whatever variations you want to make, until you feel confident you have it right.

Young (1990) has described four types of interventions for changing schemas: emotive techniques, interpersonal techniques, cognitive techniques, and behavioral techniques. Hypnotherapy can be especially useful in the first area; indeed, Young states that schema-focused cognitive therapy is not only characterized by more focus on childhood origins of problems, but also makes more use of emotive techniques.

Creating Imaginary Dialogues

This technique can be used to create a dialogue with a significant person who was present earlier in the client's life. Young (1990) recommends that the dialogue be conducted with the client's eyes closed; it is just a short step to conducting the dialogue while in a hypnotic trance. Clients can play either themselves or the significant person, or alternate between the two, or the therapist might role-play one of the two individuals. The client is asked to respond as she would have liked to, not as she actually did. For example, I once had a client whose grandfather (an important person in her life) had died suddenly before she had a chance to say goodbye to him. While in a trance, she was able to imagine his presence and say goodbye to him in a way she had not done earlier. The hypnotic routine went something like this:

Now imagine your grandfather standing before you as he did when he was alive. You know he's there but you also know he won't be there much longer. Tell him how important he has been to you, how much you love him, and how much you (will) miss him.

After several repetitions of this routine or variations of it, the client reported feeling much relieved and was able finally to put a closure to this significant death.

Emotional Catharsis

Gestalt therapists have long stressed the importance of discharging affect to reduce the distress due to unfinished emotional business. However, expression of this often negative affect may be partially blocked by cultural and familial strictures against the expression of strong affect. Hypnosis, by lowering resistance to such expression, may allow the client to express what has hitherto not been allowed. For example, a client who has unexpressed (and unresolved) anger toward his father may be encouraged to talk to his father while in a trance. Although hypnotic catharsis can lead to temporary emotional relief, it is important that there be subsequent discussion of the current reality of that anger and that behavioral steps toward resolution of it be taken as well, so that the expression of negative affect is not reinforced. Encouragement of the expression of negative affect may simply lead to a future *increase* of it by the reinforcement principle rather than a *reduction* of it by the cathartic principle.

Age Regression and Review of Past Memories

Age regression can also be used to modify core cognitive schemata as well as identify them. As mentioned earlier, core cognitive schemata identified by age regression can then be reevaluated nonhypnotically in the light of current conditions and reality. However, a reevaluation of a core schemata can also be initiated hypnotically. Dowd (1992) has provided an example of how this might be done. He used hypnotherapy with a client who had an excessive fear of the dark and was able, through age regression, to trace the fear back to her third year by asking her to stop counting backwards when she reached a month and year which "has special significance for your problem." He then used the following hypnotic routine to restructure her childhood thoughts and feelings in an adult context:

> Young people, because they are small and weak, feel helpless and scared because bigger people seem so much more powerful . . . perhaps you feel that way too. . . . As we grow older we become bigger, stronger, and more powerful. Often, however, the old feelings of fear remain; perhaps you feel that way too. We sometimes don't realize, do we, that we eventually become the person who once seemed so big and so important to us. We still feel like the frightened, helpless child . . . but we need not fear as adults the things we feared as children.

This last sentence was used like a refrain as this hypnotic routine was repeated and progressively elaborated.

Other examples of the use of age regression and the hypnotic review of past memories can be found in Dowd (1996) and Smith (1996). In the former case, an Erickson-like hypnotic routine was used to restructure tacit cognitions about parental relationships and enable the client to engage in new implicit learning about his enuretic problem. In the latter case, age regression was used to elicit early memories about several traumatic events that were then used nonhypnotically to evaluate a powerful cognitive schema.

Modifying Past Memories

There has been a great deal of recent controversy about the veridicality of past memories, especially in the area of sexual abuse. It is likely, however, that memories do change over time, often in a self-enhancing direction, although it is not necessarily clear which memories change and which don't. One need only recall the war veterans whose elaborated memories of war stories over the years place themselves increasingly at the center of the action. Fleming and colleagues (1992) have presented evidence indicating that three variables manipulate the subjective experience of memory: context, attention, and the number of times an episode is recalled. *Context* indicates that clients may learn or remember better in situations that are similar to those in which the original learning took place. *Attention* indicates that memory is different if the attention was divided rather than focused. *Number of times an event is recalled* indicates that events more often recalled were remembered less accurately but with more familiarity, elaboration, and certainty.

There are important implications for the practice of cognitive-developmental hypnotherapy. First, by using age regression to bring clients back to an earlier time, the recall of significant information may be enhanced by contextual similarity. Furthermore, new learning may be enhanced as well. Second, using divided attention, as is commonly done in Ericksonian hypnotherapy, may result in lowered resistance, since clients may attribute the source of the hypnotic message to themselves rather than to the therapist. Research has also shown that hypnosis may influence the recall of experimenter-delivered messages, so that they are experienced more like remembered events, a phenomenon that was especially pronounced for the more hypnotizable subjects. Third, the "repetition principle" may be especially important, since clients' memories may be shaped by therapists using repeated recall, in a hypnotic trance, of significant events. For example, a client who remembers a rape as one for which she was responsible or contributing by negligence may be assisted in reducing her self-blame by the repeated recall of the event during which the therapist shapes the guided recall to suggest that perhaps she really wasn't responsible for it and didn't contribute to it. This technique already appears to underlie much psychotherapy and even ordinary conversations (not always in a positive direction!) but may be enhanced by the deliberate use of hypnotic suggestions to shape memory in psychologically healthy ways. As Alloy and Abramson (1988) have noted, depressives may perceive situations more realistically than nondepressives, and self-enhancing cognitive biases may be associated with less depression. A little cognitive distortion may be healthy!

Hypnotic (Counter)conditioning

Conditioning, or counterconditioning, has been a part of the therapeutic armamentarium for a long time. Originally developed as a behavioral technique, it entered the cognitive therapy literature as *covert sensitization and conditioning* (Cautela 1975). The essence of the technique is that a problematic situation is covertly paired with an incompatible response, usually relaxation. In its hypnotherapeutic variant, a psychologically distressing event or situation identified earlier is evoked while the client is in a trance and is then paired with the relaxation associated with the trance. Although a hypnotic trance does not necessitate relaxation, in hypnotic counterconditioning it is especially important to ensure that the client is deeply relaxed before the problem image is recalled. For example, a client troubled by an overly aggressive boss might be asked to recall an image of his boss shouting at him for a mistake, then asked to relax deeper into a trance as he allows the image to develop in his mind. Developmentally, this image might be further linked with earlier possible difficulties with an aggressive parent or other significant caregiver. This approach, along with many standard images, is fully described in Kroger and Fetzler (1976).

A CAVEAT

One further point must be made. The examples in this chapter and other writings in hypnotherapy can give the reader the impression that one-session hypnosis interventions are sufficient to solve the client's problem. As in all other psychotherapeutic interventions, hypnotherapy requires repetition across several, perhaps many, sessions. Strongly entrenched cognitive schemata do not yield easily to any interventions! Therefore, it is important that the hypnotherapist, especially one following a cognitive-developmental approach, be prepared to use the same routines in successive interviews, varying them as necessary to avoid boredom on the part of both client and therapist.

Hypnosis has much to offer to cognitive-developmental hypnotherapy. Potentially, it can help access core tacit schemata by lowering or displacing resistance. It can help clients to retrieve and rework early memories that still play a powerful role in shaping current cognitions and behaviors. It can help provide powerful challenges to existing cognitive schemata in ways that lower expressed resistance. Finally, it can provide clients and others with an important self-control strategy that they can use for coping with a variety of problems.

REFERENCES

Alloy, L. B., and Abramson, L. Y. (1988). Depressive realism: four theoretical perspectives. In *Cognitive Processes in Depression*, ed. L. B. Alloy. New York: Guilford.

Beck, A. T. (1987). Cognitive models of depression. *Journal of Cognitive Psychotherapy: An International Quarterly* 1:5–38.

Cautela, J. R. (1975). Covert conditioning in hypnotherapy. *International Journal of Clinical and Experimental Hypnosis* 23:15–27.

Dowd, E. T. (1992). Hypnotherapy. In *Comprehensive Casebook of Cognitive Therapy*, ed. A. Freeman and F. M. Dattilio, pp. 277–283. New York: Plenum.

——— (1993a). Motivational and personality correlates of psychological reactance and implications for cognitive therapy. *Psicologia Conductual* 1:131–140.

——— (1993b). Cognitive-developmental hypnotherapy. In *Handbook of Clinical Hypnosis*, ed. J. W. Rhue, S. J. Lynn, and I. Kirsch, pp. 215–232. Washington, DC: American Psychological Association.

——— (1996). Hypnotherapy in the treatment of adolescent enuresis. In *Casebook of Clinical Hypnosis*, ed. S. J. Lynn, I. Kirsch, and J. W. Rhue, pp. 293–310. Washington, DC: American Psychological Association.

——— (in press). La evolucion de las psicoterapias cognitivas (The evolution of the cognitive therapies). In *Manual de psicoterapias cognitivas: Estada de la cuestion y proceso terapeutico (Handbook of cognitive psychotherapies)*, ed. I. Caro. Barcelona: Editorial Paidos, S.A.

Dowd, E. T., and Courchaine, K. E. (1996). Implicit learning, tacit knowledge, and implications for stasis and change in cognitive psychotherapy. *Journal of Cognitive Psychotherapy: An International Quarterly* 10:163–180.

Dowd, E. T., and Pace, T. M. (1989). The relativity of reality: second order change in psychotherapy. In *Comprehensive Handbook of Cognitive Therapy*, ed. A. Freeman, K. M. Simon, L. E. Beutler, and H. Arkowitz, pp. 213–226. New York: Plenum.

Fleming, K., Heikkinen, R., and Dowd, E. T. (1992). Cognitive therapy: the repair of memory. *Journal of Cognitive Psychotherapy: An International Quarterly* 6:155–173.

Freeman, A., Pretzer, J., Fleming, B., and Simon, K. M. (1990). *Clinical Applications of Cognitive Therapy*. New York: Plenum.

Golden, W. L., and Friedberg, F. (1986). Cognitive-behavioural hypnotherapy. In *Cognitive-Behavioural Approaches to Psychotherapy*, ed. W. Dryden and W. Golden, pp. 290–319. London: Harper & Row.

Guidano, V. F. (1987). *Complexity of the Self.* New York: Guilford.

Kroger, W. S., and Fetzler, W. D. (1976). *Hypnosis and Behavior Modification: Imagery Conditioning.* Philadelphia: Lippincott.

Rosen, H. (1989). Piagetian theory and cognitive therapy. In *Comprehensive Handbook of Cognitive Therapy*, ed. A. Freeman, K. M. Simon, L. E. Beutler, and H. Arkowitz, pp. 189–212. New York: Plenum.

Smith, W. H. (1996). When all else fails: hypnotic exploration of childhood trauma. In *Casebook of Clinical Hypnosis*, ed. S. J. Lynn, I. Kirsch, and J. W. Rhue, pp. 113–130. Washington, DC: American Psychological Association.

Young, J. E. (1990). *Cognitive Therapy for Personality Disorders: A Schema-Focused Approach.* Sarasota, FL: Professional Resource Exchange.

3

CASE FORMULATION IN COGNITIVE-BEHAVIORAL THERAPY

Michael A. Tompkins

A case formulation or conceptualization is a hypothesis about the underlying psychological mechanisms that drive or maintain a patient's problems. Case formulations are used by therapists to guide and focus therapy, and are particularly useful when a patient's difficulties are numerous and complex, when the patient is not compliant with treatment recommendations, or when the therapist–patient relationship is problematic. A case formulation is generally theory-driven, that is, problems or psychopathology are explained on the basis of the structures and processes of a particular psychological theory. Unfortunately, little is written about case formulation in cognitive-behavioral therapy (except Persons 1989, Turkat 1985, Turkat and Maisto 1985). This chapter explains the role of case formulation in cognitive-behavioral therapy, describes a model of cognitive-behavioral case formulation, applies this model to a clinical case, and demonstrates the use of the case formulation to make clinical decisions and interventions.

ROLE OF THE COGNITIVE-BEHAVIORAL
CASE FORMULATION

The central role of the case formulation is to improve treatment outcome. In this sense, the therapist adopts a functional approach to establishing the quality of a formulation (Hayes et al. 1987). Other roles of the case formulation include guiding the therapist's choice of treatment modality, helping the therapist select intervention strategies within a modality, guiding the therapist in creating homework assignments and working effectively with homework noncompliance, helping the therapist understand and intervene appropriately with patient behaviors that threaten the therapeutic relationship or undermine treatment, and obtaining a better understanding of how the patient's maladaptive patterns of relating manifest themselves in the patient's life and in the therapy itself (Persons 1993).

COGNITIVE-BEHAVIORAL CASE FORMULATION MODEL

The model of case formulation described here is based on the work of Persons (1989, 1993), and Persons and Tompkins (1997), which draw from the cognitive therapy of Beck (1976) and from functional analysis as described by Nelson and Hayes (1986). Beck's cognitive model of psychopathology states that problems and symptoms result from the activation of underlying core beliefs by stressful life events. Cognitive therapy focuses on altering the cognitive structures and processes that cause and/or maintain problematic behaviors. Functional analysis, which concerns itself with the functional relationships that direct and/or maintain maladaptive behaviors, focuses on the identification of overt problematic behaviors, on the contingencies that maintain and/or direct the behaviors, and on the role of behaviors as objective measures of treatment outcome. The contributions of these two theories to the cognitive-behavioral case formulation model are apparent in the structure of the case formulation worksheet (Table 3–1). A description of the components of the case formulation follows, and then a clinical application of this model (Table 3–2).

Problem List

The problem list is a comprehensive list of the patient's problems, stated in simple, straightforward language that includes a description of the cognitions (automatic thoughts) considered responsible for maintaining the problematic behavior and/or mood. The link between cognitive-behavioral

Table 3–1. The Cognitive-Behavioral Case Formulation Worksheet

Identifying information

Problem list

Core and conditional beliefs

Origins

Precipitants and activating situations

Working hypothesis
    Goals
    Interventions

Predicted obstacles to treatment

case formulation and Beck's cognitive theory is apparent in that each problem on the problem list is described in terms of the three key components of Beck's model: problematic behavior and/or mood, underlying core beliefs, and the life events that activate the core beliefs. For example, a problem like "Work Difficulties" is best described in terms of the problematic behaviors or moods at work (e.g., avoidance of work-related assignments, angry outbursts, anxiety); the accompanying cognitions (e.g., "I can't do this." "They should treat me better"); and the activating events (e.g., criticism by a co-worker). In addition, it is important to describe problems in a form that can be observed and measured whenever possible. In this way the problem leads to a clear treatment goal that can be monitored and recorded. For example, if panic attacks are a problem, then the frequency and duration of the attacks can be recorded and tracked. Likewise, if one of the problems on the problem list is depressive symptoms, an objective measure like the Beck Depression Inventory can be used to establish the level of depression at pretreatment and to monitor it during treatment.

Core and Conditional Beliefs

Cognitive-behavioral theory views cognitions as central to the maintenance of problematic behaviors and moods. Core beliefs are the therapist's conjectures about the patient's views of self, others, and the world that appear to direct or maintain the patient's problematic behaviors and symptoms. For example, anxious patients commonly believe that they are weak and helpless and that the world is dangerous and unpredictable (Beck et al. 1985). Also, Beck and colleagues (1990) have proposed that patients may have conditional (if–then) beliefs that contribute to their symptoms. For example, socially anxious patients commonly hold conditional beliefs such as,

"If I make a mistake, then people won't like me," or "If others disapprove of me, then I won't be able to handle it."

Precipitants and Activating Situations

These are the external situations and circumstances thought responsible for activating underlying core beliefs that produce problems and symptoms. The precipitant is a situation that activates a patient's underlying core beliefs to such a degree that his/her usual coping skills become ineffectual and they experience distress and become symptomatic. Generally, the precipitant is the situation that brings the patient into treatment. Activating situations, on the other hand, are specific events that the patient can identify as producing discomfort or problems. For example, a medical resident reported that he was experiencing panic attacks and drinking too much alcohol since beginning his residency (precipitant). He had to make important decisions each day and became particularly anxious and fearful when he had to interview a patient and make treatment recommendations while being observed by his instructors or other students (activating situation).

Origins

In this section, the therapist briefly describes one or two incidents or circumstances of the patient's early life thought responsible for the development of the maladaptive core and conditional beliefs. Beck's cognitive model proposes that core beliefs are shaped by seminal experiences in early childhood, particularly experiences with parents or other caregivers. Modeled behaviors or failures to learn important skills can also be included in this section. For example, a patient who was raised by a critical and demanding father and a passive

and overly compliant mother might find it difficult to be assertive with others since he did not have a model of appropriately
assertive behavior when he was growing up.

Working Hypothesis

The working hypothesis is the heart of the cognitive-
behavioral formulation and ties together the problems on the
problem list, the core and conditional beliefs, and the activating events. The working hypothesis is what most clinicians
refer to when they think of a case formulation. It guides
interventions and explains both progress and problems in the
therapy. The working hypothesis is retained, altered, or discarded depending on the outcome of the treatment. If the
patient does not make good progress or relapses, the working
hypothesis is revised and used to develop a revised treatment
plan. The recursive nature of this process—formulation, treatment based on the formulation, monitoring outcome, and
revised formulation based on the outcome—is the hallmark of
behavioral case formulation, in which treatment is viewed as a
single-case empirical study (Barlow et al. 1984).

Treatment Plan

The treatment plan (treatment goals and interventions) flows
from a well-defined problem list and working hypothesis.
Although the treatment plan is not part of the formulation per
se, it is based on the formulation. For example, if a therapist
hypothesizes that a patient's test anxiety results from poor
preparation and test-taking skills, then the treatment plan will
include skill building in this area. If, instead, the therapist
hypothesizes that a patient's test anxiety results from activation of a maladaptive core belief like "I can't do this," the

treatment plan will include cognitive restructuring. Or, if the therapist suspects that the anxiety results from activation of a maladaptive conditional belief like "If I fail, then I'll be punished," the patient and his therapist might develop behavioral experiments to test this assumption.

Predicted Obstacles to Treatment

This section of the cognitive-behavioral case formulation lists potential difficulties that may arise in the therapeutic relationship and other aspects of the treatment. The therapeutic relationship and the parameters of the treatment may activate a patient's problematic beliefs. For example, a patient who believes, "If I don't perform perfectly, then others will become angry and reject me," may be reluctant to complete his therapy homework for fear that the therapist might be dissatisfied with his work. The case formulation enables the therapist to predict problems that might arise in the therapy and thereby avert an early termination or unproductive therapist-patient interactions.

USING THE COGNITIVE-BEHAVIORAL FORMULATION

This section illustrates five specific ways in which the case formulation can be used in therapy: securing collaboration, selecting intervention points and guiding inquiry, selecting intervention strategies, selecting homework assignments, and ensuring compliance.

THE CASE

Jill is a 42-year-old divorced physician's assistant who lives with her 14-year-old daughter. Jill's chief complaint was that she was very depressed following an incident with a demanding physician at work and was looking for a "social coach to help me learn to interact with difficult people and not take it so hard." Jill was severely depressed (Beck Depression Inventory score was 22) and her chief depressive symptoms were sadness, loss of satisfaction in once pleasurable activities, fatigue, difficulty getting things done, self-criticism, and long periods of tearfulness. Jill reported that she was spending too much time alone. When she was asked out by friends or colleagues from work, she declined, saying, "I don't think I have much to offer people." Jill's mother and two of her sisters lived nearby, but Jill seldom saw them because she experienced them as critical and unsupportive. Jill rarely protested their treatment of her; when she did, her mother ignored her. Jill was also worried about her relationship with her daughter and whether she was being a good mother. Jill stated that she had trouble saying "no" to her daughter's unreasonable requests and that they often argued. Jill remembered one occasion when her daughter screamed at her, "Leave me alone. I can't breathe around you," which caused Jill to run to her room and cry for an hour or more.

Jill has a long history of depression beginning in adolescence. She is the oldest of nine children and remembers her life as caring for her siblings, with little time for herself. Jill remembers her father as a harsh and critical man who frequently called her "fat" and "lazy," while praising her siblings. Jill believed her mother viewed her as the "hired help," and she frequently complained when Jill asked to attend a party or spend time with friends.

Securing Collaboration

Cognitive-behavioral therapists expect their patients to actively participate in their therapy: to monitor and record their moods, thoughts, and behavior; to design and execute experiments to test their beliefs; and to provide feedback on the effectiveness of the therapist's strategies and manner. The case formulation helps the therapist secure a collaborative stance with the patient who may be unfamiliar with therapy or unfamiliar with a model of therapy that emphasizes such active participation on his/her part.

J. S. Beck (1995) has described several ingredients necessary to good patient–therapist collaboration, including a rationale for interventions and homework assignments, and agreed-upon goals for therapy. The case formulation can help the therapist build these ingredients into the therapy. For example, the cognitive-behavioral therapist can secure collaboration early in the therapy by sharing the formulation with the patient. The formulation serves as a common language for discussing the patient's difficulties and as the basis for the rationales given for all interventions and homework assignments:

Therapist (after listening and empathizing for several minutes): Jill, it sounds as if you're very upset because your car was vandalized today and you had to make all the arrangements, including getting to your therapy session, on your own. I'm thinking that something sounds familiar about this.

Jill: What do you mean?

T: Well, remember the story you and I came up with to describe the reasons you get upset when you have to do things on your own.

J (pause): Oh, yeah. That I get really upset because people don't care?

T: Yes. That's right. And the other piece to that story is that sometimes you have the belief that being on your own means being worthless. Do you remember that discussion?

J: Yeah (*patient becomes tearful*). I think that if I was worth something I would have someone in my life to help me with these things.

T: That's how I remember it too. What do you think, could this be part of why this particular event is so upsetting to you?

J: Yes, I think so.

T: And what do you think? Is this thought, "If I was worth something, I would have someone in my life," accurate and helpful?

J: Not when I really think about it.

T: So how about if you and I talk about this situation a bit more and see if we can come up with some thoughts that are more helpful.

J: Good. I hate feeling this way. When we talk about it, I can see that it doesn't make any sense.

In addition to educating the patient about the cognitive model and providing a rationale for treatment, the cognitive-behavioral case formulation contains explicit goals for the treatment. As mentioned earlier, the treatment goals and interventions come directly from a comprehensive problem list and working hypothesis. These goals are developed with the patient and updated as the therapy proceeds. Since the goals are part of the formulation, the patient can clearly see that treatment is based on his/her particular difficulties and the underlying cognitive structures and processes thought responsible for their problems.

Selecting Intervention Points and Guiding Inquiry

How does the therapist select which problematic behavior to work on? Select which maladaptive belief to take up in therapy? Whether to take up a problem now or to wait till later in the therapy? The cognitive-behavioral case formulation helps the therapist make these decisions and to focus the session on the problem most closely related to the patient's central difficulties.

For example, Jill, who holds the belief, "If I ask for what I want, then I'll be ignored or rejected," and a pattern of failing to assert herself with others, calls to tell me that she will be late again due to a recent change in her responsibilities that makes her usual appointment time difficult to keep. She arrives to the session fifteen minutes late and in a panic. She sits down and quickly begins to discuss a recent incident with a co-worker, but doesn't raise the topic of her lateness or the difficulty she had in keeping the appointment. Attending to the formulation, I know that I need to ask about the difficulty and why she hasn't discussed with me the possibility of changing her appointment time.

The case formulation also guides the therapist's inquiry about a situation or problem. For example, Jill, who holds the belief, "I don't count," began her therapy session with the statement, "I had several things I wanted to talk about today, but they don't seem so important anymore." Without the case formulation, I might have responded to this statement by saying, "Well, why don't we review your homework and perhaps you'll remember one of the things as we go along," hoping that this would lead to something productive. However, attending to the case formulation, I knew to spend some time discussing with Jill her decision to disregard what was important to her a few moments before. Perhaps Jill has thoughts like, "This isn't important," or "Why bother him with this trivia," which caused her to disregard topics of importance to her. Without a case formulation, I might have missed an important therapeutic opportunity.

Selecting Intervention Strategies

The therapist uses the cognitive-behavioral case formulation to select the most appropriate intervention strategy. Often the therapist must decide whether to focus on behaviors that increase adaptive functioning (e.g., skills training) or on cognitions that maintain the problematic mood or behavior.

For example, Jill came to a therapy session upset by what she described as her "chronic procrastination." Jill explained that every month she fails to pay her bills on time even though she has money in her account. At this point I might have hypothesized that Jill's procrastination was due to a skills deficit and said to her, "Well, let's look at how you approach this task," and reviewed with Jill her organizational and time management skills. However, attending to Jill's case formulation, I remembered that Jill frequently underestimates her ability to handle situations in which she has good skills because she tells herself, "I'm worthless," and that this belief could be activated in situations in which she felt independent or on her own and that this could cause her to avoid this task. The formulation suggested a better intervention would be for Jill and me to complete a Thought Record together to identify the thoughts that underpin her sadness and the problematic behavior of avoiding paying her bills on time.

On another occasion Jill came to a session upset with her progress and insisted that she be given more therapy homework. When asked about this, Jill stated, "I'm not working hard enough. If I did more homework I'd be less depressed." Jill's request made a certain amount of sense. She had a tendency to wait to the last minute to do her homework and on several occasions she did not complete it. Also, Jill's mood had improved some (Beck Depression Inventory score of 12) but she was still prone to tearful periods. Despite these considerations, I replied "I wonder if this is a good idea. I know you think you're not working hard enough, but I sometimes think you're working too hard. What do you think? Is there any chance that you're working too hard?" Why did I propose that Jill might be working too hard rather than going along with her interpretation of the problem? The answer, of course, is in the formulation. Based on the formulation of her case, I hypothesized that Jill's conditional belief, "If I don't do something perfectly, then I'm flawed," may cause her to be overcritical about her homework performance and maintain her negative mood. To have Jill focus more on her homework performance might not be a good strategy. A better strategy might be one that helps her see the connection, if any, between the unrealistic demands she places on herself and how depressed she feels.

Jill and I discussed the situation and she agreed that the best evidence of whether she was working hard enough would be a change in her mood. She reasoned that her mood would deteriorate if she did less therapy homework so she agreed to do one hour less each week and keep a careful log of her mood to see whether there was an effect. In following the formulation, I helped Jill learn that her negative mood was connected more with her tendency toward perfectionism and self-criticism than on the quality or quantity of her therapy homework. Interestingly enough, this intervention improved Jill's mood whereas the intervention Jill suggested would simply have reinforced her perfectionism and tendency toward self-criticism.

Selecting Homework Assignments

Assigning homework in cognitive-behavioral therapy is not a simple task. Often the therapist must consider many aspects of the patient and the therapy before assigning homework, including the relevance of the assignment to the problem being worked on in the session and whether the assignment is realistic given the patient's general intelligence, skill set, and motivation. A cognitive-behavioral case formulation helps the therapist make appropriate homework assignments.

For example, Jill's belief, "If I ask for what I want, then I'll be ignored or rejected," prevented her from making suggestions about activities she would like to do with friends and acquaintances. As a result, she seldom initiated new friendships. When she was invited out but did not like the activity a friend suggested, Jill declined and spent another evening alone rather than suggest an alternative. Her isolation further reinforced her belief, "I'm worthless and unimportant."

Jill's case formulation suggested that an appropriate homework assignment would enable her to test the assumption that she will be rejected if she asks for what she wants. To that end, Jill and I developed a strategy whereby Jill predicted the acceptance-to-rejection ratio that would result if she asked twenty-five people over the next three weeks for something she wanted. Jill and I then role-played a number of situations in which she was able to ask for something. We also developed a coping plan in the event that she was rejected. After three weeks, Jill reported that she had greatly overestimated the number of times she expected to be rejected and had started to make bolder requests that she would never have dreamed of previously. Jill also stated that she was far less upset than she predicted when her requests were rebuffed, particularly in light of the greater number of acceptances she received.

Ensuring Compliance

The cognitive-behavioral case formulation (see Table 3–2) is particularly helpful in ensuring that the patient complies with treatment recommendations, homework assignments, and other aspects of the therapy that increase the likelihood of a positive outcome. In addition, the success of cognitive-behavioral therapy depends on the quality of the collaboration between therapist and patient. The dilemma for the therapist is how to ensure compliance while maintaining a collaborative alliance with the patient.

Linehan (1993) uses the term *therapy-interfering behaviors* to refer to patient behaviors that will, if not addressed, interfere with a therapy and result in treatment failure. To appropriately address therapy-interfering behavior, Linehan believes that the therapist must understand the function the behavior serves for the patient—that is, the therapist must have a formulation.

A common therapy-interfering behavior is homework non-compliance. The cognitive-behavioral case formulation can help the therapist understand possible reasons for homework noncompliance and generate strategies to deal with it. For example, early in the therapy, Jill failed to complete a homework assignment. After discussing the assignment with Jill, I was certain she understood the rationale for the homework as well as what she was supposed to do. I considered her cognitive-behavioral formulation and hypothesized that she may have tried the homework, but her conditional belief, "If I don't do something perfectly, then I'm flawed," prevented her completing it or bringing it to the session. To test this hypothesis, I worked with Jill to remember a moment when she thought about the homework, even though she didn't work on it. We then completed a Thought Record, and Jill learned that she was overworried about doing the homework "perfectly" and that this fear prevented her from getting the most out of her therapy. We then decided that she would try to complete the homework first and *then* give herself a grade rather than grading her homework *before* she had finished it. In addition, we devised a coping card that listed positive statements designed to undermine the belief, "I have to do my homework perfectly, otherwise I'm second-rate." In this way Jill and I worked through a problem that could have stalled the therapy.

The cognitive-behavioral case formulation is also helpful in protecting the therapeutic alliance. In an early session with Jill, during which she described an early childhood event, I interrupted her to obtain additional specific information. I then noticed that she turned her head away and became tearful. Attending to the formulation, I hypothesized that Jill's belief, "I don't count," may have been activated, leading her to feel rebuked and sad. I asked her to tell me what was going through her mind as she turned her head away. Jill said, "I wasn't thinking anything. I guess I'm too sensitive." I pressed her and she responded, "I guess I felt dismissed, like you didn't care about what I was saying." This information validated my hypothesis. At my invitation, Jill looked for other evidence to support her belief that the therapist didn't care about her. She found little, and I was able to use this opportunity to explain the cognitive model to her—how certain interpersonal situations, in and out of therapy, can activate dysfunctional beliefs that lead to her feeling worthless and sad. Jill left the session feeling reassured, particularly after I encouraged her to bring up any future concerns about me or the therapy so that the two of us could learn how to work effectively as a team. In the absence of a formulation, I might have overlooked this important moment or prematurely reassured her, rather than using the moment to set the stage for future discussions of patient–therapist interactions that might undermine the therapeutic alliance.

Table 3–2. Cognitive-Behavioral Case Formulation Worksheet for Jill

Identifying Information: Jill is a bright, articulate 42-year-old divorced physician's assistant who lives with her 14-year-old daughter. She sought treatment after she "lost it" and left work in tears following an argument with a demanding physician.

Problem List:

1. Depression—Jill's score on the Beck Depression Inventory was 22, which indicates a severe level of depression. Jill is

often tearful and sad, accompanied by the thoughts, "I'm second rate. I'm useless." She is irritable and has trouble concentrating at work. She no longer enjoys once pleasurable activities and complains of fatigue and difficulty getting things done. She is extremely self-critical and at times feels hopeless that her life will improve.

2. Social isolation—Jill has few close friends and desperately wants them. She is a member of a professional organization (and has been an officer) but she doesn't pursue relationships with the people in the organization she meets. When asked out by co-workers, she often refuses, thinking, "I have nothing to offer," or "Why would they want to be around me?" Jill would like to have a boyfriend but she doesn't pursue opportunities because she thinks she is unattractive and "over the hill."

3. Procrastination—Jill delays completing important tasks at home and work. For example, she is often late paying her bills, even though she has the money. She avoids writing the checks because she becomes sad, accompanied by the thoughts, "I have no one who cares about me. I have to do everything myself."

4. Difficulties at work—Jill feels inadequate at work and is reluctant to take on unfamiliar or challenging tasks for fear of failing. Her employers in turn become more demanding, which Jill then interprets as evidence of her inability to live up to their expectations. Jill is often comparing her performance to her co-workers, accompanied by the thoughts, "They're so much better than me. Why should I even try?" These thoughts cause Jill to decline opportunities that could lead to greater responsibility and promotion. As a result, her career is stagnant, which further reinforces the beliefs that she is "worthless."

5. Difficulties in relationship with mother and siblings—Jill is angry with her mother but persists in seeking her approval despite the fact that her mother prefers her younger sisters.

For example, Jill's mother asked Jill to pick her up at the airport rather than asking another daughter who was not working and who lived closer to the airport. When Jill said that she would have to take time off from work and suggested that her mother call her sister, her mother replied, "Well, you can't be that busy. It's not like you're a doctor or something." Jill became very sad and tearful, accompanied by the thoughts, "I don't count. She doesn't care about me."

6. Parenting difficulties—Jill worries that she is an inadequate parent. She has trouble saying "no" to her daughter's unreasonable requests or insisting that her daughter do housework for fear that her daughter will think her cruel and uncaring, accompanied by the thoughts, "She won't love me," or "It's not that important. I can do it myself." Jill and her daughter are overclose because Jill has trouble doing pleasurable activities on her own. When her daughter asks for time to herself, Jill becomes sad and tearful, accompanied by the thoughts, "She doesn't care about me. I'm not a good mother."

Core Beliefs: I am worthless and unimportant. I don't count.

Others are better and more important than me.

The world is critical and unfair.

Conditional Beliefs: If I don't do something perfectly, then I'm flawed.

If I ask for what I want, then I'll be ignored or rejected.

Origins: Jill was the oldest of nine children and provided much of the day-to-day care for her younger siblings. For her efforts she was either ignored by her mother or criticized by her father. From this experience Jill may have concluded that she was worthless.

Jill's father was an alcoholic career military officer who was stern and unpredictable. He often hit Jill and ridiculed her, calling her "fat" and "ugly." Jill's mother tended to ignore these abuses, telling her, "You must have deserved it."

Although Jill was bright, her parents did not encourage her to excel in school or to think about a career, telling her, "You don't have what it takes." Instead, her brothers were given the benefits of a good education and were expected to attend college. As a result, Jill lacks confidence in her abilities and does not feel entitled to her successes.

Precipitants and Activating Situations: Jill entered treatment following an argument with a superior at work who criticized her professional judgment and yelled, "What's wrong with you?" Jill was extremely upset and was not able to work for several weeks. Activating situations for Jill appear to include situations in which (1) she feels independent and on her own (e.g., when paying her bills, at the end of a relationship); (2) she is criticized; (3) she must assert her needs over the needs of others.

Working Hypothesis: Jill's beliefs, "I'm worthless," or "I don't count," cause her to feel depressed, inadequate, and inconsolable when she is criticized or in a situation in which she feels alone or unsupported. These beliefs, and the belief that "Others are more important," may cause her to be unassertive with friends and co-workers. She then may be less successful at work, have fewer friends, and delay important tasks at home and work, which reinforces the belief, "I'm worthless," or, as a consequence of her setting aside her needs in the favor of the needs of others, she may become resentful. She may then become angry for which she feels guilty and reinforces the belief, "I'm worthless." At times Jill is able to overcome her sense of worthlessness and assert herself, but because she is unskilled in assertive behavior, her requests come across as angry or demanding. As a result, she may be criticized or fail to get what she wants, thereby reinforcing the beliefs that there is something wrong with her and that she is undeserving.

Treatment Plan:

Goals:

1. Decrease depressive symptoms (monitor depression weekly with the Beck Depression Inventory).
2. Increase assertive behavior with co-workers, friends, family, and the therapist.
3. Increase pleasurable activities.
4. Decrease social isolation.
5. Decrease reactivity to criticism and the demands of others.

Interventions:

1. Teach the formulation; show Jill that her moods and behaviors depend on whether or not she thinks she is worthless or second-rate.
2. Through skill building and role-play, work with Jill so that she is better able to assert her needs over the needs of others.
3. Role-play assertively handling the criticism and disapproval of others.
4. Cognitive restructuring of the maladaptive beliefs (with the use of Thought Records and positive data logs out of session).
5. Teach Jill about the role that the beliefs "I'm not important" or "No one cares" play in her avoiding certain tasks (procrastination) and the accompanying negative mood. Help Jill learn alternative ways of coping with these thoughts and feelings and teach time management skills if needed.
6. Work with Jill on more appropriate parenting of her daughter that recognizes her rights as a parent and her daughter's need for time alone and with friends.

7. Help Jill acquire more friends on which she can call and depend.
8. Work with Jill to be more assertive with her mother and siblings. Teach her how to communicate to her family that she is worthwhile and that her time and interests are important.

Predicted Obstacles to Treatment:

1. Jill may feel dismissed or unimportant in therapy, particularly if the therapist forgets important information or changes topics or the direction of the interview.
2. Jill may not be assertive in the therapy session, particularly if she feels she must choose between her needs and the needs of the therapist.
3. Jill may be reluctant to comply with homework, set the agenda in a session, or offer suggestions to the therapist for fear that she may be wrong or fail in some way.

CONCLUSION

As Persons (1989) has noted, although the cognitive model tells the therapist that mood can be changed by changing cognitions and behaviors, it does not tell the therapist what intervention to choose for a particular problem at a particular moment in the therapy. A formulation helps the therapist to generate strategies relevant to the problem at hand or to predict problems that might arise to compromise the therapy or undermine the therapeutic alliance.

Standardized treatment protocols generally do not provide guidance to clinicians who must work with less motivated patients or with patients who have problematic ways of relating to others. In the absence of such guidance, clinicians may resort to cajoling or haranguing their patients in an effort to maintain treatment compliance. There is some work under way to address the apparent conflict between researchers' needs for standardized protocols and clinicians' needs for flexibility. For example, Eifert (1995) has suggested that protocol treatment and individualized treatment might be combined by nesting standardized components within an individually tailored treatment. Research to establish the efficacy, effectiveness, dropout, and relapse rates of individualized versus standardized treatments is urgently needed.

REFERENCES

Barlow, D. H., Hayes, S. C., and Nelson, R. O. (1984). *The Scientist-Practitioner: Research and Accountability in Clinical and Educational Settings*. New York: Pergamon.

Beck, A. T. (1976). *Cognitive Therapy and the Emotional Disorders*. New York: International Universities Press.

Beck, A. T., Emery, G., and Greenberg, R. (1985). *Anxiety Disorders and Phobias: A Cognitive Perspective*. New York: Basic Books.

Beck, A. T., Freeman, A., and Associates (1990). *Cognitive Therapy of Personality Disorders*. New York: Guilford.

Beck, J. S. (1995). *Cognitive Therapy: Basics and Beyond*. New York: Guilford.

Eifert, G. H. (1995). Why we need to match treatments to clients and not to labels—at least some of the time. Paper presented at World Congress of Behavioural and Cognitive Therapies, Copenhagen, Denmark, July.

Hayes, S. C., Nelson, R. O., and Jarrett, R. B. (1987). The treatment utility of assessment: a functional approach to evaluating assessment quality. *American Psychologist* 42:963–974.

Linehan, M. M. (1993). *Cognitive-Behavioral Treatment of Borderline Personality Disorder*. New York: Guilford.

Nelson, R. O., and Hayes, S. C. (1986). The nature of behavioral assessments. In *Conceptual Foundations of Behavioral Assessment*, ed. R. O. Nelson and S. C. Hayes, pp. 3–41. New York: Guilford.

Persons, J. B. (1989). *Cognitive Therapy in Practice: A Case Formulation Approach*. New York: Norton.

———— (1993). Case conceptualization in cognitive-behavior therapy. In *Cognitive Therapy in Action: Evolving Innovative Practice*, ed. K. T. Kuehlwein and H. Rosen, pp. 33–53. San Francisco: Jossey-Bass.

Persons, J. B., and Tompkins, M. A. (1997). Cognitive-behavioral case formulation. In *Handbook of Psychotherapy Case Formulation*, ed. T. D. Eells. New York: Guilford.

Turkat, I. D., ed. (1985). *Behavioral Case Formulation*. New York: Plenum.

Turkat, I. D., and Maisto, S. A. (1985). Personality disorders: application of the experimental method to the formulation and modification of personality disorders. In *Clinical Handbook of Psychological Disorders: A Step-by-Step Treatment Manual*, ed. D. H. Barlow, pp. 502–570. New York: Guilford.

4

RESISTANCE
AND SELF-LIMITATION

Robert L. Leahy

Although cognitive therapy is often an efficient and direct method of intervention for depression and anxiety, it is not uncommon for patients to resist the therapist's recommendations. Some therapists may take a "consumer model" toward resistance and claim that if the patient is not willing to change, then the therapist should not or cannot intervene effectively. Patients are viewed as consumers who direct the therapist toward goals that the patient is either willing or not willing to pursue. The therapist might take the view, "If the patient is not willing to change, then he is not ready for therapy." Although I recognize that the final choices are up to the patient, I believe that the consumer model, taken to this extreme, is naive and does not recognize the potential for the therapist to help the patient analyze and evaluate the resistance as part of the patient's treatment for depression or anxiety. In this chapter I explore a social cognitive model of resistance that expands on the cognitive model and has proved useful in helping patients understand and modify their self-limiting patterns.

DEPRESSION AS ADAPTATION

A common assumption, guiding a variety of models of depression, is that depression is a "failure" or "malfunction" on the part of the patient. Biological models propose that depression is the result of deficiencies in biochemical functioning, behavioral models suggest that depression results from deficiencies in rewards or excesses in aversive experiences, skill-acquisition models posit deficiencies in assertiveness, social skills, and problem solving, and the traditional cognitive model points to distortions in thinking or maladaptive assumptions. Although all of these models are valid, they do not account for the apparent motivated resistance of some patients who are resistant to change. For example, why would a man who is depressed resist or vigorously argue against the "rational responses" offered by the therapist? Does the patient fail to recognize that the rational response, or the alternative suggested, will readily end his hopelessness and self-criticism and provide him with the opportunity to get over his depression?

The view I present here is that depression, in various forms—like anxiety, anger, aggression, and phobia—is a universal phenomenon that is present in a wide variety of species. Given its universality, one might wonder whether there is anything that might be adaptive in depression in the evolution of the organism. For example, we view fever as a symptom of disease, but indeed fever is better viewed as an adaptation to fight off disease. To eliminate fever, in some cases, prolongs disease (Nesse and Williams 1994). The view that "diseases" of various kinds, especially "mental diseases," are attempts to adapt to a primitive reality (that may no longer be present) has been advanced by a variety of writers in the field of evolutionary psychiatry (Wenegrat 1990). Fears of snakes, the dark, strangers, heights, being left alone, dogs, and closed spaces are fears that may in some primitive environments confer adaptive value (Bowlby 1969, Marks 1987). Bowlby argued that depression, protest, and reattachment are universal responses to the loss (and rapprochement) of a love object and that these responses help strengthen the attachment bond necessary for protection against predators, access to food, procreative functioning, and socialization of the species (Bowlby 1969, 1980).

Consider some of the symptoms of depression as possibly adaptive given an environment of recent loss, failure, and scarcity. Loss of energy, loss of appetite, and decrease in behavior decrease the need for calories in a scarcity environment. Loss of interest in sex decreases the likelihood of sexual competition for partners who believe (perhaps incorrectly) that their partner has abandoned them. Further, loss of sexual interest may be adaptive if important resources, such as food, protectors, and nesting sights are scarce. Self-criticism may be a useful way to terminate losing behavior and to learn how to correct oneself. Hopelessness, in fact, may be a helpful temporary self-limitation for individuals who have taken too many risks or who have few resources available. In fact, some have argued that submissive posturing, so common with the sad, downcast visage of the depressive, may be an attempt to appease those higher in the dominance hierarchy or, in some cases, to activate nurturant altruistic responses in others who might provide resources the depressive lacks.

I propose that one can make a case for strategic pessimism. Resistant depressives adapt a cognitive, behavioral, and interpersonal strategy whose purpose is to prevent further depression. It is the belief of many depressives that increasing hope may confer greater risks and greater exposure. Given the belief that current and future resources or assets are limited, risks are to be avoided. The depressive may adapt a pessimistic strategy because he believes that this protects him against further loss. Depression, from this model, is not only a function of the negative schemata of the depressive, but also the attempt to control costs. *Depression is a risk management strategy.*

DEPRESSIVE PORTFOLIOS

In order to develop this model of resistance, I have borrowed from microeconomic models of decision making in finance theory (Becker 1976, Leahy 1996, 1997a,b, Tomassi and Ierulli 1995). I am not interested in how depressives invest their money or play the stock market, but rather in how they make mundane decisions about how to "invest" their time, effort, status, and other personal resources. One can view individuals as differing in the *portfolio theories* that they hold. A portfolio theory is your view of your current and future assets, your purpose in investing (protecting assets, growth), your perception of the duration of investing (short term versus long term), your tolerance of risk (risk averse, risk neutral, or risk lover), the replications of investment, and the value attached to gains and losses.

Depressive individuals pursue a minimization strategy— that is, they wish to minimize the chance of any further loss. They believe they have few assets, little possibility of offsetting current losses with future "earnings," a low value for gains (since they are anhedonic), and a high added cost for loss. The higher valuation of loss is due to the fact that they believe losses are to be avoided at all costs.

Since the goal is to avoid losses, depressives put in high stop-loss orders for themselves. For example, when the depressive sees (or imagines) that he will begin to lose, he "stops out" and quits. This, of course, corresponds to "learned helplessness"—that is, giving up in the face of failure—but for many depressives it appears to have a rational and utilitarian function: it avoids further losses. Why not stop out and conserve whatever meager assets you have available? Indeed, for some depressives the beginning of a loss implies a cascade of losses—that is, losses will continue, unabated, with increasing velocity. Once losses begin, the depressive may believe that they cannot be stopped. Cost cascades imply an increasing acceleration of losses into a chasm of failure, emptiness, and destruction. For example, the therapist may ask the patient, "Why would it bother you if you failed (at this task)?" The depressive may believe that failure in a single task marks the beginning of other failures in his life, resulting in loss of a reason to live. Thus losses are to be anticipated, avoided, and cut short as soon as possible. High stop-loss orders appear rational, given the negative schemata that foretell scarcity, failure, and depletion. Better to be sadder but wiser than to have everything lost.

DEPRESSIVE RISK MANAGEMENT

The experienced clinician wishes to avoid sounding like a Pollyannish optimist wherein a sophistic distortion leads him to argue that this is the best of all possible worlds. There are many possible worlds better than this one, as anyone who has done even a cursory reading of the "progressive" twentieth century may attest. Depressives adapt risk-management strategies to prevent further loss in a world viewed as volatile, potentially uncontrollable, scarcity-based, competitive, and even dangerous. Indeed, one might view much of human history as a description of volatility, uncontrollability, scarcity, and danger, where the solace for many was in superstition, subservience, immediate pleasure (often from alcohol), and the hope of a painless death. I do not wish to sound like the voice of doom, but the history of our species is hardly a tale of a city on a hill following a beacon of light.

Depressives attempt to manage their risk by adapting high stop-loss orders, hedging, discounting gains, and taking an ambivalent position regarding hope. Depressives use high stop-loss criteria when, at the first sign of frustration or failure, they quit and pull back. They hedge by seldom putting all their effort into one goal, generally holding back by waiting, observing, and anticipating loss. They are ambivalent about hope because they view getting their hopes up as a risk of becoming overly optimistic, taking too many chances, and becoming overexposed.

All of this is meant to keep the depressive from becoming too highly exposed to future losses, which are viewed as untenable and devastating. As indicated earlier, the depressive "stops out" early to avoid the cost cascades of a perceived linear downtrend. He hedges, by keeping one foot in and one foot out, so that he can rest somewhat assured that he has not risked everything. These hedging moves are like probes to see if there is anything positive in the horizon: if rewards are not immediately forthcoming, then he closes out and pulls back. Depressives discount gains because the world is viewed as potentially dangerous and providing scarce rewards. Gains are not viewed as predictive of further gains or as an indication of the individual's potential for producing positives. In the negative schemata of depression, gains are viewed as an aberration, a fluke that might mislead one into becoming hopeful and thereby risk greater exposure. Consequently, depressives are often ambivalent about hope: they wish to experience the improved mood associated with optimism, but they fear the risk of added exposure. Gains are viewed as carrying the weight of gravity. For the depressive, what goes up will almost certainly come crashing down. Therefore, the depressive decides to pull out with a small gain before the anticipated ax falls.

SELF-HANDICAPPING STRATEGIES

Two of the losses that depressives try to protect against are loss of self-esteem and loss of face. One strategy that depressives use is *disattribution*. For example, depressives who fail to do self-help homework assignments are able to disattribute their lack of rewards to lack of effort or to the failure of the therapist. We know that when depressives actually engage in behavior, exerting some effort, and they fail, they are biased toward attributing their failure to lack of ability, thereby lowering their self-esteem: "I failed because I'm incompetent. I am a failure." Strategizing, or resistant, depressives may avoid this unwanted attribution by refusing to try, thereby resulting in the face-saving cognition, "I did not succeed because I didn't even try." Thus we really do not know if the depressive is "incompetent"—perhaps if he tried he would have succeeded. Perhaps he has potential. In this financial metaphor one can say that the depressive takes an "option" on trying—he can always try in the future.

Another disattribution strategy is to blame the therapist for the patient's not trying: "I'm not getting any better because you are not helping me," or "You don't care about me." This distracts both patient and therapist to the issue of dependency and empathy rather than to the patient's choices in not engaging in self-help. The patient may be "invested" in not trying to avoid any full exposure to self-evaluation: by blaming the therapist or by sabotaging the therapy, the depressive may conserve whatever self-esteem is left by externalizing the problem and handicapping the self. The resistant depressive appears to be saying to himself, "If I don't give it 100 percent and I can blame the therapist, I avoid any true evaluation of myself."

Some patients self-handicap by establishing impossible goals that allow them to maintain a narcissistic ideal self-image (to be attained in the future). For example, one patient held an extraordinary view of her need for a perfect partner: to abandon this demand for a perfect partner would imply, she said, that she was "ordinary." The view of ordinariness was equivalent, in her value system, to the quality of worthlessness. Thus, as long as she held onto a perfectionistic goal for her partner, she could maintain her idealization of her potential. If she did not achieve the perfect partner, it would mean that she was not able to achieve what no one else achieved anyway. The great fear was to aim for the less-than-perfect partner and find that even that was difficult to attain.

Another self-handicapping strategy is to invest the self in the idealization that others have of the self—that is, to attempt to live up to the expectations of others who view you as a laudable character. By investing in the idealized self, the patient preserves the illusion of special status or special person and does not have to abandon the belief that "Once I get over this depression I will be able to get everything I want." Some patients resist change because to accept less would lower their status in the eyes of others. For example, a female patient from an affluent family claimed that she could not work due to her bipolar disorder. The fact was that she had few job skills and therefore could hope to pursue only work viewed as lower in status than that of her friends and family. Her therapist encouraged her to engage in volunteer work with a "high status" group. She pursued this on a regular basis for two years, working twenty hours per week, but was able to reconstrue it as volunteer work rather than a low-status job. Consequently, she was able to obscure evaluation of herself by claiming that she was bipolar (but special) and that she was volunteering (rather than acknowledging her inability to pursue more "prestigious" work).

Some resistant depressives become anxious when others, like the therapist, have increased expectations about the patient. Although the therapist, and the patient's friends, may view these expectations as supportive, they create anxiety for a variety of reasons: first, they raise the standard that the patient feels he must live up to and risk failing at; second, they encourage the patient to become optimistic, thereby running the risk of overexposure; and third, the increased expectations of others conflict with the patient's risk-management strategy of looking for reasons not to change. Consequently, the therapist who directs the patient to evidence of his competence will often find the patient arguing that he is more incompetent than the therapist could ever imagine.

Another self-handicapping strategy is to transfer the problems to others. This lateral pass of the problem is common in marital conflict: the husband, recognizing that he has a problem with his own anger, transfers the problem to his wife by making her responsible for his angry outbursts. His problem now becomes her failing. Similarly, the depressed patient, fearful of taking risks, blames the therapist and others for his not getting better.

For the patient to overcome his resistance he must find a way to make a change that does not make him seem foolish for not having made the change in the past. Some patients adapt a model of "parallel difficulty"—"I have been depressed for ten years, it should take me ten years to get better. If I get better in ten weeks, it must mean that I am an idiot for not having done that in the past." Patients adhering to the model of parallel difficulty may prefer biological cures rather than therapeutic cures since the former imply little personal responsibility for lack of improvement.

Thus far I have proposed that depression may be viewed as a strategy to avoid further loss. Depressives adapt a risk-management strategy in which they may self-handicap to prevent further loss of self-esteem and face. In the remainder of the chapter, I describe how this conceptualization of resistance was helpful in treating a highly resistant depressed male who, as I will suggest, was locked in his own "existential prison."

The Existential Prison

Tom was a 45-year-old married male who came to therapy after a ten-year depression. Tom complained of anxiety, depression, indecisiveness, procrastination, low self-esteem, loneliness, fears, inactivity, self-criticism, and marital problems. He scored 20 on the Beck Depression Inventory (BDI), with elevations on sadness, hopelessness, self-critical items, lack of satisfaction, loss of interest, and the need to push himself to get anything done. On the SCL 90R he had elevated scores on depression, anxiety, and obsessiveness. On the SCID II questionnaire and interview he revealed evidence of compulsive, self-defeating, and narcissistic personality.

Tom traced his depression back ten years (which appears to correspond with the dramatic increase in his wife's career success and his withdrawal from his wife). His depression was further aggravated by a career change six years prior to intake. He had been a middle-level executive who accepted a buyout of his contract when the company moved its operations to another city. Tom planned to become an entrepreneur. His wife, an executive, was doing well financially, so he felt little financial pressure of his own.

Tom's consulting business failed to generate income. This resulted in his self-critical thoughts: "I'm not good at selling," "I'm doing nothing," "It's a totally wasted life," "I'll get rejected (if I pursue more clients)," "I'm no good," "I don't belong anywhere." Tom equated his worth as a person with financial success. His wife's financial success created ambivalent feelings in him. On the positive side it provided him with financial security and, he claimed, he could vicariously take partial credit for her success since he "counseled" her on business matters. On the negative side he felt like a "loser" compared to his wife, making him feel like he was dependent and "needy."

Tom reported growing up in a working-class family. Owing to his small stature, compared to other children his age, he generally felt inferior. He would compensate for this by macho bravado and impulsive angry outbursts that intimidated his peers. Tom indicated he generally avoided pursuing girls (or, later, women) who were intellectually his equal, because he felt intimidated by them. He met his wife when he was 20 and she was 18. They married two years later. Tom appeared to occupy a dominant role in the relationship for the first twelve years, since he was earning more and his wife appeared to defer to his "superior knowledge about business."

INTERVENTIONS

The initial interventions focused on establishing short-term and long-term goals and examining (1) his interest in developing his consulting business, (2) his self-criticism, and (3) his interest in maintaining the marriage. Overtly, Tom appeared highly cooperative and enthusiastic about therapy. We examined the advantages and disadvantages of developing a "successful small business." The advantages were "money—to help me deal with a divorce if we get divorced, keep me busy, feel I have a place, and feel productive." The disadvantages were "not prestigious, not secure, uncertainty of income flow." Tom indicated that building a small business negated his "rightful entitlement" to a stake in his wife's earnings, a stake that he believed was partly his because of his support of her.

Tom could not settle on any long-term goals with his wife. His thoughts about her were "I'm a house pet," "I don't have any rights," "I'm dependent on her," and "I got screwed." He thought of divorce, but rejected it as unacceptable because of his belief that they might still be able to work it out, they had a long history with each other, and he would be worse off financially.

Since financial demands were a central part of his feelings of dependency and failure, we examined the costs and benefits of needing $150,000 per year versus $70,000 per year—the difference between what he could expect in a "successful business" versus pursuing less demanding financial goals (see Table 4–1).

In examining the consequences of having less money, Tom indicated that he would not have as nice a car, he would lack financial security, and he could not take people to expensive restaurants. Moreover, having less money was equated with not being special, feeling like a "geek," and fears of becoming destitute (and ending up in the old working-class neighborhood). However, as Tom examined his financial goals he realized that he generally did not spend a lot of money and that he was often satisfied with less expensive things. If anything, he had been purchasing more expensive clothing to please his wife. Left on his own, he claimed, he would prefer casual clothing and a less extravagant life-style.

Table 4–1. Needing $150,000 per year

Advantages	Disadvantages
I can attain this (with wife)	Might be unrealistic
Raise my self-esteem	Disappointment
	Depending on wife's income
	Pass up something that could make me happier

Resistance to Change

Tom agreed that being able to live on less money could help him feel less dependent and allow him the option of pursuing other work. However, although he indicated that everything we talked about made sense, he did little to change and he seldom thought about therapy between sessions. As was typical of him at this point in therapy, Tom used cognitive avoidance as his main defense against anxiety.

I provided Tom with a conceptualization of his resistance, focusing on five factors:

1. *Discomfort dodging*: He avoided business contacts that made him uncomfortable, just as he avoided asserting himself with his wife. Similarly, he avoided thinking about therapy in between sessions and he avoided confronting his wife with their problems;
2. *Entitlement*: He believed that he owned a piece of his wife's success and that, since he was "smart and good," he deserved more than the average person;
3. *Expectations of stability*: He believed that everything would remain the same—that his wife would not divorce him and that she would continue to support him financially;
4. *Unwillingness to compromise*: He believed that to accept less money would lead to deprivation. He believed that he should not compromise on being very successful at something—especially in his business. If he could not be very successful, he would not accept less;
5. *Shame*: He avoided people when he was at home during the day, lest they wonder why he was "unemployed." He was concerned that his family and his in-laws would view him as a failure if he made any career changes.

I asked Tom to list the advantages and disadvantages of each of these issues (Table 4–2). As inspection of the table

Table 4–2. Dimensions of Resistance

Discomfort Dodging

Advantages	Disadvantages
No hassles	Become soft
Easy life	Intolerance of problems
Don't have to deal with problems	"Forget" how to deal with problems
	Miss opportunities to learn
	Insulated from real life
	Avoid good and bad things

Entitlement

Advantages	Disadvantages
(None)	Feel weak . . . like a housecat
	Don't rely on myself
	False security
	What if the one I depend on fails?
	Dislike myself

Things Remain the Same

Advantages	Disadvantages
Predictability	Never try anything new
Security	Boring
	Lose interest in everything

Won't Accept Less—No Compromise

Advantages	Disadvantages
Could get more	Missed opportunities

Shame-Avoidance of Others

Advantages	Disadvantages
Won't look like a failure to others	Must live a lie
	Probably unnecessary
	Others don't really care
	Forget who I am

indicates, he believed that the disadvantages outweighed the advantages. Since many depressed patients have difficulty seeing themselves overcoming difficulties, I asked Tom to describe a period in his life when he successfully overcame obstacles and focused on his own goals rather than avoidance and discomfort dodging. Tom indicated that for most of his adult life, until his depression, he had been extremely focused on his goals—working his way through college, getting an MBA with honors, and securing promotions at work. His satisfaction in achieving goals changed with the onset of his depression, when money became the only goal.

As inspection of each of these comparisons reveals, there was general support for the position that Tom would be better off if he did not pursue resistance—that is, if he did not pursue discomfort dodging, entitlement, stability, unwillingness to compromise, and shame-avoidance. Moreover, Tom's motivation in therapy dramatically increased with our analysis of his resistance. Having analyzed the schemas underlying his resistance, we needed to address two important issues that maintained his resistance. First, we needed to examine his "portfolio theory" in order to modify his perception of risk and investment in his future. Second, we had to find a face-saving strategy that would allow him to maintain his public esteem while he simultaneously acknowledged that his business had failed. In order for him to move forward he had to find a rationale and a publicly acceptable strategy to give up the past.

PORTFOLIO THEORY OF TOM'S RESISTANCE

At this point we have enough information to analyze how Tom viewed his alternatives and assets. Turning to the portfolio theory described earlier, we can analyze how Tom could modify his pessimistic resistance and develop a more positive, risk-oriented, growth "portfolio."

Tom's Pessimistic Portfolio Theory

Current assets (What has he to offer?): Tom believed that he had almost nothing to offer anyone. He believed that he had very little money and he doubted that he would be attractive to women.   **Low**

Future assets (What could he earn?): He believed that he would never be able to do well in business and that he would become less desirable over time.   **Low**

Utility of gains (What is the value of increases in income or rewards?): He believed that any future earnings would be offset by taxes and that the extra work involved made it useless. Furthermore, he saw little value in challenge, learning, or growth.   **Low**

Potential loss (What is the potential decrease in status and self-esteem?): Tom thought that change risked substantial losses to his self-esteem through the risk of failure, public exposure, and humiliation.   **High**

Risk tolerance (How much risk could he take?): He wished to avoid risks because he believed that change was threatening and could lead to a series of further losses.   **Low**

Diversification (How many different sources of rewards did he have?): He felt that he was highly dependent on his wife for financial support and that he had few sources of rewards or competence outside the relationship.   **Low**

Time frame (Was he in it for the long term or the short term?): His time frame for seeing rewards was that he had to see a payoff immediately or it would not

be worth pursuing. He did not take a long-term
investment strategy to his life.   **Low**

Regret-orientation (Did he criticize himself for making
   mistakes?): Change was potentially costly because
   he would criticize himself if things did not work
   out.   **High**

Stop-loss (How quickly would he pull out once negative outcomes occurred?): He would give up quickly
   in the face of frustration or discomfort. Even *thinking* about change was unpleasant, so he would
   quickly cease thinking of change lest he become
   more anxious.   **High**

Hedging (Does he keep one foot in and one foot out?):
   Tom kept one foot in his marriage and one foot
   in his consulting business that was doing poorly.
   Whenever he thought of making more commitment
   to one or the other, he would pull back in the
   opposite direction. He would not put 100 percent in
   either.   **High**

In conceptualizing Tom's resistance to change, it was necessary to modify each of the elements of Tom's portfolio
theory. In addressing these issues, we examined his potential
for change from a positive perspective, emphasizing greater
assets, future earnings, longer time frame, and diversification.
This is depicted below.

A Positive Portfolio Theory

Current assets: He had substantial capital, intelligence,
   business experience, and personal skills.   **High**

Future assets: Many of his current assets could improve over time. He could also obtain additional
   training and skills.   **High**

Utility of gains: He had been too focused on the marginal utility of more income. We could focus on new reward categories—learning, challenges, novelty, and personal growth.   **High**

Potential loss: Since he was depressed, he had nothing to lose but his depression. If his wife was going to stay, he would have to make some changes. If he was to get divorced, he would need some new direction.   **Low**

Risk tolerance: He had to recognize that maintaining the status quo was risky, since it assured his depression and had high opportunity cost. We could reframe "risk" as "resourcefulness," putting it in a positive light.   **Moderate**

Diversification: We could increase his alternatives by examining what he could do in addition to his current consulting and management of his financial assets.   **Moderate**

Time frame: He had been too focused on a magic bullet that would solve everything immediately. We could examine changes that he could work on over a longer period of time.   **Moderate**

Regret-orientation: We could focus on increasing the value he would place on making changes, taking risks, and praising himself for being different from others who do not take risks. If things did not work out perfectly, it only meant he was a "player."   **Low**

Stop-loss: Rather than quitting before he made a move, we could focus on the intrinsic rewards of learning, novelty, and challenges, and look at changes as an investment that had its ups and downs.   **Low**

Hedging: He always seemed to hold part of himself back in making a change. We needed to focus on the idea that satisfaction comes with commitment. He had to recognize that he could risk the security of

his financial dependence (and live on less) in order
to make changes. **Low**

The new positive portfolio theory was aimed at providing
Tom with a conceptualization of how he could view decision
making from an empowered view that he had a variety of
assets, that rewards could be diversified, and that he could
take an investment strategy that encouraged him to view
change as a long-term commitment. By diversifying his assets—
for example, he thought of going back to school, either law
school or graduate school—he could magnify his future earnings. We identified new rewards other than money—for example, we examined how learning, challenge, novelty, helping
people, and getting out of a rut could be new sources of
rewards for him. Finally, we examined what his thinking was
like in earlier periods of his life when he was successful at
accomplishing tasks. This included the willingness to work
hard, the ability to learn difficult subjects, his assertiveness
and skill with people, and his ability to take an investment
strategy over time. These past successful traits were added to
his current "assets" or personal resources. His personal assets
depended less on what he owned than on who he was.

OVERCOMING SELF-HANDICAPPING

The examination of Tom's alternatives appeared to encourage
him, but he still had difficulty deciding which course to take.
At this time he was considering corporate work, law school, or
teaching. Tom reported a dream that disturbed him. "I was in
kindergarten class. I was afraid of going to a big building—
filled with uncertainty. Overwhelming. The class was all adults,
like me. The teacher gave a test on ABC's. I couldn't do it. I got
an average grade. I left the room, but got lost looking for a
bathroom."

We interpreted this dream as his fear of regressing, humiliation in failing, and his lack of direction. Tom indicated that his biggest fear now was that people who thought he was a successful consultant would think less of him.

We examined the possibility of directly confronting this fear of others' expectations by telling his family about his real work situation. Tom indicated that the advantages of this were, "I would be free to be myself, wouldn't have to playact, I can feel young again." The disadvantages were, "They'd think less of me, pity me, see me as a failure." I indicated to Tom that he was living in an existential prison in which he was the warden who prevented himself from leaving. I assigned Sartre's play, *No Exit*, for him to read. The play depicts the dilemma and interaction of several characters who find themselves in a room they soon recognize to be Hell. As each discusses his or her life story, it becomes clear that they are more caught up in trying to justify themselves to each other than in trying to leave the room and get out of Hell. When the main protagonist discovers a door, he chooses to stay in the room to continue his discussions of himself. I thought that Sartre's existential play would help Tom recognize his dilemma in making a choice—that is, he was more concerned with justifying himself to others (and to himself) than in getting out of the apartment that he had made into his existential prison.

Tom was enthusiastic at the next meeting. We decided that "Hell is other people's expectations of you." Tom correctly viewed himself as locked in an existential prison of his own choice with himself as the warden who would never let himself out. We examined a variety of strategies that he could use to "save face." First he could reattribute his business problems to the "recession." Second, he could normalize the problem: "All consultants are having the problem." Third, he could reduce others' expectations by indicating that he was considering getting out of consulting. When he presented this to his family and in-laws, he was surprised to learn that they supported his idea of making a change.

Tom decided that the best alternative would be in an entirely new field—becoming a therapist. We worked on "expanding the criterion for success" by setting aside financial success as his goal and pursuing the idea of helping people and learning entirely new skills. As Tom pursued his course of study over the next six months, his depression completely lifted. He had found a way out of the existential prison in which he had trapped himself. He could now feel comfortable telling everyone that he had decided in his late forties to set aside his old business interests to pursue something entirely new—becoming a therapist. I asked Tom to evaluate how he had changed in the past year. His responses are shown in Table 4–3.

As indicated earlier, this patient became more highly motivated in therapy when we analyzed his resistance. By providing the patient with a conceptualization of his resistance—that is, his assumptions and schemas about entitlement, illusions of stability, discomfort dodging—and by helping him examine his theory of "choice" by evaluating his portfolio theory, we were able to work collaboratively toward decisions that could break him free from his depression and immobility.

CONCLUDING COMMENTS

Tom's depression was completely alleviated. He reported no sadness, no hopelessness, and no self-criticism a year later. We continued to meet sporadically as he enjoyed relating his enthusiasm about his new course of study. Ironically, although he had told everyone that his consulting business was not working out, he began getting new clients and he began to feel somewhat overloaded with combining both schoolwork and consulting work. He decided to remain partially separated

Table 4–3. Patient's Summary of Change

Topics	Last Year	Today
Self-handicapping	Thought I was finished in my career. Resisted change.	Feel like I could "rule the world," excited about new possibilities.
Discomfort dodging	Avoid discomfort at all costs.	Faced most discomfort squarely.
Entitlement	Totally entitled. Loss "can't happen" to me.	Still feel somewhat entitled, but will deal with loss if it happens.
Expectations that things remain the same	Wanted *nothing* to change.	Want *everything* to change
Loss (and need) of money	Couldn't live without a lot of money.	Still don't want to live without, but the prospect is not unthinkable anymore.

from his wife, whom he continued to see on weekends; despite my efforts to get him to confront the marital issues, he still believed that he could wait for the marriage to work itself out one way or another. Just as he had used discomfort dodging and the illusion that everything could remain the same in his work problems, he also used these strategies in his marital avoidance. However, that was the agenda he chose to follow.

This case illustrates the value of directly analyzing the patient's resistance from the perspective of a cost-benefit utility model based on portfolio theory and self-handicapping strategies. The task of the therapist was to go beyond the traditional cognitive therapy techniques to evaluate with the patient why he was committed to resisting change. Utilizing concepts such as hedging and self-handicapping was helpful in providing the patient with a conceptualization of change and why he actively resisted change. The utility and self-handicapping models of resistance were appealing to this patient, partly because of his capability in working with a logical utilitarian model and partly because resistance was framed in terms of adaptation (that is, as an attempt to provide further loss). This made sense to him and appeared less pejorative. However, once his depression lifted—due to his ability to understand his resistance, modify it, and foresee meaningful work and an acceptable role for himself—he was less interested in addressing these issues as they pertained to his marriage. The continued resistance in this area of his life reflected his assessment that the costs outweighed the benefits of change.

REFERENCES

Becker, G. S. (1976). *The Economic Approach to Human Behavior.* Chicago: University of Chicago Press.

Bowlby, J. (1969). *Attachment and Loss: I. Attachment.* New York: Basic Books.

—— (1980). *Attachment and Loss: III. Loss: Sadness and Depression.* London: Hogarth.

Leahy, R. L. (1966). *An investment model of depressive resistance.* Paper presented at meetings of the Association for the Advancement of Behavior Therapy, New York, November.

—— (1997a). Depression and resistance: an investment model of decision-making. *Behavior Therapist* 20:3–6.

—— (1997b). An investment model of depressive resistance. *Journal of Cognitive Psychotherapy*, in press.

Marks, I. M. (1987). *Fear, Phobias, and Rituals: Panic, Anxiety and Their Disorders.* Oxford: Oxford University Press.

Nesse, R. N., and Williams, G. C. (1994). *Why We Get Sick: The New Science of Darwinian Medicine.* New York: Random House.

Tomassi, M., and Ierulli, K., eds. (1995). *The New Economics of Human Behavior.* Cambridge, UK: Cambridge University Press.

Wenegrat, B. (1990). *Sociobiological Psychiatry: A New Conceptual Framework.* Lexington, MA: Lexington Books.

II

APPLICATIONS TO PSYCHIATRIC DISORDERS

5

DEPRESSION

Ruth L. Greenberg

*A*s the scene opens, the cognitive therapist finds the depressed
patient caught in a devouring web of troubles. He is trapped by
the symptoms of his depression and snagged by features of his
personality; he is at the mercy of biological forces and psychological ones, individual attributes and environmental stressors,
past experiences and present dilemmas. He has perhaps some
hope of extricating himself, some sense of his own strengths, but
he cannot mobilize his resources, and he may fear significant
change.

Perhaps another conflict has taken place offstage that has
helped to secure the patient in this hapless pose: the conflict
between his need for treatment and his willingness to seek it.
Perhaps only the sense of last resort, the sense that there are no
alternatives, has at last propelled the patient into the therapist's
office. Yet the cognitive therapist applies a simple set of principles to help the patient release himself from a complex

predicament, hoping to produce a cost-effective treatment with long-term advantages for relapse prevention.

COGNITIVE THERAPY OF DEPRESSION

Cognitive therapy, a short-term, structured treatment for depression, derives from the model of depression described by Beck (1970). In Beck's model, depression comprises emotional, cognitive, motivational, and physical manifestations, but the cognitive aspects of depression are viewed as playing a pivotal role in the maintenance of the syndrome. The depressed patient's thinking is seen as dominated by the "cognitive triad"—patterns of negative thinking about the self, the world (the patient's experiences), and the future. He (or she) experiences a stream of negative "automatic thoughts"—thoughts that occur without reflection or reasoning, but are plausible to the patient, although they may appear highly distorted to an outside observer. These thoughts are seen as producing a direct effect on mood and motivation. If, for example, the patient's automatic thoughts involve predictions that his efforts are doomed to failure, he is likely to feel discouraged and unwilling to take action to try to help himself.

Beck (1970) posited further that the patterns of negative thinking in depression resulted from the activation of latent idiosyncratic schemas, which he defined as structures "for screening, coding, and evaluating the stimuli that impinge on the organism" (p. 283). While functional schemas allow the individual to orient himself or herself in time and space, evaluate and make sense of experiences, some schemas develop that are potentially maladaptive. These schemas, generallly characterized by their content, represent broad, negative generalizations about the self—for example, "I am stupid," "I am socially unacceptable." Like adaptive schemas, the maladaptive schemas filter information from the environment and organize the way the individual interprets experience; unlike the more adaptive schemas, they are relatively rigid and closed to new information. While maladaptive schemas may remain latent for long periods of time, they become increasingly active as depression progresses, and in time the negative content dominates the patient's thinking and functioning.

Cognitive therapy of depression attempts to counteract the force of these negative schemas and thus lift the patient's mood and outlook. The therapy embodies a collection of techniques designed to modify distorted beliefs about self, world, and future. Classically defined by Beck and colleagues (1979), it attempts to counter the depressed patient's helplessness and hopelessness by overtly structuring the therapy, employing such devices as the creation of a problem list, the setting of an agenda for each session, and even scheduling of activities between sessions. The rationale for cognitive therapy is presented to the patient, and the interview is used to elicit and identify negative "automatic thoughts." When the patient has identified specific problems, these are addressed, with the goal of developing solutions. Behavioral experiments are used as empirical tests of the patient's negative predictions, and also to provide experiences of mastery and pleasure, which help to disrupt the depressed mood. As the patient learns to identify and evaluate negative automatic thoughts, he or she is asked to record and challenge them between sessions.

On the basis of these collections of automatic thoughts, as well as other data, the therapist forms a hypothesis about the underlying beliefs and shares it with the patient, who then is encouraged to define the hypothesis. The validity of dysfunctional beliefs may then be evaluated. Throughout, the therapist maintains a collaborative relationship with the patient; the validity of thoughts and beliefs is challenged through a Socratic style of questioning rather than through lecture or exhortation. Finally, homework is typically assigned throughout the course of treatment and is viewed as a means of helping the patient take responsibility for his or her own treatment, so that the patient is prepared from the outset for termination. In my view, the essential simplicity of the principles of cognitive therapy is a significant advantage in that patients are frequently able to understand and apply them on their own.

Numerous writers and clinicians have contributed to the range and repertoire of cognitive therapy since it was originally described (see, for example, Kuehlwein and Rosen 1993). Among the innovations relevant to the treatment of depression is the emerging literature on the treatment of personality disorders. Beck and associates (1990) and Young (1990) related the formation and maintenance of personality disorders to the operation of maladaptive schemas, much as Beck (1970) had earlier related depression to schema development. These authors have developed such treatment methods as re-creating childhood experiences through imagery and role-play, and using in-session experience to arouse and modify affect and behavior related to the functioning of maladaptive schemas. Since enduring, self-defeating patterns of relating to others are found not uncommonly in the population of depressed patients (Shea et al. 1990), these techniques are frequently integrated into the treatment of depression, as I will attempt to illustrate with the case of John.

A DOUBLE DEPRESSION

John suffered from "double depression": recurrent major depression superimposed on chronic dysthymia. *DSM-IV* (1994) defines the criteria for a major depressive episode as five or more of a list of symptoms briefly summarized as follows: depressed mood, loss of interest or pleasure in activities, significant weight loss or weight gain, insomnia or hypersomnia, psychomotor agitation or retardation, fatigue or loss of energy, feelings of worthlessness or guilt, loss of ability to concentrate or make decisions, recurrent thoughts of death. The symptoms must include either depressed mood or loss of interest or pleasure, must have been present during the same two-week period, and must represent a change from previous functioning.

The dysthymic patient (*DSM-IV* 1994) also experiences a continuing depressed mood and, in addition, problems with appetite, sleep, energy, self-esteem, concentration or decision making, and feelings of hopelessness, but only two of these additional symptoms are required to make the diagnosis. However, symptoms must have been present for at least a two-year period; during that period, symptoms may have been absent for no more than two months. Further complicating John's treatment were an assortment of avoidant and dependent personality features. In the language of *DSM-IV*, for example, John viewed himself as "socially inept, personally unappealing, or inferior" (p. 665), and had "difficulty initiating projects or doing things on his . . . own" (p. 668).

THE CASE OF JOHN

John appeared in my office with the haunted look of a man who had neither slept nor eaten very much for the past few weeks, as indeed, it developed, he had not. At work every day his effort was strained and anxious, and by the time he came home he felt unable to do anything but watch television and try not to think or feel. His many friends phoned to no avail: he refused to see them and told me he felt unable to connect to anyone. John complained of misery and unhappiness, of having little will or initiative, and of doing only what he must to maintain his meager income. He informed me that there were a lot of things wrong with him: he made many mistakes at work, failed to learn things properly, and couldn't retain information. Although he felt he should be studying at night so that he would be more effective in his job, he felt paralyzed each evening, then full of self-reproach the next day.

"I have a blatant dislike of everything." John told me he felt critical not only of himself, but of the people around him, and bitter about "things in general": art, culture, politics, his prospects for work and career. At 23 he was not suicidal, but cynical, despairing, and lonely. While he admitted that his problems in the past few weeks had been more severe than usual and probably the result of stresses at work, John told me all his problems were long-standing. He had been depressed since childhood and, despite an ability to be sociable, felt he never really got along with people and avoided getting close to them. "I don't care about other people. They annoy me. I just horse around with them or try to get away." He had had girlfriends, but characterized his relationships with them as problematic: "When I have a girfriend, I don't like to be away from her, but I'm mad at her all the time; my relationships just don't work out." In his very complaints John illustrated Beck's cognitive triad: negative views of himself, his experiences, and his future.

John's history had been tragic. His parents had been immigrants who had struggled hard in this country until his father died of cancer when John was 8. Mother's remarriage had ended with a fatal car accident four years later, leaving John, at 12, with a gruff and domineering stepfather, and no siblings to share his ordeal. Yet the situation had its advantages, from John's point of view. Stepfather, a factory worker, worked nights, leaving John on his own most of the time. With no college aspirations and no idea of a vocational path other than to follow his step-father into the factory, John "messed around" throughout high school, spending his abundance of unsupervised time with similarly undirected friends.

One day, on a whim, John had applied to a local university, and was eventually admitted. Remarkably, as John sat before me, he was a summa cum laude graduate of that university. He had achieved this status, however, at the cost of nearly disabling anxiety, vomiting, and shaking before exams and while writing papers. It was obvious that there were cognitive distortions involved in John's apparent view of himself as incompetent or defective. John's history also suggested that additional negative self-schemas might underlie his avoidant and dependent personality features, dousing his relationships with dissatisfaction and unfulfillment.

Treatment Begins

Where to start?

As always in working with a depressed patient, I wanted my initial intervention to strike a blow at John's hopelessness and lighten his sense of helplessness. I wanted to offer help with short-term problems, while offering reasonable assurance that longer-term issues would be attended to. It is a daunting task for any therapist to select such an intervention, and so I used the classic cognitive-behavioral solution: ask the patient to set some goals.

John elected to work first on his sense of paralysis and his difficulties at work; although he had no expectation of success in tackling his problems with relationships, he agreed we might discuss them at a later time. It was clearly important to help John restore a sense of self-efficacy, so I looked for a small task that might provide a "success experience." John believed that he should be studying computer programs every night so that he would be better equipped to carry out the responsibilities of his bookkeeping job during the day. While it seemed perfectionistic of John to expect this of himself, especially when he was suffering from depletion and fatigue, working toward this goal seemed a way of engaging him both in

collecting negative automatic thoughts and setting more realistic standards.

> "I wonder what you are feeling when you come home at
> night, intending to spend some time on this project?"
>
> "I don't know. I just turn on the TV."
>
> "And what if you didn't?"
>
> "I'd just feel bad, I guess."
>
> "And what do you imagine would be going through your
> mind? What thoughts? What images?"
>
> "That I can't do it—I can't learn enough to make a differ-
> ence."
>
> "So perhaps you are making a prediction about how much
> you will accomplish, and how meaningful it will be."

By continuing to question John, I was able to execute some
indispensable first-session maneuvers (Beck et al. 1979). I
gained his agreement that he was experiencing a series of
negative automatic thoughts, that it was possible they were
distorted in some way and plausible that they had an effect on
his mood and behavior. I explained the "cognitive model" and
told him something about its history. I managed to whittle the
task he had set for himself from three hours each night to a
half hour or an hour on each of two or three nights. I engaged
him in challenging his tacit assumption that the study was
worthwhile only if it entirely overcame his sense of inadequacy
at the job—and he grudgingly adopted the notion that whatever time he put in would have some utility. Again in classic
fashion, I carefully defined his homework so that it was
practically "no-lose": he was to complete the task or at least
turn the TV off long enough to try to notice the negative
thoughts that stopped him.

Finally, I explained to John that with the cognitive model as
an investigative tool, we would later be able to explore his
feelings about friendships and intimate relationships, his doubts

about the future, and the terrible performance anxiety that had so often brought his heart to his stomach.

A Few More Sessions

It was clear that John's mood had lightened somewhat when I next met with him; he stated that he felt more in control. He had spent two hours at his evening task, and while he was disappointed that he had not accomplished more, he recognized that he was no longer completely "stuck"; doing his homework had rewarded him with some sense of mastery. Skeptical of the cognitive model, he was nevertheless willing to try to apply it to the issue on his agenda: his feelings of incompetence at work.

At work, it emerged, John had been feeling anxious, depressed, and angry. When given an assignment, he reported, his automatic thoughts were, "I can't do it." He would then attempt to find someone to help him, but if others refused he would become angry, and had automatic thoughts such as, "They don't care about me." At this point he might try to work on the assignment, but he would experience a stream of self-critical thoughts, such as, "Others would know how to do this," "What I'm doing can't be right," "I should have learned how to do this before," or "There's something wrong with me." In fact, co-workers were less willing to help John than they had been, irritated by his frequent requests.

John agreed that his seeking help might be part of the problem. Whenever he did succeed at a task, he attributed it to his co-workers' assistance and thus accumulated no sense of personal competence. I proposed a dual approach. First, we would attempt to evaluate the belief, "I am incompetent," based on available evidence. John promptly began to list many errors he had made on his last job, and argued ardently that they signified a learning disability, a "defect." Yet he was

willing to admit that the errors had been inconsequential, and
further, that it was possible that they had been due to poor
concentration, a symptom of his depression and anxiety. (We
agreed that once his emotional distress had been alleviated,
we might reevaluate the question of learning disability.) Evidence against the belief was plentiful, once my questioning
opened its mental hiding place. Even at the current job, for
example, John had succeeded in solving some problems that
had stumped his co-workers. On a flash card, we recorded
John's conclusion—"I *am* capable of doing this job"—and the
evidence to support it.

The second element of our strategy consisted of a homework assignment. For one week John would avoid his usual
strategy of asking for help with assignments. Instead, he would
record each assignment in a notebook, followed by a rating of
how strongly he believed he could accomplish it, on a scale of
zero to 100 percent. If it was a large task, he would break it into
smaller steps and rate each one. Later he would rate how well
he had done with each task or step. This exercise would
provide some new information that would help test the belief,
"I am incompetent." Further, I reframed the anxiety he was
likely to experience as a good thing, a sign he was starting to
break old patterns of dependency and self-doubt, and proposed that he think of himself as starting to develop some
tolerance for such anxiety.

By the next session John's depression had eased some
more, and with it some of his skepticism. Although his ratings
of performance reflected his perfectionism, they were still
higher than his ratings of *expected* performance, and he had
experienced some relief from the tension of trying to obtain
help from busy, preoccupied people. John admitted his findings cast more doubt on the idea that he was incompetent. We
agreed that he would continue these ratings for another week.

The following week, John, usually quiet and reticent, was
less communicative than usual. I asked what he was con-

cerned about—if he thought I would react badly to what he had to say—and watched tears gather in the corners of his eyes.

"I don't know. I just feel bad, I guess."

John had made vague, undifferentiated statements like this before, but now, for the first time, it occurred to me that John would have to work hard just at identifying his feelings—recognizing them, labeling them, and, perhaps most of all, feeling safe in expressing them. After I shared these thoughts with John, who nodded agreement, I went on to ask whether he had felt free to express feelings in his family. John replied that he hadn't: "Not sure why." His mother was warm, and popular with the neighborhood children, but John had always felt himself an "outsider" around her, never thought he should bother her. Father had rarely been present, stepfather unapproachable.

John was now talking more freely. I asked what he had been feeling earlier, when he had begun to cry, and he began, hesitatingly, to tell about his loneliness. He had returned to "hanging out" with friends, but felt distant from them. They liked him, he was certain, because of his mocking, sardonic views, but was certain they would dislike him if they really knew him. This seemed not entirely unreasonable, as he had mocking, sardonic views of them: "I just think their problems are stupid. They have no idea what I have to deal with. They have parents to help them if they mess up. They expect you to sympathize with them when their worries are ridiculous." Still, John thought there was something wrong with *him*: "I have no empathy. I should care and I don't."

Despite these negative feelings about people, John told me, he had begun to feel attracted to a young woman at work. Again with some hesitation, he told me he feared approaching her—feared not a possible rejection but a possible success and the repetition of his own destructive patterns, which he was certain would ensue. "When I'm with a girl, I act rude to her, or I act goofy, or I'm mad at her." John craved a relationship, in part because of a feeling of calm, an ability to focus, that he sometimes experienced around a girlfriend. At home by himself, he agreed, he was often nervous and restless; his recent "homework" successes notwithstanding, he had trouble focusing on activities that were not passive or "mechanical": he could watch TV or do laundry, but he could not easily read a book.

Spontaneously, John related his performance anxiety in college, and his recent "paralysis of the will," to an inability to take action *alone*. With a sudden twinge of my own anxiety, I realized that my patient's future—his ability to love and his capacity to achieve—depended on the resolution of these dilemmas. John seemed anguished, listless, tucked suddenly into an envelope of helplessness.

Identifying Core Beliefs

What beliefs about the self, what impulses, what mechanisms, might compel such behavior? I asked John to tell me what he was feeling when he was "rude" or "goofy" with friends and girlfriends.

> "I don't know. I just don't know what to do. I don't think they're really interested in me, so I cover up."
> "And why don't you think they are interested in you?"
> "I'm different from other people, I guess."

And so he was. The college-educated, middle-class crowd who were currently his friends did not seem to share his modest background or his history of neglect. Yet John had felt himself an outsider even in his early years.

> "You see yourself as an outsider, different in a bad way."

"Right."

"And so you don't express very much about yourself."

"Yes."

"And what about feeling mad at girlfriends, what are you feeling then?"

"I don't know. I don't like what they're doing, and I have to put up with it."

So many "I don't know"s! I took these as further signs that John was unaccustomed to expressing his feelings, or perhaps fearful that they would be dismissed, demeaned, misunderstood. I questioned further. Although John's responses remained sparse and tentative, he gradually managed to suggest what some of his basic beliefs, attitudes, and compensatory mechanisms might be. I offered this summary to John:

"I am incompetent and cannot function on my own, but I am socially unacceptable, different. I need others to depend on, but they will not like me if they really know me. Thus I rarely express my intimate thoughts, feelings, or preferences—in fact, I cover them up with sarcasm and insults, and by clowning around. But inside I feel distant from others, and sometimes resentful that they do not know or understand me better."

John agreed that this summary described him pretty well. For homework he was to try to notice automatic thoughts he experienced around his friends when he was uncomfortable. I also encouraged him to consider asking the young woman for a date—in therapy, he would have a chance to reflect on and modify his maladaptive patterns. And, of course, he was to try to continue his more independent behavior at work.

Automatic Thoughts, Automatic Behaviors

John's sleep and appetite had by now improved dramatically, and his other depressive symptoms had moderated. He brought a short list of observations he had made of his feelings around friends—and around his date.

One day a friend had asked him to a foreign film. John was sick and could not go; the friend, however, intended to go alone, and spoke excitedly about the excellent reviews. John's response was quick sarcasm: "Well, aren't you special? *You're* going to a movie." The sarcasm was typical—automatic behavior for John—but this time John had stopped to make note of his feelings and automatic thoughts. He had felt sad and a little angry, and had the thought, "He's going and I'm not."

This was my chance to introduce the Dysfunctional Thought Record; I had John record, on the form, the situation, his feelings, and his automatic thoughts. But the automatic thoughts John had noted were merely a statement of fact—he had not yet expressed the negative meaning of the event. I illustrated the "downward arrow" technique (Burns 1980), drawing an arrow downward below John's "automatic thought," and asked: "What did it mean to you, that he was going and you were not?"

"That I'm not too important to him." This statement was recorded beneath the arrow.

John acknowledged readily that the meaning of the event was related to a core belief, "I'm socially unacceptable." He accepted my explanation of how core beliefs, or schemas, filtered his perceptions so that, over and over, he experienced the world in a way that was consistent with those beliefs (Beck et al. 1990, Young 1990). It was our task, I told him, to try to readmit some of the information that had been filtered out along the way.

"So let's test out the thought, 'I'm not too important to my friend.'"

John thought he did have evidence to support this thought—after all, he didn't *feel* important to his friend. But this was "emotional reasoning" (Burns 1980), I explained: feeling it, no matter how strongly, did not make it true. And John had considerable evidence against the thought. His friend, for example, had kept phoning John throughout the worst of his depression, despite John's repeated attempts to push him away. John was reluctant to accept the emerging conclusion, and began to laugh a wry, disgusted laugh.

"Yeah, sure, I'm important to him."

"Perhaps it's hard to believe something different. Perhaps the thoughts contain a kernel of truth—the two of you would be closer if you weren't always pushing him away, if you let him in on your feelings. But if you continue to accept the negative thoughts uncritically, you will continually re-create these patterns."

With this, John agreed to record a "rational response": "The evidence shows I am important to him"—and listed the signs his friend did care.

The second observation John had recorded related to the young woman he had asked for a date. As John had predicted, this co-worker had accepted, and the two had shared dinner in a restaurant. At dinner he had felt increasingly depressed, and was able to identify the thought, "Why should she like me? I'm ugly and boring."

Again we used the Dysfunctional Thought Record as a framework for testing the thought, this time with less resistance from John. Now that he understood the use of the Thought Record, I assigned it as homework. John was to use it to record uncomfortable feelings and automatic thoughts. If the automatic thoughts he recorded did not express the negative meaning of an event, he was to use the "downward arrow" technique, as we had done in session. Further, he was to use his typical dysfunctional behavior as a cue to look inward to discover his feelings and automatic thoughts. Together, in the following sessions, we would try to develop rational responses.

Refining Our Strategy

As John began to gain skill in identifying his feelings and in using the Thought Record, his depressed mood decreased further. Happily, his dates with the young woman also continued, and became a pleasant respite for him. Soon John was "back to normal"—his chronic level of depression and low self-esteem. He was no longer expressing as many extreme, negative statements about himself. But it was increasingly apparent that his relationships were in fact replete with maladaptive patterns. He was rude to his girlfriend to "test" whether she liked him; he would virtually never express a preference regarding how they spent their time together, and end up resenting the loss of control over his time. If the acute depression had placed a magnifier on John's negative beliefs about himself, this period of relatively benign mood had shifted the glass to his interpersonal behavior. If John were to gain lasting relief from depression, we would have to further modify his dependent behavior and avoidance of intimacy, as well as his perfectionism and inhibiting fear of failure.

In the collaborative fashion typical of cognitive therapy, I explained my concerns to John. He had mixed feelings about having the problems enumerated in this way. "I'm really a mess," he said. But he was glad to have them named clearly. We decided to target two types of behavior. John wanted to look for a better job, and by taking steps toward this goal he would be increasing autonomy as well as confronting his fear of failure. Second, he would look for opportunities to express his feelings and preferences and thus his experience of intimacy. John thought he could manage to take one step in each of these areas each week. To assist him, he would use Dysfunctional Thought Records, anxiety tolerance, and some anxiety management skills I promised to teach him. We would use the next few sessions to review his difficulties and try to specify the next step in each homework domain.

But each session became an examination of John's avoidance. Relaxation training, and further practice in recognizing schema-related thoughts and behavior, seemed to have no effect. The core beliefs clearly had a strong hold on him, and we would have to mount a fiercer attack on them to move forward. I wanted now to discuss John's childhood experiences, to understand the impact of the loss of his parents, and to grasp how these events might have contributed to the development of his schemas. John, however, had few memories of childhood; he did little but shrug his shoulders when I asked about them. Reluctantly, I concluded this path was unproductive.

But these thoughts led me to reflect on the *process* of therapy. In John's therapy I had been more forceful than usual in defining problems and goals; perhaps, as in the larger world, John had avoided stating what he needed and allowed others to impose a direction, then reacted with continuing, unexpressed ambivalence or anger, lacking a felt connection to a mutual endeavor.

John, I decided, needed to experience actively embracing his own goals. Next session, I described the impasse as I perceived it, but resisted the impulse to define the problem further or help John to solve it. After thirty frustrating minutes, watching him struggle with increasing anxiety, I heard him say, "I guess I wasn't taking responsibility for the problem. I really need to stop talking about it and start looking for a job."

After this session John became more active in pursuing his vocational and interpersonal goals, and more creative and independent in applying cognitive techniques to help himself. We were able to further challenge his core beliefs and articulate "new beliefs." Perhaps because of increased comfort with me and with the process of therapy, John was able to share some memories of childhood. Through imagery he was able to achieve some compassion for the lonely, neglected child he had been, and help the "child" challenge the belief that he was not worth much to others. With further resolution of the depression and clear evidence of change in his feelings and behavior toward friends and intimates, we were able to taper the frequency of sessions and finally to terminate treatment.

I end my references to John with a short but indispensable note about antidepressant medication. John elected to work without medication, and I supported his choice. However, I believe the therapist has an obligation to ascertain that the depressed patient is aware of the option of medication and educated about its possible advantages and disadvantages. If, in the therapist's view, the patient is refusing needed pharmacotherapy, the therapist must help the patient evaluate his or her attitude toward medication, just as the therapist would challenge other dysfunctional beliefs.

It may be of interest to note that, as many patients enter therapy already taking medication, the need for some of the classic cognitive therapy techniques designed to cope with the most disabling symptoms of depression may be reduced, while enduring, maladaptive interpersonal patterns may be more salient from the outset. Hence, techniques drawn from the cognitive therapy of personality disorders may be an increasingly important component of the cognitive therapy of depression. In any event, the treatment of depression is inevitably intertwined with the treatment of personality issues, as schemas relevant to personality dysfunction seem almost invariably to be activated in depression.

EFFECTIVENESS OF COGNITIVE THERAPY

Cognitive therapy has long been regarded as an effective psychosocial treatment for depression (see, for example, Hollon et al. 1991, Shapiro et al. 1994). In most studies it has performed as well as or better than comparison treatments, including pharmacotherapy. In addition, evidence suggests that cognitive therapy may reduce the chance of symptom return after treatment is terminated. However, in a 1993 review, Hollon and colleagues point to methodological limitations in the literature to date; they conclude that cognitive therapy is a "particularly promising, but as yet not fully proven, clinical intervention" (p. 274). These cautions notwithstanding, cognitive therapy represents, at least for many patients, a powerful training not only in coping with depressive symptoms but in modifying their responses to potentially depressogenic stressors over the course of a lifetime.

REFERENCES

Beck, A. T. (1970). *Depression: Causes and Treatment*. Philadelphia: University of Pennsylvania Press.

Beck, A. T., Freeman, A., and Associates (1990). *Cognitive Therapy of Personality Disorders*. New York: Guilford.

Beck, A. T., Rush, A. J., Shaw, B.F., and Emery, G. (1979). *Cognitive Therapy of Depression*. New York: Guilford.

Burns, D. (1980). *Feeling Good*. New York: Signet.

Diagnostic and Statistical Manual of Mental Disorders (DSM-IV) (1994). 4th ed. Washington, DC: American Psychiatric Association.

Hollon, S. D., Shelton, R. C., and Davis, D. (1993). Cognitive therapy for depression: conceptual issues and clinical efficacy. *Journal of Consulting and Clinical Psychology* 61:270–275.

Hollon, S. D., Shelton, R. C., and Loosen, P. T. (1991). Cognitive therapy and pharmacotherapy for depression. *Journal of Consulting and Clinical Psychology* 59:88–99.

Kuehlwein, K. T., and Rosen, H., eds. (1993). *Cognitive Therapies in Action*. San Francisco: Jossey-Bass.

Shapiro, D. A., Barkham, M., Rees, A., et al. (1994). Effects of treatment duration and severity of depression on the effectiveness of cognitive-behavioral and psychodynamic-interpersonal psychotherapy. *Journal of Consulting and Clinical Psychology* 62:522–534.

Shea, M. T., Pilkonis, P. A., Beckham, E., et al. (1990). Personality disorders and treatment outcome in the NIMH Treatment of Depression Collaborative Research Program. *American Journal of Psychiatry* 147:711–718.

Young, J. E. (1990). *Cognitive Therapy for Personality Disorders: A Schema-Focused Approach.* Sarasota, FL: Professional Resource Exchange.

6

PANIC DISORDER*

Mary Ann Mercier

DESCRIPTION OF THE DISORDER

Since *panic disorder* was introduced as a new diagnostic category in the third edition of the American Psychiatric Association's *Diagnostic and Statistical Manual of Mental Disorders* (*DSM-III*) (1980), its criteria have been modified to reflect our increasing knowledge of its central features. It was initially defined as a minimum of three panic attacks within three weeks, each marked by a discrete period of fear or apprehension having at least four of twelve symptoms. *DSM-III-R* (1987) required four attacks within four weeks, four of thirteen symptoms, and it specified those attacks must be unexpected and have a sudden onset. Sudden onset generally means panic

*The author wishes to acknowledge the assistance of Mary Guardino, Director of Freedom from Fear.

will peak within ten minutes, although Barlow and colleagues (1994) suggest that a criterion of five minutes might better show the true nature of the alarm reaction in panic. A clear demarcation of the abruptness of the attack is necessary to differentiate panic from other anxiety states.

The recognition that panic attacks occur across anxiety disorders, not just in panic disorder, led the APA to place the definition of panic attack at the beginning of the "Anxiety Disorders" section in *DSM-IV* (1994). It also led to a typology of panic attacks: unexpected, situationally bound, and situationally predisposed. Unexpectedness is an important factor in differentiating between panic disorder and other types of anxiety in which panic attacks occur.

Panic attacks in specific phobias (formerly simple phobia) occur in response to the feared stimulus; for example, an animal phobic's panic attack would occur when confronted by a dog, but not during an electrical storm. Likewise, a social phobic might experience an attack when told he must deliver a half-hour speech, but not while standing in an empty parking lot. Both are examples of situationally bound or situationally predisposed panic in which the phobic's fear is of the situation—the dog, or having to give a speech and the possible embarrassment that might cause—not of the panic attack itself.

On the other hand, in panic disorder the fear is *of having a panic attack*. The unexpectedness of attacks leads to the fear of having other attacks. Even in panic disorder with agoraphobia, in which the panicker comes to fear a particular situation in which she has had panic attacks in the past, her fear is not of the situation itself but of having other attacks.

Rapee and colleagues (1992) compared the typical symptoms of unexpected panic attacks with those reported by anxious patients without panic, and found the following to be common among those with panic disorder: fear of dying, fear of going crazy or losing control, paresthesia, dizziness, faintness, unreality, and shortness of breath. The two cognitive symptoms, fear of dying, or fear of loss of control or going crazy, reflect concern about the implications of, or consequences of, an attack. Although neither has to be present for an individual to meet criteria for panic disorder, both help differentiate panic from other anxiety disorders. "Thus, cognitive symptoms may be viewed as epiphenomenal to the experience of panic" (Barlow et al. 1994, p. 557).

DSM-IV's definition of panic disorder no longer emphasizes a specified number of panic attacks within a certain time period, but focuses on the impact of the attacks, thus zeroing in on the essential features of panic disorder. It is now defined as recurrent unexpected panic attacks, *and* at least one of the following over a period of one month after a panic attack: subsequent persistent concern about having other attacks; worry about the implications of, or consequences of, the attack (loss of control, suffering a heart attack, going crazy); and/or a change in behavior as a result of the attack (e.g., urge to escape the situation).

Panic disorder may occur with or without agoraphobia. Agoraphobia is the fear and avoidance of being outside the home, on a bridge, in a crowd or standing in line, or traveling by car, bus, or train. In each of these situations escape may be difficult or embarrassing, or help may not be present if one suffers a full-blown or limited-symptom panic attack (*DSM-IV* 1994).

Treatment Approaches

Biological theories, which view panic as distinct from non-panic types of anxiety and as due to differences in underlying biological processes (Klein 1981), have generated a tremendous amount of research, especially experiments involving the provocation of panic in the laboratory (see e.g., Liebowitz et al. 1985). Not surprisingly, the treatment of choice among biologically oriented specialists is psychopharmacologic.

One psychological theory suggests that panic results from normal fear that occurs inappropriately, leading to the fear of additional attacks and a sense of uncontrollability (Barlow 1988, Barlow et al. 1994).

Cognitive models of panic emphasize the role played by a persistent tendency to misinterpret the meaning of bodily sensations or anxiety symptoms as being more dangerous than they actually are (Beck 1988, Clark 1986); for example, "I'm dying," "I must be crazy." These repetitive catastrophic misinterpretations lead to an increase in the severity of physical symptoms that then results in a panic attack. Cognitive treatment focuses on identifying these misinterpretations; finding other noncatastrophic interpretations for the bodily sensations; testing the validity of the new interpretations; and exposure to feared sensations or, in the case of the agoraphobic, to feared situations associated with past panic attacks (Clark 1986, 1989).

CASE IDENTIFICATION

Tom was a 29-year-old unmarried aircraft mechanic who sought treatment for a fourteen-year history of anxiety attacks. The second oldest of five children, two girls and three boys, he lived with his parents in an urban area.

PRESENTING COMPLAINT

Tom's main complaint was his worsening anxiety following the breakup of a six-month-long relationship with his girlfriend. He reported feeling more sluggish than usual, chronically off-balance or unsteady, short of breath most of the time, and frequently dizzy. Multiple, daily "anxiety attacks" were becoming the norm. Although he had exhibited moderate phobic avoidance for several years by opting to take cabs rather than walking, it had worsened to the point that he hated standing alone in wide-open areas such as an airport tarmac. Walking, whether it be across wide streets or in giant aircraft hangars, troubled him because of his fear that he would collapse or faint if he wasn't near some structural support like a wall or railing.

HISTORY

Tom's first panic attack occurred on his way to school at age 15. Although it lasted for only two or three minutes, he was left feeling shaky, faint, fearful of losing bladder control, and short of breath. Other attacks followed regularly, but school attendance never became an issue. Importantly, coincident with his first panic attack was Tom's initial history of alcohol use, which later met criteria for abuse and dependence. As a teenager he was apparently able to continue to engage in most of his regular activities as long as he could self-medicate with alcohol, usually beer. He graduated from high school and attended a community college for two years prior to joining the United States Navy.

During his four years in the Navy, Tom continued to experience panic attacks almost daily, though he exhibited little phobic avoidance. However, his alcohol use increased. Nonetheless, he apparently functioned reasonably well in the service and was honorably discharged. Tom's panic worsened greatly following his discharge, when he became employed as a civilian aircraft mechanic. Although he reported never having a panic attack while actually working on an airplane, crossing large parking lots and walking through gigantic hangars was becoming increasingly difficult for him, especially on hot, humid days. His means of coping with his growing anxiety was with progressively larger amounts of alcohol. On some days he would consume as much as a case of beer by himself. Within three years of taking the job he was dependent upon alcohol. Over the next two years he required detoxification five times. After his fifth detox he never used alcohol again, but turned to marijuana and cocaine for several months. By the time he sought treatment he had been clean of all drugs, including alcohol, for more than two years.

He had no history of depression or other anxiety disorder. Despite numerous medical workups, including a consultation with a pulmonary specialist, he had no significant medical problems.

ASSESSMENT

Tom was referred to me as part of a ten-week combined treatment program of psychoeducation, pharmacotherapy, and cognitive therapy. At intake into the program he was assessed by an intake coordinator and his treating psychiatrist. An interview based on the Structured Clinical Interview for *DSM-III* (SCID) was used.

Prior to his first panic attack at age 15, Tom reported no significant difficulties in any area of his life. Since then he had experienced hundreds if not thousands of panic attacks. His attempts at managing them were limited to three strategies. Self-medication with alcohol occurred first. It wasn't until his final (and longest) detoxification in a rehabilitation center eleven years later that Tom discovered the panic-predisposing attributes of a hangover, and stopped drinking. During his alcohol treatment he learned yoga techniques and assertiveness training. Although he found these to be somewhat helpful in managing everyday affairs, they did not lessen the frequency or severity of his attacks. In fact, he reported a sudden burst of anxiety while attempting relaxation training, the description being entirely consistent with relaxation-induced panic. When neither marijuana nor cocaine helped prevent the attacks, he stopped using those drugs on his own.

Usually Tom tried to "tough it out," demanding that he go to school, on dates, and to work, but avoiding large open spaces. Whenever possible, he would "cover" his problem by walking alongside fences or near walls, and parking close to buildings to avoid having to cross large lots. He attempted to engage in those activities necessary to his vocational and personal life, but used avoidance to keep from getting into situations where he might feel dizzy or faint, and have another panic attack.

Despite Tom's sadness over the breakup with his girlfriend, he showed no signs of depression and reported no past history of any mood disorder.

Panic Attacks

The assessment of Tom's panic attacks followed the procedure suggested by Clark (1989), and involved questioning him about several recent attacks and the completion of a panic log. The combination of both of these showed that his most frequently occurring symptoms were shortness of breath, dizziness, faintness, feelings of unreality, and chest pain. Sometimes he also experienced nausea, a fear of dying, or a fear of losing control. In most cases his attacks came on suddenly and lasted for no more than three minutes.

The number of his symptoms and their abruptness meet *DSM-IV* criteria for panic attacks. His daily attacks easily qualify as "recurrent." Tom's core symptoms, except chest pain, correspond with those reported by Rapee and colleagues (1992). Despite the suggestion of situationally bound panic or at least situationally predisposed panic because of his avoidance of wide-open spaces, his main fear was of having another panic attack. He did not experience panic every time he was in these situations, nor did he know when an attack might actually occur. Thus this uncertainty about the timing, as well as the inevitability of an attack, meets the unexpectability requirement. His avoidance patterns reflect his worry about having another attack.

In summary, Tom was diagnosed:

Axis I: Panic disorder with agoraphobia of fourteen years' duration; moderate phobic avoidance
Alcohol dependence, in remission
Alcohol, cannabis, and cocaine abuse in remission
Axis II: None
Axis III: None
Axis IV: Mild (breakup with girlfriend)
Axis V: 61–70

SELECTION OF TREATMENT

At intake Tom was offered three treatment options: a comprehensive program of psychoeducation, pharmacotherapy, and cognitive therapy; pharmacotherapy and psychoeducation; or cognitive therapy. He chose the combined treatment package.

COURSE OF TREATMENT

My first contact with Tom was two weeks after he started the program. By then he had completed two of five group psychoeducation meetings, and was taking 50 mg of imipramine, a tricyclic antidepressant useful in the treatment of panic disorder (Klein 1981). Although his attacks were less frequent, he was still having at least one daily.

Session 1

The cognitive model of panic (Clark 1986) was presented during our first session. Because the model emphasizes the misinterpretation of bodily sensations, internal or interoceptive cues were sought as the trigger stimulus. Wide-open spaces were clearly his external trigger. In questioning Tom about the sequence of his symptoms, it became clear that although he complained most of dizziness, the first symptom he noticed a second or less before an actual attack started was shortness of breath. We agreed this was probably his internal trigger stimulus. The moment he experienced shortness of breath, he saw it as threatening and became increasingly apprehensive. This growing apprehension resulted in several anxiety symptoms including dizziness, faintness, chest pain, and nausea. In severe attacks he feared dying, losing control, or going crazy, but generally his main fear was of fainting. Once sure he would faint, his anxiety peaked.

Although he found the model interesting, Tom wasn't sure how it applied to him. He agreed to continue monitoring his panic, pay attention to his breathing when in wide-open spaces, and return for cognitive therapy. Additionally, having reviewed his history and being convinced of his having had a relaxation-induced panic attack, I asked for and received his permission to meet with his group leader to adapt relaxation training to minimize the probability that an attack would occur. We decided to have him use a focal point rather than closing his eyes during relaxation, and to have him wiggle his fingers whenever he feared losing control.

Session 2

Our second session was one week after the first. It had been an unusually hot week and he complained of feeling even dizzier than normal. Self-monitoring of his breathing convinced him that he often held his breath, then would repeatedly try to fill his lungs with air, but would end up feeling shorter of breath. He became pale just expressing his fear of fainting.

Tom was not a psychologically minded man. He rarely endorsed cognitive symptoms despite his admission, upon questioning, that he feared having panic attacks because he might lose control. Therefore, I decided to conduct an in-session experiment to demonstrate what effect his pattern of breathing was having on him. In this way I could review the model of panic in specific terms that might be meaningful to him.

As a first step in the procedure we practiced paced breathing. He was instructed to inhale to his own slow count of three, then to exhale to a similarly slow count of three. Once he could do this, we turned to voluntary overbreathing. I explained that it consisted of rapidly filling his lungs with air, then emptying them, then refilling them completely, and so on, followed by a brief demonstration.

Within seconds Tom was settled into his basic pattern of overbreathing. I then asked him to stand in the middle of the room, away from all furniture and walls. He paled at this suggestion and beads of sweat formed on his forehead, but he complied with my request. Encouraging him with patter such as "That's good," or "That's it," he continued to overbreathe despite his rapidly increasing discomfort in doing so. Although Clark and Salkovskis (1987) recommend overbreathing for two minutes, Tom was symptomatic within ten to fifteen seconds. I asked him to describe how he felt. His reply was faint, extremely dizzy, sweating, short of breath, and very fearful that he would faint at any moment. When asked how similar this was to one of his panic attacks, he said it was just like it except that he wasn't as scared because I was there and he knew I wouldn't let anything happen to him.

Because of his judgment that this was like one of his panic

attacks and his sureness that he would faint, I asked what he was doing to keep himself from fainting even though the answer was obvious to me. He was standing at attention, his knees locked, his arms stiff, and his fingers curled into fists. Once he admitted to this physical posture, I asked him to bend his knees and move his head around in circles. His paleness as he initially complied with this request made his skin pure white, and his face glistened with sweat, leaving little doubt that he was experiencing a full-blown panic attack. I then asked him to bend over at the waist and circle around to the front, sides, and back. In spite of his 100 percent prediction that he would faint once he did any of these motions, he did not. As soon as Tom was convinced that he was not going to faint, I led him into paced breathing by repeatedly counting to three at a slow pace. This entire experiment required less than two minutes. Once he was breathing normally, I asked him to sit down again. We reviewed the cognitive model of panic, inserting his reactions into the cycle, and he agreed that it fit him well.

Tom's homework for the week was to experiment in order to find out if stopping overbreathing when he felt dizzy or lightheaded gave him relief. Because of his lack of confidence that he could do paced breathing when frightened, he was instructed to breathe into his cupped hands. He was also asked to practice paced breathing at home when he was relaxed.

NOTE: Although I have found that this behavioral experiment often produces considerable anxiety in my patients, this case was unusual in the degree to which this happened. Many panickers will not identify the resulting symptoms of overbreathing as being a panic attack, but will admit to similarities. Therapists usually must ask for more information about the physical sensations that the patient is experiencing, because they are usually not as obvious as they were with Tom. Some psychologists contend that such behavioral experiments are ineffective with persons on antipanic medications such as imipramine or benzodiazepines. My experience is that patients may not experience as wide a range of symptoms or the same intensity, but they are nonetheless of sufficient severity to demonstrate the connection between their breathing and their other symptoms.

Session 3

Our next scheduled meeting was two weeks later. By this time Tom reported a marked improvement in his panic, having had six attacks in two weeks, all of them rated as mild. Whether this improvement was due to cognitive therapy or medication (100 mg imipramine) could not be determined. However, Tom found that slowing down his breathing helped him to feel less dizzy and lightheaded. On those occasions when he did experience panic, he said he knew what it was and just rode it out. His only phobic avoidance other than staying near walls, occurred on two of the hottest days of the summer when he opted to take a cab rather than walk. At other times, when he became dizzy while walking, he slowed his pace while focusing on his breathing until his symptoms subsided, then continued walking at a normal pace.

Session 4

We met again two weeks later. By then Tom's psychiatrist had increased his medication to 200 mg. In the two weeks since I had seen him, Tom had had four panic attacks, all but one rated as mild. However, he was doing more things like walking across parking lots rather than around their perimeters where he would be close to a fence. He could also walk through large hangars without thinking about how far he was from the walls.

His only instance of phobic avoidance was taking a cab one evening when he was particularly tired and humidity levels were in the nineties.

Although it is impossible to separate the effects of therapy from medicine, his changes in behavior suggested he was learning to react to his panic in constructive ways; for example, doing paced breathing or breathing into his hands whenever he felt dizzy or lightheaded.

At this session he asked to speak of stressful events in his life. He was being considered for a promotion at work, and was helping his parents to build an extension onto their home. Traditional cognitive exercises were introduced like a cost-benefit analysis for deciding whether he should accept the promotion. The main focus of the session, though, was on defining normal anxiety, which is often a problem for people who have suffered from panic disorder for long periods of time. Because they are used to experiencing very high levels of anxiety, and because they falsely assume other people in anxiety-producing situations experience either very low levels of anxiety or none, they don't know what constitutes a normal and reasonable level of anxiety. We decided to use a 100-point scale to measure anxiety, with 90–100 being a full-blown panic attack. His homework was to ask his family and friends how much anxiety they would have in various situations, including accepting a promotion. We agreed to meet again in one month.

Session 5

In the month since our last session Tom reported having only one panic attack, which dissipated within ten seconds—this despite his having accepted the promotion and being in training school. He experienced no anticipatory anxiety or expectation of having another attack as a result of this brief attack, and had no phobic avoidance. After ten weeks in the comprehensive program, Tom's panic disorder was in remission.

By this time Tom was finding walking to be a pleasant form of relaxation. He was also aware that the more frequently he walked, the less likely he was to become anxious when he had to cross wide-open spaces. We discussed other forms of relaxation including progressive relaxation exercises (which were *not* inducing panic after the changes mentioned in Session 1) and listening to music that had a beat slower than his resting heart rate. We listed other activities that had been pleasurable to him at other times in his life, and he agreed to engage in them now that he wasn't consumed with concern about having panic attacks.

Because this was our last scheduled session as part of his program, we reviewed what techniques had been useful to him in stopping his panic, and in coping with anxiety. A follow-up session was scheduled in two months. Unfortunately, the patient did not come in for follow-up cognitive therapy. Although he was grateful for his impressive and rapid recovery, he was unsure how well cognitive techniques would work if he wasn't taking medicine. He continued on imipramine for another year and a half, being fearful of coming off it. Had I been able to work with him at this time, I would have helped him to prepare to reduce his medication in several ways: (1) a "strategy card" could act as a reminder of those techniques (e.g., paced breathing) that he routinely found useful; (2) after identifying situations in which he was currently experiencing anxiety, we could determine whether its level was "normal and reasonable" and discuss ways to cope with that anxiety; (3) it was important that Tom learn that nothing bad would happen to him if he suffered another panic attack. We could approach this from two directions, cognitive and behavioral. By developing a series of rational responses, he could demystify and decatastrophize his beliefs about panic attacks and what it meant about him that he had them (e.g., "I'm weak," "I'm not in control of my emotions"). By repeatedly provoking panic attacks in session, Tom would learn his role (overbreathing) in their development, especially on hot and humid days when he was most likely to overbreathe. This would have shown him the benign nature of the attacks, and would have allowed him to learn to stop the attacks altogether. Once armed with this information, he could begin to reduce his dosage of medication as directed by his psychiatrist.

My own evaluation of Tom's therapy is that the medication speeded his learning and his recovery. His fear of reducing this dosage, though, shows that despite his changes in behavior, his thinking had not changed sufficiently. This is not surprising given his lack of psychological-mindedness, his fifteen-year history of panic disorder, and most important, that we had met for only five sessions. Until his thinking was changed in such a way that he no longer engaged in catastrophic interpretations of his physical sensations, Tom was likely to relapse.

Two years after starting treatment, Tom had reduced his medication to 50 mg of imipramine and was in the process of decreasing it further. He was having infrequent panic attacks and very limited phobic avoidance. Overall, he expressed satisfaction with his progress.

REFERENCES

Barlow, D. H. (1988). *Anxiety and its Disorders*. New York: Guilford.

Barlow, D. H., Brown, T. A., and Craske, M. G. (1994). Definitions of panic attacks and panic disorder in the *DSM-IV*: implications for research. *Journal of Abnormal Psychology* 103:553–564.

Beck, A. T. (1988). Cognitive approaches to panic disorder: theory and therapy. In *Panic: Psychological perspectives*, ed. S. Rachman and J. D. Maser, pp. 91–109. Hillsdale, NJ: Erlbaum.

Clark, D. M. (1986). A cognitive approach to panic. *Behavior, Research, and Therapy* 24:461–170.

———— (1989). Anxiety states: panic and generalized anxiety. In *Cognitive Behaviour Therapy for Psychiatric Problems*, ed. K. Hawton, P. M. Salkovskis, J. Kirk, et al., pp. 52–96. Oxford: Oxford University Press.

Clark, D. M., and Salkovskis, P. M. (1987). *Cognitive treatment for panic attacks: therapist's manual.* Unpublished manuscript, Oxford.

Diagnostic and Statistical Manual of Mental Disorders (DSM-III) (1980). 3rd ed. Washington, DC: American Psychiatric Association.

———— *(DSM-III)* (1987). 3rd ed. rev. Washington, DC: American Psychiatric Association.

———— *(DSM-IV)* (1994). 4th ed. Washington, DC: American Psychiatric Association.

Klein, D. F. (1981). Anxiety reconceptualized. In *Anxiety: New Research and Changing Concepts*, ed. D. F. Klein and J. Rabkin. New York: Raven.

Liebowitz, M. R., Gorman, J. M., Fyer, A. J., et al. (1985). Lactate provocation of panic attacks II: biochemical and physiological findings. *Archives of General Psychiatry* 42:709–719.

Rapee, R. M., Sanderson, W. C., McCauley, P. A., and DiNardo, P. A. (1992). Differences in reported symptom profile between panic disorder and other *DSM-III-R* anxiety disorders. *Behavior, Research, and Therapy* 30:45–52.

7

GENERALIZED ANXIETY DISORDER

John H. Riskind

INTRODUCTION

Generalized anxiety disorder is a relatively new diagnostic category. First introduced in 1980 by the *DSM-III*, the diagnosis of generalized anxiety was used to include the phenomenon referred to as "free-floating" anxiety or "anxiety neurosis" within the diagnostic system. The category of generalized anxiety disorder (GAD) is characterized today in *DSM-IV* (1994) as "excessive anxiety and worry which occurs more days than not for at least 6 months, about a number of events or activities (such as work or school performance). The individual finds it difficult to control the anxiety and worry, and suffers from additional symptoms such as restlessness, muscle tension, difficulty concentrating, irritability, and sleep disturbance." The diagnosis reflects recognition today that a group of patients exists who experience chronic anxiety and worry, and are not subsumed under the rubrics of the other anxiety disorders.

GAD was first delineated as a residual category in *DSM-III* because it was not diagnosed when panic disorder, phobias, or obsessive-compulsive disorders were present. Thus it was, in effect, a "wastebasket" category. This ambiguous, secondary status of GAD was removed by *DSM-III-R* (1987), which gave the disorder status as a primary diagnostic category (not just a residual). Another major modification in the diagnosis, which has been maintained in the *DSM-IV*, is that worry has been defined as one of the major features of the disorder. Thus these shifts in the *DSM* emphasize the essentially cognitive nature of the disorder. It seems that the cognitive features of GAD, such as worry (Borkovec et al. 1991), are the defining features of the disorder, but it must be recognized that these cognitive features do not uniquely define the disorder (Riskind et al. 1991). For example, the presence of chronic worry does not ensure a diagnosis of GAD (Sanderson and Barlow 1990). Nevertheless, the absence of such worry guarantees that the disorder is not present. Moreover, Sanderson and Barlow conclude that a patient with chronic worry is twice as likely to have GAD than any other specific anxiety disorder. Their data at the Albany Center for Stress and Anxiety Disorders indicate that chronic worry is significantly higher in GADs than in other anxiety disorders; however, worry is also elevated in other categories of anxiety disorder as well.

A high degree of comorbid prevalence of social phobia occurs as a secondary diagnosis in GADs (Sanderson and Barlow 1990). Such findings suggest that worries about social evaluation are often common themes in GAD, but must be accompanied by other worry themes as well to justify a diagnosis of GAD.

OUTCOME STUDIES

Although GAD has been described as a "stubborn" condition to treat, a number of recent studies have demonstrated the efficacy of cognitive-behavioral therapy (Barlow et al. 1984, Blowers et al. 1987, Borkovec et al. 1987, Butler et al. 1987, 1991, Durham and Turvey 1987, Power et al. 1989). These studies indicate that the treatment gains are relatively stable (Butler and Booth 1990). Furthermore, as Butler and Booth review, several of the studies show a superiority of cognitive forms of treatment over other forms, including behavior therapy.

Despite the general efficacy of cognitive therapy, many GADs don't respond to treatment. The cognitive treatment in these studies typically involves twelve or fewer sessions. The limited number of sessions leaves open the possibility that more extended cognitive treatment would benefit those patients who are initially nonresponders. Be this as it may, in some of the treatment studies a third of the GAD patients in the cognitive treatment groups failed to show a significant difference from their pretreatment levels of functioning (Butler and Booth 1990). A further problem for future research is that the twelve sessions of cognitive therapy worked less well for those who needed it the most: patients who were initially highest in anxiety and in their tendency to impose threatening interpretations on ambiguous information, as assessed by Butler and Mathews's (1983) "Interpretations Questionnaire."

Butler and Booth (1990) emphasize the need for creative use of the cognitive model when treating GADs. Unlike simple phobia, where a concrete "series of steps to bring about change can be recommended" (p. 205), in GAD the "path to progress is more blurred and less distinct" (p. 205). They suggest that the varied and complex nature of the condition, and the variety of methods that GADs can use to reduce their anxiety, requires a flexible and creative approach in piecing together a series of steps with a patient. Such flexibility and creativity, of course, requires a solid grounding in the cognitive model of anxiety and its methods.

The need for flexibility and creativity is illustrated by the familiar phenomen of "relaxation-induced" anxiety among GADs (Borkovec et al. 1987). This refers to the phenomenon of anxiety rising after relaxation training in GADs. Anxiety induced by relaxation training may reflect the idiosyncratic meaning that many GADs attach to loss of personal control, and perhaps the idiosyncratic control they attach to tension states. The phenomen indicates the need to conceptualize each unique patient in their distinct terms, and to tailor and modify intervention approaches so they will uniquely work with them.

COGNITIVE MODEL OF ANXIETY

According to the cognitive model, anxiety stems from a series of almost simultaneous judgments about the dangerousness of a situation (Beck 1976, Beck and Emery 1985). Taking a cue from Lazarus and Folkman (1984), Beck and Emery assert that the initial judgment, or primary appraisal, identifies the situation as a threat and assesses the probability, imminence, and degree of the potential harm. The next judgment, the secondary appraisal, is an estimate of the ability to counter harm, or to neutralize or cope with the danger. Finally, the maximum anxiety results from an identification that a situation is a threat coupled with a judgment that one lacks ability to cope with or control the danger.

According to the "hierarchical" component of Beck's cognitive model (Beck et al. 1983), cognitive phenomena are understood to contribute to the origins of psychological problems, including anxiety, at multiple levels. The different levels can be likened to a pyramid. At the top of the pyramid are stream-of-consciousness cognitions or automatic thoughts—parts of the immediate disorder or episode of the problem.

Lower down, in the wider middle of the pyramid, are more enduring ideational themes such as a pervasive sense of personal vulnerability in anxiety, as opposed to a sense of hopelessness in depression. These ideational themes are considered a separate class of cognitive phenomena from transient cognitions.

At the wide base of the pyramid are enduring erroneous beliefs, concepts, and attitudes, the underlying patterns or cognitive schemas that occupy a nearly central position in cognitive theory. Schemas are kinds of cognitive patterns or mental knowledge structures that organize all an individual's facts, memories, beliefs, and attitudes. They also determine how the individual thinks and reasons about ambiguous threat scenarios. For example, they assist the individual to interpret threat cues, and make predictions about the personal meaning or significance of a situation even on the basis of minimal information.

Schemas are the basic cognitive mechanism in psychological disorders that shape information processing. The schemas that guide thought associations, interpretations of ambiguous situations, or inferences at any time are the currently operative ones, and can be distinguished from other stored and enduring organized schemas that are *not* immediately or actively represented in the working memory or ongoing stream-of-consciousness of the individual at any given moment (see, e.g., Riskind and Rholes 1984). Once activated or primed, the idiosyncratic set of schemata of a given individual gives shape to the individual's ideas that characterize that disorder and its symptoms. In generalized anxiety disorder it is assumed that danger schemas that organize the individual's beliefs and concepts of personal danger are activated virtually constantly. As a result, the individual reaches predefined conclusions ("I am in danger," "There is a threat to my survival or well-being") with minimal cues, makes negative predictions, and worries about catastrophic scenarios.

According to Beck (1967), schemas include not only complex taxonomic systems for classifying stimuli, but also structured logical elements consisting of premises, assumptions, and even fully developed syllogisms. For example, the cognitive schemas that underlie anxiety may contain taxonomic systems for identifying the dangerousness of situations, as well as assumptions ("If-then") and negative syllogisms ("Thus," . . .). Once activated or operable, such schemas act as cognitive filters that affect what the individual attends to and focuses on, fills in gaps in missing information, and increases the likelihood that stimuli will be classified or recognized as danger signals (even if, objectively, they are not).

Research provides support for the general outlines of the cognitive formulation. For example, studies show that GADs have more of a tendency than other subjects to attend to threatening information (Mathews and MacLeod 1985) and impose threatening interpretations on ambiguous stimuli (Butler and Mathews 1983, Davey et al. 1992). They also often show a memory bias for threatening material (Greenberg and Beck 1989).

CLINICAL MODEL

The cognitive clinical model of GAD provides clear guidelines for treatment. A first goal is to normalize the anxiety and help the patient to understand the symptoms. A related goal is also to prepare patients for collaboration in therapy and to present the treatment model to them. One specific aim of the cognitive therapist is to help unify, normalize, and explain the diverse anxiety symptoms to the patient. Often patients are terrified of the variety of the different intense symptoms they have (fear of fear) and often exacerbate anxiety by misinterpreting the symptoms as manifestations of other disorders. To help unify and normalize the symptoms, as well as explain them, the following statement (or something like it) is useful:

Anxiety and fear are natural reactions that humans have to danger. We all have the capacity for anxiety and fear. Anxiety is like a smoke alarm system that we all have. It is a part of what it is to be human. The different symptoms that you are having— feelings of edginess, tension, sleep disturbance, distraction— are all symptoms of anxiety. You have one basic problem, not many. The problem is anxiety.

While anxiety is very unpleasant, some of the major under- lying causes of the anxiety are controllable. That is, anxiety is often caused by threatening thoughts. Anyone who has threat- ening thoughts and worries much of the time, even if they are exaggerated or distorted, would feel anxious. We have found that many people with anxiety like yours can be helped by helping them to identify and then cope with the thoughts that make them anxious.

The next general treatment goal is to assess and then counter anxiety by targeting spontaneous threatening auto- matic thoughts concerned with the theme of physical, social, or psychological danger. This involves teaching the patient to recognize when he or she is engaging in distorted thinking that either overestimates the presence of threats or underesti- mates the client's ability to cope with the threats. It also involves teaching the patient coping skills with which to counter the thoughts and refute them. Later, a goal is to help the patient to recognize the negativistic internal framework of maladaptive cognitive patterns and beliefs that are producing the distorted thoughts of danger and anxiety.

The standard cognitive therapy protocol (see e.g., Beck and Emery 1985) involves using thought diaries, role-playing, hypothesis testing, and a variety of cognitive-behavioral exercises. Imagery exercises are useful, as Beck and Emery describe, and can be used to restructure overestimates of threat or underestimates of coping potential.

Another component of cognitive therapy is to assist the patient in developing an individualized "coping kit" of techniques, counterarguments, and other materials to help them cope with their anxiety. Emphasis is placed here on identification of procedures that work for them personally (e.g., regular physical exercise, thought diaries, specific kinds of counterarguments).

These standard cognitive techniques can be supplemented with worry—stimulus control procedures (Borkovec et al. 1983). For example, patients who have particular problems with worry can schedule regular half-hour sessions of worrying at a preassigned time and place. Patients often find it helpful to engage in such worry sessions while they take a hot bath. After rehearsing their worries in these circumstances, they can use thought diaries to counter the negative ideas. The cognitive therapist can also assess subtle avoidance that occurs in anxious patients, such as tendencies not to want to think about unpleasant matters in their current lives, and counter this (Butler and Booth 1990).

As seen earlier, the standard cognitive clinical model has proved useful for patients with GAD. As the outcome literature shows, however, many patients don't respond to the standard cognitive treatments, despite their overall efficacy. Hence the standard clinical model could benefit from augmentation. This is not to say that a cognitive approach is not basically valid, but simply to propose that a cognitive framework might be recast or extended to provide a better basis for maximally effective intervention.

OTHER MODELS: LOOMING VULNERABILITY MODEL

One possible constraint on the utility of the standard cognitive model of anxiety for at least some patients is that it simplifies the cognitive events that produce fear into a static picture: it is as if the anxious person is represented as looking out on a frozen landscape or timeless, unchanging space. Another cognitive formulation, called the *looming vulnerability* model (Riskind in press), emphasizes that the conventional cognitive model, in effect, parses the individual's cognitions about an ongoing stream of events in a danger situation into static snapshot assessments at a particular moment. In contrast, the looming vulnerability model emphasizes the importance of cognitions about the time rate or velocity of change of the dangerous situation, that is, the speed with which threat seems to be progressing moment by moment down a logically predicated sequence of events toward fruition. The model assumes that differing amounts of anxiety result as a function of the degree to which a threat situation is assessed as time-dependent and rapidly advancing in time or space moment by moment toward its climax. A threat that advances slowly, and has a slow "delta," could produce minimal anxiety.

This sense of the rapid growth and approach of threat over time, or looming vulnerability, is viewed as the core cognitive content that instigates anxiety states. Moreover, while the sense of looming vulnerability would be expected to correlate with other assessments of threat (such as of its probability, imminence, or controllability), it is not reducible to these or synonymous with them. The conventional variables or cognitive assessments are too general or coarse-grained to account for specific cognitive differences between emotional dysfunction such as anxiety versus depression. That is, overestimates of the probability of negative events, and underestimates of one's ability to cope with the events, are characteristics common to anxiety and depression (see, e.g., Butler and Mathews 1983, Riskind in press). The overlap could stem in part from the too-general and too-static concept of danger implicit in current cognitive models. Of relevance to the present chapter, it is possible that considering the looming vulnerability model could increase the responses of many GADs to treatment. Before we consider a case study, it is useful to briefly review some past research on looming vulnerability in anxiety.

The static characterization of the standard cognitive model is related to its use of the structural concept of cognitive schemas. Schemas of the usual kind have an implicit spatial organization and lack the fluidity or dynamic characteristics that enable them to represent rapid change processes. Even conceptual hierarchies are spatial. In contrast, the looming vulnerability model invokes a specialized form of schema—the cognitive script—that is pertinent to the representation of change (Riskind in press). Scripts are temporally organized. They are useful for representing sequential changes in a flow of events, such as the sequential events involved in (1) a birthday party where one gives presents, gets cake, sees the presents being opened, and so on; (2) a restaurant when one sees a menu and then orders food; or (3) the events involved in a fearful fantasy about getting fired. Scripts have sequence rules (e.g., before one can order food, one must see a waiter or menu) and thus provide a logical basis for understanding the catastrophizing sequence by which GADs proceed from worry about minor events to worry about catastrophic events. Thus, before a patient can be fired for incompetence and then homeless and destitute, he or she must first make serious mistakes at work.

RELEVANT PAST RESEARCH

Although conducted independently of, and prior to, the looming vulnerability model, past studies show that individuals with small-animal phobias exaggerate the physical movement of the phobic stimuli (Hekmat 1987, Rachman and Cuk 1992, Weerts and Lang 1978). Additionally, studies directly testing the looming vulnerability model confirm that phobic individuals generally exaggerate the fast rate at which their phobic stimuli (e.g., spiders or germs) are moving forward or looming toward them (Riskind and Maddux 1993, 1994, Riskind and Wahl 1992, Riskind et al. 1992, 1995). Those studies bring the study of anxiety closer to developmental and ethological observations that young children (Reingold and Eckerman 1973) and other animal species (Schiff et al. 1962) respond with fear to objects that loom rapidly closer. For example, Schiff and colleagues showed that fiddler crabs, chicks, humans, turtles, and rhesus monkeys responded with evidence of fear when exposed to a looming silhouette on a screen that resulted in the visual experience of a looming object. Rhesus monkeys, including infants less than 8 months of age, were found to withdraw rapidly in response to the looming silhouette, making alarm cries and leaping to the rear of the cage. Further studies document that other species of animals, including hens (Evans et al. 1993), rats (Westby 1990), fish (Dill 1990), and nonhuman primates (both infants and adults) (King and Cowey 1992), automatically react to looming or optically expanding stimuli with focal fear and defensive behaviors (such as ducking, crouching, or hiding). In much the same way as these other species, human infants and adults respond to unfamiliar objects that approach them (or grow rapidly in size) with fear, agitation, and defensive head movements characteristic of avoidance (Ball and Vurploot 1976, King et al. 1992). Similarly, children show greater "stranger anxiety" to unfamiliar persons who approach them rapidly rather than slowly (Reingold and Eckerman 1973, Trause 1977). Consistent with general behavior theory, we suspect that the same basic principles relating the antecedent and subsequent factors of perceived rate of growth of threat and fear response have generality and application to generalized anxiety in humans.

Thus it is possible that GADs are perpetually construing events in the world through a construct of rapidly changing, quickly evolving danger. In effect, they are responding to the same basic principles that affect turtles, fiddler crabs, fish, frogs, and nonhuman primates. The specifics of the fear-eliciting situations differ, as do the conceptual abstractness of the stimulus events perceived as threats, but the role of the growth rate of threat and fear response is the same. A prior study suggests that many individuals with GAD have a chronic tendency to construe threats in this way, and this tendency is referred to as a looming maladaptive style. For example, anxious people with the style might repetitively worry about rapidly evolving danger when driving their cars on the highway—about the engine blocks rapidly cracking, the tire treads peeling, the fan belts cracking, and so on. Similarly, anxious people with the style might worry about their relationships in such a way that they imagine them as fraying and rapidly breaking apart. In general, the looming maladaptive style colors the perceived world, gives the anxiety-prone person the impression that things are tottering, slipping, on the verge of rapidly changing, and that threats are dynamically evolving.

Results of several studies indicate that the sense of looming vulnerability is not simply interchangeable with other familiar cognitive assessments of a situation's dangerousness (such as probability, imminence, uncontrollability, or unpredictability). According to the looming vulnerability model, the sense of looming vulnerability (or rapidly evolving and dynamic "looming" nature construed for danger) should correlate with other cognitive assessments (such as the probability or imminence of harm). But the sense of looming vulnerability assesses a conceptually separate appraisal component and is a more effective way to identify the cognitive core that instigates anxiety. Specifically, results supporting the hypothesis that the sense of looming vulnerability is a more effective predictor of anxiety were provided in two correlational studies (Riskind et al. 1992). A specific sense of looming vulnerability to the threat posed by spiders emerged consistently as a unique predictor of fear of spiders, whereas subjects' assessments of the probability, imminence, and unpredictability of harm by spiders did not.

My two studies (Riskind and Wahl 1992, Riskind et al. 1992) also supported the hypothesized distinctness of the association between the more generalized "looming maladaptive style" and the predisposition to experience anxiety. This is a questionnaire measure of the looming style developed for generalized anxiety states. A measure of the looming maladaptive style was still robustly correlated with anxiety after partialing depression, but not with depression after partialing anxiety (Riskind et al. 1992). Several further studies summarized in my work (1996) show that (1) a sense of looming vulnerability predicts subsequent avoidance behavior, such as avoidance of situations where threats are expected; (2) a sense of looming vulnerability also predicts increases in the frequency of worry as well as hostility, fear, and sadness over six weeks in time. Subjects who have a higher sense of looming vulnerability show increases in worry, fear, anxiety, hostility, and other negative emotions beyond the levels of the emotions at the time that their sense of looming vulnerability is assessed. Other studies show that it instigates typical anxiety-relevant automatic thoughts from Beck's Cognition Checklist, as well as vigilance behavior. Also, the sense of looming vulnerability differentiates GADs from depressives and normal controls without psychopathology, where standard threat variables (such as the probability of occurrence of harmful events) do not.

TREATMENT IMPLICATIONS

Since the looming vulnerability model proposes an etiological chain for anxiety, each part of the chain presents a possibility for intervention. Targeting the dysfunctional anticipatory style by Socratic questioning ("What is the evidence that the danger is evolving rapidly?") could be undertaken. The therapist can help the client to use logic and reason to test the assumptions that the problems can develop as quickly as they do. Modifying passive behavior to more active problem solving can also reduce the sense of vulnerability, as in standard cognitive therapy.

Of particular interest in the treatment of GAD is the additional possibility that imagery might be useful. If the looming vulnerability paradigm is correct in its prediction that a sense of a rapidly evolving danger is critical, then it would also tend to follow if a person is anxious about a source of danger, using imagery to *reduce* his sense that danger can rapidly grow would greatly reduce his anxiety or fear. It is plausible, in the context of looming vulnerability theory, that a patient could reduce his or her fear by using imagery to stop the rapid growth rate of threat.

In several recent studies we tested this reasoning by having subjects watch videotapes of contamination scenes (e.g., toilets, trash cans). We then experimentally manipulated the subjects' cognitive perspective of the tape using imagery instructions. Half of the subjects were simply led to view the video clips of a contamination scene such as a filthy public toilet (Control Condition). The other half of the subjects in the "freeze" (Experimental) Condition were led to view the video clips with instructions that the contaminants were "frozen" and unable to spread from their position. We obtained evidence that subjects experienced lower fear and threat in the experimental condition in which they used imagery to "freeze" the spread of the contamination (Riskind et al. in press). Specifically, as expected, participants were far less anxious and worried by video clips of contamination scenes when they were asked to apply the instructions to freeze the spread of the contamination. Some of the most interesting findings were obtained using indicators of phobic avoidance behavior. When they had practiced the freeze imagery, subjects were willing to stand nearer a contamination site (a dirty toilet) and were more likely to take a cookie from a tray placed near a large trash can. The findings of these studies are consistent with the predictions generated by looming vulnerability theory.

We turn our consideration at this time to an actual clinical patient's case.

DESCRIPTION OF PATIENT WITH GAD

A 34-year-old unmarried woman with GAD was treated using some of these techniques. Her initial presenting complaints included chronic feelings of worry, tension, anxiety, nervousness, and episodic feelings of intense comorbid depression. She reported she also got "edgy and snappy and bickered with my fiancé." A major focus of her worry was her continuing fear of failure in the relationship and ultimate rejection. She also had secondary worries and fears about her personal and sexual adequacy, the security of her status with her employer in her job, the security of her two sisters and mother, her financial future, her ability to save money, the risk that she would go crazy, and a variety of minor concerns such as the risk of her contaminating the health of friends when she had a cold.

She presented herself initially as having a "negative, pessimistic attitude" she wanted to change, and stated that "things may even be worse than I actually think they are." At the same time, she described herself as an individual who worried a lot and was a "crisis manufacturer." The patient stated that she was very sensitive to criticism, lacked self-confidence, and suffered from indecision over what she wanted to do. Reflecting a depressive component, she said that she "perceives obstacles as insurmountable." At times when she was actively experiencing periods of depression, she had thoughts such as "Everything is hopeless," "I can't change anything about myself," "There is no point in trying to work on anything." Thus, as expected by cognitive theory, she identified the causes of her expected failures within herself in unchangeable personal defects. However, the depressive ideation was responsive to standard cognitive interventions.

Background

The patient, Debbie, was the youngest of three sisters in the family. She was born in the District of Columbia area in suburban Maryland, but her family moved during her childhood to Ohio. Her father, however, who had a serious medical condition, stayed in the D.C. area for nine years. Every time he left Ohio for Maryland after a visit, she would think she might never see him again. A result of his absence is that she felt an absence of attention. Further, she described her mother as a "very negative, even misanthropic person." Her mother's negativity was a factor that influenced the patient's current anxiety. For example, her mother would say, "How can you get a nice guy like Larry to want to be involved with you? You are so abrasive and obnoxious."

In high school she was not a happy person, and viewed herself as defective because she had a "weird family background" and saw her parents as having a "screwed-up" marriage. She developed a very negative, sarcastic sense of humor, was very cynical, and described herself as having been a painfully shy person who had "no self-confidence and was very depressed." The first time she kissed someone was when she was 20 at the university. She was "terrified of men." At the time of the initial clinical intake, she said she was "fairly outgoing," and "wanted to make up for lost time."

She had excellent grades at the university, but mainly studied and worked two days a week. Thus she had little social life. Her first real relationship was when she was 24 and moved to Pittsburgh. In her words, it was a "real disaster." She reported that he was a "charmer," but later changed and became "mean and cheated" on her. During this relationship, moreover, she never had actual intercourse, and was uneasy about sex. The boyfriend later "dumped" her, increasing her anxiety about men.

A few years later her father died, and she went into a depression. She began to think that her father hadn't really loved her, and that no guy had "wanted" her. Thus these painful experiences further accentuated and reinforced her initial cognitive vulnerability to anxiety.

She met her current boyfriend, whom she was engaged to and had been living with for several months, at a folk dancing club in northern Virginia. She believed that Larry often got frustrated around her for being so negative. One of her fears was that she was a "drain" and "burden" on the boyfriend, and that he would realize that he didn't like having her around. She was also intensely unhappy with her job as a marketing assistant, and she felt she wanted to move up to a higher level on the career ladder. But she wasn't sure how to do it, had recurring doubts about her ability to get another job or to keep it, and disparaged herself for this ("I'm not smart enough to do more," "Other people are smarter than me").

Typical Automatic Thoughts

Debbie's typical automatic thoughts contained several threads that served to initiate and exacerbate her anxiety and comorbid depression. As expected from standard cognitive theory, many of these thoughts involved dire predictions of impending catastrophe. Examples of these recurring ideational themes are presented below:

Typical Anxious Thoughts

"I'm uneasy that things are going so well. Something is going to go wrong. I'm trying to sabotage things. I can't be happy."

"Past relationships that I thought would work out didn't."

"We're headed for a major crash."

"Larry's sister thinks I am a snob."

"I am more vulnerable and at risk because I'm committed" [when she agreed to become engaged].

"He might leave me because I'm anxious."

"I can't let myself be happy—the breakup will only hurt more."

"My anxieties are about getting married."

"What if I gave my friend who has cancer a cold? He'll die."

"I'm going nuts. I'll have to sign myself into St. Elizabeth's. I'll have to be put in a straight jacket and be flipped out" [when she had intense anxiety and a "general feeling of nervousness"].

"See, I'm a loser" [when frustrated with herself].

As is evident from some of the above thought samples, much of this patient's automatic thinking was characterized not just by a preoccupation with danger, but a sense of *rapidly evolving dangers* and looming vulnerability (e.g., "We're headed for a major crash").

Debbie's comorbid depression and mixed anxiety and depression symptoms were linked to typical thoughts as well. As expected by cognitive theory, many of these thoughts were characterized by self-derogation and hopelessness.

"Larry is waiting for me to turn into a nicer, more thoughtful person before he completely accepts me. I'm like a fixer-upper."

"I'm a burden on him. I'm no good for him. Our relationship is doomed."

"I'm failing at everything. I'm not happy at my job. I'm not treated well at work and hate it. I'm worried about our sex life. I'm getting behind in school. I'm not in control of my life. I feel kind of old" [on her birthday, which reminded her of all she hasn't accomplished].

Underlying Beliefs

Debbie's underlying belief system seemed to include the following maladaptive generalizations and conclusions:

"I'm incapable of having a successful relationship."

"I'm an unlucky person. I'm not a person who gets breaks."

"I am defective."

"I sabotage all my relationships."

"Everybody leaves eventually."

"I must be very kind and compassionate or he will leave me."

"I'm setting myself up to be hurt if I let my guard down and let someone get close to me."

"I don't know how to keep a marriage."

Behaviors

Debbie's problem behaviors included hypervigilance and subtle forms of avoidance of closeness with her fiancé. These included bickering with him whenever she felt threatened by closeness. These behaviors also included inhibition of sexual desire. She reports that she "never really enjoyed sex."

Case Conceptualization

Debbie's maladaptive belief system seemed to predispose her to interpret many ordinary, and even positive, situations with her fiancé in very threatening ways. Debbie drew on the generalizations she had made from the past and then expected that she was incapable of having a relationship with men and that they would inevitably leave her. These maladaptive beliefs, which formed the basis of an anxiety-producing danger schema, seemed strongly rooted in the stinging sense of abandonment by her father that she had experienced as a child. The beliefs in her personal defectiveness, and ultimate likelihood of failure, made her view her intimacy with her fiancé as highly threatening. The same beliefs provided the source for negative automatic thoughts concerning her inadequacy at work and other situations.

To cope with the anxiety produced by her negative cognitions, Debbie appeared to have developed defensive, compensatory beliefs. These included beliefs such as, "You should not be defined by the person you go out with. You should not be completely dependent or you will be more devastated if the person hurts you." Additionally, her unwillingness to risk being vulnerable seemed to drive her bickering and criticism of her fiancé as well as inhibit her sexual arousal.

In all these areas Debbie manifested a variety of classic cognitive errors, including fortune-telling ("It won't work out"), overgeneralization ("Men always leave me"), labeling and internalization ("I am defective"), and emotional reasoning ("I feel worthless, so it must be true"). Such cognitive errors reflect the distortions inherent in the broad generalizations used by her in interpreting her experiences.

Goals

Debbie's immediate goals obviously included reduction and better control of her anxiety. She also wanted to improve her relationship, work on her difficulties with inhibition of sexual desire, and work on a better career.

Treatment Plan

The treatment initially followed the standard cognitive model, including helping Debbie to identify recurring negative automatic thoughts and find effective ways to counter them. The decatastrophizing technique (Beck and Emery 1985) was used effectively. In addition, a number of other cognitive techniques were helpful. For example, one set of exercises helped Debbie to practice making a distinction between irrefutable facts ("We had an argument") and unlikely or at least unmaterialized possibilities ("He will leave me"). Socratic questioning and homework was successfully used to challenge Debbie's negative assumptions ("I can't let myself get too dependent and vulnerable," "I may be sexually defective") and automatic thoughts that inhibited her sexual enjoyment with Larry. A reattribution technique was used to help her to see that her lack of enjoyment was due to her nervousness and negative thinking rather than to any inherent personal defect in herself or the relationship. Similarly, Debbie found it helpful to think about differences in the quality of her previous unsuccessful relationships with men and the quality of her relationship with Larry. By means of this logical analysis, Debbie realized that she "didn't want the previous relationships to work out." This gave her a greater sense of control. A further intervention that helped her to increase her self-esteem was to change the cognitive anchors and reference point she used to evaluate herself: She practiced training herself to compare to zero (instead of comparing herself to an ideal of what "should be"). For example, she would evaluate her sexual enjoyment against a zero baseline and better realize that she *was* enjoying herself sexually, rather than compare herself against an idealized picture of what she might expect herself to experience.

Several cognitive interventions derived from the looming vulnerability model also proved particularly helpful to Debbie, particularly when she seemed less responsive to standard interventions. Debbie realized that she tended to look on change that took place in her life as basically negative and rapidly evolving. Change was an issue in looking for another job, as well as moving forward in her relationship ("This could be a disaster. This could be worse"). Socratic questioning was used to help her to challenge her beliefs about the essentially negative character of change and its too-rapidly evolving nature. For example, Debbie found it helpful to review evidence for and against the thoughts that change was always negative in her past and that it always evolved more rapidly than she could adapt.

A useful imagery-based intervention was used when Debbie began a session with particularly high feelings of anxiety and worry. She was worried about leaving her job to go back to school, and about not having money after she got married. She was further worried that her lack of income would cause her husband to leave her ("I'm worried that I'm almost 35 and have no money saved. I'm supposed to get married soon. I'll end up doing menial temp work and still not have any money, and Larry will leave me").

Debbie was asked to imagine each set of worries as a chain of catastrophic steps leading to disaster. She herself likened them to a "train rushing down the track" toward her. She was asked to "picture the chain of disasters in your mind as a train rushing forward toward you." She rated herself as anxious (90 on a 100-point scale) and worried (95 on a 100-point scale).

Next, when she was asked to imagine this chain or train of

disasters as moving in "very small increments" toward her, such as a train that moved down the track one inch every ten minutes, then she reported that "I have more control." Her ratings of anxiety worry on a 100-point scale fell from 90 and 95, respectively, to 5.

In one further scenario Debbie was asked to exaggerate the speed or onrushing scene of disasters first. This exaggeration in itself led her to vocalize herself that things were "not moving so fast" and gave her an enhanced sense of control as well.

Outcome

Shortly after the interventions above, Debbie's anxiety improved dramatically. She felt better able to control her anxiety now and long after the termination of therapy. She and the therapist judged her to be greatly improved. While the standard cognitive interventions were important to her improvement, Debbie felt that the interventions based on reducing the "looming" of her fears had been particularly helpful.

REFERENCES

Ball, W. A., and Vurploot, E. (1976). Perception of depth in infants. *Anee-Psychologique* 2:83–399.

Barlow, D. H., Cohen, A. S., Waddell, M. T., et al. (1984). Panic and generalized anxiety disorders: nature and treatment. *Behavior Therapy* 15:431–449.

Beck, A. T. (1967). *Depression: Clinical, Experimental, and Theoretical Aspects.* New York: Hoeber.

———— (1976). *Cognitive Therapy and the Emotional Disorders.* New York: International Universities Press.

Beck, A. T., and Emery, G. (1985). *Anxiety Disorders and Phobias: A Cognitive Perspective.* New York: Basic Books.

Beck, A. T., Epstein, N., and Harrison, R. (1983). Cognitions, attitudes and personality dimensions in depression. *British Journal of Cognitive Psychotherapy* 1:1–16.

Blowers, C., Cobb, J., and Mathews, A. (1987). Generalized anxiety: a controlled treatment study. *Behavior Research and Therapy* 25:493–502.

Borkovec, T. D., Mathews, A. M., Chambers, A., et al. (1987). The effects of relaxation training with cognitive therapy or nondirective therapy and the role of relaxation-induced anxiety in the treatment of generalized anxiety. *Journal of Consulting and Clinical Psychology* 55:883–888.

Borkovec, T. D., Shadick, R., and Hopkins, M. (1991). The nature of normal and pathological worry. In *Chronic Anxiety: Generalized Anxiety Disorder and Mixed-Anxiety Depression*, ed. R. M. Rapee and D. H. Barlow. New York: Guilford.

Borkovec, T. D., Wilkinson, L., Folensbee, R., and Lerman, C. (1983). Stimulus control applications to the treatment of worry. *Behavior Research and Therapy* 21:247–251.

Butler, G., and Booth, R. G. (1990). Developing psychological treatments for generalized anxiety disorder. In *Chronic Anxiety: Generalized Anxiety Disorder and Mixed Anxiety Depression*, ed. R. M. Rapee and D. H. Barlow. New York: Guilford.

Butler, G., Cullington, A., Hibbert, G., et al. (1987). Anxiety management for persistent generalized anxiety. *British Journal of Psychiatry* 151:535–542.

Butler, G., Fennell, M., Robson, P., and Gelder, M. (1991). A comparison of behavior therapy and cognitive-behavior therapy in the treatment of generalized anxiety disorder. *Journal of Consulting and Clinical Psychology* 59:167–175.

Butler, G., and Mathews, A. (1983). Cognitive processes in anxiety. *Advances in Behavioral Research and Therapy* 5:51–62.

Davey, G. C., Hampton, J., Farrell, J., and Davidson, S. (1992). Some characteristics of worrying: evidence for worrying and anxiety as separate constructs. *Personality and Individual Differences* 13:133–147.

Diagnostic and Statistical Manual of Mental Disorders (DSM-III) (1980). 3rd ed. Washington, DC: American Psychiatric Association.

———— (*DSM-III-R*) (1987). 3rd ed. rev. Washington, DC: American Psychiatric Association.

———— (*DSM-IV*) (1994). 4th ed. Washington, DC: American Psychiatric Association.

Dill, L. M. (1990). Distance-to-cover and the escape decisions of an African cichlid fish. *Environment, Biology, and Fish* 27:147–152.

Durham, R. C., and Turvey, A. A. (1987). Cognitive therapy vs. behavior therapy in the treatment of chronic general anxiety: outcome at discharge and at six month follow-up. *Behavior Research and Therapy* 25:229–234.

Evans, C. S., Macedonia, J. M., and Marler, P. (1993). Effects of apparent size and speed on the response of chickens, Gallus gallus, to computer-generated simulations of aerial predators. *Animal Behavior* 46(1):1–11.

Greenberg, M. S., and Beck, A. T. (1989). Depression versus anxiety: a test of the content-specificity hypothesis. *Journal of Abnormal Psychology* 98:9–13.

Hekmat, H. (1987). Origins and development of human fear reactions. *Journal of Anxiety Disorders* 1:197–218.

King, S. M., and Cowey, A. (1992). Defensive responses to looming visual stimuli in monkeys with unilateral striate cortex ablation. *Neuropsychologia* 30:1017–1024.

King, S. M., Dykeman, C., Redgrave, P., and Dean, P. (1992). Use of a distracting task to obtain defensive head movements to looming visual stimuli by human adults in a laboratory setting. *Perception* 21:245–259.

Lazarus, R. S., and Folkman, S. (1984). *Stress, Appraisal, and Coping.* New York: Springer.

Mathews, A., and MacLeod, C. (1985). Selecting processing of threat cues in anxiety states. *Behavior Research and Therapy* 23:563–569.

Power, K. G., Jerrom, D. W. A., Simpson, R. J., et al. (1989). A controlled comparison of cognitive-behavior therapy, diazepam and placebo in the treatment of generalized anxiety. *Behavioral Psychotherapy* 17:1–14.

Rachman, S. J., and Cuk, M. (1992). Fearful distortions. *Behavior Research and Therapy* 30:583–589.

Reingold, H., and Eckerman, C. O. (1973). Fear of a stranger: a critical examination. In *Advances in Child Development and Behavior*, vol. 8, ed. H. W. Reese. New York: Academic Press.

Riskind, J. H. (in press). Looming vulnerability to threat: a cognitive paradigm for anxiety. *Behavior Research and Therapy*.

Riskind, J. H., Hohman, A. A., Moore, R., et al. (1991). The relation of generalized anxiety disorder to depression in general and dysthymic disorder in particular. In *Chronic Anxiety: Generalized Anxiety Disorder and Mixed Anxiety-Depression*, ed. R. M. Rapee and D. H. Barlow, pp. 29–51. New York: Guilford.

Riskind, J. H., Kelly, K., and Moore, R., et al. (1992). The looming of danger: Does it discriminate focal phobia and general anxiety from depression? *Cognitive Therapy and Research* 16:1–20.

Riskind, J. H., and Maddux, J. (1993). Loomingness, helplessness, and fearfulness: an integration of harm-looming and self-efficacy models of fear and anxiety. *Journal of Social and Clinical Psychology* 12:73–89.

——— (1994). Loomingness and the fear of AIDS: perceptions of motion and menace. *Journal of Applied Social Psychology* 24:432–442.

Riskind, J. H., Moore, R., and Bowley, L. (1995). The looming of spiders: the fearful perceptual distortion of movement and menace. *Behavior Research and Therapy* 33:171–178.

Riskind, J. H., and Rholes, W. S. (1984). Cognitive accessibility and the capacity of cognitions to predict future depression: a theoretical note. *Cognitive Therapy and Research* 8:1–12.

Riskind, J. H., and Wahl, O. (1992). Moving makes it worse: the role of rapid movement in fears of psychiatric patients. *Journal of Social and Clinical Psychology* 11:349–364.

Riskind, J. H., Wheeler, D., and Pacerno, M. (in press). Effects of freeze imagery and loom imagery on obsessional fears of contamination. *Behavior Research and Therapy*.

Sanderson, W. C., and Barlow, D. H. (1990). A description of patients diagnosed with *DSM-III-Revised* generalized anxiety disorder. *Journal of Nervous and Mental Disease* 178:588–591.

Schiff, W., Caviness, A., and Gibson, J. J. (1962). Persistent fear responses in rhesus monkeys in response to the optical stimulus of "looming." *Science* 136:982–983.

Trause, M. A. (1977). Stranger responses: effects of familiarity, stranger's approach, and sex of infant. *Child Development* 48:1657–1661.

Weerts, T. C., and Lang, P. J. (1978). Psychophysiology of fear imagery: differences between focal phobia and social performance anxiety. *Journal of Consulting and Clinical Psychology* 46:1157–1159.

Westby, G. W. M. (1990). Output pathways from the rat superior colliculus mediating approach and avoidance have different sensory properties. *Experimental Brain Research* 81:626–638.

8

OBSESSIVE-COMPULSIVE DISORDER

Stephen J. Holland

Obsessive-compulsive disorder (OCD) is the fourth most common psychiatric diagnosis in the United States. One out of every forty adults will meet criteria for OCD at some point in their life (Karno et al. 1988). Behavioral treatment, consisting of exposure and response prevention, is widely recognized as the treatment of choice for OCD. Approximately 75 percent of patients with OCD show substantial improvement with behavioral treatment (Steketee 1993). These gains are generally maintained after treatment has stopped. In addition, serotonin agonists, such as Anafranil, Prozac, and Paxil, have been found effective in treating OCD. However, relapse rates can be as high as 89 percent after medication is discontinued, unless behavioral treatment is also used (Steketee 1993).

In recent years there has been a small but growing literature on cognitive treatments for OCD. Three recent studies have found cognitive therapy or rational emotive therapy as effective as exposure and response prevention (van Oppen and Arntz 1994). Salkovskis (1989) has suggested that adding cognitive elements to behavioral treatment for OCD has the potential to decrease dropout and improve the effectiveness of treatment.

This chapter describes a treatment model that uses both cognitive and behavioral techniques to target the schemas that are hypothesized to maintain OCD.

CLINICAL PRESENTATION OF OCD

In order to be diagnosed with OCD under *DSM-IV* (1994) criteria, a patient must have either obsessions or compulsions. Obsessions are recurring thoughts, impulses, or images that cause distress. Compulsions, also known as rituals, are repetitive behaviors or mental acts that the patient feels driven to do in order to reduce this distress. Most patients, in fact, have both obsessions and compulsions. Many OCD patients show substantial avoidance of situations that are likely to trigger obsessive fears and/or compulsive actions.

BEHAVIORAL MODEL OF OCD

The behavioral model of OCD emphasizes the role of conditioning in maintaining the disorder (Steketee 1993). Surveys show that 80 percent of the normal population reports occasionally having intrusive thoughts similar to the obsessions that plague OCD sufferers (Barlow 1988). However, OCD patients appear to be particularly distressed by these thoughts. Often the thoughts run counter to deeply held beliefs or values. The emotional distress patients feel eventually becomes associated with the thoughts through classical conditioning. In essence, because patients feel distressed every time the thoughts occur, they develop a conditioned phobia of their own thoughts.

Patients often attempt to cope with their obsessive thoughts by trying to avoid thinking them. In addition, they may engage in certain actions to try to reduce their anxiety. For example, fearing contamination, they may wash their hands. They may also avoid situations that trigger obsessive thoughts. Such actions generally produce a temporary reduction in anxiety, which then serves to reinforce the behavior.

There are two problems with these avoidance and compensatory behaviors. The first is that attempting not to think about something makes it more likely that one will think about it (Wegner 1989). In other words, by attempting to avoid their obsessive thoughts, OCD patients make them appear more frequently. Second, the relief provided by compensatory actions is only temporary. As the thoughts recur, the actions must be repeated. The result is that OCD patients engage in an escalating cycle of obsessive thought, attempted avoidance and compulsive behavior, and recurring obsessive thought.

The standard behavioral treatment for OCD is designed to break these conditioned responses. It consists of two elements: (1) exposure to the feared thoughts, and (2) prevention of the usual responses of avoidance and/or compulsions. Exposure allows patients to discover that if they focus on the feared thoughts rather than avoid them, no negative consequences occur and their anxiety eventually diminishes. Response prevention is necessary because patients may use their rituals to avoid the anxiety associated with exposure, thereby reducing its effectiveness. Research has demonstrated that neither exposure nor response prevention alone is as effective as the two combined (Steketee 1993).

COGNITIVE MODELS OF OCD

Salkovskis (1989) and van Oppen and Arntz (1994) have proposed similar cognitive models of OCD. Both models regard intrusive thoughts as normal. What makes the thoughts disturbing and sets off the OCD cycle is patients' beliefs about their intrusive thoughts. Patients tend to overestimate (1) the likelihood of the occurrence of negative events; (2) the damage that would result; (3) the degree of responsibility that they would bear; and (4) the consequences of being held responsible. In other words, OCD sufferers have overactive schemas of danger and responsibility. Guidano and Liotti (1983) emphasize OCD patients' need for perfect certainty in all matters, including safety. Cognitive therapy for OCD targets patients' beliefs about their obsessive thoughts, not the thoughts themselves.

CASE EXAMPLE

The cognitive-behavioral treatment model that was used for this case has three phases. The first phase consists of assessment, educating the patient, and preparation for treatment. The second phase consists of exposure and response prevention. The third phase is open-ended and targets the schemas that maintain both the symptoms of OCD and the difficulties the patient has in various life roles. Since the procedures for exposure and response prevention have been extensively described elsewhere (e.g., Steketee 1993), this chapter concentrates on the third phase of treatment.

Background

My first contact with Robert was a phone call from his mother. She told me that her 25-year-old son had suffered from OCD for a number of years. She had recently taken him to a psychiatrist, who had prescribed Prozac. However, Robert became concerned when he read about the side effects, especially nausea, and had discontinued the medication. She reported that she had suffered from anxiety for years and that her mother had OCD. After interviewing me regarding my qualifications, she made an appointment for her son.

Robert presented at the first session as an attractive, slightly built, personable young man who was quite anxious. He described a history of obsessive fears and ritualizing—mostly involving repeating actions—since the age of 10. He said that his condition had worsened in the last two years, and attributed this to anxiety he was feeling about getting started in his career as a photographer. He currently was ritualizing many hours a day. For example, he would spend up to an hour and an half a night taking his pants on and off. Other rituals included opening and closing computer files at work, reprinting photographs in the darkroom until he felt he had completed a print without having an obsessive thought, complex patterns of tapping various objects in a room, and a number of bathroom rituals. His repetitions often ran into the hundreds.

Robert's obsessive fears included vomiting, the number 13, having his face disfigured in a car accident, being in an airplane crash, and a member of his family dying. He avoided buses, boats, and airplanes. He avoided walking down certain streets that had become associated with obsessive thoughts. He avoided buying CD's by musicians who had died in plane crashes. He also avoided eating certain foods for fear they would make him sick.

Robert reported that he grew up in an upper-middle-class suburban home. His parents had divorced five years earlier, and he had a sister who was two years his elder. His father was an attorney, whom he described as a largely absent figure. He reported having a close, confiding relationship with his mother. However, he also reported that she was highly anxious and constantly afraid that something would happen to one of her children. For example, she had walked them to school every day until they were in middle school. Even now that they were both in their twenties, she insisted on always knowing exactly where they were and having a phone number where she could reach them at all times. Robert lived with his mother and sister. When he discussed possibly moving into an apartment of his own, his mother told him he should wait until he was married. This was not the cultural norm in their community.

Robert aspired to a career as a commercial photographer. However, he was currently managing the office of a small company, and had done little to pursue photographic work. His college girlfriend had broken up with him three years earlier, largely because of his ritualizing. He had not dated and had had only a couple of sexual experiences since that time.

Phase 1: Preparation

Sessions 1–9: After gathering the information outlined above, I began to educate Robert regarding OCD. He was asked to begin reading the self-help book *Stop Obsessing* (Foa and Wilson 1991). Robert was then taught several relaxation techniques. For homework he was asked to write down all the ways his life would be better if he no longer ritualized. This was used to create a list of advantages and disadvantages of undergoing exposure and response prevention. After this exercise, Robert expressed a strong desire to proceed with treatment.

Robert was next asked to log all of his rituals for a week. The log revealed almost constant ritualizing. Robert reported that this self-monitoring exercise had led to some decrease in ritualizing, and was very pleased by this. He was next asked to experiment with disrupting his rituals by either performing them very slowly, doing odd-number rather than even-number repetitions, or postponing them. He was surprised to discover that when he postponed a ritual for even a few minutes, the urge to ritualize often went away.

Finally, we made a schedule for exposure and response

prevention over the next three weeks that included a ninety-minute session early in the week for in-session imaginal exposure to Robert's obsessive fears and a forty-five-minute session later in the week to review progress and plan self-directed in vivo exposure to his avoided situations. Robert was told that he would have to stop ritualizing once exposure work was initiated, and was asked to consider whether he would prefer to stop all rituals at once or to gradually give up the rituals associated with each obsessive fear as we moved up the exposure hierarchy.

Phase 2: Exposure and Response Prevention

Sessions 10–14: At the start of the next session Robert reported that he had gone "cold turkey" on rituals and had not ritualized at all over the last several days. He was praised for this, but also warned that relapse was likely and not to be discouraged if it occurred. Imaginal exposure was then initiated.

When doing imaginal exposure, the therapist narrates a scenario that involves the patient's fears while the patient is asked to imagine himself in the situation. In order to help the patient visualize the scene and become emotionally involved, the patient is asked to add details to the story, such as what emotions or physical sensations he experiences or what actions he takes. Throughout the scenario, the patient's anxiety level is monitored by asking him to periodically rate his distress from zero percent (not anxious) to 100 percent (maximum anxiety). The scenario is audiotaped so the patient can listen to it again. Typically, as the patient repeatedly listens to the tape, first in session and then as homework, his anxiety level in response to it decreases. This habituation indicates that the conditioned link between the obsessive thought and anxiety has been weakened.

The first item on Robert's hierarchy was having his face disfigured in a car accident. Before proceeding, I inquired about the details of the fear. Robert reported that he was most concerned that he would be too ugly to get a job and that no woman would want to date him. I then narrated a detailed scenario in which he has an accident, wakes up in the hospital and realizes his face is disfigured, and ultimately finds himself unable to obtain work and rejected by every woman he approaches. Robert's anxiety ratings never got above 40 percent, and he habituated quickly.

We then moved on to his second fear—vomiting. Unfortunately, in the middle of this exposure Robert's anxiety peaked suddenly and there was insufficient time to allow him to habituate fully. His anxiety did drop from a high of 90 percent to 60 percent, but it was necessary to use a distraction technique (having him describe objects in the office) to reduce his anxiety before he left the session.

In the next session, held two days later, Robert reported that he had felt very anxious after the previous meeting and had performed some rituals. He had been unable to listen to the tape on his own. I recommended that rather than proceeding with our agenda, which had been to plan in vivo exposure, we redo the exposure to his fear of vomiting. I offered to extend the session to be sure to allow sufficient time for his anxiety level to decrease. Robert agreed to this plan. When I narrated the scenario again, however, Robert's anxiety never got above 25 percent. He was amazed by this. I explained that this was the result of habituation. Robert was assigned homework to begin to expose himself to the first items on his hierarchy of avoided situations.

The experience of having his anxiety, which had initially felt very threatening, reduce so quickly encouraged Robert and motivated him to continue treatment. Over the next two weeks we moved through the rest of the items on his hierarchy of obsessive fears. Robert habituated quickly to all of them. He did show some reluctance to listen to exposure tapes between sessions because they made him feel "unclean." I told him this was a form of avoidance and encouraged him to listen to the tapes daily. Robert also continued self-directed exposure to the hierarchy of avoided situations.

By the end of the planned three weeks of exposure and response prevention, Robert was reporting considerable progress. He was much less troubled by his obsessive thoughts. His ritualizing had decreased from hours a day to a few minor incidents during the week. He was able to do things he had felt unable to do previously, such as ride a bus, walk down streets he had avoided, and purchase CDs he had been afraid to buy. He also reported progress in areas that had not been targets of treatment. For example, he said he was able to disagree with his mother without feeling so guilty and that he was apologizing less at work. In addition, he had begun working on his photography portfolio.

I discussed with Robert the option of doing a few more sessions to solidify his gains and work on relapse prevention and then terminating treatment. However, both he and I felt that there were several areas of his life that could benefit from continued therapy. Specifically, we identified fears about pursuing his career, his lack of romantic/sexual involvement, and his conflict about moving out of his mother's house as targets of treatment. We agreed to continue meeting once a week.

Phase 3: Schema-Focused Therapy

Sessions 15–52: During the next seven sessions several themes emerged, which were then dealt with in greater depth during the rest of the therapy. Robert reported that he had always associated going against his mother's wishes as being bad, and feared that it would lead to something bad happening, such as vomiting. He began to experiment with expressing disagreement with her, and identified his constant apologizing as a ritual meant to ward off any negative consequences. He reported the thought, "I should always be nice to my mother. If she's happy, I'm happy." A few sessions later, Robert reported getting into an argument with his mother and having the spontaneous thought, "Why don't you die?" He felt very guilty and ritualized after this.

Robert began to make some progress in his career. He was hired to assist on a photography shoot, but felt anxious about it. He said his goal was to feel no anxiety at the shoot. I suggested that this was an unrealistic goal, and that a more appropriate goal would be to accept anxiety. The relationship between anxiety and performance was discussed, and Robert was told that peak performance occurs at moderate levels of anxiety. Robert also began working on a portfolio of his own photographs, but reported having trouble completing it because "it has to be perfect." This notion was challenged, and the fact that perfection was another unattainable goal was discussed. In the next session, Robert reported that he had finished his portfolio and had begun trying to set up appointments to show it to potential employers.

Robert also discussed his wish to have a girlfriend. However, he stated the beliefs that he was not attractive, that there was something wrong with him, and that no one would want to go out with him. He also said that he felt that he would have to take "unbelievable risks" to ask anyone out.

During these sessions Robert continued doing exposure and response prevention. One week he was assigned to print some photographs without ritualizing. He came back the following week and reported that he had done well until he was almost finished, and then he had reached for a can of soda in order to repeat taking a sip, which was a common ritual for him. He spilled the soda and ruined a batch of photographs. He reported that just before this occurred he had the thought, "Just one for safety." Robert was then asked to write the advantages and disadvantages of doing just one ritual for safety. He concluded that the only advantage was a temporary reduction in anxiety, and the disadvantages—including wasted time and effort, possible accidents, and reinforcing his OCD symptoms—were far greater.

After a couple of months, Robert reported that he had gotten his first small assignment as a freelance photographer. He was very excited, but also quite anxious. He reported the thoughts, "I could get an anxiety attack and not be able to do it," and, "They will think I'm not an amazing, top-quality photographer." Over the next several sessions we worked on anxiety management techniques, including progressive muscle relaxation, rational responding to his negative thoughts, focusing on the task at hand, accepting anxiety, and acknowledging to others that he was anxious.

Robert found these techniques helpful, and several weeks later reported that the job had gone very well. However, he also said that he was afraid that if he got any other photography jobs he would be anxious for weeks before and that he wouldn't be able to stand it. His thought was, "You should only feel anxious two hours before a job, otherwise it's not normal."

Over the next several sessions we explored these fears. It was pointed out that his anxiety was likely to decrease with experience. Then he was asked to consider whether anxiety was normal as people move up in their careers. For homework he was assigned to ask other people if they felt anxious in similar circumstances. He was too afraid to ask anyone, but reported hearing of well-known people who did experience such anxiety. I also shared with him my experience of being anxious for several months as I began graduate school.

At one point Robert said, "This is all very nice, but no one wants to be anxious." I said to him that if that were true, why were there things like roller coasters and horror films? Robert seemed surprised by this question. He then began to consider the idea that his anxiety could be part of the excitement of starting his career and that without some anxiety it wouldn't feel like a challenge. As he got a number of freelance assignments over the next several months, Robert focused much more on his feelings of excitement and much less on his anxiety.

During these sessions Robert reported some increased difficulty with ritualizing, although nothing that approached the level of compulsive behavior he engaged in prior to therapy. While he was religious about not ritualizing to anxious thoughts regarding upcoming photography jobs, he would sometimes ritualize about other obsessive thoughts for fear that if he didn't, his anxiety would spill over and hurt his work. He also showed a reluctance to engage in exposure work, again fearing that it would make him more anxious prior to shoots. Examination of evidence was used to point out that, in fact, while he sometimes felt temporarily more anxious if he did not ritualize, refraining from rituals actually decreased his overall level of anxiety and reduced the frequency of obsessive thoughts. Robert was encouraged to continue exposure and response prevention, and reported a decrease in ritualizing.

As Robert began to get freelance work on a semiregular basis, a new theme emerged: feelings of guilt and fears that unless he atoned for his guilt by ritualizing, some catastrophe, such as a family member dying, would occur. This manifested in several ways. First, he reported feeling guilty because he was beginning to experience success in his career while friends of his who were also in creative fields were still struggling. In addition, as he worked more, Robert began having some normal conflicts with coworkers over creative decisions. However, he felt very guilty about getting angry and disagreeing with others, even when the final decisions were clearly his to make. He reported thoughts such as, "I don't deserve all this," "I don't want to do anything that doesn't make someone else 100 percent happy," and "It's not nice to say negative things to people. If I don't ritualize something bad will happen."

These fears were again explored, first using cognitive techniques to point out that (1) many people do "bad" things without having plane crashes kill their families; (2) other people are more responsible for their own happiness than he is; and (3) unless he asserted his point of view and demanded that people live up to certain standards he could not do his job. Robert was then assigned homework over a number of weeks to practice asserting himself in a variety of situations. Over time, Robert reported increased comfort and success in being assertive at work and with friends.

When Robert's feelings of guilt about being successful and asserting his own wishes first began to appear, he again reported an increase in ritualizing, this time more extensive than before. At one point he reported that he had ritualized for an hour after accidentally coming across a picture of an airplane on a computer file. As we discussed his efforts to control this latest bout of ritualizing, it became clear that Robert was relying primarily on response prevention, setting goals for days or weeks to be "cold turkey," while at the same time almost completely avoiding doing exposure.

After this problem was pointed out, we did some additional imaginal exposure during sessions, including a scenario in which he imagined dying in a plane crash. Robert was then asked to plan his own exposure homework without consulting with me. This was done to minimize his tendency to use my sanctioning of exposure assignments to reduce his feelings of responsibility and anxiety.

Robert responded to these interventions with a marked decrease in ritualizing. He came to understand that response prevention alone was not sufficient, and at one point stated, "Exposure is like a pill I have to take for the rest of my life. I really don't mind it." After this he never again resisted exposure work and did not report anything more than minor ritualizing.

Around this time Robert also began talking about stopping therapy. He reported that he was feeling more confident in his ability to control his OCD and said, "It's a little like leaving home. Eventually I have to go." We decided to set a tentative goal of ending therapy within the next two months.

The exposure work around Robert's fear of flying led to another interesting discussion. He reported that his mother had always said, "I refuse to accept death." We talked about the advantages and disadvantages of refusing to accept the inevitable, and I pointed out that part of his fear of flying seemed to be linked to the idea that he or his family could somehow avoid ever dying. He reported that he found the idea of accepting the inevitability of death very useful.

Throughout the sessions described above the topic of dating would periodically come up. Robert was going to more social events where he met women, but felt very anxious about making any kind of advance unless there was unmistakable evidence that the woman was interested in him. Robert began to talk about one particular woman named Judy, to whom he was attracted. He reported the thoughts, "I won't be able to get her," and "I can't face rejection." We discussed the advantages and disadvantages of requiring absolute certainty before taking a risk, and Robert was encouraged to consider flirting and making his interests known as a form of exposure.

The issue of sex and dating heated up after Robert reported that his mother, who not been involved with anyone since the divorce, had started an affair. Robert reported feeling that she was acting like a fool and being very angry at her. In the next session Robert reported a fear that he had not previously disclosed. He said he had some bumps on his penis, which he thought must be genital warts. He had been to six doctors, all of whom had assured him the bumps were normal. The results of a biopsy were negative. Robert wasn't sure he could trust the doctors and had consulted a number of medical books. He reported the thoughts, "I'm doomed and can't get married. If I get together with a girl she'll see it and won't want to be with me. I'll never be comfortable unless it's totally smooth skin. I'm not perfect. I'm inadequate."

We attempted to address these thoughts using cognitive techniques over several sessions. However, while Robert reported an immediate decrease in anxiety, the anxiety always returned. Robert then consulted a seventh doctor, who again told him there was nothing abnormal about the bumps. At this point I suggested that we conceptualize his fears about his penis as another form of OCD. During this period Robert was spending more time with Judy, but it was not clear whether she was interested in him romantically. I pointed out that his obsessive fears about his penis seemed worst when he was most anxious about what was going on with her. I recommended that we initiate exposure and response prevention to deal with this fear. His homework was to refrain from looking at medical books or consulting any more doctors and to tape-record an exposure scenario in which he went to bed with a woman who then rejected him because of the bumps on his penis.

The following week Robert reported that he had had sex. His partner had been a woman he had known for a number of years and whom he had always been attracted to. He was very pleased and reported a sharp decrease in obsessive thoughts about his penis. He said he had come to realize that everything came down to taking risks, and that some things were worth taking risks for. Interestingly, he had noticed that the woman had some hair on her breasts and concluded that "everyone has imperfections."

At one point during these sessions I had to cancel an appointment with Robert due to an emergency. Robert reported that he felt he had handled this situation well and was feeling ready to be on his own. We both acknowledged that there were other issues to work on: Robert was still living at home and had not yet entered an ongoing romantic relationship. However, he was feeling able to control his OCD, his work was going well, and he wished to concentrate his time and money on his career. I agreed to ending treatment, with the understanding that he could return at any time and that it was likely he would want to continue therapy at some point.

In our last session Robert noted that he had a big freelance job the next day that he had not even discussed with me. He reported feeling no anxiety about it. When I asked what had made the difference, he replied, "Accepting anxiety." He was actively meeting women at social events, and several of them seemed interested in him. He did admit that he still felt anxious about approaching Judy to clarify their relationship. We also discussed the fact that his mother starting an affair had made it easier for him to pursue a relationship of his own without feeling guilty.

When I followed up with Robert three months later, he reported that his career continued to go very well and his ritualizing was still minimal. He had flown in an airplane without any significant anxiety. Finally, he was now involved in an exclusive relationship with Judy. However, he also admitted having feelings of anxiety and jealousy about her, and said he was considering returning to therapy.

DISCUSSION

Robert entered therapy with moderately severe OCD. This was initially targeted with standard behavior therapy, i.e., exposure and response prevention. Although Robert responded well, he continued to have problems in life-role functioning, and so therapy was continued. In the process several core assumptions and schemas related both to his OCD and his general functioning became apparent:

1. Any anxiety is bad, and therefore to be avoided.
2. Things have to be perfect to be acceptable.
3. All risks should be avoided and one must be 100 percent certain of safety before doing anything.
4. If I put my own needs or wishes before someone else's, I'm being bad, and something bad will happen as a result.
5. I am responsible for what happens to others.
6. There is something wrong with me. I am inadequate and unacceptable.

These schemas were targeted using both exposure and cognitive techniques. Robert continued to have some problems with recurring bouts of ritualizing until it became apparent that he was avoiding exposure to his obsessive fears. Once he realized the importance of exposure, he felt much more confident in his ability to manage his symptoms.

It is interesting to note that some of Robert's schemas are consistent with a traditional psychoanalytic formulation of OCD, namely, that rituals represent a defensive undoing meant to counter unacceptable impulses, such as anger. Certainly his relationship with his mother appeared to play a role in his conflict over dating and sex. In this treatment, however, the schemas were addressed using a structured, directive approach that both reduced Robert's OCD symptoms and allowed him to make substantial progress in his life-role functioning.

REFERENCES

Barlow, D. H. (1988). *Anxiety and Its Disorders: The Nature and Treatment of Anxiety and Panic.* New York: Guilford.

Diagnostic and Statistical Manual of Mental Disorders (DSM-IV) (1994). 4th ed. Washington, DC: American Psychiatric Association.

Foa, E. B., and Wilson, R. (1991). *Stop Obsessing: How to Overcome Your Obsessions and Compulsions.* New York: Bantam.

Guidano, V. F., and Liotti, G. (1983). *Cognitive Processes and Emotional Disorders: A Structural Approach to Psychotherapy.* New York: Guilford.

Karno, M., Golding, J. M., Sorenson, S. B., and Burnam, M. A. (1988). The epidemiology of obsessive-compulsive disorder in five U.S. communities. *Archives of General Psychiatry* 45:1094–1099.

Salkovskis, P. M. (1989). Obsessions and compulsions. In *Cognitive Therapy in Clinical Practice: An Illustrative Casebook*, ed. J. Scott, J. M. G. Williams, and A. T. Beck, pp. 50–77. London: Routledge.

Steketee, G. S. (1993). *Treatment of Obsessive Compulsive Disorder.* New York: Guilford.

van Oppen, P., and Arntz, A. (1994). Cognitive therapy for obsessive-compulsive disorder. *Behavior Research and Therapy* 32(1):79–87.

Wegner, D. M. (1989). *White Bears and Other Unwanted Thoughts: Suppression, Obsession and the Psychology of Mental Control.* New York: Viking.

9

HYPOCHONDRIASIS*

Mark Sisti

INTRODUCTION

Sociological writing has described how hypochondriasis has fallen in and out of favor culturally. This type of complex somatic and psychological symptom presentation was at one time the stock and trade of physicians. Since modern Western medicine has discovered the germ paradigm it has since excelled in conceptualizing and treating specific as opposed to complex psychobiological syndromes. Historically associated with an artistic sensitivity or temperament, hypochondriasis was once considered a disease of the elite and sophisticated, again a cultural position that has largely reversed itself. Today chronic somatization patients often make health professionals

---

*Originally presented as *Hypochondriasis: new treatment strategies* at the American Psychiatric Convention, May 26, 1994.

feel ineffective and are too often seen as self-centered victims or complainers. Whether culturally in fashion or not, hypochondriacal symptomatologies are ubiquitous. Fifty percent of all patients seen by physicians have hypochondriacal symptoms.

We all ruminate, inevitably, sometimes catastrophically, about our health. What percentage of time our thoughts are focused on these health-related ruminations and the ability to dismiss them when it is appropriate to do so is primarily all that separates anyone from a diagnosis of hypochondriasis. It is estimated that 30 percent to 60 percent of all visits to primary care physicians are by the "worried well," that is, those who have no serious medical disease (Baur 1988). In addition to hypochondria's extremely high prevalence rate, it has an extremely high comorbidity rate. This high comorbidity problem has perhaps been the single largest factor in complicating, obscuring, and legitimizing this disorder. Despite all its complexities, its high degree of comorbidity, and historically its lack of response to treatment, hypochondriasis has been recognized as a distinct syndrome since Hippocrates.

While no comprehensive epidemiological studies have been conducted, it is estimated that approximately 2 percent of the general population suffers from a clinical level of hypochondriasis. It is likely that this figure is largely underestimated, given that patient samples taken from medical settings report the prevalence of hypochondriasis varies between 6 percent and 9 percent. Age of onset is commonly in the early twenties, with a waxing and waning but ultimately chronic course. Symptoms often increase in frequency as a patient becomes elderly. While most surveys indicate an equal gender distribution, surveys with broader diagnostic criteria, that is, inclusion of somatization disorder, often show much higher prevalence rates among women. Currently *DSM-IV* (1994) allows for multiple overlapping diagnosis (e.g., obsessive-compulsive disorders [OCD], hypochondriasis, and MDD). While allowing for this multiple diagnostic overlap may provide a realistic description of a patient's symptoms, it hasn't necessarily clarified the nature of hypochondriasis.

DEFINING AND DIFFERENTIAL CRITERIA

Seventy-nine percent of hypochondriacal patients also meet criteria for another concurrent diagnosis, most commonly depression and anxiety disorders (Barsky et al. 1992). The distinction that still appears in the literature between primary (pure) and secondary (comorbid) hypochondriasis may be fast disappearing because of the extremely high comorbidity problem. The fact is that hypochondriasis rarely appears alone. While it may ultimately be more realistic to think of hypochondriasis as being present in various degrees of severity among various diagnostic groups, it must not be forgotten that some percentage of patients genuinely have hypochondriacal symptoms with such severity and persistence as to constitute a legitimate diagnostic category and treatment target. In spite of the comorbidity problem there are certainly patients for whom the duration, frequency, and intensity of health-related obsessions are clearly the predominant feature and legitimately a central symptom interfering with a patient's quality of life. Too many clinicians have often made the error of simply interpreting or reframing a patient's symptoms into psychologically or socially acceptable form. In practice this often translates into ignoring the reality of hypochondriacal obsessions and compulsions. Making an accurate diagnosis is essential to conceptualizing the case, and to subsequently providing appropriate patient feedback and treatment. *DSM-IV* currently defines hypochondriasis with the following primary criteria: (1) a belief that one *has* a serious disease, which is not of delusional intensity (one can acknowledge the possibility that the belief is unfounded), (2) persistence of the belief despite medical reassurance, (3) six-month duration. Differentiating somatization disorder from hypochondriasis is a matter of ascertaining whether a patient's preoccupations center around the fear of *having* a specific disease or, as in somatization disorder, on preoccupations with the *symptoms and discomfort* of the disease. Differentiating hypochondriasis from OCD or generalized anxiety disorder (GAD) is a matter of assessing how central (in terms of frequency and duration) health-related ruminations are relative to other general ruminations (e.g., family, financial). Distinguishing OCD from hypochondriasis is largely predicated on the distinction between *getting* as opposed to *having* a disease. If a person is obsessed with getting a particular disease, this may be OCD, also referred to as "illness phobia" (e.g., fear of contracting AIDS, cancer). If a patient believes he actually has the disease, a diagnosis of hypochondriasis is warranted. However, if this belief in the disease is highly overvalued (is of delusional intensity, with no room for doubt), then delusional disorder, somatic type, is the proper diagnosis.

CONCEPTUALIZATION

In a seminal study on hypochondriasis by Pilowsky (1967) a factor analysis revealed three principal dimensions: bodily preoccupation, conviction of illness despite reassurance, and disease phobia. Rotating the relative emphasis on these factors can aid the clinician in arriving at a working conceptualization. As one emphasizes or deemphasizes the various combinations of these dimensions, the clinician begins to clarify the subtle differences among the somatic diagnoses. When generally bodily preoccupation predominates, somatization disorder emerges; when conviction predominates, one moves toward the hypochondriacal or delusional disorders; when fear of getting a disease dominates the presentation and conviction is weaker, an OCD conceptualization or "illness phobia" emerges (Fallon et al. 1993). It is not uncommon to diagnose both an anxiety disorder (e.g., OCD) and hypochondriasis simultaneously or to see these diagnoses shift in emphasis over the course of time in the same patient.

CASE 1

Mr. A. was a middle-aged man who avoided compulsively any contact with anything or anyone associated with AIDS, and obsessed for hours each day that he would contract it. Over the course of months and just prior to entering treatment he shifted to a belief that he had contracted HIV. Since that time he spent what amounted to three or four hours per day, and the majority of his interrupted sleep, obsessing about *having* AIDS (he slept a total of only two or three hours per night during this phase). He had engaged in multiple medical exams, all except the HIV test itself, because he believed he would go crazy or become severely depressed if he were 100 percent certain that he had AIDS. But he was nearly certain he did. After all, he had the sweats, chronic sore throat, fatigue, weakened immune system, and so on. He had compulsively seen many health professionals for reassurance, and sought multiple reassurances from the therapist and friends. Over the course of therapy he eventually shifted from a high degree of certainty that he had AIDS to attempting to entirely eliminate any remaining doubts that he didn't. He began to devise elaborate schemes as to how to collect information that would eliminate some of his doubt about not having AIDS.

A patient's cognitions and behavior may go from initially being illness-phobic ("I must do everything I can to avoid getting cancer," "I should avoid touching that person, scientists aren't 100 percent certain how it is transmitted") to a conviction that they have the disease ("My life is awful, I have cancer," "I cannot get tested, it would only confirm my worst nightmare, and life wouldn't be worth living"), and possibly to the symptom preoccupation of somatization disorder ("I know it's not cancer, but I can't live with the feeling of cysts in my breasts," "I couldn't enjoy myself with this much discomfort, so why bother going out"). Over the course of treatment, or even across time without treatment, patients may cycle through these various stages of conviction and focus. Each of these presentations offers the clinician a different point of entry into building an alliance and proceeding into treatment. As treatment proceeds, the clinician must be prepared to shift focus if the patient shifts from one of these conceptualizations to another. Not all patients shift in these ways; many stay within a particular diagnostic conceptualization and hopefully decrease in the duration, frequency, and conviction of the obsession over the course of treatment.

Increasingly the literature conceptualizes conviction as a continuum, a spectrum of certainty as opposed to discrete disorders based on frozen degrees of conviction. *DMS-IV* has begun to recognize this in asking the clinician to note the degree of insight that accompanies OCD. At the far end of such a spectrum, where insight into the irrational nature of the ideation is low and therefore conviction is at 100 percent, is the severe delusional disorder, somatic type; at the milder end of the continuum, illness phobias and somatization disorder. This spectrum of conviction concept has also contributed to the literature supporting a spectrum of obsessive-compulsive related disorders (OCRD). The similarity between obsessing about getting a disease (OCD) and obsessing about having a disease (hypochondriasis) or obsessing about a particular body part (BDD) challenges more rigid diagnostic distinctions. Wider diagnostic considerations for OCRD also include trichotillomania, eating disorders, and sexual and gambling compulsions. For some of these later diagnoses the added problem of deciding whether they might be better conceptualized and distinguished as impulse control disorders is highly complicated and an unresolved theoretical controversy (Hollander 1993). While no full epidemiological studies have assessed the prevalence of hypochondriasis among OCD patients, one study found a 33 percent lifetime prevalence rate of hypochondriasis among OCD patients (Hollander 1993). The other primary similarity between OCD and hypochondriasis is of course the behavioral similarity. Both groups of patients tend to report urges to perform and engage in active (ritualistic) and passive (avoidant) compulsive behaviors: checking of various types, reassurance seeking, multiple medical tests, compulsively checking medical texts, body scanning and/or checking, repeating reassurances to oneself mentally, compulsively avoiding a particular test, compulsively avoiding particular conversations, movies, and so on (related to illness or death), and compulsively avoiding certain places or activities/objects associated with illness.

Once a patient becomes entangled in hypochondriacal thinking and behavior, a classic self-perpetuating, self-amplifying OCRD cycle becomes established. The three primary points in this cycle are (1) contact with an internal and/or external trigger, that is, bodily sensation or changes, illness-related information; (2) physiological activation, and activation of obsessions, that is, access to cognitive schemas regarding vulnerability and perfectionism, intolerance of doubt, general attributions of danger, a sense of self in which one is unable to withstand such mental and physical threats, beliefs regarding the need for hypervigilance; and (3) active and passive forms of compulsiveness, that is, checking, repeating, avoiding, hypervigilant body scanning. The cycle is self-perpetuating in the classic sense that avoidant and compulsive behaviors may offer the patient some immediate reward: the anxiety is temporarily relieved through locating some reassuring piece of information. The temporary nature of this relief and the tendency over the course of time for compulsive forms of relief to grow into increasingly unmanageable amounts of time make this cycle ultimately self-defeating. The self-amplification nature of such a cycle perpetuates itself via self-confirming feedback. This feedback loop is brought about by the main strategy of the hypochondriac, that is, hypervigilance regarding any doubts about the body's health. The assumption underlying hypervigilance would be, "I must be aware of and do something about all bodily change and sensation." The hypervigilant mode of mental and behavioral checking creates further physiological activity (at times exacerbating or creating physical symptoms) and cognitively creates a selective attention problem in which mental filtering errors disqualify incongruent information. While such a confirmatory cognitive bias has not actually been empirically demonstrated with hypochondriacal patients, information- and mood-congruent processing bias has been generally demonstrated with anxious and depressed individuals (Teasdale and Russell 1983). Finally, if a patient is engaged in bodily manipulation during checking, such checking often irritates the affected region to the point of physical exacerbation, further confirming a patient's suspicions of illness.

CASE 2

Ms. B. is a young woman who presented with constant thoughts of anxiety regarding the possibility of having cancer. She had already had one benign but "irregular" cyst removed surgically from her breast, had multiple aspirations and biopsies, and was currently interviewing numerous surgeons to have another suspicious cyst removed when she came in for treatment. While reporting that she usually checked her breasts only the requisite one time per month, upon further assessment this figure changed when she was "monitoring a suspicious cyst." Suspiciousness legitimized physically checking and manipulating her breast up to several times per day. After approximately a month, she "confirmed" a painful, irritated, and therefore abnormal cyst whose size and feel seemed to change. She proceeded to recruit several expert opinions until she found one that believed in fact that it was suspicious and it should be removed. Physicians who encouraged watchful waiting were at this point rejected.

Educating patients regarding the nature of this self-perpetuating, self-amplifying, and ultimately self-defeating cycle and weakening the various links in this cycle by offering alternatives to obsessive beliefs and compulsions is the primary thrust of cognitive-behavioral therapy (CBT) for hypochondriasis. Since the focus of this article is cognitive-behavioral in nature, no direct mention has been made of biological conceptualizations other than mentioning the aroused autonomic states presented by these patients. The above cycle describes the maintenance, perpetuation, and exacerbation of hypochondriacal symptoms in CBT terms. What predisposes individuals to develop such cycles is probably an interaction of various developmental circumstances and biological predispositions. If it turns out that hypochondriasis is truly an OCRD, then accumulating current research seems to suggest that initially a genetic predisposition puts a patient at risk and subsequent developmental experiences play a contributing role in the initial manifestation and subsequent course of the obsessive-compulsive symptoms (Mavissakalian et al. 1985).

TREATMENT

The cognitive-behavioral treatment presented is based on the previously described theory that hypochondriasis is an obsessive-compulsive related disorder. Such a conceptualization is theoretically and practically consistent with cognitive-behavioral treatments that target the core symptoms of any anxiety disorder, that is, reducing the anxiety itself through desensitization, reducing behavioral compulsions through extinction, and reducing obsessions through cognitive restructuring. The benefits of each of these strategic elements overlap in a complementary fashion. In treating any OCRD it is often helpful when first introducing the treatment rationale to present autonomic overactivity (anxiety) as the "fuel" and compulsive behaviors as the self-defeating attempts to decrease the anxiety. The two primary methods described below for reducing the anxiety are replacing these self-defeating attempts at anxiety reduction with (1) new cognitive-behavioral coping skills and subsequently (2) exposure/desensitization strategies. Three primary phases of treatment are outlined: engagement and assessment, skill building and restructuring, and exposure and maintenance. Such a phase-oriented approach to cognitive-behavioral therapy is very similar to Meichenbaum's (1985) stress inoculation training (SIT) and is common to many short-term CBT protocols. Depending on the skill deficits and/or strengths of the individual patient and the comorbid difficulties, such an approach can be expanded to address more significant pathology (characterological difficulties, multiple diagnosis) over the course of treatment. While treatment will be presented as phases, in actuality these treatment phases overlap and are by no means unidirectional.

Engagement and Assessment

The first phase of therapy contains three primary goals: (1) building of a working alliance, (2) ongoing cognitive and behavioral assessment by both therapist and patient, and (3) acclimation of the patient to CBT rationale and conceptualization.

Unfortunately, working alliances with somatically centered patients are often notorious for being problematic. If the patient isn't the first to become disenchanted from prior treatment frustrations, the health care provider may become frustrated over the patient's insistence on focusing on physical symptoms, in spite of there being no real cause for concern. Often this mutual frustration and confusion as to which "symptoms" are actually the target of treatment has led psychologists and physicians alike to focus on something other than the hypochondria itself, leaving the patient with hypochondriasis misunderstood and dissatisfied. While the reluctance of these patients to see a mental health professional (most present to physicians and do not follow through on a recommendation to see a mental health practitioner) is understandable given the above scenario, an attempt is currently being made by cognitive-behavioral therapists to directly address the hypochondriasis itself, without necessarily ignoring accompanying physical complaints (as in somatization disorder).

After the initial differential diagnostic interview, the rationale of a cognitive-behavioral therapist to a potential patient (who is primarily in a somatizing mode) is that they are suffering from an OCRD, and that these illness-related obsessions, anxieties, and compulsive behaviors worsen the physical symptoms in an escalating and reciprocal cycle. Patients are not told that the physical complaints are necessarily baseless or entirely emotional. If a patient presents with hypochondriasis without physical complaint, then the OCRD conceptualization and rationale is even more straightforward, that is, reducing psychological symptoms (obsessions, compulsions, anxiety) is the primary target. Obviously, patients need to be given definitions and descriptions of how obsessions and compulsions are manifested in their particular case.

Hypochondriasis that presents an illness phobia (OCD) is not particularly focused on solving actual physical symptoms but on the fear of developing such symptoms. Illness phobics may be better off prognostically if for no other reason other than having greater insight and therefore a stronger initial alliance with a mental health professional. The most basic tenets of cognitive-behavioral therapy are presented during the initial sessions: the reciprocal relationship between thoughts, emotions, and behavior; the idea that one can often choose one's emotional state and behavior; that one cannot do this without hard, ongoing work.

A central tenet of an OCRD/CBT approach to hypochondriasis is that checking in excess is self-defeating and must be reduced. Compulsive checking is presented as having only short-term benefits if it works at all. The self-defeating nature of compulsions is a point that some patients are more convinced of than others. For most patients the necessity of reducing checking is a belief that needs continuous reinforcement by the therapist. A further case that can be presented to the patient is that compulsions maintain and even exacerbate self-defeating and anxiety-provoking beliefs—the patient never has a chance to see if not giving into compulsive urges will result in intolerable anxiety or the imagined catastrophic consequences. The patient needs to be warned, however, that such beliefs have been overlearned. Since it has taken so long to learn these ideas and behaviors, it is going to take a sustained, systematic effort over the course of time to unlearn them. Furthermore, the anxiety likely to arise if a person resists compulsive urges will seem intolerable only in the beginning. The patient must be informed that the anxiety that occurs when they resist compulsive urges will fade over time as they learn alternate ways of coping.

The skill-building phase of therapy will assist them in being increasingly able to confront the typical triggers for anxiety without giving into compulsions and therefore allowing desensitization to take place. Depending on the patient and the time constraints of therapy, the extent to which a patient shares these and other fundamental CBT conceptualizations of treatment can be explored socratically and not simply stated as dogma. Patients' doubts are addressed in the context of collaborative empiricism, in which ideas that the patient does not particularly believe are put to the test in some way, for example, "Anxiety will go down after repeated exposure, and so will the urge to check." This example of a belief in extinction is often challenged and makes for a good place to eventually recommend that a patient "hypothesis-test" the idea empirically (Beck et al. 1979). Choose a modern anxiety target, and warn the patient that it may take several exposures and/or two hours or more for the anxiety to begin to diminish. Other doubts can be addressed in a similar fashion and relevant evidence can be collected. Reviewing the extent of concordance between the therapist's recommended targets/goals and the patient's can be crucial in avoiding later difficulties. Goals likely to succeed are decreasing illness-related anxiety, decreasing time spent on illness ruminations, increasing social and occupational interaction, decreasing illness-related behavior, increasing pleasurable activity, and lessening the physiological symptoms if present (as in somatization disorder).

In addition to the above general elements of building a therapeutic alliance, the assessment process continues beyond the initial diagnostic assessment. Ongoing efforts to perform a cognitive and behavioral functional analysis should be constantly guiding the course of therapy and feedback should constantly be solicited from the patient as to their thoughts on the course of therapy. Also essential in these initial sessions is the simultaneous distribution of information where one finds a lack of basic information regarding the inevitable questions regarding cause and prognosis, and so on. As part of this initial distribution of treatment information, a patient should be made aware of OCRD-relevant medication information such as SSRI's as a potential adjunct to cognitive-behavioral therapy and the decreased likelihood of relapse after discontinuing medications for those who have success-fully completed a course of CBT.

Guided discovery is the preferred means through which information is exchanged and the therapist's notes should be supplemented with the patient's own guided attempts at self-monitoring. Not only will this facilitate the therapist's assessment, but reviewing self-monitoring records together will give the therapist a chance to make certain that the patient understands the rationale of therapy. Self-monitoring should include *triggers*; environmental and/or somatic triggers that precede anxiety and/or compulsive urges (discriminative stimuli, relevant sensations, bodily changes, medical informa-tion, contact with illness cues, etc.); and *cognitions*, attributions regarding sensations and how or whether to remove them, catastrophic beliefs regarding not performing compulsions, basic assumptions regarding vulnerability/safety, and beliefs regarding self-efficacy and risk taking. Identifying the degree of conviction (one to 100 percent) for these cognitions can also be helpful. Finally, self-monitoring should also include *behav-iors*, the various compulsive urges including the urge to avoid, repeat, check, and seek reassurance as well as other forms of avoidance such as inactivity. Self-monitoring includes the amount of time spent compulsively checking medical concerns and the myriad ways in which this is done (time spent scanning; reassuring oneself; reading medical texts; seeking reassurance through others; getting to, waiting for and being examined by a physician). This is the time for the therapist to be assessing the functional analysis of triggers, behaviors, and cognitions, but, if successful, the engagement and assessment phase also familiarizes the patient with the basic tenets of cognitive-behavioral therapy and methods of challenging self-defeating beliefs. After these initial sessions the patient should feel like a respected collaborator in treatment; have a better understanding of the presenting problem, its prognosis, and treatment options; have begun practicing homework outside of session; and be ready to face temporary increases in anxiety for the sake of long-term reduction in symptoms.

Skill Building and Restructuring

In the skill-building and restructuring phase of treatment the emphasis is on rehearsing the skills introduced and outlined in the alliance stage. Goals for this phase of therapy include restructuring both obsessive thoughts and compulsive behaviors. Cognitive restructuring at this stage not only continues to identify automatic thoughts and generate rational alternatives, but ideally deepens the patient's conviction in these alternative beliefs. Patients must be reminded of the ongoing effort needed to maintain a new perspective on, for example, the proper significance of medical tests and the realistic probability of serious illness. At this point in therapy the patient has already begun homework assignments (self-monitoring) and an increasing emphasis on the importance of between-session work is underscored. The rationale at this phase of treatment has now been given in general CBT terms, but also in personal terms, thanks to self-monitoring and ongoing assessment. The patient must believe in the conceptualization enough to make a further commitment to use the strategies in and especially out of session. If a patient is ambivalent about further restructuring his/her cycle of fears and compulsions, then several alternatives are available: taking more time to explore the CBT rationale and thereby potentially strengthening motivation (getting the patient from the contemplation stage to the action stage), moving on only to general stress-management-type coping strategies (such as deep muscle relaxation) without beginning to interrupt compulsive habits yet, or asking the patient if he/she would rather return to therapy at a future time when he/she has further ruled out other solutions and is ready to proceed.

This may also be a time for the therapist to help the patient reconsider a dual psychopharmaco-CBT approach in order to maximize the benefits of both (a brief note should have already been made to the patient in earlier sessions regarding this treatment option). If they seem sufficiently oriented, then further introduction and rehearsal of general coping strategies proceeds. General anxiety reduction strategies should be rehearsed first under ideal practice situations, then slowly moved into increasingly difficult situations in which they can begin to replace compulsive habits. General coping strategies include any and all CBT strategies that may assist the patient in targeting the highly aroused physiological states that often accompany and drive compulsiveness. These skills and strategies include but are not necessarily limited to pleasure planning, assertiveness training, thought stopping followed by distraction, progressive muscle relaxation (PMR), breathing retraining (BR, paced and/or diaphragmatic), cue-controlled relaxation (CCR), rational responding, and self-instruction. PMR, BR, and CCR are direct attempts to lower physiological reactivity and should be presented as such. Patients should be reminded that if these strategies are not practiced under ideal conditions once a day for at least a month, they will probably fail to lower autonomic reactions when used under anxiety-provoking conditions—practice is essential (see Barlow and Cerny 1988, Jacobson 1938, McMullin 1986 for further details on these strategies).

Which of these skills are chosen and emphasized is a clinical judgment call based on the best fit between a patient's deficits and strengths and an analysis of relevant triggers. Reviewing the nature of the triggers preceding hypochondriacal ruminations should help, as should the initial diagnostic conceptualization of the case. Illness phobics (whose triggers often cluster around coming into contact with illness-related information) would benefit more from gearing coping skills toward facilitating and engaging in exposure and desensitization, while somaticizers whose triggers appear to be related to more general forms of stress may require more emphasis on counterconditioning and/or habit reversal strategies. The themes observed among the general stressors identified may also help to choose among interventions for this type of case. Teaching these more general somaticizers to identify what patterns exist among stressful times and triggers builds a case for reframing and acknowledging *with conviction* that the somatizations are misguided and magnified attributions for a stress response. Learning to respond to these stressors in new ways that are ideally incompatible with their old responses (habit reversal) is the goal here. For some of these more general somaticizers triggers may often include poor use of free time, an inability to shift their thinking/behavior, and/or poor social and assertiveness skills. As skill building continues past the point of practicing only under ideal conditions, the patient is increasingly encouraged to begin replacing compulsive coping efforts with CBT coping skills. This often includes attempts at resisting some type of checking or reassurance seeking. Often compulsive urges overwhelm these initial attempts at resistance; suggesting initially that the patient plan only to *delay* giving into the urge while coping is rehearsed is an intermediate step to total response prevention.

Since, for hypochondriacs, checking often happens through family, friends, and/or physicians, some discussion about these top enablers is also in order. Exploring these relationships and encouraging independence and self-soothing can be an essential step. Often hypochondriacal patients have become dependent on excessive reassurance from family and physicians. Altering the frequency of reassurance seeking, time between reassurances, and the number of people used for reassurance are often the most realistic targets for initial response-delay and response-reduction interventions. Discouraging doctor hopping and establishing one physician as a medical gatekeeper is also a useful guideline. Assisting the patient in learning to communicate assertively (not aggressively) with these individuals—possibly even inviting central significant others to a session and establishing guidelines limiting checking and reassurance—is a consideration. Limiting all illness-related self-checking to absolute minimum reasonable levels is an essential treatment target. Offering the rationale that, since on average the yearly or biyearly visit to the "medical authority" should be sufficient to maintain good health for most people, all other self-checking should be seen as inconclusive and therefore unnecessary. For women, of course, monthly self-breast exams are permissible.

Given today's climate of preventative medicine, it is an absolute necessity for anxious/obsessive patients to fight vigilantly to keep medical tests in perspective. With today's incredibly detail-sensitive preventative testing, patients will be bombarded through life with constant information regarding tests that encourage "watchful waiting." If preventative testing cannot be put into the context of being undeserving of worry and a sense of impending danger seen as unwarranted, then the patient will be in a constant state of anticipatory anxiety. Helping patients to place medical information into this preventative context may include a discussion of the nature of preventative medicine, the sensitivity of modern medical tests, recent cultural fascination with health/illness, and the effects of malpractice and liability on physician-to-patient feedback. Ultimately arriving at the assumption that varying degrees of bodily wear and their accompanying discomforts are inevitable physical changes, and not seeing health as a static, symptom-free state, is an essential goal of cognitive restructuring. Any other rational responses, constructed mutually by the therapist and patient, that allow the patient to resist unnecessary checking also play an essential role for cognitive strategies. It is at this point that therapists encourage the *prevention* (not just the delay) of compulsive urges to check, in which coping techniques and exposure-oriented strategies really begin to overlap. It is at this phace of therapy that the emphasis shifts to exposure and response-prevention (ERP) while the newfound coping skills continue to be practiced.

EXPOSURE AND MAINTENANCE

As previously mentioned, the treatment stages are overlapping and therefore a good deal of exposure-type work has already begun at this point in therapy. Technically, exposure for hypochondriacal patients may work best for the illness phobic, the patient who fears *getting* a particular illness. It is these patients who most closely fit the OCRD format and for whom this phase of therapy is absolutely essential, but the strategies are also useful for other types of somaticizers. For those who are not classic illness phobics, exposure should be part of a total treatment package that will better prepare the patient for using the newly acquired coping skills under high-stress conditions. Patients must be ready to make a final commitment of time, effort, and heightened anxiety to continue with this last stage of therapy.

Once again, therapist and patient monitoring charts are used to identify clusters of common elements or themes among identified triggers. Hierarchies are constructed around specific illnesses (AIDS, cancer, etc.), situations/events (hospitals, death, medical discussions/information, tests, doctors, sick people or more general triggers—criticism, social conflict, etc.), sensations (palpitations, dizziness, pain/injury, anger, etc.), or actions (strains, sports, swallowing, eating certain foods, specific movements, etc.). Exposure-response prevention (ERP) assignments are planned for both in and out of session; they entail exposure to the hierarchy triggers, without engagement in compulsive responses; and response prevention (avoiding, escaping, or excessively distracting, seeking reassurance, etc.). Such in vivo exposure work can also be supplemented with imaginal exposure. Imaginal exposure can often help to desensitize patients to what they cannot yet face in vivo or to what is impossible to face literally, for example, actually having cancer, hearing the doctor announce positive findings, living with such news, imagining one's family living with such news, even death itself. Imaginal exposure work can be supplemented with video- or audiotapes of relevant imagery. Audiotapes with repetitive phrases or preconstructed verbal scripts describing certain scenes can supplement imaginal exposure homework assignments. Prerecorded videotapes of relevant imagery or themes may also be useful. Patient and therapist alike should explore local medical libraries or even feature films that may contain the relevant themes. All such exposure to in vivo or imaginal scenes should be accompanied by a notation of the subjective units of distress (SUD) level (one to 100). Over the course of ERP, SUD ratings help to guide therapists in deciding how hard to push patients (try to work in the 60 to 70 range) and when to move up the hierarchy. Therapist and patient are engaged in an ongoing juggling act during exposure work, that is, between helping the patient to attend fully to exposure cues while intermittently rehearsing various coping skills. A balance between these two modes facilitates patient compliance. Rational responses can also help to inhibit patient urges to immediately escape/terminate further exposure or engage in other forms of compulsive behavior. As one prevents compulsive urges, it is also an opportunity to identify and disprove a patient's catastrophic assumptions regarding not giving into compulsive means of coping ("If I don't go to the doctor immediately when I have a pain, I will miss something serious"; "I cannot tolerate living with this doubt, I need the immediate reassurance of a doctor").

Present the rationale that ERP prepares the patient to deal

with the triggers that often precede the reemergence of habitual obsessional thinking and compulsive behaviors. A natural extension of ERP work is a preparation for lapses. An exploratory discussion of relapse prevention should include an attempt to foresee and prepare for upcoming general stressors. Patients should be warned to expect lapses, but the importance of not surrendering one's new skills entirely when inevitable challenges or lapses occur should be stressed. Inform the patient that lapses into such obsessions or compulsions are inevitable and not a sign of failure but a cue to use the new thinking and behaviors as fully as possible. Patients should be encouraged to rehearse both coping skills and intermittent exposure exercises before lapses occur, not simply when they are in crisis. If they wait for high-anxiety situations to apply these new skills, without ongoing practice on lesser anxieties, they will usually fail. The fact that realistic treatment success is not the total elimination of such flare-ups but a reduction in the number, duration, and intensity of these lapses should be emphasized. Finally, booster sessions for coping with particularly difficult situations should be encouraged.

CONCLUSION

While the need for research is still great regarding CBT for hypochondriasis, early research efforts are showing favorable results (see Fallon et al. 1993 for recent review). Improvement has been measured in various ways, from decreased number of doctor visits, to less time spent ruminating about health, to less compulsive behavior. Also showing favorable results for hypochondriasis is group CBT, though much of this research lacks control groups (Barsky et al. 1988). Finally, CBT for somaticizing is even catching on internationally, with investigators reporting 73 percent improvement (compared to 59 percent control) in unexplained physical symptoms in a Dutch sample (Marton 1996).

Through CBT's focus on eliminating obsessional beliefs and accompanying compulsive routines, and replacing such routines with healthier habits, patient and therapist have a unique opportunity to come to terms with the common waxing and waning of hypochondriacal tendencies, and ultimately to attempt to decrease the degree of disability—real or perceived. The assumption that living as full and active a life as possible (within one's limits), if not without physical pain, emotional distress, and discomfort, then in spite of it, is a major underlying assumption of CBT for hypochondriasis. Helping these patients to diversify their activities and to actively engage in physical, social, professional, spiritual, and creative activities while spending as little time as possible engaging in illness-related behavior—and as much time as possible in health-related behavior—is the overall goal of CBT for hypochondriasis.

REFERENCES

Barlow, D. H., and Cerny, A. C. (1988). *Psychological Treatment of Panic*. New York: Guilford.

Barsky, A. J., Geringer, E., and Wool, C. A. (1988). A cognitive-educational treatment for hypochondriasis.*General Hospital Psychiatry* 10:322–327.

Barsky, A. J., Wyshak, G., and Klerman, G. L. (1992). Psychiatric comorbidity in *DSM III-R. Archives of General Psychiatry* 49:101–108.

Baur, S. (1988). *Hypochondria, Woeful Imaginings*. Berkeley: University of California Press.

Beck, A. T., Rush, J. A., Shaw, B. F., and Emery, G. (1979). *Cognitive Therapy of Depression*. New York: Guilford.

Diagnostic and Statistical Manual of Mental Disorders (DSM-IV) (1994). 4th ed. Washington, DC: American Psychiatric Association.

Fallon, B. A., Klein, B. W., and Liebowitz, M. R. (1993). Hypochondriasis: treatment strategies. *Psychiatric Annals* 23:374–381.

Hollander, E., ed. (1993). *Obsessive-Compulsive–Related Disorders*. Washington, DC: American Psychiatric Press.

Jacobson, E. (1938). *Progressive Relaxation*. Chicago: University of Chicago Press.

Marton, K. I., ed. (1996). Treating patients with unexplained physical symptoms. *Journal Watch for Psychiatry* 2(2):15.

Mavissakalian, M., Turner, S. M., and Michelson, L. (1985). *Obsessive-Compulsive Disorder: Psychological and Pharmacological Treatment*. New York: Plenum.

McMullin, R. E. (1986). *Handbook of Cognitive Therapy Techniques*. Ontario: Penguin.

Meichenbaum, D. (1985). *Stress Inoculation Training*. Elmsford: Pergamon.

Pilowsky, I. (1967). Dimensions of hypochondriasis. *British Journal of Psychiatry* 113:89–93.

Teasdale, J. D., and Russell, M. C. (1983). Differential effects of induced mood on recall of positive, negative, and neutral words. *British Journal of Clinical Psychology* 22:163–171.

10

POST-TRAUMATIC STRESS DISORDER

Mervin R. Smucker

INTRODUCTION

PTSD Symptomatology

The existence of post-traumatic stress disorder (PTSD) as a clinical syndrome is well documented in the scientific litera-ture. According to the American Psychiatric Association's fourth edition of the *Diagnostic and Statistical Manual of Mental Disorders* (*DSM-IV* 1994), PTSD develops in the aftermath of a psychologically traumatic event that is outside the range of usual human experience. The characteristic symptoms of a PTSD syndrome involve (1) recurrent and intrusive recol-lections of the traumatic event (e.g., recurring flashbacks, dreams, nightmares), often accompanied by intense emotional distress; (2) avoidance of trauma-related stimuli and/or numbing of general responsiveness; and (3) increased arousal (e.g., hypervigilance, exaggerated startle response, sleep disturbance, irritability). PTSD tends to be more severe and longer lasting when the traumatic event is of intentional human design (e.g., sexual abuse, physical torture, war, or concentration camps, in contrast to accidents or natural disasters such as floods or earthquakes).

Type I versus Type II Traumatic Events

An important consideration in the assessment and treatment of PTSD is whether the stressor producing this syndrome is a Type I or Type II trauma (Meichenbaum 1994, Terr 1991). Briefly, a Type I trauma is an unexpected, isolated traumatic event of limited duration (e.g., a single incident of rape, physical assault, sniper shooting, natural disaster, or industrial accident) from which a quick recovery is likely. By contrast, a Type II trauma is more long-standing in nature and involves a series of expected, repeated traumatic events (such as ongoing childhood sexual or physical abuse) that lead to a negatively altered schematic view of self and the world. Type II traumas frequently develop into a more complex and chronic PTSD response associated with other psychiatric conditions, including higher rates of substance abuse, eating disorders, mood disorders, depressive and anxiety disorders, panic disorders, chronic relationship problems, and long-standing characterological disturbances evidenced by emotional lability, self-abusive behaviors, and suicidality (See North et al. 1994 for a discussion of comorbidity and PTSD).

COGNITIVE CONCEPTUALIZATION OF PTSD

From a cognitive processing perspective, PTSD results from inadequate emotional processing of traumatic events, and

PTSD symptoms abate once adequate or successful emotional processing has occurred (Foa and Kozak 1986, Horowitz 1986, Smucker et al. 1995). Thus it is the individual's response to trauma—and *not* the traumatic events—that produces a PTSD syndrome. Similarly, it is the individual's response to his/her PTSD symptomatology that determines the course of recovery.

Indicators of Emotional Processing

A number of theorists have recently elaborated on the nature of emotional processing and how it may be impeded or facilitated. As noted by Horowitz (1986), many trauma victims use denial, numbing, amnesia, or other dissociative strategies as protection from "information overload" and the affective distress associated with their traumatization. While the use of such cognitive and affective avoidance responses may have been adaptive survival responses at the time of the traumatic occurrence(s), their continued post-trauma use is viewed as a maladaptive avoidance strategy that thwarts or delays successful emotional processing.

Rachman (1980), who defined emotional processing as a process by which emotional responses decrease, concluded that successful emotional processing (of fear) could "be gauged from the person's ability to talk about, see, listen to or be reminded of the emotional events without experiencing distress or disruptions" (pp. 51–52). Expanding on Piaget's theory of adaptation, Horowitz (1986) noted that traumatic material is complete once the cognitive schemata have been altered to incorporate and integrate new information. He observed the presence of a "completion tendency" with PTSD sufferers, whereby intrusive traumatic recollections (e.g., recurring flashbacks, repetitive nightmares) continue to emerge until the traumatic material is fully processed. While successful emotional processing is often delayed by means of denial and numbing,

Horowitz concluded that the oscillation between PTSD intrusions and denial/numbing responses is a naturally occurring feature prior to a complete integration of the traumatic material.

Foa and Kozak (1986), who defined emotional processing as "the modification of memory structures that underlie emotions" (p. 20), asserted that two conditions are essential for successful emotional processing of traumatic material to occur: (1) activation of the entire fear memory (including cognitive, affective, and primary sensory stimuli), and (2) incorporation of "corrective" information that is incompatible with traumatic elements of the existing fear structure.

Van der Kolk and van der Hart (1989) noted that recurring traumatic memories involve primary sensory sensations (e.g., visual, auditory, kinesthetic, tactile) that must be transformed into language before they can be adequately processed and integrated into existing mental schemas. The authors described the raw, unprocessed nature of traumatic memories as follows:

> Trauma stops the chronological clock and fixes the traumatic moment in memory and imagination. Such traumatic memories are *not* usually altered by the mere passage of time. These traumatic memories become fixed and the intense vehement emotions interfere with their natural processing. These traumatic memories are *not* organized on a linguistic line. [p. 447]

Traumatic versus Nontraumatic Memories

The nature of traumatic memory itself has implications for how trauma-related material is accessed and processed within a therapeutic context. According to van der Kolk and van der Hart (1989, 1991), traumatic memories are encoded and accessed differently from nontraumatic or narrative memories. They reported that, in contrast to narrative memories, traumatic memories (1) lack verbal narrative and context, (2) are state dependent, (3) are encoded in the form of vivid sensations and images that cannot be accessed by linguistic means alone, (4) are difficult to assimilate and integrate because they are "stored" differently and are often dissociated from conscious awareness and voluntary control, and (5) often remain "fixed" in their original form and unaltered by the passage of time.

Similarly, Vardi and colleagues (1994) found more primary sensory stimuli (visual, kinesthetic, auditory) contained in the traumatic memories of rape and incest victims than in their nontraumatic memories. They also reported that the traumatic memories of incest victims were more fragmentary and less continuous than those of rape victims, suggesting that the nature of traumatic memories may vary according to whether the trauma is of a Type I or a Type II nature.

Traumagenic Schemas

For survivors of Type II traumas, especially when they are experienced in childhood, PTSD symptomatology is often embedded in trauma-based schemas (Smucker and Niederee 1995), which serve as cognitive templates that filter and organize mental processes and significantly influence how subsequent events are perceived, interpreted, encoded, and recalled. The continued presence and activation of these "traumagenic schemas" (e.g., schemas of powerlessness, worthlessness, culpability, unlovability) serve to keep the trauma survivor in a perpetual state of perceived victimization long after the abuse has ceased and lay the foundation for the development of a chronic PTSD syndrome. For Type II trauma survivors in particular, the trauma-based "powerlessness schema" seems to form the nucleus of their PTSD syndrome, often leaving them in a state of "functional paralysis" such that they have enormous difficulty coping with the daily "knocks" of life without being thrown into a major emotional crisis. Thus the PTSD sufferer's sense of powerlessness becomes a primary target of cognitive therapy with this population.

AN EXPANDED COGNITIVE TREATMENT PARADIGM

While clearly embedded in information-processing theory and schema theory, cognitive therapy with PTSD is also conceptually rooted in attachment theory and object-relations theory. In an expanded cognitive therapy paradigm, imagery interventions are used in promoting a therapeutic secure base, fostering introject change, modifying trauma-related primary sensory stimuli, and facilitating schematic shifts at both a primary and secondary process level.

Attachment Theory and Cognitive Therapy

In attachment theory, psychotherapy is viewed as a process of reappraising and reworking inadequate, dysfunctional, outdated schematic models of the self and attachment figures (Bowlby 1988). A central therapeutic task is thought to be the development of a "secure base," from which patients can begin the arduous task of exploring and reworking their internal working models (Bretherton and Waters 1985).

Similarly, a primary task of the cognitive therapist's work with PTSD patients is to provide a "secure base" or "safety zone" that serves as a therapeutic anchor, from which the patient's painful traumatic material can be successfully reprocessed. The therapist facilitates cognitive and affective shifts back and forth from this secure therapeutic base into the traumatic material. (This procedure may be viewed as analogous to Wolpe's systematic desensitization treatment that involves facilitating patient shifts from a state of relaxation to exposure to phobic stimuli, followed by a return to the relaxed state.)

Object-Relations Theory, Introjects, and Cognitive Therapy

Consistent with a basic tenet from object-relations theory (Bretherton and Waters 1985, Cashdan 1988), a therapeutic goal for trauma victims is to internalize this secure base by developing a "positive therapist introject," which serves as the patient's focal point in forming a new schematic template. (Although the term *introject* has traditionally been used within a psychodynamic context, it may also be viewed as a useful cognitive construct denoting how an individual has schematically "internalized" the treatment received by early caregivers, and is reflected in how one views and treats oneself today. While treatment by early caregivers is viewed as critical to the process of introject formation, introjects are subject to further development and modification across the lifespan [Henry et al. 1990].) When activated or "summoned up" by the patient, this internal cognitive representation of the therapist (often visual and auditory in nature) may have a calming/soothing effect on the patient's mood, especially during times of emotional distress. Eventually, this new therapist introject may become integrated into the patient's schematic internal representation of self.

Imagery and Cognitive Therapy[1]

The use of imagery as a primary therapeutic agent is an important component of cognitive therapy with patients suffering from PTSD.[2] As noted by van der Kolk and van der Hart (1991), traumatic memories and their associated meanings are often encoded as vivid images and sensations not accessible through linguistic retrieval. Since much of the cognitive disturbance associated with traumatic memories (e.g., recurring flashbacks, repetitive nightmares) is embedded in the traumatic imagery, directly challenging and modifying the PTSD victim's distressing imagery becomes a potent means of providing "corrective" information and facilitating the processing of the traumatic material.

In cognitive therapy, imagery-focused interventions are thus used as primary therapeutic agents to facilitate alleviation of PTSD symptomatology and modify trauma-related beliefs and schemas (e.g., powerlessness). *Imaginal exposure* (i.e., activating the "fear memory" via visual and affective reenactment of the trauma) is used in combination with *imaginal rescripting* (i.e., modifying the traumatic imagery to produce a more favorable outcome). The goal of imagery rescripting is essentially to replace victimization imagery with mastery imagery, such that patients may "experience" themselves responding to the trauma scene as empowered adults no longer "frozen" in a powerless state of victimization. Through the visual rescripting process, the traumatic images are modified and the traumagenic beliefs are identified and challenged.

---

1. See Anderson (1980), Beck and colleagues (1985), and Edwards (1990) for a review of clinical applications of imagery in cognitive therapy.

2. Numerous cognitive-oriented clinicians have elaborated on the process of modifying traumatic imagery as a means of reframing traumatic events and their meaning (Beck and Freeman 1990, Peterson et al. 1991, Smucker et al. 1995, Smucker and Niederee 1995, Staton 1990).

Primary and Secondary Cognitive Processing
in Cognitive Therapy

In cognitive therapy with PTSD, an important distinction is noted between primary cognitive processing and secondary cognitive processing. ("Primary cognitive processing" and "secondary cognitive processing" are extensions of the Freudian terms "primary process" and "secondary process," which Freud coined to reflect two fundamentally different modes of psychic functioning. Freud viewed the primary process as the earliest, most primitive and illogical form of mentation that is primarily iconic in nature, lacking in temporal dimension, and reflected in such mental activities as dreams, fantasies, and daydreams. By contrast, he viewed the secondary process as governed by reality-based logical thought, and exemplified by delayed gratification and active problem-solving activities [Moore and Fine 1990].) The interweaving of these two levels of processing is crucial in the successful emotional processing of traumatic material. Briefly, the activation and reworking of imagery is viewed as a "primary cognitive process" (i.e., nonverbal, nonlinguistic mental activity that is primarily visual and auditory in nature). By contrast, the linguistic processing of thoughts and feelings about an event (e.g., verbalizing one's cognitions through talking or writing) is viewed as a "secondary cognitive process."

In cognitive therapy with PTSD, processing traumatic material at both primary and secondary levels is considered essential for successful emotional processing to occur. Primary cognitive processing is at work whenever imagery is activated in the therapy session, although secondary cognitive processing usually occurs simultaneously. Verbalizing aloud traumatic images in the session is in itself a form of secondary cognitive processing, as it involves putting words to images. During imagery work in cognitive therapy, the patient and therapist "freeze" the imagery from time to time (i.e., put the imagery "on pause") and linguistically process thoughts and feelings about the imagery being experienced. As such, the therapist and patient typically go back and forth during a therapy session from primary cognitive processing (experiencing the imagery) to secondary cognitive processing (verbalizing thoughts and feelings about the imagery). At the end of each imagery session, patients are also asked to verbalize their thoughts and feelings about the imagery (i.e., to reprocess primary process material at a secondary level of cognitive processing). This primary and secondary cognitive processing is continued beyond the therapy session as part of the patient's homework, which involves listening daily to the audiotaped imagery session and recording reactions in a journal.

INITIAL TREATMENT INTERVIEW

At intake, information is obtained about the patient's current life situation, family history, history of traumatic experiences, current psychological adjustment, medical history, alcohol and drug use, depression, and severity of PTSD symptoms. Much of the initial clinical interview focuses on the immediate presenting problems, the degree to which they interfere with daily functioning, the response of the patient's social milieu (family, friends, employer, co-workers, etc.), and how the patient has attempted to cope with his/her symptoms. Specific questions are asked about the presence, frequency, and intensity of intrusive traumatic recollections, dissociative flashbacks, and nightmares. It is important to be sensitive to the emotional state of the patient while probing these areas. Clinical assessment measures are given that can be readministered at the termination of treatment and at follow-up. (See

Stamm 1996 for a compendium of PTSD clinical assessment measures.)

As there is some variability in the prominence of specific post-traumatic stress symptoms that emerges among traumatized patients, an important initial task of the clinician is to assess whether a patient meets full criteria for PTSD, whether the PTSD is a primary or secondary clinical diagnosis, or whether the patient is manifesting partial post-traumatic stress symptoms that are "blocking" intrusive ideation (cognitive avoidance) and preventing the onset of a full-blown PTSD syndrome (affective avoidance). Thus the symptoms targeted for treatment, as well as the specific treatment goals and interventions chosen, will depend in part on which post-traumatic stress symptoms are determined to be the most prominent, the most distressing, and the most dysfunctional, and the degree to which these PTSD-like symptoms may be functioning as cognitive avoidance or affective avoidance strategies.

TREATMENT APPLICATION

The following section focuses on the application of cognitive therapy with traumatized patients suffering from a PTSD syndrome whose most prominent and debilitating symptoms involve the visual and affective "reliving" of their trauma(s).

Specific Treatment Goals

While the general goal of cognitive therapy with patients suffering from a PTSD syndrome is to facilitate successful emotional processing of their trauma(s), specific treatment goals include (1) decreasing physiological arousal, (2) eliminating intrusive traumatic recollections (e.g., recurring flash-backs, repetitive nightmares), (3) replacing traumatic imagery with empowering imagery, (4) transforming traumatic imagery into narrative language, (5) modifying traumagenic beliefs and schemas, (6) developing more effective coping strategies for dealing with daily life stressors, and (7) developing an enhanced capacity to self-calm and self-soothe, especially during times of emotional distress.

Presentation of Treatment Rationale

Once the specific intrusive traumatic memories have been targeted for intervention, a brief description of the treatment is offered to the patient (may be paraphrased in therapist's own words):

> This therapy is designed to help you process and master your traumatic memories and leave you feeling more in control of your life. Much of our work will involve the use of imagery; that is, asking you to visually recall and reexperience the traumatic images, thoughts, and feelings that you experience during a flashback (or nightmare). We will then change the traumatic images to produce a better outcome. The aim is for you to replace your victimization imagery with mastery imagery, so that you can see and feel yourself responding to your trauma no longer as a victim, but as an empowered individual. This, of course, does not change the traumatic event itself or what actually happened, but it will change the images, thoughts, feelings, and beliefs that you have about the trauma. Do you have any questions?

Patients are fully informed of the emotional distress and heightened state of arousal that is likely to occur when traumatic imagery is induced in the therapy sessions, and are encouraged to call the therapist between sessions should the need arise. It is important to emphasize that reexperiencing painful traumatic memories in a therapy session is very different from experiencing them in the patient's everyday environment, that the trauma is not actually occurring at such times, and that the therapist's voice and supportive presence provide a "therapeutic anchor" throughout the imagery session. (See Smucker et al. [1995] and Smucker and Niederee [1995] for a detailed description of imagery and schema-focused cognitive interventions with adult survivors of childhood sexual abuse suffering from PTSD.)

Introduction of SUD

Following the treatment description, the patient is taught how to use a subjective units of distress (SUDs) rating on a zero to 100 scale to describe the degree of distress or discomfort he or she is experiencing. The therapist may explain this as follows:

> This treatment involves asking you to experience memories and scenes that will generate some anxiety and discomfort. I will be asking you to monitor and rate the degree of discomfort you experience on a scale from zero to 100. A rating of 100 would indicate that you are extremely upset, the most distressed you have ever felt. A rating of zero would indicate that you feel no discomfort at all. Using this scale, how much discomfort might you be feeling at this moment?

Imaginal Exposure

The patient is then asked to visualize (preferably with eyes closed) and describe aloud the traumatic memory in the present tense, as if it were happening at the moment. If the patient reports experiencing multiple traumatic flashbacks or nightmares, the most distressing memory is generally targeted for treatment. Any questions that the patient may have about the imagery session at this point are best addressed in a succinct and reassuring manner. During imaginal exposure, the therapist's role is facilitative rather than directive. The therapist does not intervene other than to ask the patient for more details of the abuse scene or to elaborate on specific thoughts and feelings. It is crucial that the entire "fear network" be activated during imaginal exposure, which includes visual, affective, sensory, and kinesthetic stimuli. When the verbalized account of the traumatic memory appears to have ended, the therapist may ask, "Is there anything more that happens in the traumatic memory?" Once it is clear that the patient has reexperienced the entire traumatic memory, the exposure imagery is brought to a close.[3]

Mastery Imagery

As soon as the patient has completed the imaginal exposure, the therapist may describe the mastery imagery phase as follows:

I'd like you once again to visualize the beginning of the traumatic imagery and describe, in the present, what is happening. This time, however, we will change the traumatic

---

3. For some Type I traumas experienced as an adult (e.g., natural disasters, industrial accidents, or even in some instances of rape or assault), imaginal exposure by itself may be sufficient. While not yet subjected to the rigors of empirical testing, clinical evidence and feedback received from therapists across a broad range of clinical settings does suggest that the modification or "rescripting" of traumatic imagery immediately following imaginal exposure is essential when treating Type II traumas and useful when treating most Type I traumas.

imagery to a better outcome, and I will help you with this. Are you ready to begin?

Any questions the patient may have about this phase are best deferred until the end of the imagery session. When the patient has indicated a readiness to begin, the therapist may proceed as follows:

> When you are ready, you may once again visualize the beginning of the traumatic imagery and describe in detail what is happening.

Initially, the mastery imagery phase closely resembles the exposure imagery. However, when the traumatic imagery reaches its zenith, the patient is asked to visualize him- or herself as an adult today entering the traumatic scene. (A variation of this technique would be to ask patients whether they could visualize themselves responding differently to the traumatic situation.) The therapist may facilitate this through such questions as:

> Can you now visualize yourself as an adult today entering the trauma scene?
> What happens when you, the adult today, enter the trauma scene?
> What would you, the adult today, now like to do? . . .
> Can you see yourself doing that?

The specific purpose of the mastery imagery phase is to replace victimization imagery with coping imagery. If unable to visualize themselves as adults today achieving "mastery" in the rescripted imagery, patients may "experiment" with bringing outside support people into the imagery to help.

During imagery modification, the cognitive therapist uses a guided discovery approach while employing "socratic imag-

ery"[4] (as opposed to guided imagery), and is careful not to tell
the patient what to do or suggest what should be happening
in the rescripted imagery. The therapist's role is thus primarily
facilitative, as patients are encouraged to decide for themselves what "coping" strategies to use in the mastery imagery.
(See Smucker and Niederee [1995] for a more detailed elaboration on the clinical application of socratic imagery.)

Self-Nurturing Imagery

Following completion of the mastery imagery, the therapist
fosters self-nurturing imagery, in which the adult today is
encouraged to interact directly with the traumatized self. The
therapist and patient may refer to the patient's traumatized
self as "the child" (if applicable), "the wounded self," or any
other idiosyncratic description that seems appropriate. The
therapist may facilitate this by asking such questions as:

> What would you, the adult today, like to do or say to the
> traumatized self? . . . Can you visualize yourself doing (or
> saying) that?
> How does the traumatized self respond?
> And how would you, the adult today, like to respond?
> What do you, the adult today, see when you look into the
> eyes of the traumatized self?

The self-nurturing imagery continues until it appears that
the adult today has offered sufficient nurturance to the trau-

---

4. Socratic imagery, which is essentially socratic questioning applied in
the context of imagery modification, derives from the notion that it is
healthier and more empowering for trauma victims to develop their own
mastery/coping imagery than to have it be directed, dictated, or suggested
to them by the therapist.

matized self. When the patient indicates a readiness to bring the imagery to a close, the patient is asked to let the imagery fade away and open his or her eyes.

Processing and Debriefing

Reactions to the imagery work are discussed and processed. To facilitate such processing, the therapist may ask such questions as:

How was that for you?
How are you feeling at this moment?
What thoughts or feelings do you have about the work we
  just did?

It is important to allow sufficient time for patients to gain control over their emotions prior to leaving the session. The therapist also inquires about the patient's general ability to self-calm and self-nurture, especially when feeling upset. The therapist and patient then collaboratively explore various self-calming/self-nurturing strategies for the patient to experiment with between sessions. If there is a history of self-abuse, it is imperative that the patient contract for safety.

Homework

Homework involves asking the patient to (1) listen daily to the audiotape of the entire imagery session just completed[5] and record SUDs levels prior to and after listening to the audiotape; (2) write in narrative form subjective reactions to the

---

5. All imaginal exposure and rescripting sessions are recorded for the patient on an audiotape for daily listening and processing.

audiotaped imagery session immediately after listening to it; (3) reframe the traumatic event(s) that gives personal meaning to the pain and suffering experienced; (4) document efforts in a journal to self-calm and self-nurture, especially when feeling upset; (5) record frequency and intensity (on a zero to 100 scale) of flashbacks experienced between therapy sessions; (6) if the traumatic event was of human design and involved deliberate perpetration acts, write at least one letter weekly to the perpetrator (letters not to be sent) expressing thoughts and feelings about the perpetration; (7) contract for safety. Although the homework assigned may appear rather ambitious, homework adherence does yield comparatively better results and significantly enhances successful emotional processing of the traumatic material.

Cognitive therapy continues more or less in the above manner until either successful emotional processing of the material has occurred, as evidenced by a significant reduction or elimination of PTSD symptomatology combined with an absence of avoidance behaviors, or the patient feels able to effectively manage the remaining PTSD symptoms without continued therapeutic support. With Type I traumas, cognitive therapy typically lasts for five to ten sessions, whereas treatment of Type II traumas generally lasts considerably longer.

TREATING "PERIPHERAL" POST-TRAUMATIC STRESS SYMPTOMS

Not infrequently, traumatized patients seeking treatment show signs of PTSD-like symptoms, but their symptom profile does not include repeated "reexperiencing" of the traumatic event (e.g., via visual flashbacks), which is viewed as the "nucleus" of a PTSD syndrome. In the following section, examples of such "peripheral" post-traumatic stress symptoms are noted and guidelines are offered for their conceptualization and treatment within a cognitive therapy context.

Increased Arousal

Symptoms of increased arousal sometimes emerge as the most prominent and distressing clinical symptoms (e.g., hypervigilance, exaggerated startle response, chronic sleep disturbance, generalized fear/anxiety). Although upsetting and disruptive, such responses may be "peripheral" manifestations of a PTSD syndrome not yet fully activated that serve to "block out" intrusive traumatic recollections, flashbacks, and associated affect. While increased arousal symptoms may serve to keep specific trauma-related stimuli outside their conscious level of awareness, such individuals appear extremely tense, rigid, fearful, and anxious, and are unable to relax as they are constantly on the lookout for the "next bomb to drop."

The initial focus of cognitive therapy with such patients is on identifying the specific problems for which the patient is seeking help, and then establishing specific, mutually agreed upon treatment goals. If the treatment goal is to significantly reduce or eliminate the increased arousal symptoms, it should be made clear to the patient that achieving this goal could lead to a short-term exacerbation of PTSD symptoms (e.g., intrusive images or flashbacks of the traumatic event), but that the emergence of such symptoms would facilitate emotional processing of the trauma, and thus be beneficial to the patient's long-term recovery. If the patient responds to this caveat with some hesitation, it may be useful to conduct a cost-benefit analysis together with the patient, weighing the pros and cons of reducing or maintaining the increased arousal symptoms.

If the patient decides that reducing the increased arousal symptoms is a desirable treatment goal, a two-pronged approach can be employed. This involves identifying and challenging the beliefs and schemas underlying the increased arousal symptoms (e.g., schemas of vulnerability and powerlessness), while simultaneously helping the patient to develop more adaptive coping strategies for daily functioning. Thus the cognitive therapist may employ schema-focused interventions (see Young 1994) along with standard cognitive therapy and stress inoculation training[6] interventions (e.g., dysfunctional thought records, relaxation training, self-calming imagery training, focused breathing, skills acquisition training, grounding techniques), and pharmacological interventions.

In instances where patients are too fearful of change and are not yet ready to give up their "defenses," cognitive therapy may not be warranted unless clear and reasonable therapeutic goals can be identified.

Dissociation

Some traumatized patients present with a more generalized psychogenic amnesia accompanied by the presence of frequent dissociative episodes, an autohypnotic skill that functions as an "affective anesthetic." While dissociation may serve to shield individuals from painful trauma-related stimuli, as well as afford them an escape from unpleasant affect associated with tensions and stress of daily living, it can also interfere significantly with their productive functioning and lead to aversive consequences (e.g., putting individuals at risk for losing their job or marriage because the boss or spouse will no longer tolerate their dissociative episodes and their "high-maintenance" unproductivity).

With the dissociative patient, cognitive therapy begins with

---

6. See Foa et al. (1991) and Meichenbaum (1993) for a detailed description of the clinical application of stress inoculation training.

educating the patient on the nature and function of dissociation, how it is often a very adaptive coping response at the time of a traumatic event, but how it tends to be increasingly dysfunctional and maladaptive when part of a prolonged post-trauma response. After collaboratively examining how dissociation may have been a useful survival strategy for the patient in the past, the therapist invites the patient to assess the costs and benefits of the continued use of dissociation as a coping strategy today. As is the case when working with addicts, patients must be highly motivated to want to change before any therapeutic interventions are likely to be effective. Above all, patients must be clearly convinced that the long-term pain caused by continuing to dissociate is more costly than its short-term benefits or secondary gain. Moreover, it must be clear to patients that a likely short-term cost of not dissociating (i.e., of giving up the "addictive response") will be to experience frequent and intense waves of painful affect, and that the pain could feel unbearable at times.

Once it is clear that the patient is indeed motivated to give up dissociation as a coping strategy, cognitive therapy can proceed, with the focus on developing strategies to increase the patient's tolerance for emotional pain while simultaneously developing alternate coping strategies to replace the dissociative episodes. Thus, if the specific treatment goals are to (1) significantly decrease and eventually eliminate all dissociative episodes, and (2) increase the patient's emotional pain threshold—and these seem like reasonable therapeutic goals to both therapist and patient—a range of cognitive interventions may be employed on a trial-and-error basis including prolonged exposure,[7] affective tolerance training, focused breathing, relaxation training, skills acquisition training, and

---

7. See Foa and Kozak (1986) and Foa et al. (1993) for a description of the theory, rationale, and application of prolonged exposure in the treatment of rape victims suffering from PTSD.

grounding strategies that include intensive daily physical workouts, together with pharmacological interventions.

If patients are reluctant to give up their dissociation "defenses" at present, cognitive therapy may need to be suspended until clear and reasonable therapeutic goals can be identified and the patient is motivated and seriously committed to the attainment of these goals.

Generalized Emotional Numbing

Some traumatized patients attempt to escape and avoid all pain associated with their trauma by completely shutting down emotionally. They are afraid that if they allow themselves to feel anything at all, they will be consumed and overwhelmed by negative affect. While "protecting" trauma victims from feeling the pain of their trauma and from feeling overwhelmed by negative affect, such affective avoidance strategies keep trauma survivors "stuck" in their traumatization, prevent them from being able to experience the range of normal human emotions, and lead to a lonely existence devoid of intimacy and human bonding.

Here again, before beginning treatment with such patients, it is important to clarify the specific problem areas for which help is being sought as well as the specific treatment goals. If the patient's stated treatment goal was to become "emotionally alive" again, it would be important for the therapist to understand why and how the patient has come to that decision. It should also be clear to the patient that becoming emotionally alive again could well lead to an exacerbation of PTSD symptoms and heightened negative affect. If the patient nevertheless appeared motivated to proceed in this direction, an array of cognitive and behavior interventions could be employed, on a trial-and-error basis, that focus on increasing affective tolerance (e.g., affective enhancement exercises in and out of the therapy session) and increasing intimate contacts with others.

On the other hand, if the patient's defenses are beginning to crumble and he or she is beginning to feel overwhelmed with the emergence of heightened affect, it is especially important to clarify what the patient would like from therapy. If, for example, the patient is seeking assistance in developing more effective strategies to shut off all emotions, the therapist might explain how people stay "stuck" when they try to bury their emotions, that emotional processing of a traumatic event is required for recovery from it, that one has to go through the traumagenic pain to get beyond it. Again, cognitive therapy can be most useful within the context of clearly defined treatment goals.

Partial Intrusive Ideation

Patients who oscillate between PTSD intrusions and denial/ numbing responses or who report experiencing partial trauma-related flashbacks may also be blocking out painful parts of their traumatic memories, which they may not yet feel ready to address or handle emotionally. Prolonged imaginal exposure may in some instances be used to facilitate activation of the entire traumatic "fear network" so that emotional processing of the trauma can be enhanced.

For patients who report vague or nebulous memories of traumatic events, care must be taken not to be too directive or suggestive. To be sure, the cognitive therapist does not want to engage in so-called "memory reconstruction" work that could lead to the creation of "false memories." Likewise, the use of hypnotic interventions for "memory retrieval" has not proven reliable or effective and is not used in cognitive therapy.

CASE EXAMPLE

Maria was a 40-year-old female who had been raped at age 19 by the grandfather of the children for whom she was babysitting. Although this was a Type I trauma, she complained of suffering from recurring nightmares of the rape several times weekly over the past 21 years. She reported experiencing the nightmare each time in its original form (exactly how she had remembered experiencing the rape at age 19), and that each time she had the nightmare she felt "violated and raped all over again." In addition to suffering from PTSD, which was her primary diagnosis, Maria was experiencing chronic sleep disturbance as well as some generalized anxiety and depression. In spite of many years in psychiatric treatment, Maria reported receiving no help with her repetitive nightmares.

Maria was referred for a cognitive therapy treatment consult by her psychiatrist, who asked if Maria could receive help with her nightmares. (At the time, she was on an inpatient unit at a psychiatric hospital.) Because she lived out of state and was soon going to be discharged from the hospital, the therapist did not have much time to work with her clinically.

During the consult, Maria was asked if she would be willing to do some imagery work with the nightmare. She readily agreed, noting that she had been "haunted" by this terrifying nightmare for over half of her life and was therefore willing to try almost anything. Maria was then asked to close her eyes, visualize the beginning of the nightmare/rape scene, and verbalize in detail what she experienced. Maria was able to vividly visualize and verbalize the entire nightmare/rape scene along with a great deal of affective distress. When the imaginal exposure phase was complete, the imagery rescripting phase began. At the beginning of this phase, Maria again verbalized the rape scene from the beginning. When the traumatic imagery seemed to be at its peak, Maria was asked what she might like to do differently at that point. She replied that she'd like to kick him (the perpetrator) hard in the crotch, but she was afraid to do so. The therapist asked Maria if she would be willing to experiment with this in the imagery, to which she agreed. Maria was then asked if she could visualize herself kicking the perpetrator as hard as she could in the crotch, which she was readily able to do. She was then asked how the perpetrator was responding to her kick, to which she replied: "He's lying on the floor, screaming out in pain and holding his crotch with his hand." This became an "empowering moment" for Maria as she proceeded, in imagery, to kick him a few more times. Maria was then able to visualize herself expressing directly to the perpetrator her thoughts and feelings about the abuse (something she had not been able to verbalize previously), letting him know exactly what she thought of him, how she had suffered from his "beastly" act for so many years, and that it was now his turn to suffer.

By the end of the imagery session, Maria's affect had dramatically shifted. She was not only smiling, but appeared elated. That night, Maria again experienced the same nightmare; this time, however, she was able to overpower the perpetrator in her nightmare just as she had done in the imagery session the previous day. Although no further therapy sessions were conducted, the therapist did continue to follow up with her by phone on a regular basis in the following months to inquire whether she had had any more nightmares. With each contact, Maria reported a complete absence of nightmares. The therapist's last contact with Maria was at the six months' follow-up, at which point she continued to be completely free of nightmares.

Although this was an unusually short-term use of cognitive therapy with a PTSD patient, this case does demonstrate how effective cognitive interventions can sometimes be under limited circumstances. Conceptualizing Maria's affective distress within a cognitive framework, one sees evidence of the most basic tenet of cognitive therapy in action—that emotional pain is directly linked to negative/upsetting cognitions (thoughts or images), and that modifying or changing the upsetting cognitions can lead to rapid and significant alleviation of the associated affective distress. The target cognitions in Maria's case were the victimization images embedded in her recurring nightmare. With the therapist providing facilitative assistance in the context of a "therapeutic secure base," Maria was able to directly confront her powerlessness schema in one session by "contaminating" the rape-related victimization imagery and replacing it with empowering imagery. She was then able to take these "rescripted" mastery images with her from the session and modify the victimization imagery in her nightmare as well, and thereby eliminate her terrifying nightmares altogether.

REFERENCES

Anderson, M. P. (1980). Imaginal processes: therapeutic applications and theoretical models. In *Psychotherapy Process: Current Issues and Future Directions*, ed. J. J. Mahoney. New York: Plenum.

Beck, A. T., Emery, G., and Greenberg, R. L. (1985). *Anxiety Disorders and Phobias: A Cognitive Perspective*. New York: Basic Books.

Beck, A. T., Freeman, A., and Associates (1990). *Cognitive Therapy of Personality Disorders*. New York: Basic Books.

Bowlby, J. (1988). *A Secure Base: Parent-Child Attachment and Healthy Human Development*. New York: Basic Books.

Bretherton, I., and Waters, E., eds. (1985). Growing points of attachment. *Monographs of the Society for Research in Child Development* 50(1–2), Serial 209.

Cashdan, S. (1988). *Object Relations Therapy: Using the Relationship*. New York: Norton.

Diagnostic and Statistical Manual of Mental Disorders (DSM-IV) (1994). 4th ed. Washington, DC: American Psychiatric Association.

Edwards, D. J. A. (1990). Cognitive therapy and the restructuring of early memories through guided imagery. *Journal of Cognitive Psychotherapy: An International Quarterly* 4:33–51.

Foa, E. B., and Kozak, M. J. (1986). Emotional processing of fear: exposure to corrective information. *Psychological Bulletin* 99:20–35.

Foa, E. B., Rothbaum, B. O., Riggs, D. S., and Murdock, T. B. (1991). Treatment of post-traumatic stress disorder in rape victims: a comparison between cognitive-behavioral procedures and counseling. *Journal of Consulting and Clinical Psychology* 59:715–723.

Foa, E. B., Rothbaum, B. O., and Steketee, G. S. (1993). Treatment of rape victims. *Journal of Interpersonal Violence* 8:256–276.

Henry, W. P., Schlacht, T. E., and Strupp, H. H. (1990). Patient and therapist introject, interpersonal process, and differential psychotherapy outcome. *Journal of Consulting and Clinical Psychology* 58(6):768–774.

Horowitz, M. J. (1986). *Stress Response Syndromes*, 2nd ed. Northvale, NJ: Jason Aronson.

Meichenbaum, D. A. (1993). Stress inoculation training: a twenty year update. In *Principles and Practices of Stress Management*, ed. R. L. Woolfolk and P. M. Lehrer. New York: Guilford.

——— (1994). *A Clinical Handbook/Practical Therapist Manual: For Assessing and Treating Adults with Post-Traumatic Stress Disorder (PTSD)*. Waterloo, Ontario: Institute Press.

Moore, B. E., and Fine, B. D. (1990). *Psychoanalytic Terms and Concepts*. New Haven, CT: Yale University Press.

North, C. S., Smith, E. M., and Spitznagel, E. L. (1994). Violence and the homeless: an epidemiologic study of victimization and aggression. *Journal of Traumatic Stress* 7:95–110.

Peterson, K. C., Prout, M. F., and Schwartz, R. A. (1991). *Post-Traumatic Stress Disorder: A Clinician's Guide*. New York: Plenum.

Rachman, S. (1980). Emotional processing. *Behavior Research and Therapy* 18:51–60.

Smucker, M. R., Dancu, C. V., Foa, E. B., and Niederee, J. L. (1995). Imagery rescripting: a new treatment for survivors of childhood sexual abuse suffering from post-traumatic stress. *Journal of Cognitive Psychotherapy: An International Quarterly* 9(1):3–17.

Smucker, M. R., and Niederee, J. L. (1995). Treating incest-related PTSD and pathogenic schemas through imaginal exposure and rescripting. *Cognitive and Behavioral Practice* 2:63–93.

Stamm, B. H., ed. (1996). *Measurement of Stress, Trauma, and Adaptation*. Lutherville, MD: Sidran.

Staton, J. (1990). Using nonverbal methods in the treatment of sexual abuse. In *Violence Hits Home: Comprehensive Treatment Approaches to Domestic Violence*, ed. S. M. Stith, M. B. Williams, and K. Rosen. New York: Springer.

Terr, L. C. (1991). Childhood traumas: an outline and overview. *American Journal of Psychiatry* 148:10–20.

van der Kolk, B. A., and van der Hart, O. (1989). Pierre Janet and the breakdown of adaptation in psychological trauma. *American Journal of Psychiatry* 146:1530–1540.

——— (1991). The intrusive past: the flexibility of memory and the engraving of trauma. *American Imago* 48:425–454.

Vardi, D. J., Fisler, R. E., and Koenen, K. (1994). *Qualitative aspects of traumatic and nontraumatic memories: a preliminary study*. Poster session presented at the 10th annual meeting of the International Society for Traumatic Stress Studies, Chicago, November.

Young, J. (1994). *Cognitive Therapy for Personality Disorders: A Schema-Focused Approach*. Sarasota, FL: Professional Resource Press.

11

SUBSTANCE ABUSE

Cory F. Newman

Cognitive therapy has been applied in the treatment of substance abuse disorders for over twenty years (see Beck and Emery 1977). However, until about 1990 relatively little was known about the cognitive model of substance abuse, as the major treatments in the field continued to be pharmacotherapy (see Jaffe 1995, Kosten et al. 1992), twelve-step fellowships (e.g., Alcoholics Anonymous 1955), confrontive "reality" therapy (Glasser 1981), and social-learning approaches (see Abrams and Niaura 1987, Sobell et al. 1988).

A multisite collaborative study by the National Institute on Drug Abuse, examining the efficacy of psychosocial treatments for substance abuse, brought cognitive therapy closer to the forefront, and was accompanied by the publication of a comprehensive treatment manual (Beck et al. 1993).

Cognitive therapy is a highly active treatment that strives to help clients not only to work toward the ultimate goal of abstinence from harmful, addictive substances, but also to learn new life skills. For example, many clients with long histories of substance abuse have failed to develop problem-solving, communication, organizational, time-management, assertiveness, and self-monitoring skills to a degree that would be sufficient to live a productive and fulfilling life. Cognitive therapy focuses heavily on the acquisition of such skills, so that clients can build self-efficacy and reduce life stress, and thus reduce the likelihood of cyclical relapses.

COGNITIVE THERAPY IN RELATION TO OTHER TREATMENTS FOR SUBSTANCE ABUSE

Cognitive therapy is compatible with and complementary to the aforementioned models of treatment. Clinically, it has been observed at the Center for Cognitive Therapy at the University of Pennsylvania that clients respond well to multiple treatments, such as individual cognitive therapy, methadone maintenance, and twelve-step support groups, and there is evidence that combinations of treatments can be particularly efficacious (Onken et al. 1995). Anecdotally, the main obstacles to the application of multiple, simultaneous treatments for substance abuse have been economic unfeasibility and the rigid views of some treatment providers who are partisan to their own approaches and thus discourage clients from seeking other forms of help.

Cognitive therapists recognize that social support is extremely important for substance abusers, and therefore generally support their clients' participation in twelve-step meetings. Likewise, pharmacologic treatments, from general psychiatric medications to chemical agonists and antagonists, are encouraged when appropriate and medically supervised. Cognitive therapy, because of its strong emphasis on skills acquisition, is hypothesized to be particularly strong in helping clients to *maintain* therapeutic gains over the long run. Given that substance abuse is a relapsing disorder, this benefit cannot be overemphasized.

DIAGNOSTIC ISSUES

The diagnostic areas of substance abuse and substance dependence are very broad indeed (NOTE: For purposes of convenience, the term *substance abuse* will be used throughout this chapter, inclusive of the phenomenon of physiological dependence). Experienced users of standardized, structured, diagnostic interviews know how much time can be spent on the substance abuse module of the assessment. Nonetheless, it has been very difficult to come to agreement on what precise behaviors constitute substance *abuse* and what behaviors meet the criteria for partial remission, full remission, and relapse.

A full explication of these diagnostic issues is beyond the scope of this chapter. However, it is instructive to examine the common denominator that appears on almost all the lists of criteria for substance abuse that were ever devised—the notion that the use of the chemical causes marked impairment and consequences in important areas of concern in life, such as family, work, health, and cooperation with societal rules—and yet the addicted individual continues using the substance nonetheless. This pattern often results in a downward spiral of heavier substance abuse and more serious life problems. Ultimately the abuser is faced with a crisis, and it is at this time that treatment is most likely to ensue, though this is by no means certain to occur. The annals of family and medical histories are replete with unfortunate stories of people who have gone to their graves without ever accepting treatment for their substance abuse problems. Therapists who treat substance abusers know that a primary clinical goal is to help the client to acknowledge the fact that he or she has a serious problem. Indeed, the main thrust of this cognitive therapy case chapter will be to demonstrate how to achieve this goal so that further interventions may be utilized.

THE COGNITIVE MODEL OF SUBSTANCE ABUSE AND RELAPSE

For the most part, the cognitive model of substance abuse is not an etiological model. The root causes of substance abuse are multiple, varied, and interactive (Woody et al. 1992). Hereditary predisposition, cellular adaptation, modeling of parents and peers, socioeconomic factors, peer pressures, faulty beliefs about the effects of substances, poor self-image, inflated estimates of personal control over substances, ease of accessibility of substances, avoidance through self-medication, and many other factors can account for the onset of substance abuse.

However, the cognitive model is a particularly instructive conceptual system in which to understand the *maintenance* of substance abuse behaviors, the tendency toward *relapse*, and the areas in which therapeutic *interventions* may occur. The cognitive model breaks down the phenomena of substance abuse into seven components, each of which represents a link in the chain of events that perpetuates the problematic behavior, and each of which suggests a potential area for therapeutic intervention.

1. *High-risk stimuli*: These include *external* stimuli such as the "people, places, and things" to which twelve-step groups refer. Examples include the drug dealer who telephones the client to ask if he would like some of the new "stuff" that has just come in, the hand-held mirror that the client previously used in order to create and snort lines of cocaine, a beer

commercial on television, the street corner where the client used to "score" her dope, and other stimuli that reside outside one's person. Many of these stimuli can be avoided with careful planning and vigilant awareness, though complete avoidance is practically impossible. Therefore, many other interventions are necessary to help a substance abuser remain abstinent. Still, a reduction in exposure to the sorts of drug cues listed above is a positive step toward sobriety.

Internal high-risk stimuli are represented by emotional and physiological states that either remind the substance abusers of times they have used in the past, or that stimulate a desire to alter their consciousness, either as a way to avoid the internal state (e.g., trying to "blot out" feelings of anxiety) or to enhance it (e.g., trying to magnify a sexual experience). Twelve-step groups have used the acronym HALT to represent the internal high-risk stimuli of being "hungry, angry, lonely, and tired." Clients cannot expect (though they often hope) to avoid these internal states forever. They must learn to cope with them actively. Cognitive therapy is especially strong in this area.

2. *Maladaptive beliefs about drugs*: These are the faulty points of view that many substance abusers maintain about substances and their use. Sometimes they hold these beliefs owing to misinformation (in which case they need psychoeducation), and sometimes they are self-serving myths that enable the substance abuser to continue denying the harmful effects of the drug abuse behavior (in which case they need to learn and apply the skills of self-monitoring and rationally reevaluating their beliefs).

Many of these beliefs focus on the feelings of relief that the drug would produce, to the exclusion of awareness of the associated consequences (e.g., "I need a few lines of coke after work to unwind"). Other beliefs pertain to the strong allure of the drug (e.g., "Once you get the feeling you want to use, there's no stopping it until you use"). Still other maladaptive beliefs are incorrect assumptions about the effects of the drugs (e.g., "I can drink as much beer as I want, because beer isn't really alcohol," or "As long as I snort cocaine I'm okay, because it's only addictive and dangerous if you smoke it or shoot it").

Another set of dysfunctional beliefs about drugs stems from and interacts with the sorts of beliefs that are associated with other psychological disorders. For example, a person with social phobia may believe that "I have to be buzzed in order to deal with people without being a nervous wreck." Similarly, a person suffering from depression (or more seriously, borderline personality disorder) may believe that "I don't deserve to have a good life anyway, so I may as well go ahead and slowly kill myself with drugs that will give me a little pleasure while I go downhill." These types of beliefs are commonly encountered in clients with dual diagnoses, and they represent a strong area of intervention in cognitive therapy.

3. *Automatic thoughts*: These are the instantaneous ideas and images that clients get when they are on the verge of experiencing a magnification of their physiological cravings and urges to use psychoactive chemicals. Therapists commonly encounter clients who, in retrospect, said, "F— it!" or "I don't care what happens" to themselves as a prelude to the exacerbation of their craving and their intentions to use. Other frequently assessed automatic thoughts include images of the first "hit," words such as "party time," or "let's do it," and anticipatory thoughts about the experience of being "high." These spontaneous thoughts help propel the substance abuser toward deciding to use drugs.

Cognitive therapists teach their clients to monitor these thoughts, to become more aware of the effects of these thoughts on their physical sensations and on their decision-making process regarding using. It is vitally important that clients learn not to accept these automatic thoughts at face value, and instead question their validity and adaptiveness.

4. *Cravings and urges*: These are the physiological sensations that substance abusers report make them feel uncomfortable and make it difficult to decide not to use drugs. Many of our clients maintain the faulty belief that the only way to quell the cravings is to use the drug. They are partially correct in that physiological withdrawal symptoms temporarily abate when the chemical is introduced into the body. However, this only serves to exacerbate the client's dependence on the drug, and future cravings and urges worsen in their intensity.

Cognitive therapists educate their clients about the cyclical nature of cravings (indeed, the cyclical nature of human drives in general). They help their clients to experiment with delaying acting on the cravings so that they learn that the sensations will subside on their own if not acted upon. Cognitive therapy clients learn ways in which to distract themselves from the cravings, and to add a period of reflective delay between the urge to use and their actual pursuit of the drug. This buys some valuable time, and often interrupts the almost "unconscious" nature of impulsive drug use (e.g., "I don't know what happened, Doc—I was fine, but *the next thing I knew* I was in the bar and getting smashed").

5. *Permission-giving thoughts*: In the parlance of more traditional psychotherapies, this is the phenomenon known as "rationalization," whereby the client silently (and sometimes openly) argues that there is a good reason to use drugs, and/or not enough of a good reason to abstain at this time. This cognitive process serves to clear the path for the substance abuser to use the drug without feeling guilty, at least for the moment. Commonly encountered "permission-giving" thoughts are, "I've been 'good' [abstinent] for long enough, therefore it

couldn't hurt to take a little 'holiday' from sobriety and use today," and "I need to use so I can test myself to see if I can control my use—maybe I am at the point where I can use a little bit and not be addicted like I used to be." Some clients evidence more openly defiant permission-giving thoughts, such as, "Whether I use or not is nobody's business but my own, so I'll use if I damn well please," and "As long as nobody else knows, it's okay if I use, because the problem is not that I do drugs, it's that I get caught."

Clients in cognitive therapy are taught to examine their permission-giving thoughts, to label them as such, and to understand the deceptive nature of this process of thinking. For example, clients who minimize their intention to drink a beer by thinking, "I'm only going to have a beer" are asked to repeat this thought aloud, but without the word "only," which gives the sentence its implicit permissive tone. Clients learn to make such cognitive changes as a matter of habit, so that self-deception is lessened.

6. *Instrumental strategies*: This refers to the behavioral steps that substance abusers take in order to procure and use the drug. Examples include going to the closet to get one's secret stash, paging the supplier, going out to a bar, driving by a particular street corner, and soliciting money from friends and relatives (usually under false pretenses), among others.

Cognitive therapists assist their clients in recognizing their standard methods of obtaining their drugs of choice, as well as the ways in which they subtly set themselves up to be conveniently situated to do so. It follows that an important therapeutic strategy is to help clients structure their lives so that it is as inconvenient as possible to get hold of the drugs. This is especially challenging to accomplish when the client is faced with household members who use, and/or lives in a neighborhood in which drug dealing is rampant.

7. *Using the addictive substance*: The final stage in the seven-step model is the client's actual using of the drugs or alcohol. This is considered to be a stage in the *process* of substance abuse, not simply an *outcome*. It is a process in that the cognitive model, similar to social-learning and harm-reduction models (see Marlatt et al. 1993), does not view drug relapse as an all-or-none phenomenon in which the client reverts back to square one once the substance is used. Instead, each sip of an alcoholic beverage, each puff on a pipe of crack, and each pill that is popped is seen as a new point on the client's decision-making continuum.

Unfortunately, the decision to cease and desist from further use does become more difficult as the substance abuser becomes more and more impaired by the substances used up to that point. Further, this seventh step in the chain of events often feeds back into the first step of the cycle, as the substance abuser often will feel remorseful and/or will suffer a depressive "crash" or other negative consequences as a result of the episode of using. This becomes a new set of high-risk stimuli, and the vicious cycle is well under way. Therefore, one of the fundamental goals of cognitive therapy is to provide clients with as many tools of self-assessment and self-intervention as possible to break the cycle (e.g., not to let a single "slip" lead to a full-blown relapse because the client felt hopeless and maintained the maladaptive belief that "I already blew my sobriety, so I might as well go on a huge binge").

Although the cognitive model is presented (for simplicity's sake) as an orderly sequence of phenomena from high-risk situations all the way through to the actual using of the drug, the reality is that the process of substance abuse can be triggered at any link along the chain, and the sequence may vary. Still, the model provides an exceptionally useful heuristic for clinicians and clients alike.

ENCOUNTERING DENIAL

One of the obstacles that therapists of substance abusers must contend with is the clients' minimization or outright denial of their problems with substances—indeed, their unwillingness at times even to admit that they have *used* the substances, even when the objective evidence to the contrary is compelling (Bishop 1991, Levy 1993). Therapists of court-remanded substance abusers are well aware of this phenomenon, and the case study reviewed here will be about just such a client.

Prochaska and colleagues (1992) have written persuasively about the "stages of change" that substance abusers go through, from complete unwillingness to acknowledge a problem to earnest commitment to become abstinent and to remain so for the long term. Clearly, therapists can establish a collaborative therapeutic agenda with substance abusers more readily if the latter are closer to the "commitment to change" end of the continuum than if they are exhibiting denial or ambivalence about change. Nevertheless, therapists who treat substance abusers must be prepared to find common clinical ground with those clients who are relatively unprepared for change, as these clients make up a fair proportion of the substance-abusing population in treatment, especially when such clients are ushered into treatment by relatives, employers, and judges. Unless therapists find a way to collaborate with clients who exhibit denial, it is likely that clients will disregard the therapists' assessment and interventions (Levy 1993). On the other hand, therapists must not collude with the clients' tendency to minimize and overlook their very real problems lest the clients receive little or no treatment. Therapists face the daunting challenge of being both confrontive and collaborative with their clients, a task that is quite congruent with the methods of cognitive therapy (Newman 1988).

Although the concept of "denial" is not expressly a part of

the cognitive model of substance abuse outlined above, it can be seen to be a part of Steps 2 (maladaptive beliefs about drugs) and 5 (permission-giving beliefs). In Step 2 the clients believe that they have no issues surrounding substance abuse, believe that they have nothing to fear from substances, and see themselves as impervious to the ill effects that others suffer. Indeed, they may even believe that they have not used a substance at all, such as when a client reasons that "a beer really isn't alcohol," and therefore does not perceive that his daily six-pack represents a departure from sobriety. In Step 5 the clients may admit that they have ingested a chemical substance, but will give themselves bogus rationales that "justify" having done so. For example, a client may argue that he smoked crack because "It has been one month since I last used, and it was necessary for me to test my ability to control my use." This is certainly a form of denial in that the client has not yet incorporated the adaptive belief that all manner of using drugs entails undue risk when compared to choosing not to use at all.

Yet another manifestation of denial—perhaps the most difficult kind to confront effectively—is the client's deliberate dishonesty. Here the clients know that they have engaged in substance use, but state forthrightly to the therapist that they have not. This may be construed as part of Step 2 in the model, where the client's general belief is that "honesty doesn't pay, because I will simply be punished for pleading guilty." Clients who have come through the court system are quite familiar with the benefits of pleading "not guilty," or plea bargaining. If they are on probation or parole, their admissions of substance abuse may be reported to the courts. In this respect they are well trained by life experience to circumvent the truth as a matter of self-preservation. However, even if the client believes that an admission of substance use to a counselor will be kept confidential, the client may still deny using if he or she holds the belief that "My therapist will judge me to be a bad person if I admit that I have used." Therefore, embarrassment, shame, and a fear of abandonment may motivate clients to be dishonest about their recent substance abuse episodes.

Therapists who suspect that their clients are being dishonest face a difficult set of choices about how to proceed. If they choose not to confront the clients' denial, perhaps as a way to prevent the clients from prematurely bolting from treatment, the therapists' task is to find a way to make therapy relevant. If therapists choose to address the denial directly, their task is to make it as educative, validating, and nonthreatening a process as possible. The successful application of these strategies requires considerable effort, skill, experience, and luck. The following case study will illustrate this process.

THE CASE OF "DELLA"

Della was a 42-year-old woman who commenced treatment as a condition of her parole. She had spent ten months in prison on a conviction of possession of crack cocaine. Della was aware that her progress in cognitive therapy was being monitored by "Jackie," her parole officer, and that absences from therapy and/or episodes of drug relapse could result either in residential treatment or reincarceration. In addition to her participation in treatment at the Center for Cognitive Therapy, Della was required to submit to weekly urinalyses in order to detect illicit drug use. As a result, the cognitive therapist was not required to report Della's drug use to the parole officer. The urinalyses served this purpose. However, the therapist was required to file monthly therapy attendance reports.

Background and Diagnostic Issues

Della lived in an impoverished, urban neighborhood with her 24-year-old daughter and 8-year-old grandson. Della was unmarried, but had a boyfriend who reportedly was clean and sober, and employed as an auto mechanic. Della, having just been released from legal custody, was not yet reemployed.

At intake Della met diagnostic criteria for major depression in addition to her substance abuse (which was not considered to be in remission as she had been in a controlled environment). Axis-II issues were unclear, as Della's long history of heavy abuse of crack cocaine made it difficult to determine whether her "borderline personality-like" behaviors were characterological or sequelae to long-term substance abuse.

Della's mother had been alcoholic, and her father had been absent since Della's infancy. Della finished high school, but her plans to attend community college were abandoned when she became pregnant. She gave birth to a daughter and raised her as a single parent, still living in a chaotic household with her hard-drinking mother. Della managed to gain employment from time to time, but was never able to make advancements or to sustain a given job for very long. Della reported that she suffered from untreated depression for much of her adult life to date, and that the only "relief" she felt from this condition was when she was introduced to crack cocaine by a neighbor when she was 33 years old. She used the drug for eight years, until her legal apprehension. In the meantime, her daughter quit high school, gave birth to a son at the age of 16, and abdicated her responsibilities as a parent by using drugs and staying out until all hours of the night. Della noted that one of the reasons for her depression was her shame, guilt, and worry over her daughter's life-style.

First Six Cognitive Therapy Sessions

Della was very receptive to treatment, as she expressed thanks for receiving her first individual therapy for her depression. Interestingly, she did not identify her substance abuse history as a problem until the therapist prompted her. Della maintained that her addiction to crack cocaine was a "thing of the past" given that she had been abstinent for ten months in prison. She was adamant that her problem was "depression over my life," made worse by her ongoing travails with her drug-abusing, child-neglecting daughter. The therapist chose to work with this agenda, as it provided the best window of opportunity to engage Della in active treatment. Still, the therapist humbly offered that Della's unhappiness, coupled with her reimmersion into her neighborhood, served as significant high-risk stimuli for potential drug relapse. Della assured the therapist that relapse would not occur.

Della was very responsive to cognitive therapy for the initial six sessions. She expressed appreciation for the therapist's taking her life problems seriously, for giving her a lot of feedback during sessions, and for teaching her how to "think like a confident person and to solve problems" rather than fall into despair. Della complied with the homework assignments, which included adjunctive readings (e.g., *Feeling Good*, by David Burns [1980]) and Daily Thought Records to monitor and modify her typically hopelessness-engendering thoughts.

Unfortunately, Della was not as receptive to the therapist's attempts to teach her about the cognitive model of substance abuse per se. She believed it was irrelevant to spend valuable time in session discussing an issue that was "a thing of the past." The therapist reasoned that, at the very least, Della could learn how she overcame her substance abuse problem, step by step and principle by principle, so that she could practically apply these methods under any conditions throughout her life. Della responded that staying sober was simply a matter of willpower, and that she already demonstrated she had it, and that was that. The therapist gave her credit for having "willpower," but expressed the opinion that willpower comprised a number of *skills*, similar to the ones she was learning in order to overcome her depression. The therapist added that perhaps Della could use her Daily Thought Records not only for monitoring and reevaluating her depressive thoughts, but also as a way to recapitulate some of the cognitive processes she went through in order to assert her "willpower" against cravings for crack cocaine.

Della grudgingly agreed to do this. The therapist, noticing Della's half-hearted reaction, asked the quintessential cognitive therapy question: "What is going through your mind right now?" Della replied, "You don't believe me when I say I'm over the drug thing. I guess that's your job, so what can I do?" The therapist, taking pains to express a respectful and empathic tone, stated that he believed in Della's character and commitment to therapy, and that his goal was to be "thorough to a fault" in making certain that Della learned everything she could so as to maintain her sobriety as well as overcome her depression.

In the sixth session Della reported that her daughter was "missing." Della remained stonefaced the entire session as she and her therapist discussed the situation and brainstormed courses of constructive action that Della could take. Toward the end of the session, the therapist humbly asked whether this upsetting turn of events had rekindled Della's old desire to blot out her emotional pain with alcohol or crack, and whether this suggested that another session should be held soon to deal with issues of avoiding relapse. Della bristled, and tersely noted that she had "more important things on my mind right now." The therapist empathized with her extreme worry over her daughter, but added that "your well-being is the most important thing on *my* mind right now."

Signs of Relapse

Della did not show up for her next session. When the therapist attempted to reach her by phone on repeated occasions, nobody picked up. At the same time the following week, Della again did not show up. The same pattern occurred when the therapist tried to reach her by phone. Two days later Jackie, the parole officer, telephoned the therapist to inform him that Della had had two "hot" urines in the past two weeks (one of which occurred *prior* to the most recent therapy session!), signifying that she used crack cocaine. She stated that she had driven to Della's house three times, and the place was deserted. The therapist and parole officer agreed to keep each other informed if Della reappeared, and they agreed that the therapist later would assess whether Della could continue to be treated on an outpatient basis.

Two days later Della walked into the Center for Cognitive Therapy unannounced, stating that she was there for her appointment. The therapist said that he was glad to see her, but that he had other clients scheduled. Della affected surprise and replied, "But isn't my appointment for today?" The therapist retorted, "No, your last two times were supposed to be on Monday, and the Monday before." The therapist went on to say that Jackie had informed him about the two hot urines, and that this had to be at the top of the agenda next session, which was scheduled for first thing the next morning. Della again expressed shock and dismay, saying that "there has to be some sort of mistake," and agreed to come in the following morning.

Collaboratively Confronting the Denial

The therapist expected three possible reactions from Della as a result of the interaction above. First, Della might not show up the next morning. Second, she might arrive, but be angry about being "falsely accused" of relapsing on crack cocaine. Third, Della might admit her "fall," and implore the therapist to help her, not to abandon her. Interestingly, none of these scenarios occurred. Instead, Della arrived for her session, denied that she had used any substances at all, and seemed completely composed, at peace, and not at all angry. The therapist found himself quite off balance, and was reminded of the hazards of "fortunetelling," one of the cognitive distortions as outlined by Burns (1980).

When a cognitive therapist finds himself or herself stymied and stumped in a given therapeutic interaction with a client, the appropriate response is to gather more data, either via questionnaires, or more commonly by asking the client a series of open-ended questions. Therefore, in this instance, the therapist looked at Della's responses to the Beck Depression Inventory (Beck et al. 1961), the Beck Anxiety Inventory (Beck et al. 1988), and the Beck Hopelessness Scale (Beck et al. 1974), saw that the scores were all "zero" (thus indicating no negative affective symptoms whatsoever), and followed up with some questions about what had transpired in Della's life over the past two to three weeks.

The following are condensed segments of the dialogue that ensued:

Therapist: Della, as I said when you came in yesterday, we will need to discuss your absences from therapy, as well as the hot urines. First, however, I want to ask you about your daughter. Is she okay? What happened to her? (The therapist chose this tact to maximize the likelihood that Della would speak freely in this potentially contentious or secretive session. Also, it would lead to a discussion of Della's mood, which seemed oddly calm given the circumstances of her family life and drug-testing.)

Della: Oh, she's fine. She was just hangin' out, you know. She came home a couple of days ago.

Therapist: But what happened? Last time you were here, you were sick to death about her. You were so worried. We talked about calling the police and everything. And then *you* were missing, and *I* was extremely concerned. Can you fill me in on what's been going on?

Della: I'm really fine. Don't be concerned. (It was clear that Della was not going to divulge very much information voluntarily, and that the therapist's concern alone would not be sufficient to inspire Della to be open and honest.)

Therapist: Okay (pause). It's just that I would be reacting so differently if I were in your place, Della. If my daughter had been missing for two weeks, I would be a nervous wreck. On top of that, if somebody told me that I came up positive for crack cocaine *twice*, I would be fixing for a fight, or I would be feeling very guilty, sorry, and vulnerable. So, I'm trying to empathize with you, but I'm getting it all wrong. Can you straighten me out? Can you help me understand why you feel so calm?

Della: I know I'm okay. I don't know why I got the hot urines. I've been drinking, but cocaine? No. No. Not at all. Not at all. No way. I'm fine.

Therapist (Since Della seems to have answered the question by admitting that she has been drinking, the therapist will pursue the drug abuse angle, and drop the topic of the daughter for now.): Della, I want to believe what you're saying, but I'm really in a conflict about this. I value our relationship, and I value the fact that we have done some really good work together for our first six sessions, so I don't want to spoil things by making you think I doubt you, and I don't want you to think of me as being a hardass.

Della: Oh no. Everything is fine between us. I know you got a job to do. I understand. I'm here to answer anything you got to ask me.

Therapist: That's part of the conflict I'm talking about. I want to get along with you, but if I don't use my clinical judgment and question the things you say, then I may be shortchanging you, because I'm being *too* nice to you and not doing my

job, which is to help you with your depression and substance abuse.

Della: Don't be concerned about me. I'm fine. Do whatever you
have to do. I know you want to help me. I appreciate it.

At this point in the session the therapist has succeeded on
two counts. First, he has nurtured the maintenance of the
therapeutic relationship in spite of potential rupture. Second,
he has managed to get Della to admit to her use of alcohol.
However, it is clear that Della is not predisposed to discuss
much of anything that is substantive, and her friendly de-
meanor, coupled with her repeated protestations that "everything is fine," puts the therapist in a double bind of sorts. The
therapist will have to find another way to encourage Della to
discuss her absences from therapy and cocaine use.

The therapist is committed to achieving these admissions,
as this is a rare and powerful opportunity to demonstrate to
Della that doing "cognitive therapy of substance abuse" *is*
relevant to her. The therapist is concerned that if he does not
support the data at this point, the efficacy of the approach will
be severely compromised. As a result, Della is almost certain
to continue her relapse episode, and she will be lost from treatment. The therapist must pull out all the stops to get Della to
collaborate in discussing her drug use. Only then will he be
able to offer the full course of treatment as it is intended to be
offered. Nevertheless, the therapist must continue to be solici-
tous and accepting in tone, even as he contests the veracity of
the client's responses, or the therapeutic relationship will be
unduly strained. The following is an attempt to walk this fine
line.

Therapist: If I didn't know you . . . if we hadn't worked so well
together . . . and somebody just gave me a report to evaluate . . . saying that a person missed two sessions, dropped

out of sight, and had two hot urines . . . well, what would *you* say about that person?

Della: I would say that person was using something. But since you *do* know me, you know I wouldn't be using.

Therapist: That's my dilemma, exactly. If it were anybody else, I would be dead certain that they had relapsed on crack, and that they needed the best of my help and support immediately to get back on track again. And I would gladly be there for them and do all that I can. But since we're talking about *you*, it's hard for me to imagine that you're using again, especially since you're telling me you're *not* using. (The therapist's comment was intended to drop the hint that he would be very helpful and caring even if the client admitted that she had been using.)

Della: Because you trust me, and I appreciate that. (Whether by intention or not, this is another double bind, as the therapist has been given the message that further pursuit of this matter may be tantamount to a *lack* of trust, which the client will *not* appreciate.)

Therapist: I know you want me to trust you, and I definitely want you to trust me too. But you know what? *Trust is not a perfect thing.* And one time of doubt between two people does not have to destroy the trust, especially if they respect each other and want to work things out. I want to work things out between us. (The therapist tries to dispel the client's implicit belief that trust is an all-or-none phenomenon. This gives both client and therapist some margin for error. The therapist can be forgiven for doubting the client's word, and the client can be excused for distrusting what the therapist will really do if he finds out that the client has been using cocaine.)

At this point in the session the therapist temporarily shelves his pursuit of the breaching of the client's denial, though he comes back to it later. Now he returns to a discussion of "what has happened the past two to three weeks." What he discovers, with no surprise, is that Della cannot account for her whereabouts to any meaningful degree. Her chronological depiction of events is internally inconsistent, and at times downright magical. The "opening" for the therapist once again to address the denial occurs when Della answers questions about how she "recovered" from worrying about her daughter. Della makes the following key comment:

Della: I can't even remember what happened last session. I can't even believe it has been three weeks since we last had a session together. Sometimes when I get upset, I just block everything out. I can't even remember a thing. (Later the therapist will need to assess whether this represents a cognitive deficit, a dissociative response, a drug-induced loss of short-term memory, a confabulation, or combinations thereof. For now, it is sufficient to use this comment to imply that Della may also have forgotten all about her drug use during the past three weeks.)

Therapist: You know, Della, you may have just solved the mystery. You're telling me that you've been so upset since we last met, and so calm now, that there's a big gap of time and memory for which we can't account. This may be where our answer is. Listen to this, Della. Is it possible, given your experience with memory loss during times of upset, that you used some crack cocaine but you have forgotten? Is it possible that, in your disappointment with yourself, you couldn't bear the thought that you had broken your promise to yourself, so you blanked it right out of your mind?

Della: (dumbstruck, then tongue-tied)

Therapist: This could explain the whole thing. People forget things, especially under terrible stress, but a drug test never forgets. So while this thing could look like a mistake in the drug test, or it could look like you're not being truthful, the reality might be that *neither* of these things is going on.

The real truth could be that the test was right, and you're being as honest as you can be, but you can't remember the days when you were using crack. What do you think of that, Della? (This is a way to make sense of contradictory data, and it might even be an accurate hypothesis, but at the very least it gives Della a face-saving way to admit that she may have been using drugs.)

Della: It might have happened. I guess it might have happened. What now?

Therapist: We just made a breakthrough discovery. We learned something incredibly valuable that's going to help you. What do you think we learned?

Della: That I can't remember what happened?

Therapist: And what makes that important?

Della (pause): I don't know. Maybe . . . I don't know.

Therapist: What does it mean if you can't account for your time? What could that be a signal for? What could it be a wake-up call for?

Della: Relapse or something?

Therapist: Exactly. A relapse. If you can't remember things, and time seems to get past you before you know it, that's your opportunity to consider the possibility that you need some extra support from people such as your NA sponsor, me, your boyfriend, and even Jackie. What do you think of that?

Della: Yeh, I would let you know.

Therapist: Most important of all, would you let *yourself* know? Would you be willing to admit to yourself that you probably had a lapse or a relapse? Would you be willing to try to nip the problem in the bud before it got worse, rather than try to protect yourself from the truth?

Della: Yeh, I would do that.

Therapist: Are you willing to do that now? Can we talk about what might have happened in the past two to three weeks that might have led to your using? Can we explore that right now?

Della (sad expression): Yes.

Therapist: You seem very sad right now. What are you thinking?

Della: That I was doing so good. I was trying so hard.

Therapist: I know that. It wasn't a waste. We can use what you have learned so far, and it will help you to overcome this lapse, and to move forward. We're in much better shape than we were even thirty minutes ago when you believed that everything was fine. Now we know what we're up against, and we deal with things up front. Now we have a chance. This is an opportunity. We just turned the corner, and now we're going in the right direction.

Outcome

Della and the therapist agreed to meet with the parole officer during the following session. It was decided that Della would temporarily switch to a residential drug-abuse treatment program so as to maximize the chances that she could gain a renewed period of sobriety before reentering outpatient cognitive therapy.

At this time Della has returned to treatment with her cognitive therapist, and has established a good attendance and sobriety record. Much therapeutic work continues to focus on relapse prevention with regard to both her substance abuse and her depression.

The most significant risks to Della's maintaining her therapeutic gains continue to be her daughter's problems, the prevalence of drugs in her neighborhood, and her frustration over not being able to find gainful employment. On the other hand, Della feels a great deal more pride and self-confidence, understands and can spot both her internal and external high-risk situations, and has become adept at monitoring and responding to the automatic thoughts that minimize her problems and therefore mitigate against her therapeutic vigilance. Cognitive therapy with Della will also focus on general problem-solving skills, and will continue to help her to develop meaningful activities and relationships with people who are not substance users. She will continue in treatment for the remainder of her parole period, which is over a year.

REFERENCES

Abrams, D. B., and Niaura, R. S. (1987). Social learning theory. In *Psychological Theories of Drinking and Alcoholism*, ed. H. T. Blane and K. E. Leonard, pp. 131–178. New York: Guilford.

Alcoholics Anonymous: The Story of How Many Thousands of Men and Women Have Recovered from Alcoholism (1955). New York: Alcoholics Anonymous World Services, Inc.

Beck, A. T., and Emery, G. (1977). *Cognitive Therapy of Substance Abuse*. Unpublished therapy manual. University of Pennsylvania.

Beck, A. T., Epstein, N., Brown, G., and Steer, R. A. (1988). An inventory for measuring clinical anxiety: psychometric properties. *Journal of Consulting and Clinical Psychology* 56(6):893–897.

Beck, A. T., Ward, C. H., Mendelson, M., et al. (1961). An inventory for measuring depression. *Archives of General Psychiatry* 4:561–571.

Beck, A. T., Weissman, A., Lester, D., and Trexler, L. (1974). The measurement of pessimism: the hopelessness scale. *Journal of Consulting and Clinical Psychology* 42(6):861–865.

Beck, A. T., Wright, F. D., Newman, C. F., and Liese, B. (1993). *Cognitive Therapy of Substance Abuse*. New York: Guilford.

Bishop, D. R. (1991). Clinical aspects of denial in chemical dependency. *Individual Psychology: Journal of Adlerian Theory, Research, and Practice* 47(2):199–209.

Burns, D. (1980). *Feeling Good: The New Mood Therapy*. New York: William Morrow.

Glasser, W. (1981). *Stations of the Mind: New Directions for Reality Therapy*. New York: HarperCollins.

Jaffe, J. H. (1995). Pharmacological treatment of opioid dependence: current techniques and new findings. *Psychiatric Annals* 25(6):369–375.

Kosten, T. R., Gawin, F. H., Kosten, T. A., and Morgan, C. (1992). Six-month follow-up of short-term pharmacotherapy for cocaine dependence. *American Journal on Addictions* 1(1):40–49.

Levy, M. (1993). Psychotherapy with dual diagnosis patients: working with denial. *Journal of Substance Abuse Treatment* 10(6):449–504.

Marlatt, G. A., Somers, J. M., and Tapert, S. F. (1993). Harm reduction: application to alcohol abuse problems. *National Institute on Drug Abuse Research Monograph Series* 137:147–166.

Newman, C. F. (1988). Confrontation and collaboration: congruent components in cognitive therapy. *The Cognitive Behaviorist* 10(3):27–30.

Onken, L. S., Blaine, J. D., and Boren, J.J. (1995). Medications and behavioral therapies: the whole may be greater than the sum of the parts. *National Institute on Drug Abuse Research Monograph Series* 150:1–4.

Prochaska, J. O., DiClemente, C. C., and Norcross, J. C. (1992). In search of how people change: applications to addictive behaviors. *American Psychologist* 47:1102–1114.

Sobell, L. C., Sobell, M. B., and Nirenberg, T. D. (1988). Behavioral assessment and treatment planning with alcohol and drug abusers: a review with an emphasis on clinical application. *Clinical Psychology Review* 8:19–54.

Woody, G. E., Urschel, H. C. III, and Alterman, A. (1992). The many paths to drug dependence. In *Vulnerability to Drug Abuse*, ed. M. D. Glantz and R. W. Pickens, pp. 491–507. Washington, DC: American Psychological Association.

III

SPECIAL POPULATIONS AND ISSUES

12

MARITAL CONFLICT

Norman Epstein

Although there has been a recent leveling off of the dramatic climb in divorces that characterized the past few decades, approximately half of marriages end in divorce, and many couples who choose not to divorce still live with chronic conflict and distress. There is evidence that marital conflict coexists with many of the disorders covered in this volume, such as depression (Beach et al. 1990), anxiety disorders (Craske and Zoellner 1995, Goldstein and Chambless 1978), substance abuse (McCrady and Epstein 1995), and sexual dysfunction (Heiman et al. 1995, Hof 1987), and that relationship problems can play causal roles in the development and maintenance of individual psychopathology. In turn, an individual's disorder can be a major stressor and disrupt partners' abilities to meet each other's needs within a relationship. Therefore, whether or not a clinician specializes in the treatment of marital problems,[1] he or she is highly likely to encounter members of distressed couples in the course of clinical practice, and it is important to be aware of ways in which individual and couple characteristics interact, and how couples therapy can be either the primary or an adjunctive treatment for a variety of presenting problems.

Cognitive-behavioral couples therapy represents an integration of traditional behavioral marital therapy (BMT) procedures for modifying couples' destructive interaction patterns, cognitive therapy concepts and procedures for altering cognitions that contribute to relationship conflict and distress, and family systems concepts concerning the functioning of dyadic and larger family groups. Outcome studies evaluating behavioral marital therapy (including behavioral contracts, communication training, and problem-solving training) have indicated that it is more effective than no treatment or nonspecific treatments in reducing negative behavioral interactions and marital distress (Baucom et al. 1996b). Furthermore, studies that have compared the relative effectiveness of BMT components (communication training, problem-solving training, behavioral contracts) have shown them to have equally positive impact. However, evidence that a considerable minority of couples remained at least somewhat distressed after BMT (Jacobson et al. 1984) was one of the factors that has led to the integration of cognitive restructuring procedures into BMT much more systematically than was traditionally the case. Initial studies have either substituted some cognitive restructuring sessions for behavioral interventions, and compared the cognitive-behavioral combination to BMT that included no

---

1. Although the term *marital therapy* is used for convenience in this chapter, the general principles and procedures described are applicable in any intimate relationship, including same-sex relationships. The term *couples therapy* will be used as well, to connote this broad range of applicability.

specific focus on cognitions, or have compared cognitive restructuring alone to BMT. Both types of studies have demonstrated
that cognitive interventions (alone or in combination with behavioral interventions) produce constructive cognitive changes
and enhance marital satisfaction. Because the existing outcome studies included only brief (e.g., three sessions) cognitive restructuring that was presented separately rather than
integrated with communication training and other behavioral
interventions, there is a need for further studies that evaluate
cognitive-behavioral couples therapy as it is conducted in
clinical practice. Nevertheless, the results of the initial studies
have been promising.

ASSESSMENT OF COUPLES' RELATIONSHIP PROBLEMS

Apart from the psychiatric diagnoses that may apply to one or
both members of a couple, *DSM-IV* (1994) offers little to the
clinician in terms of diagnosing problems in the relationship
itself. The very brief description of the V61.1 "Partner Relational Problem" coding category refers to

> a pattern of interaction between spouses or partners charac-
> terized by negative communication (e.g., criticisms), distorted
> communication (e.g., unrealistic expectations), or noncommu-
> nication (e.g., withdrawal) that is associated with clinically
> significant impairment in individual or family functioning or the
> development of symptoms in one or both partners. [p. 681]

Although there are continuing efforts to devise a diagnostic
system for categorizing types of dysfunctional relationships
(Kaslow 1993), assessment of couples tends to be more
complex than individual diagnosis (Snyder et al. 1995). For
example, Snyder and colleagues describe how evaluation of a
couple includes assessment of the two individuals, their

dyadic interactions (a case in which the whole certainly is greater than the sum of the parts), their relationships with other nuclear family and extended family members, and the influences of broader community and cultural systems. Assessment also has to take into account both overt behaviors and the partners' subjective experiences. The systems theory concept of circular causality guides assessment in that an individual's symptoms can simultaneously be a response to another person's actions and a stimulus for the other's responses.

In spite of the complexity of couple relationships, theoretical and empirical literature has identified a number of variables that appear to be central to well-functioning relationships, and clinicians who work with couples are likely to see repetitive patterns in a couple's interactions that involve these factors. These factors tend to fall into three domains central to a cognitive-behavioral approach to marital therapy: behaviors, cognitions, and affect. The following are brief descriptions of the major factors in each of these domains that tend to differentiate distressed from nondistressed couples. Rather than attempting to fit couples into discrete relational diagnoses, the clinician can evaluate each couple's functioning in each area, identifying specific changes in behavior, cognition, and affect that would be likely to reduce the partners' conflict and distress. In a cognitive-behavioral model of relationship dysfunction (Baucom and Epstein 1990, Epstein and Baucom 1993), each individual's behaviors, cognitions, and affects are viewed as interacting in determining his or her pattern of interacting with the partner, as well as his or her level of satisfaction with their relationship. Although the complexity of the relationships among behavior, cognition, and affect cannot be described sufficiently in a brief chapter (see the above references for more detail), the following sections highlight key variables for assessment and treatment planning in couples therapy.

BEHAVIORAL FACTORS IN COUPLE RELATIONSHIPS

There is considerable empirical evidence to support the social exchange theory (Thibaut and Kelley 1959) view that members of distressed relationships exchange more displeasing behaviors and fewer pleasing behaviors than members of nondistressed relationships, and that exchanges of negative behavior in unhappy couples tend to be reciprocal (Baucom and Epstein 1990, Weiss and Heyman 1990). It often is striking how even couples who report that they were highly attracted to each other when they met and shared many positive experiences with each other in the past now engage in very low rates of positive exchanges and relatively high rates of aversive exchanges. Although it is beyond the scope of this chapter to consider the range of factors that can contribute to such a shift in a couple's behavioral exchanges over time, it is important for the process of treatment planning that the couples therapist (particularly within a cognitive-behavioral framework) conduct a systematic assessment of the conditions that have been associated with positive versus negative couple interactions. For example, the treatment implications for a couple who have spent less leisure time together due to competing demands from work and family may be quite different from those for a couple who have been alienated since one partner engaged in an extramarital affair. However, in either case one of the foci of assessment and treatment will be the particular behavioral patterns that the couple has developed that tend to maintain or exacerbate their subjective distress.

When couples complain about a lack of intimacy, a systematic assessment of their relationship history often reveals that they currently spend much less time together engaged in mutually enjoyable activities than they did in the earlier stages of the relationship. It is important to evaluate whether the couple's current lack of shared positive activities developed due to competing demands on their time, or reflects a pattern of withdrawal due to the partners' unhappiness with each other (or both processes). Another factor that can maintain a pattern of few shared positive activities is that the individuals may have developed a negative expectancy that if they spend time together they will discover that they no longer have much in common. Thus, in a cognitive-behavioral approach to couples therapy (Baucom and Epstein 1990), the clinician needs to assess both the couple's pattern of positive and negative shared activities and their cognitions about spending time together.

The quality and quantity of a couple's communication also are important behavioral components of their relationship that the clinician needs to assess and possibly treat. Although the *DSM-IV* criteria concerning forms of problematic communication cited above are vague, they do address a substantial body of clinical and research literature pointing to the crucial role of communication in relationship functioning.

Although initial studies found a correlation between partners' global marital distress and their lower scores on self-report questionnaires assessing overall communication quality (e.g., "We understand each other when we discuss issues") rather than specific behaviors (e.g., Bienvenu 1970), more recent self-report scales, such as Christensen's (1988) Communication Patterns Questionnaire, ask partners to report the frequencies of more specific dyadic interaction patterns such as mutual constructive communication, demand–withdraw patterns, and mutual avoidance/witholding. Important gains in the behavioral assessment of couple relationships have been made through the development of systems for observing and coding dyadic behavioral exchanges. Behavioral coding systems are designed to identify specific acts by each partner, as well as reciprocal acts between partners, that contribute to pleasing or distressing interactions, in the present or longitudinally. The major systems that have been developed by clinical researchers for coding couples' interactions on an act-by-act basis are the Marital Interaction Coding System (Heyman et al. 1995), the Couples Interaction Scoring System (CISS) (Gottman 1979, Notarius and Markman 1981), and the *Kategoriensystem fur Partnerschaftliche Interaktion* (KPI) (Hahlweg et al. 1984). Although empirical studies have indicated that specific behavioral codes are not reliably associated with conflict and distress in individual couples (see Baucom and Epstein 1990), a number of communication patterns have been identified that are strongly related to deterioration in marriages over time. For example, using a more global behavioral coding system called the Rapid Couples Interaction Scoring System (RCISS) (Krokoff et al. 1989), in which each speaking turn for each partner is rated on a set of codes based on verbal content and nonverbal behaviors, Gottman (1993a,b) has found that partners who exhibit higher frequencies of complaining/criticizing, defensiveness, contempt, and stonewalling are more likely to separate and divorce. Revenstorf et al. (1984) coded couples' problem-solving discussions and found that distressed couples were more likely than nondistressed couples to engage in "problem escalation," in which one partner's statement of a problem was followed by the other partner's negative expression (e.g., blaming), which was then followed by the first individual's negative expression (e.g., blaming the person in return). Nondistressed couples also were able to stop this "distancing" (negative reciprocity) sooner than distressed couples. Similarly, Gottman et al. (1977) found that distressed couples were more likely to engage in "cross-complaining" (partners exchanging descriptions of problems), whereas nondistressed couples were more likely to identify problems and then discuss potential solutions. Thus the clinician who is evaluating a distressed couple can structure assessment sessions to include observations of the partners discussing relationship issues and identify specific patterns in the interactions that impede resolution of conflicts and that contribute to the individuals' frustration, anger, and hopelessness about their relationship.

The aspects of communication that are most often the foci of cognitive-behavioral couple therapists are (1) skills for expressing thoughts and emotions clearly and constructively, (2) skills for empathic listening, and (3) skills for problem solving. The most common model used for teaching couples expressive and empathic listening skills is Guerney's (1977) Relationship Enhancement approach, which focuses on partners practicing specific communication guidelines as one partner takes on the role of expresser and the other the role of listener. For example, the expresser is responsible for phrasing descriptions of his or her thoughts and emotions concisely and for stating those views as subjective rather than as the absolute truth. In turn, the listener is to focus on trying to understand the subjective experience that the expresser is describing and to communicate that understanding to the expresser by subsequently paraphrasing the messages, without interjecting his or her own opinions. Detailed guidelines for assessing couples' deficits in expressive and listening skills, and for teaching the skills, can be found in the volumes by Guerney (1977), Baucom and Epstein (1990), and Markman and colleagues (1994).

Problem-solving communication is a process in which the partners are instructed *not* to express feelings about an issue, but rather to engage in systematic behavioral definition of a problem, identification of one or more possible (i.e., feasible *and* acceptable) behavioral solutions to the problem, and a concrete plan to try the solution in daily life. Detailed procedures for teaching couples problem-solving skills are presented by Baucom and Epstein (1990), Holtzworth-Munroe and Jacobson (1991), Jacobson and Margolin (1979), O'Leary and Turkewitz (1978), and Stuart (1980).

COGNITIVE FACTORS IN COUPLE RELATIONSHIPS

Baucom et al. (1989) identified five types of cognition that affect conflict and distress in couples' relationships: (1) selective attention, in which each individual notices some aspects of the events occurring in the couple's interactions but overlooks others, (2) *attributions*, or inferences that each person makes about causes of positive and negative events in their relationship, (3) *expectancies*, or predictions about the likelihood that particular events will occur in the relationship in the future, (4) *assumptions*, involving beliefs about the characteristics of relationships (in general or one's own) and how they function, and (5) *standards*, or beliefs that each individual holds about characteristics that relationships (in general, or one's own) "should" have. Research on marital cognitions has indicated that distressed spouses tend to attribute relationship problems to stable, global characteristics of their partners, including negative personality traits, negative intent, and a lack of love (Baucom and Epstein 1990, Bradbury and Fincham 1990). The clinician can use self-report scales such as Pretzer and colleagues' (1991) Marital Attitude Survey, Fincham and Bradbury's (1992) Relationship Attribution Measure, and Baucom and colleagues' (1996a) Relationship Attribution Questionnaire to assess couples' attributions.

Research with Eidelson and Epstein's (1982) Relationship Belief Inventory, which was developed to assess unrealistic beliefs about close relationships (e.g., the assumption that partners cannot change a relationship; the standard that partners should be able to mindread each other's thoughts and emotions), has supported theoretical and clinical observations that adherence to such beliefs is associated with marital distress, negative communication, and lower commitment to one's relationship. Baucom et al. (1996c) found that individuals who hold high "relationship-oriented" standards (favoring few boundaries between partners, equal distribution of power, and high investment of time and energy in one's relationship) tend to be more satisfied with their relationships and communicate in more constructive ways. Furthermore, individuals who reported being satisfied with the manner in which their standards were met in their marriages also scored higher in relationship satisfaction.

Although there has been much less empirical research on cognitions other than attributions, assumptions, and standards, the existing findings support the relevance of cognitive assessment and interventions for relationship problems. There is a clear need for longitudinal studies to provide more information about causal relationships between forms of cognition and partners' behavioral and affective responses toward each other.

AFFECTIVE FACTORS IN COUPLE RELATIONSHIPS

Weiss (1980) described a process of "sentiment override" in which an individual's preexisting general affect and attitude toward his or her partner determines the affective and behavioral responses to the partner's current behavior more than the qualities of the partner's behavior. For example, an individual who is angry at his or her partner concerning past events in their relationship may be irritated even when the partner behaves in what a therapist or other outsider perceives as a constructive manner. Whether sentiment override is based on conditioned emotional responses or cognitive mediation (e.g., an attribution that the partner's positive behavior is based on an intent to manipulate the individual), it can contribute to the pattern of negative behavioral escalation described earlier. Consequently, therapists need to identify such emotional processes when observing couple interactions and assist partners in counteracting such global affective responses and potentially distorted cognitions that may fuel them. Similarly, individuals who have anger control problems that influence escalation of conflict with their partners may require specific interventions, such as cognitive-behavioral training in anger reduction (Deffenbacher 1996). Furthermore, as noted at the beginning of this chapter, affective disorders and anxiety disorders in one or both members of a couple are likely to have major impacts on couple functioning. The clinician must conduct a careful evaluation of whether relationship factors play an etiological role in the affective symptoms, and thus may be alleviated through couple therapy (Beach et al. 1990), or whether the affective or anxiety disorder requires individual therapy.

CASE EXAMPLE

Carl (age 46) and Marie (age 45) were referred for marital therapy by Marie's individual therapist, who had been treating her for depression for four months. The couple had separated a month earlier after twenty-one years of marriage, based on Marie's insistence that she could not tolerate living with Carl any longer. However, her individual therapist noted some ambivalence on her part concerning divorce and recommended a trial period of marital therapy to her. Although the couple had a brief previous attempt at marital therapy three years earlier, which ended when they found themselves arguing in the therapist's office and Carl refused to continue, Marie stated that seeking conjoint therapy one more time was "the right thing to do," given the couple's long history together and the distress that the separation had produced in their children (Robert, age 19, and Ann, age 17). Carl was eager to begin couples therapy, because he was opposed to the separation and hoped to effect a reconciliation.

Evaluation of the Couple

During the initial joint session, the therapist[2] first asked the partners to describe the issues that led them to call for an appointment. Carl began by stating that Marie had insisted on a separation due to her chronic unhappiness with him, and that he had never seriously considered separation or divorce a solution to their marital problems. He said that he loved his wife and had been happy with their relationship overall. Carl added that he and Marie tended to have different opinions on a variety of issues, such as childrearing, finances, and social relationships, and that they had "communication problems." When the therapist asked Carl to specify what he meant by communication problems, he replied that "we each seem to stick to our own opinion and put down the other's ideas." Marie quickly interjected, "No, I listen to your ideas, and you put *mine* down." The couple then debated this point, with each person criticizing the other or defending himself or herself against the other's criticism. The therapist used this as an opportunity to sit back and observe the process of the couple's interaction for a few minutes. He observed how quickly the negative escalation occurred, and how neither partner used effective expressive and listening skills. Finally, he noted how, after several negative exchanges, Marie expressed exasperation nonverbally (through her facial expression and a loud sigh), and withdrew from the discussion after turning to the therapist and saying, "This is why I want to live by myself."

When the therapist asked Marie about her reasons for coming to therapy, she stated that she had mixed feelings

---

2. This case example is based on a couple treated by the author. Their identities have been disguised, but the basic issues that they presented and the events that occurred during the therapy sessions are described accurately while maintaining confidentiality.

about being there. On the one hand she did not like the idea of breaking up their family, especially because their children had told them that they should "get professional help" rather than divorcing. On the other hand she had felt very frustrated, angry, and depressed for many years, due to what she described as "Carl's stubbornness, self-centeredness, and critical nature." She felt pessimistic about the chances of those characteristics changing, which had led her to insist on the separation. She said she was somewhat surprised at how strongly Carl had opposed separation, given how detached he often seemed, and at how much he said he wanted a reconciliation.

The therapist asked Marie to provide examples of the upsetting characteristics in Carl's behavior, noting that in his cognitive-behavioral approach to therapy it is important to identify behavioral patterns that are sources of distress between members of a couple. Thus the therapist was asking for behavioral data *and* introducing the couple to the concepts and procedures of therapy. As in other applications of cognitive-behavioral therapy, in couple therapy the clinician engages the clients in collaborative efforts to identify and modify sources of problems in their relationship. At this point the therapist also was aware that this couple tended to "cross-complain" and that one of the reasons they ended their previous couple therapy was that they perceived themselves as continuing their frustrating arguments in that setting. Consequently the therapist had to balance his need to hear about each partner's areas of dissatisfaction in the marriage, to observe a sample of the couple's communication patterns, and to give them some evidence that therapy would not consist of aversive arguments. He used his request to Marie for behavioral examples regarding Carl as an opportunity to share these goals with the couple.

Therapist: In order for us to identify specific positive changes that could be made in how the two of you communicate and relate to each other, we need to focus on the behaviors that tend to make one or both of you upset, as well as those that you find more satisfying. Because I don't know much about you at this point, I need to have you describe these behaviors, but I realize that you could easily experience this as a gripe session, similar to ones that you may have at home. It is important that therapy be a place where you can work on constructive changes, not a place that you'd want to avoid because your partner gets a chance to criticize you. So I'd like us to agree on some ground rules for discussing the behaviors that each of you finds upsetting. You may not agree with some of the things that you hear each other saying, but the key at this evaluation stage of our work together is for all three of us to get a clear picture of what *specific* things make you happy in your relationship and what things bother you. Let's talk for a couple of minutes about some ground rules for avoiding trading complaints here.

The therapist then engaged the couple in devising a few basic rules that they would try to follow when describing each other's behavior (e.g., describing each other's actions and not using pejorative labels—such as "selfish"—that generally make the other person defensive). The therapist then resumed his inquiry about Carl's behaviors that upset Marie.

Marie stated that for as many years as she could remember, Carl had placed his personal priorities ahead of hers and those of their children. When asked by the therapist for behavioral examples, she described how he often missed family dinners because he changed his plans and stayed late at work, and how he often made social plans for himself (e.g., a card game with friends) on short notice without discussing them with her. In contrast to this lack of involvement with the family, she said that when Carl was at home he would insist on having things done his way, refusing to negotiate with her or with the children. As an example, she described a relatively recent incident when their daughter, Ann, was invited to join friends at a Saturday matinee movie, but Carl "forbade her to go" because she had not finished some yard work that he had assigned to her. When Ann suggested that she would complete the yard work later in the afternoon, after she returned from the movie, Carl became angry, shouted at her that she was irresponsible, and ordered her to stay home and do the work. Marie told the therapist that incidents like that occurred fairly often, and that she sometimes felt a need to intervene on the part of Ann or Robert, which usually led to an argument between Carl and herself. The therapist asked Carl if Marie's description was a pretty good representation of how the events unfolded during the incident concerning Ann's going to the movie, and he said that it seemed accurate to him. He added, "It also is a good example of how Marie teams up with the children and makes me the bad guy."

After Marie had provided behavioral examples of problems in the relationship, the therapist turned to Carl and noted, "Earlier, you said that the two of you had communication problems; it would help if you could give me some more details about what aspects of your communication together doesn't seem to go well." After Carl gave some examples, the therapist reminded him that he had mentioned his perception that Marie "teamed up" with the children, and asked him to describe his memories of exactly what occurred at such times.

The therapist considered each partner's reports of couple interactions as subjective and possibly influenced by the individuals' own values, intent, and "sentiment override." Nevertheless, there was already some correspondence between the spouses' reports of their typical interactions and the samples of their communication that had occurred during the assessment session. Consequently, the therapist was formulating some hypotheses about dysfunctional interaction patterns, not only in terms of the couple's behavioral sequences (e.g., negative reciprocity) but also concerning the cognitions that each person had about the other (e.g., attributions about negative personality traits and negative intent). At this point he directed the assessment toward cognitions and affect.

Therapist: You have given me a lot of useful information about specific patterns in your relationship, and I also have gotten to see how you communicate with each other here. However, I also have noticed that your upset feelings toward each other seem to be related to how you interpret each other's behavior. In cognitive-behavioral therapy we look at how an individual often has a strong emotional reaction to his or her partner's behavior because the behavior means something significant to him or her. I'd like all of us to to get a sense of how you interpret each other's behavior.

The therapist then guided each individual in exploring his or her perceptions, attributions, expectancies, assumptions, and standards concerning the partner and their relationship, using Socratic questioning typical of cognitive therapy (see Beck 1995). Some of Carl's key cognitions included attributions that Marie did not respect him and that she felt stronger love for the children, an attribution that his children disobeyed because they did not respect him, the expectancy that no one in the family would take him seriously unless he took a hard-line stand and refused to "cave in" to their requests, an assumption that children are naturally lazy and will lose motivation to work hard if parents praise them (and need to be prodded), and standards that a man's primary duty to his family is to provide a good income and life-style, and that his family should appreciate his efforts and not bother him about engaging in some leisure activities to get a break from the pressure of his work. Among Marie's key cognitions were the attributions that Carl's behavior reflected stubborn, self-centered traits as well as a lack of love for her and their children, an expectancy that the only action on her part that could truly convey to Carl that their relationship was unacceptable to her in its present form was to live separately, and a standard (which apparently had influenced her behavior for many years, until she became depressed and very angry toward Carl) that a wife/mother should do whatever it takes to keep her family peaceful and together.

The therapist also asked the couple to provide a brief developmental history of their relationship, starting with how they met, what attracted them to each other, how they made the decision to get married, and any significant events over the years that influenced their marriage in a positive or negative way. The therapist noted that the historical information would help him put their current difficulties in perspective, and that knowing how a relationship deteriorated often provides clues about ways to improve it.

The couple described how they met in college, dated exclusively for several months and became engaged on graduation day. Marie said that she had been attracted by Carl's good looks, his intelligence, his seriousness about his work, his clear life goals, and his sense of humor. Carl said that he had liked Marie's physical attractiveness, her outgoing personality, her sense of humor, her intelligence, and their similar values and religious backgrounds. For the first few years of their relationship, the couple had spent a large amount of time together, sharing and talking about common interests (e.g., tennis, movies). After they were married, Carl completed a master's degree in business while Marie worked as a sales representative for a technology company. Once Robert was born, Marie stopped working until both children were in elementary school all day. Marie commented that she believed the tension in the marriage started to build when she was at home with two young children and Carl increasingly spent time at work. Whenever she felt frustrated, she would attempt to raise the issue of feeling abandoned by Carl, but the couple would typically argue and then avoid each other for a while. She also said that the problem seemed to worsen when Carl received a promotion at work and had more responsibilities placed on him. Carl agreed with Marie's portrayal of their relationship history. The therapist then asked the couple about areas of strength that they saw in their relationship. Marie and Carl agreed that they still shared basic values about life and that in spite of their long-standing differences about childrearing, they both would take quick action to protect their children if they perceived that they were in danger.

The evaluation session ended with the therapist thanking Marie and Carl for answering all of his questions and stating that he had gathered a lot of information about the history of their relationship and their current difficulties and strengths. He summarized the major initial findings from the session, including evidence that the couple's pattern for discussing conflictual topics tended toward cross-complaining and criticism, minimal validation of the other person, and stalemates. He also noted that each person attributed the other's negative behavior to stable, negative traits and intentions, and that it was not surprising that they were so upset with each other if they interpreted the other's behavior as due to such un- changeable traits and a lack of love and respect. He proposed that if the couple worked with him, they would focus on developing more constructive communication patterns, which would result in each partner feeling understood and re- spected, as well as better problem-solving skills for resolving their differences in ways acceptable to both of them. He also noted that in cognitive- behavioral therapy the couple would be assisted in becoming more aware of how their interpretations of each other's behavior influence their emotions and behavior toward the other person, and in becoming adept at examining the validity of those cognitions. He suggested that if behaviors that were interpreted as reflecting a lack of love were in fact based on the partners having different personal

standards about how one demonstrates love for another
person, it would be very important for them to discover that.
In such a case, rather than facing a loveless relationship,
perhaps they would be dealing with a more solvable problem
concerning even some relatively small behavioral changes that
could make the other person feel more love (and respect). He
also noted that at times couples are more able to accept
differences in their personal styles when they have more
confidence that there is a foundation of caring and commitment in the relationship. Marie and Carl replied that they
found the session constructive and wanted to continue with
therapy.

COGNITIVE-BEHAVIORAL TREATMENT STRATEGIES

I have presented a relatively extended description of the initial
assessment session and the ways in which the therapist works
to teach the couple about the therapeutic model and engage
them in therapy, based on my view that this is a major point at
which work with couples differs from individual therapy. As
in individual therapy, members of couples commonly enter
therapy with considerable ambivalence, based on hopelessness about the potential for change and some fear of what
the effects of successful change would mean for their lives.
However, members of couples also tend to be defensive and
blame each other for problems, and engaging them in therapy
requires that the therapist immediately begin to counteract
these tendencies and instill a collaborative working relationship among the three parties. Subsequent cognitive and behavioral interventions are all based on the premise that each
partner is willing to examine his or her own contribution to
circular patterns that maintain conflict. The following is a
necessarily brief summary of the interventions that were used
with Carl and Marie.

Communication Skill Training

During the second session, when the therapist inquired how the couple's week had been, Carl and Marie quickly launched into an argument about the ways in which Carl had talked to Marie about some of their joint bills. Marie described Carl's behavior as verbally abusive, and Carl defended himself, stating that Marie made him very frustrated by "refusing to take my advice about how we should handle the bills." The therapist interrupted the couple, asked them if the way they were arguing was similar to how they argue outside the office (they both said it was), and reminded them that one goal they had discussed for therapy was improving their communication skills. He then gave them a handout summarizing the guidelines for expresser and empathic listener in Guerney's (1977) Relationship Enhancement program, described their intent, reviewed each guideline with the couple, and asked whether they would be willing to practice the communication skills during therapy sessions. When the couple agreed, the therapist noted that it generally is easier to practice new skills with less emotionally upsetting topics, but it might be worth applying the guidelines in discussing their present issue during this session, while the therapist could coach them. The remainder of the session was devoted to the couple's rehearsal of the communication skills, with considerable coaching by the therapist. As homework, the couple agreed to meet twice and spend up to fifteen minutes in each of the expresser and listener roles, selecting low-conflict topics for their discussions until they were adept at using the skills. The therapist devoted approximately half of each of the next four sessions to additional work on the communication skills, and the couple practiced outside the sessions two to three times per week.

Problem-Solving Skill Training

The therapist informed the couple that use of the expressive and listening skills did not necessarily resolve problems, so it was important to practice problem-solving skills as well. He gave each partner a handout on guidelines for problem solving (see Baucom and Epstein 1990), discussed each stage of problem solving, modeled how to define a problem in behavioral terms, coached the couple in selecting an unresolved problem to discuss, and guided them through the stages of identifying and selecting a potential solution. Again, it was important to start with a problem of low to moderate intensity and to practice the skills in session before the couple attempted to use them at home. Marie and Carl were able to devise some solutions to daily problems (e.g., how to work as a team when dealing with financial concerns) that both found acceptable, and the process of using the structured guidelines resulted in both individuals feeling respected more by their partner.

Cognitive Restructuring

The basic procedures used in cognitive restructuring with couples are the same as those used in individual therapy (see Beck 1995) and will not be detailed here. These include coaching each partner to consider alternative attributions for the other person's negative behaviors, guiding them in collecting data that may disconfirm inferences (attributions and expectancies) that they make about each other, and challenging them to consider modifications in unrealistic standards that they hold for their own and each other's behavior. For example, the therapist and Carl discussed the good intentions that he had in working so hard to provide a good life for his family, but how that standard also periodically led him to feel so "burned out" that he felt a need to escape from anything that he perceived as a burden, including dealing with the daily needs of his wife and children. The therapist guided Carl in "rewriting" his standard in a manner that still included his basic values but was less likely to "set him up" for stress and avoidance: "I am committed to providing a good life for my family. One way to do that is to work hard and make a good living. However, another important way of providing a good quality of life for them is to be part of their lives personally. Often some time together can be worth more to my wife and kids than a few more hours of earning money." This was a standard that fit with Carl's values about his responsibilities and also was more attractive to Marie. The couple agreed that Carl would experiment with living according to the revised standard for a couple of weeks, and they would then evaluate the impact. They subsequently reported that they both liked the results, in terms of decreased conflict and an increased sense of cohesion.

When conducting cognitive restructuring in conjoint therapy sessions, one has the advantage of obtaining information from one partner that helps disconfirm the other's negative cognitions. On the other hand, the therapist must be prepared to structure the session so that one person's revelation of his or her negative cognitions (e.g., negative attributions) about the other person does not lead to escalation of conflict. One strategy for achieving this goal is to warn the couple that they are likely to hear some of the negative thoughts that have fueled each other's anger and upsetting behavior, but that once each person gets an opportunity to identify and test his or her own cognitions, it is more likely that any unrealistic ones can be changed. As is generally the case in conducting couple therapy, it is to the couple's benefit for the therapist to intervene actively to keep negative exchanges during sessions from escalating.

OUTCOME

Marie and Carl continued with weekly couples therapy sessions for four months, then decided to shift to sessions every other week for two more months. In spite of their history of conflict and animosity, they clearly maintained an underlying emotional bond that allowed them to tolerate the stress of working on problems in their relationship. Their feelings of satisfaction versus frustration varied from week to week, but they were fairly consistent in the efforts they invested in sessions and outside. The behavioral interventions made a significant difference in their ability to resolve conflicts and communicate in ways that were satisfying to both individuals. After three months they decided to live together on a trial basis, continuing their therapeutic work. When they decided (jointly and in collaboration with the therapist) to discontinue therapy, they agreed to a monthly follow-up session for three months. They maintained their gains and reported that they both felt more hopeful about their future together.

CONCLUSION

Working with couples conjointly presents both advantages and significant challenges. A primary advantage is the therapist's ability to observe and actively intervene with the couple's dysfunctional interaction patterns during sessions, rather than hear only about events that occur outside the therapy office. As is the case with other forms of cognitive-behavioral therapy (e.g., in the treatment of agoraphobia), efficacy appears to be enhanced when a therapist is able to engage the clients in responding in new ways in vivo. A major challenge of couples therapy is the therapist's need to manage often intense exchanges during sessions, conceptualize the patterns in rapidly unfolding interactions, and provide some evidence to distressed couples that they have the potential to relate in more satisfying ways.

REFERENCES

Baucom, D. H., and Epstein, N. (1990). *Cognitive-Behavioral Marital Therapy*. New York: Brunner/Mazel.

Baucom, D. H., Epstein, N., Daiuto, A. D., et al. (1996a). Cognitions in marriage: the relationship between standards and attributions. *Journal of Family Psychology* 10:209–222.

Baucom, D. H., Epstein, N., Rankin, L. A., and Burnett, C. K. (1996b). Understanding and treating marital distress from a cognitive-behavioral orientation. In *Advances in Cognitive-Behavioral Therapy*, ed. K. S. Dobson and K. D. Craig, pp. 210–236. Thousand Oaks, CA: Sage.

———— (1996c). Assessing relationship standards: the Inventory of Specific Relationship Standards. *Journal of Family Psychology* 10:72–88.

Baucom, D. H., Epstein, N., Sayers, S., and Sher, T. G. (1989). The role of cognitions in marital relationships: definitional, methodological, and conceptual issues. *Journal of Consulting and Clinical Psychology* 57:31–38.

Beach, S. R. H., Sandeen, E. E., and O'Leary, K. D. (1990). *Depression in Marriage: A Model for Etiology and Treatment*. New York: Guilford.

Beck, J. S. (1995). *Cognitive Therapy: Basics and Beyond*. New York: Guilford.

Bienvenu, M. J. (1970). Measurement of marital communication. *The Family Coordinator* 19:26–31.

Bradbury, T. N., and Fincham, F. D. (1990). Attribution in marriage: review and critique. *Psychological Bulletin* 107:3–33.

Christensen, A. (1988). Dysfunctional interaction patterns in couples. In *Perspectives on Marital Interaction*, ed. P. Noller and M. A. Fitzpatrick, pp. 31–52. Clevedon, England: Multilingual Matters, LTD.

Craske, M. G., and Zoellner, L. A. (1995). Anxiety disorders: the role of marital therapy. In *Clinical Handbook of Couple Therapy*, ed. N. S. Jacobson and A. S. Gurman, pp. 394–410. New York: Guilford.

Deffenbacher, J. L. (1996). Cognitive-behavioral approaches to anger reduction. In *Advances in Cognitive-Behavioral Therapy*, ed. K. S. Dobson and K. D. Craig, pp. 31–62. Thousand Oaks, CA: Sage.

Diagnostic and Statistical Manual of Mental Disorders (DSM-IV) (1994). 4th ed. Washington, DC: American Psychiatric Association.

Eidelson, R. J., and Epstein, N. (1982). Cognition and relationship maladjustment: development of a measure of dysfunctional relationship beliefs. *Journal of Consulting and Clinical Psychology* 50:715–720.

Epstein, N., and Baucom, D. H. (1993). Cognitive factors in marital disturbance. In *Psychopathology and Cognition*, ed. K. S. Dobson and P. C. Kendall, pp. 351–385. San Diego: Academic Press.

Fincham, F. D., and Bradbury, T. N. (1992). Assessing attributions in marriage: the Relationship Attribution Measure. *Journal of Personality and Social Psychology* 62:457–468.

Goldstein, A. J., and Chambless, D. L. (1978). A reanalysis of agoraphobia. *Behavior Therapy* 9:47–59.

Gottman, J. M. (1979). *Marital Interaction: Experimental Investigations*. New York: Academic Press.

——— (1993a). *What Predicts Divorce? The Relationship between Marital Processes and Marital Outcomes*. Hillsdale, NJ: Erlbaum.

——— (1993b). The roles of conflict engagement, escalation, and avoidance in marital interaction: a longitudinal view of five types of couples. *Journal of Consulting and Clinical Psychology* 61:6–15.

Gottman, J. M., Markman, H., and Notarius, C. (1977). The topography of marital conflict: a sequential analysis of verbal and nonverbal behavior. *Journal of Marriage and the Family* 39:461–477.

Guerney, B. G., Jr. (1977). *Relationship Enhancement*. San Francisco: Jossey-Bass.

Hahlweg, K., Reisner, L., Kohli, G., et al. (1984). Development and validity of a new system to analyze interpersonal communication (KPI: Kategoriensystem fur Partnerschaftliche Interaktion). In *Marital Interaction: Analysis and Modification*, ed. K. Hahlweg and N. S. Jacobson, pp. 182–198. New York: Guilford.

Heiman, J. R., Epps, P. H., and Ellis, B. (1995). Treating sexual desire disorders in couples. In *Clinical Handbook of Couple Therapy*, ed. N. S. Jacobson and A. S. Gurman, pp. 471–495. New York: Guilford.

Heyman, R. E., Weiss, R. L., and Eddy, J. M. (1995). Marital Interaction Coding System: revision and empirical evaluation. *Behaviour Research and Therapy* 33:737–746.

Hof, L. (1987). Evaluating the marital relationship of clients with sexual complaints. In *Integrating Sex and Marital Therapy: A Clinical Guide*, ed. G. W. Weeks and L. Hof, pp. 5–22. New York: Brunner/Mazel.

Holtzworth-Munroe, A., and Jacobson, N. S. (1991). Behavioral marital therapy. In *Handbook of Family Therapy*, vol. II, ed. A. S. Gurman and D. P. Kniskern, pp. 96–133. New York: Brunner/Mazel.

Jacobson, N. S., Follette, W. C., Revenstorf, D., et al. (1984). Variability in outcome and clinical significance of behavioral marital therapy: a reanalysis of outcome data. *Journal of Consulting and Clinical Psychology* 52:497–504.

Jacobson, N. S., and Margolin, G. (1979). *Marital Therapy: Strategies Based on Social Learning and Behavior Exchange Principles*. New York: Brunner/Mazel.

Kaslow, F. W. (1993). Relational diagnosis: an idea whose time has come? *Family Process* 32:255–259.

Krokoff, L. J., Gottman, J. M., and Hass, S. D. (1989). Validation of a global rapid couples interaction scoring system. *Behavioral Assessment* 11:65–79.

Markman, H. J., Stanley, S., and Blumberg, S. L. (1994). *Fighting For Your Marriage*. San Francisco: Jossey-Bass.

McCrady, B. S., and Epstein, E. E. (1995). Marital therapy in the treatment of alcohol problems. In *Clinical Handbook of Couple Therapy*, ed. N. S. Jacobson and A. S. Gurman, pp. 369–393. New York: Guilford.

Notarius, C. I., and Markman, H. J. (1981). The Couples Interaction Scoring System. In *Assessing Marriage: New Behavioral Approaches*, ed. E. E. Filsinger and R. A. Lewis, pp. 112–127. Beverly Hills, CA: Sage.

O'Leary, K. D., and Turkewitz, H. (1978). Marital therapy from a behavioral perspective. In *Marriage and Marital Therapy: Psycho-*

analytic Behavioral and Systems Theory Perspectives, ed. T. J. Paolino and B. S. McCrady, pp. 240–297. New York: Brunner/Mazel.

Pretzer, J. L., Epstein, N., and Fleming, B. (1991). The Marital Attitude Survey: a measure of dysfunctional attributions and expectancies. *Journal of Cognitive Psychotherapy* 5:131–148.

Revenstorf, D., Hahlweg, K., Schindler, L., and Vogel, B. (1984). Interaction analysis of marital conflict. In *Marital Interaction: Analysis and Modification*, ed. K. Hahlweg and N. S. Jacobson, pp. 159–181. New York: Guilford.

Snyder, D. K., Cavell, T. A., Heffer, R. W., and Mangrum, L. F. (1995). Marital and family assessment: a multifaceted, multilevel approach. In *Integrating Family Therapy: Handbook of Family Psychology and Systems Theory*, ed. R. H. Mikesell, D.-D. Lusterman, and S. H. McDaniel, pp. 163–182. Washington, DC: American Psychological Association.

Stuart, R. B. (1980). *Helping Couples Change: A Social Learning Approach to Marital Therapy*. New York: Guilford.

Thibaut, J. W., and Kelley, H. H. (1959). *The Social Psychology of Groups*. New York: Wiley.

Weiss, R. L. (1980). Strategic behavioral marital therapy: toward a model for assessment and intervention. In *Advances in Family Intervention, Assessment and Theory*, vol. 1, ed. J. P. Vincent, pp. 229–271. Greenwich, CT: JAI Press.

Weiss, R. L., and Heyman, R. E. (1990). Observation of marital interaction. In *The Psychology of Marriage*, ed. F. D. Fincham and T. N. Bradbury, pp. 87–117. New York: Guilford.

13

SEXUAL DYSFUNCTION

Jerry M. Friedman

INTRODUCTION

Problems of sexual functioning are as old as sex itself. However, it wasn't until the beginning of the twentieth century that sexual problems began to be viewed from a theoretical and methodological perspective. Sexual dysfunction was viewed, under Freud's influence, as coming from deep-rooted personality conflicts, especially a failure to resolve the Oedipus complex (Freud 1905/1962). No special adaptation of traditional psychodynamic theory was believed necessary to treat sexual dysfunction, as sexual conflict was proposed to be the cause of almost all psychopathology. In the late 1950s interventions based on learning theory were first introduced. Wolpe (1958) conceptualized sexual dysfunction as a conditioned anxiety response to a sexual situation and thus treatable by relaxation and systematic or in vivo desensitization. In the 1950s and 1960s cognitive approaches were applied to the treatment of sexual dysfunction, including thought stopping (Garfield et al. 1969), attentional training (Lazarus 1968), and rational emotive therapy (Ellis 1962, 1971). Medical interventions also date back to the early twentieth century. Until recent years these treatments were hampered by limited knowledge of human sexual physiology and an inability to differentiate sexual dysfunction along the physiological-psychological dimension (LoPiccolo and Friedman 1985).

In the late 1960s and early 1970s Masters and Johnson produced two major works (1966, 1970) that are largely responsible for the establishment of sex therapy as a distinctive therapeutic discipline. Their first work, *Human Sexual Response* (1966), made a significant contribution to the knowledge of human sexual physiology. Their second work, *Human Sexual Inadequacy* (1970), provided the field with a treatment protocol for most sexual problems. This approach was couple-oriented, brief, directive, and focused on the sexual symptoms rather than on uncovering unconscious conflict. The proposed cause of most sexual dysfunction was performance anxiety, informational and communication deficits, and the assumption of a "spectator" role during sexual activity. Over the last twenty-five years the treatment protocols proposed by Masters and Johnson remain as the foundation for most treatment programs for sexual dysfunction. Kaplan (1974, 1979) helped integrate these treatment protocols with psychoanalytic psychotherapy. She conceptualized sexual dysfunction according to a triphasic delineation of the sexual response cycle: desire, arousal, and orgasm.

Several principles underlie sex therapy and receive varying degrees of emphasis depending on the particular case.

1. Elimination of performance anxiety
2. Education
3. Promoting attitude change

4. Enhancing communication
5. Changing destructive sex roles or life-styles
6. Physical or medical interventions
7. Changing sexual behavior and teaching effective sexual technique
8. Emphasis on mutual responsibility for change

Sex therapists use a broad range of cognitive-behavioral strategies and techniqes to apply these principles to specific sexual problems in both individual and couples therapy. The dysfunctions most commonly treated are:

Orgasmic dysfunction: Delay or absence of orgasm following normal sexual excitement that is adequate in focus and duration, and not accounted for by another Axis I diagnosis or the direct effects of a substance or medical condition.

Premature ejaculation: A male dysfunction of quick ejaculation with minimal sexual stimulation before the person wishes it and not due to the direct effects of a substance.

Female sexual arousal dysfunction: The inability to attain or maintain the lubrication-swelling response that is the physical manifestation of female arousal. The problem is not due to the direct effects of a substance or to a medical condition.

Male erectile dysfunction: The inability to attain or maintain an adequate erection until completion of sexual activity. The problem is not due to a general medical conditon or to the physiological effects of a substance.

Hypoactive desire: Deficient or absent sexual fantasy and desire for sexual activity, taking into effect age and the context of the person's life. The problem is not due to the direct effects of a substance or to a medical condition.

Sexual aversion: Extreme aversion to and avoidance of all or almost all sexual contact with a partner.

It should be noted that making a diagnosis is often highly subjective. The above definitions are abbreviated from *DSM-IV* (1994) and contain such subjective terms as *deficient, adequate, normal,* and *sufficient.*

TREATMENT ISSUES

The treatment intervention most commonly included as part of most sex therapy approaches is a graded series of sexual tasks beginning with sensual massage (sensate focus) introduced as homework, along with a ban on sexual intercourse. This theoretically reduces the anxiety of having to "perform." The emphasis is on discovering new sensual experiences. The exercises have the triple purpose of removing performance anxiety by creating a no-demand experience; eliminating the spectator role by encouraging the couple to tune into their own sexual experiences and feelings; and increasing sexual communication. The sensual body massage at first is done with no breast or genital stimulation. Eventually breasts, then genitals, are introduced and finally intercourse. This in vivo desensitization is designed to keep individuals "in the moment," tuned into their physical sensations and *not* analyzing or taking on a spectator role.

The cognitive aspects of therapy may at first seem to intefere with simply tuning in to sensations. However, most sexual performance anxiety is based in core beliefs, distorted automatic thoughts, and dysfunctional schemas. Much of the cognitive work needs to be done in *preparation* for the actual sexual activity. Therfore homework (a therapy standard in both cognitive and sexual therapy) focuses on identifying self-statements that interfere with sexual response, as well as behavioral assignments (such as sensate focus).

The first stage of therapy is to help the patient(s) identify the cause of the sexual dysfunction. Sometimes it is quite simply lack of information. For example, a woman and her partner may not know where her clitoris is and that she may need direct clitoral stimulation to get aroused and have an orgasm. Frequently, problems of premature ejaculation will respond to a series of exercises best practiced through masturbation and then introduced into the couple's sex life. Cases such as these are much rarer since many self-help books and magazine articles address these issues (Heiman and LoPiccolo 1988, Zilbergeld 1978). For many cases the explanation is more complex. Cognitive therapy is particularly well suited, in the context of a brief therapy, to help patients identify the unrealistic or irrational beliefs that mediate their feelings of anxiety, aversion, anger, or despair. The most typical distorted thoughts involve equating erection with desire and manliness, equating orgasm with sexual pleasure, and equating low desire with lack of attraction. The most common term used by men (and women about men) who have a dysfunction is "I/he couldn't perform." Challenging the concept of sex as performance is often a major focus of the cognitive work.

Patients are helped to identify self-statements that mediate emotional arousal and to accept that their emotional reactions can be directly influenced by their expectations, labels, and self-statements. Individual coping statements are generated, with the aid of the therapist, to help the patient overcome the fear, anxiety, and aversion or avoidance responses that are their usual reactions to the sexual situation. Typical coping statements might include: "Just because I engage in sex doesn't mean I'm a bad person," "I know that when I was younger I learned to feel guilty about engaging in _____ and I don't want to, nor do I have to feel that way anymore," or "If I allow myself to enjoy sex, it does not mean that I will lose all control." Of course, many sexual problems are secondary to problems in the relationship and often relationship therapy is necessary prior to or concurrent with the sexual therapy. Helping patients to identify and reevaluate their worst fears about "failure" in the bedroom and to see that often the bedroom is the arena where individual and relationship issues are played out are important components of the therapy. A useful clinical tool to help patients bridge the gap between feelings and cognition is a modified transactional analysis framework (Berne 1964, Steiner 1974). Patients are asked to imagine that they have two tapes in their head (figuratively, of course) on which they have been storing important information from early childhood on. The Child tape is the repository of all of one's emotional memories. One side of the tape—the frightened/angry/needy child—stores all fear and emotional withdrawal responses. The flip side—the playful child—stores all the happy, uninhibited, and playful emotional memories. The Parent tape also has two sides. The judgmental parent contains all the dos and don'ts, should's and should not's, and other critical attitudes that have accumulated since early childhood from parents, teachers, religion, and society. The flip side of this tape is the nurturing parent, which allows not only nurturing of others but, most important, self-nurturing. Thus emotional responses come from the child tape while attitude and opinions come from the parent tape. A third element—the Adult—processes input from the environment and from the tapes to produce rational decisions.

Many people have too much frightened child and judgmental parent and not enough playful child and nurturing parent. It is explained that the work in therapy is to bring the playful child into the bedroom in order to have good sex. Frightened child and judgmental parent often work together to prevent the playful child from letting go in a playful, anxiety-free way. Judgmental parent statements directed at one's self result in anxiety, avoidance, and sometimes depression. Judgmental parent statements about others result in anger. The work in therapy is to replace some judgmental parent statements with nurturing parent statements so that the frightened/angry child can "feel safe" and thus leave room for the playful child to come out to play. Giving patients permission to let their playful child out to play often has a direct impact on sexual behavior. Judgmental parent statements often correspond to dysfunctional, distorted, automatic thoughts, especially "shoulds" about sexual functioning, mind reading about what the partner is thinking, and fortune-telling about the consequences of an "unsuccessful" sexual experience. Even if a partner responds in a nonsupportive manner to a sexual experience, judgmental parent statements about failure and defectiveness can result in a magnification of the response. Nurturing parent statements correspond to a reframed cognitive response to these thoughts.

A CASE STUDY: JOHN AND MARY

Sessions 1–4

John and Mary, an attractive couple in their late thirties, presented for therapy because of John's loss of sexual desire for Mary. The couple had been married for eight years, had one child aged 3, and had not had any sexual contact for two years. Both reported that John had lost interest in sex early in the relationship and he acknowledged that he had lost interest in a similar way in prior relationships. Both partners agreed that there was some affection but little intimacy in the relationship. They did not do a lot of sharing about feelings and most of their communication was about the business of their daily lives. John owned his own business, and Mary worked part time doing the bookkeeping for him. Mary expressed a lot of anger toward John. She felt unattractive, had lowered self-esteem, and felt frustrated by her lack of sexual outlet. She had stopped masturbating a year earlier and trained herself to turn off all sexual feelings. John also expressed anger. He felt he had no time for himself, that there was alway an implicit or explicit demand for his time and attention. He still felt sexual and continued to masturbate to fantasies of other women twice a week. Both denied any affairs.

Following the initial intake session, the next two sessions were individual history sessions with some couple time at the end of each session.

John described his family of origin as low key, with rare exression of feeling. The family members were observant Catholics and John went to Catholic schools. He rejected his religion in his late teens. He never saw affection at home, and assumes his parents had no sex life. He described himself as a loner by choice, although he did have friends.

John: I was a good boy, sweet and quiet. I didn't make waves. No one ever told me the facts of life. I discovered masturbation by accident. You know, I never felt close to my parents, and would never go to them with a problem or a personal question. I know they had a lot of anger toward each other, but the sense was not to express such feelings. Everyone was so nice, but you could tell that was not what was really going on.

John started dating in college and had lots of girlfriends and lots of sex. He found that he would be very interested in pursuing and having sex with women, but once he won them over and they were committed to him, he would lose desire, decide he wasn't really in love, and move on. When he met Mary he had an instant response. He found her more desirable than any other woman he had met. They were both in other relationships and it was a year before they actually started dating. Sex was excellent at the beginning, but within a year his desire faded slowly until it bordered on aversion. Prior to Mary, John estimates that he had twenty to twenty-five sexual partners. Over the course of his adult life he had eight years of psychodynamic therapy.

Mary, the youngest of three girls, remembers an uneventful happy childhood until age 12, when her father died. Her mother remarried a man that Mary hated, and at age 16 she went to live with an older sister and her husband. This was an unhappy marriage and Mary moved in with her other sister who was single. Mary's mother was (and still is) agoraphobic and does not leave her house. Like Mary, her mom has no friends. Mary went to Catholic school through high school, and then rejected her religion. She has a lot of anger at the church, at her mother who became unavailable to her after her father's death, and at John who now is another person in her life who she feels abandoned her. From age 18 on Mary had a series of boyfriends and a fair amount of sexual experience. She describes a pattern of low self-esteem and two relationships with men she cared about a lot that also ended in abandonment. When Mary met John, she sensed his intense desire for her.

Mary: It was an instant attraction. I know I took him away from his girlfriend. I never believed in marriage but I wanted to marry him. I felt really good being married to him. I felt safe and loved, but by the next summer I knew there was a sexual problem. I mean I wanted sex three times a day and he would give lots of reasons why he couldn't. I was doing all the initiating. We went for some help but nothing changed. Finally, I gave up on sex. I am so angry.

Mary had been in an individual psychodyamic therapy for six years and felt she had gained a lot of personal insight but was having difficulty making herself happy within this relationship. In session 4 the couple was introduced to the way therapy would proceed, including the concept of sensate focus. There was some discussion on how they had gotten to this point in their relationship and that there was a strong possibility that things could and would improve. Since John was a self-labeled workaholic, spending evening hours in his home office, they agreed to one hour of nonwork time per day to connect as a couple as positively as possible. John phoned later that week to terminate therapy. The reason given was that this was his busy season and they would wait two months to resume.

The therapist next heard from John two years later when he asked for an appointment by himself. At that time he indicated that things were still the same and that he was ready to work on the problem but that at this point Mary would not come in and he wanted to work individually.

Sessions 1–5 with John

At the first session John brought the therapist up to date.

John: I really feel ready to do something about this problem. I went back into individual therapy for eighteen months after I saw you last, but this subject wasn't even broached. Mary and I are friendly and a little affectionate. We're enjoying our son. Sometimes I make an effort to initiate but she rejects me. She is so angry that she's not willing to make an effort. I mean, that's what I used to do to her. Now she never initiates. I guess I'm really relieved when she says no. I just don't want to do it. But I'm attracted to 75 percent of the women I see and I keep masturbating.

Therapist: Sometimes when a man feels like you do, he's tempted to explore sex with other women. Tell me about any experiences or desires you've had to do that.

John: I've never cheated on Mary. But it's amazing how I'll fantasize about any and all kinds of activity with a woman, but Mary is never in the fantasy.

In sessions 2 and 3 a cognitive framework was introduced, along with the analagy of the tapes described above. By the end of session 3 John was able to make the following observation.

John: I guess I see now that what I've done is separate sex from love, romance, and commitment. You know, I just don't see those things together. I mean, my whole family, my brother and two sisters, have problems with relationships, and, boy, are my parents cold! You know, I know I've been with a lot of women, but I'm beginning to see that I'm really very shy with women. I mean I've never made the first move.

Therapist: Well, what about the sex itself? You've said you always enjoyed it at the beginning. Would you take the lead in bed?

John: Not really. I hated being with a passive woman in or out of bed. I love the feeling of sex but it feels uncomfortable too.

Therapist: Uncomfortable in what way?

John: Sort of awkward and maybe a little dirty and sordid.

Therapist: And how would you feel about these women who are assertive in bed and are doing all these things to and with you?

John: Excited. But I can't think of Mary that way. It's like that has nothing to do with the way I feel about her.

John also described a strong performance anxiety. There had been times when his interest in sex was decreasing that he had a problem with erection, which would get Mary even more upset. Now, in addition to his lack of desire, he also feared that if he did start some activity he would not get an erection and he would make things worse. John was helped to develop a set of cognitive coping statements and assigned some quiet time thinking about Mary in various pseudosexual ways, noticing the feelings that were present, seeking the thoughts that supported those feelings, and using the coping statements to minimize the anxiety/aversion.

Therapist: You know, John, that our feelings are mediated by our thoughts, and our thoughts and feelings will strongly influence what we do and don't do. And in turn, when we engage in behaviors, the way we think about the response we get from others will feed back to our feelings. So it's important not only to look at your thoughts but to actually do some things that you have been avoiding, slowly, of course, so that you have a chance to check out your worst fears. We've talked about the fact that you are fortune-telling and jumping to conclusions. Are you willing to check out some of these fears?

At session 4 the therapsit and John started creating a hierarchy of activities that could be used in both systematic and in vivo desensitization. Orgasmic reconditioning was also introduced. John was instructed to continue to masturbate as usual with his usual fantasies, but at the point of orgasm to switch to a fantasy of Mary. He was motivated to do this even though he expected it would decrease the pleasure of orgasm. The therapist was hoping that the positive reinforcer of the orgasm would be stronger than the discomfort of thinking of Mary in a sexual way, especially since concurrent cognitive work sexualizing Mary was occurring.

Sessions 5–10

The hierarchy was completed and the assignment to work with the lower items was given. John was to imagine a calming scene, then switch to the item from the hierarchy (the first item was hugging Mary in bed). In the event of anxiety at imagining this scene, John was told first to use his cognitive or nurturing statements to reduce the anxiety and stay with the scene. In the event he could not, he was to return to his calming scene for a short while, till the anxiety was gone, and then to try again, with repeated trials until he could stay in the scene with Mary with no anxiety. John proved very adept at this and over the next weeks moved up the hierarchy to the point of naked, mutual full-body massage with no anxiety. Another important theme emerged at the early stage of this assignment. At first John chose as his calming scene being alone in the mountains and then (misunderstanding the assignment) put Mary in the scene at his side. He found he was angry.

Therapist: I'd like you to stay with that feeling for a moment. Mary just came into your private place on the mountain. What are the thoughts behind the anger and resentment that you say you feel? Don't filter these thoughts. Just say them out loud.

John: It's like I'm not free. I don't call the shots. This is my private place. She doesn't belong here.

Continuing in this session, a major issue of John's setting boundaries in the relationship emerged. It became clear that John was unassertive, not only with Mary but with friends and business contacts as well. Thus assertion training became another goal in therapy. It was reframed for John that Mary was not his enemy and he needed to collaborate with her in and out of the bedroom to find mutually satisying boundaries. In the next session John reported that the orgasmic reconditioning was going well. He was able to switch to a scene with Mary somewhat before the orgasm began and was actually enjoying it. He related a dream in which he was having sex with a faceless woman and all of a sudden she turned into Mary. This startled him so that he woke up and the dream ended.

By the end of session 10 John was successfully including

Mary in all his masturbation fantasies, although only close to the point of orgasm. He was moving up the hierarchy in imagination, was practicing more assertive behavior, and had started doing some of the earlier hierarchy items with Mary in vivo, including lying in bed in a spoon position and some kissing and back massage. He was spending more quality time with Mary and his son, and had a strong feeling that she was more pleasant and less angry although they had not talked about this. John was using a lot of cognitive coping statements to deal with his anxiety during his imaginal desensitization. These included "Sex is pleasurable and I'm entitled to it. I have a beautiful woman here at my side who wants to be sexual with me. I'm not going to let my old frightened child tape keep me from the pleasure I can find"; "I don't have to be angry at Mary when she wants something from me. I'm a big boy and I can set limits. I want to get rid of my all-or-nothing thinking"; "I don't know why I started thinking that sex is sordid. It doesn't have to be. I can have sex with someone I love and maybe it will feel even better than what I used to do"; "I know that I've never been comfortable expressing my feelings. I learned that feelings are private and not to be shared. But look how I learned this. I look at my family and I see how emotionally restricted they are. I don't have to carry on this tradition, I can change this."

Sessions 11–20

The next major issue in therapy turned out to be the most difficult for John. It was suggested that John needed to talk to Mary about how things were going and to enlist her cooperation in moving forward in the in vivo assignments.

Therapist: It's really important to talk to Mary about what you've been working on. Since you're ready to introduce

sensual massage into your relationship, you need to see
how she feels about that and also to be sure that you don't
add to your anxiety by being concerned that she will expect
more. I know she didn't want to be a part of this therapy at
first, but maybe it's time to see if she will come in, even if for
only one session.

John: I'm not ready for that. I'll try to talk to her at home
(*clearly anxious*).

Therapist: You seem upset at the prospect. Let's explore what
your thoughts are about talking to her. What are your worst
fears?

John: We're getting along great. I don't want to rock the boat.

Therapist: What if you do? What can happen?

John: She may get angry. I know she still has a lot of anger.

Therapist: Let's assume the worst case for a moment, although
you need to recognize that that's a fear, not a fact. Why is it
so terrible if she gets angry?

John was able to process that again his old tapes were kicking
in—avoid strong feelings, especially anger, at all costs. An
intervention that proved particularly powerful as a coping
statement was, "You know anxiety is not pleasant, but you can
experience it, work with it, and hopefully decrease it; it is
tolerable and does not have to be avoided at all costs." John
used this statement to excellent advantage through the remainder of the therapy. Over the next sessions, with some
difficulty and occasional setbacks, John was able to do a
full-body naked massage, kiss Mary's breasts, kiss her passion-
ately, picture intercourse without anxiety in his systematic
desensitizaion, have repeated talks with Mary about his fears,
his unassertiveness, and his desire to have a good sex life with
her. John found an old photo of Mary in the nude that he had
taken at the beginning of their relationship. He was able to
masturbate frequently to this photo from the start of the

masturbatory experience till orgasm. John continued to use
cognitive strategies during the course of therapy, expecially
during some provocative times. For the most part Mary was
the ideal partner, did not put pressure on John, and remained
friendly and cooperative. She obviously saw the positive
changes and became hopeful. The following is an example of
how effective John became in his cognitive work.

John: I told Mary that I was getting closer to going further. She
said she was willing. We were playful all day, touching and
laughing. I really see what you mean about the playful child
tape for the first time. But that night we had drinks with
dinner and Mary got a little obnoxious and pushed me for
sex. I said no. It's amazing but she accepted this. The next
morning we cuddled and I played with her breasts and it felt
good. I guess I have to be careful about the alcohol. I feel as
if I ruined a great day.

Therapist: Is there any other way of looking at that experience?
We've talked a lot about reframing. How can you reframe
your automatic thought that you ruined a good day?

John: Well, I guess by turning her down I showed I could do it.

Therapist: Good, and what else?

John: I set limits and I didn't withdraw. I came back the next
day and we fooled around and she was fine with it. It's
amazing how I still fall into some of those thinking traps.
What was that, all-or-nothing thinking? Negative filter? I
guess a little of each.

In the last of the individual sessions John was pleased at his
ability to put a positive frame on several things that happened.

John: I had a great twenty-minute talk with Mary. When she
said she was really looking forward to sex with me, I didn't
get anxious. I told her I know it's slow but it will happen. I

didn't panic or withdraw or get angry. Speaking of angry, we did have an argument where it got a little heated. We both expressed our anger and I didn't hold on to it. I said what I had to say and so did she. You know, I can handle her anger now—and mine too (*laugh*).

Sessions 20–25

In sessions 20–25 Mary joined the therapy. Work on communication, problem solving, and continuation of the in vivo desensitization eventually led to intercourse. Mary and John continue monthly sessions to stay focused, maintain their gains, and deal with minor setbacks. They are planning termination of therapy in the near future.

SUMMARY

Sex therapy often requires a great deal of therapeutic eclecticism in addition to a knowledge of sexual physiology and the medical aspects of sexual functioning. In general, the earlier the sexual response is interrupted, the more complex the treatment. Problems of orgasm are often treated with brief cognitive behavior therapy. Problems of arousal often need more extensive interventions and thorough evaluation of medical factors and other psychological factors, such as depression, that may contribute to the problem. Problems of desire and aversion are most complex and often involve strong core beliefs or schema about sex, intimacy, commitment, vulnerability, and control. Cognitive therapy along with behavioral, experiential, and insight-oriented strategies is highly effective in the treatment of sexual dysfunction.

REFERENCES

Berne, E. (1964). *Games People Play.* New York: Grove.

Diagnostic and Statistical Manual of Mental Disorders (DSM-IV) (1994). Washington, DC: American Psychiatric Association.

Ellis, A. (1962). *Reason and Emotion in Psychotherapy.* New York: Lyle Stuart.

———— (1971). Rational-emotive treatment of impotence, frigidity, and other sexual problems. *Professional Psychology* 2:346–349.

Freud, S. (1905). *Three Essays on the Theory of Female Sexuality.* New York: Avon, 1962.

Garfield, Z. H., McBrearty, J. E., and Dicter, M. (1969). A case of impotence successfully treated with desensitization combined with in-vivo operant training and thought substitution. In *Advances in Behavior Therapy,* ed. R. D. Rubin and C. M. Franks. New York: Academic Press.

Heiman, J. R., and LoPiccolo, J. (1988). Becoming Orgasmic. New York: Simon & Schuster.

Kaplan, H. S. (1974). *The New Sex Therapy.* New York: Brunner/Mazel.

———— (1979). *Disorders of Sexual Desire.* New York: Brunner/Mazel.

Lazarus, A. A. (1968). Behavior therapy in groups. In *Basic Approaches to Group Psychotherapy and Group Counselling,* ed. G. M. Gazda. Springfield, IL: Charles C Thomas.

LoPiccolo, J., and Friedman, J. M. (1985). Broad spectrum treatment of low sexual desire: integration of cognitive, behavioral and systemic therapy. In *Assessment and Treatment of Desire Disorders,* ed. S. Leiblum and R. Rosen. New York: Guilford.

Masters, W. H., and Johnson, V. E. (1966). *Human Sexual Response.* Boston: Little, Brown.

———— (1970). *Human Sexual Inadequacy.* Boston: Little, Brown.

Steiner, C. M. (1974). *Scripts People Live.* New York: Grove.

Wolpe, J. (1958). *Psychotherapy by Reciprocal Inhibition.* Stanford, CA: Stanford University Press.

Zilbergeld, B. (1978). *Male Sexuality.* New York: Bantam.

14

BORDERLINE
PERSONALITY
DISORDER

Mary Anne Layden

INTRODUCTION

Cognitive therapy began as a treatment for depression and then quickly expanded to treat most other Axis I disorders. Since that time, cognitive therapy has shown itself to be rich and robust enough to expand to treat Axis II disorders as well as other kinds of problems.

The cognitive model of Axis II disorders involves three main elements: cognitions and overdeveloped and underdeveloped behaviors. The cognitions can include automatic thoughts, assumptions, and schema. The overdeveloped behaviors are compensatory strategies and the underdeveloped behaviors are missing life skills.

Automatic thoughts are at the most superficial level of thinking, involving rapid flashes of thoughts and pictures triggered by situations in which there is vulnerability. An example is thinking, "I'm failing," when you see all the work to be done on your desk. Assumptions are the conditional rules for living, which are learned through experiences, family, and societal socialization. An example would be believing, "Unless I do everything perfectly, I'm a failure." The cognitions that are the main focus of Axis II treatment are the schema. They are usually trauma-generated, unconditional, severely dysfunctional, extremely resistant to change, and produce massive affective responses when activated. The trauma can be physical, emotional, or sexual abuse or massively inappropriate parenting. An example of a schema might be, "I am completely and totally defective as a person."

The overdeveloped behavioral elements of Axis II treatment include compensatory strategies, which are coping skills developed by children to deal with the life situations in which they find themselves. Children may be in untenable situations, such as living with an alcoholic and abusive parent, experiencing sexual abuse, or living in an environment that has unspoken rules that negate the basic psychological health needs of the child. None of these are situations that children are able to get "under control," but children will try. Any strategy that works part of the time or even appears to work will often be reused rigidly. As adults, these individuals may still be relying on an extremely limited number of compensatory strategies that are overdeveloped and therefore are applied in situations in which they work and in situations in which they don't. Often these strategies, which were developed to ward off bad outcomes, produce the very bad outcomes that they were meant to prevent. When they don't produce the desired outcome, instead of trying a different strategy, the patient often decides that "they just didn't do it enough." They think they needed to do it "harder, faster, wider, deeper." So instead of giving up on behaviors that aren't working, they increase the use of the strategy when it is failing. As adults, the schema beliefs and compensatory strategies are still being activated in situations that psychologically resemble the childhood experiences.

The last element in Axis II treatment is the underdeveloped behaviors, which are life skills. Children raised by dysfunctional parents or in dysfunctional home situations did not learn many basic life skills, such as communication skills or problem-solving skills. To function in a fully healthful and adult way, the borderline patient must learn additional life skills. This allows flexibility so that coping skills can be chosen to maximize outcomes in each life situation encountered.

Axis II treatment involves accessing the schema and the compensatory strategies of the patient and restructuring them to include more accurate and functional beliefs and behaviors. It also means teaching missing life skills. All of this is done in an environment in which these new beliefs and behaviors can be practiced and learned.

BORDERLINE PERSONALITY DISORDER

Borderline personality disorder (BPD) often perplexes both the therapist and the patient. It includes a large and confusing number of very troubling symptoms, including issues of abandonment, unstable and intense relationships, identity disturbance, impulsive self-harming, suicidal and self-mutilating behavior, affective instability, feelings of emptiness, inappropriate anger, and paranoid and dissociative symptoms.

The cognitive conceptualization of BPD includes the same three elements as general Axis II conceptualization: schema, compensatory strategies, and missing healthy life skills. The typical schema of BPD patients includes abandonment, mistrust, defectiveness, incompetence, entitlement, and deprivation (Layden et al. 1993).

The typical compensatory strategies of BPD patients include avoidance, aggression, dependency, control, self-harming, "no talk–no feel" rules, and hypervigilance. These behaviors arise in response to the schema beliefs of the borderline patient. For example, when they were children, often their thoughts and feelings were invalidated and they got the message either that their thoughts and feelings were wrong and bad or that it was wrong and bad to express them. These "no talk–no feel" rules made it impossible for the child to develop a healthy self-knowledge and self-esteem. They didn't know who they were; they didn't recognize their own healthy needs or know how to ask for their needs to be met. Trauma often produces beliefs that no one can be trusted or that everyone will leave. In adult situations the childhood beliefs and behaviors are reactivated. This produces the "confusion of then with now" and adds to the reenactment of the childhood trauma by adults.

In addition, for BPD patients, the trauma has been encoded not only as content but also as a specific type of processing. The adult borderline not only still believes the childhood trauma conclusions, but processes information in these areas with cognitive strategies that are appropriate for children. They continue to use sensory motor and preoperational cognitive processing strategies on adult schema information, which maintains the beliefs. These more primitive processing skills often make the borderline patient appear incomprehensible to the therapist. Many times the patients find themselves incomprehensible as well.

The child who is abused and is developing dysfunctional and rigid coping strategies is not learning healthy life skills. They don't learn healthy communication skills, predicting skills, problem-solving skills, social skills, skills for judging whom to trust, parenting skills, assertiveness skills, self-knowledge, emotion-modulation skills, self-soothing skills, and so on. Lack of these skills causes them to involve themselves in inappropriate situations or to respond in inappropriate ways. Often they find themselves in real crisis situations that have been produced or exacerbated by the lack of healthy life skills.

The following is a list of goals for treatment of borderline personality disorder. The steps are roughly in order of presentation but a number of the steps will be repeated many times throughout the treatment and be integrated with other steps.

GOALS FOR COGNITIVE THERAPY OF BORDERLINE PERSONALITY DISORDER

1. Take a thorough history.
2. Reduce self-harming behavior and suicidality.
3. Increase self-soothing, coping, and pleasurable behaviors.
4. Teach basic life skills such as organization skills to handle mail, cleaning.
5. Teach advanced life skills such as problem solving, communication, parenting, decision making, boundary setting, emotion modulation, and relationship skills.
6. Identify schema beliefs.
7. Identify the childhood situations that produced these beliefs.
8. Identify the schema belief as an internal voice that is not one's real voice.
9. Identify whose voice it really is.
10. Encourage the patient's real voice.
11. Identify the behavior that was learned in childhood to cope with childhood situations and the beliefs those situations produced.
12. Separate then from now. What part of the current situation is similar to the old situation and acting as a trigger? What is different but not noticed?
13. Discuss other ways of behaving.
14. Practice the new behavioral life skills.

15. Verbalize the new life rules and schema from the behavioral experiments.
16. Explore identity issues.
17. Restructure images that carry schema using, for example, mental imagery, smells, and objects.

The conceptualization of this difficult disorder is complex. Treatment of the abused and confused patient by the perplexed therapist can produce less than desirable results. Understanding the cognitive and behavioral structure not only can clarify the conceptualization, but also can help to map the pathway to health.

EARLY STAGE OF THERAPY

Presenting Problems

Sophia is a 29-year-old white female who is divorced and currently works as a civil servant for the U.S. Postal Service in Philadelphia. She presented for therapy upon her release from the hospital after a ten-day stay. Her treating psychiatrist suggested she needed both individual outpatient treatment and group treatment arranged in order for her to be released. The psychiatrist referred her to me.

It was Christmastime and she told me her life at home was in disarray. She was living at home with her mother and father after her divorce. Her room, like her life, was a "disaster area." She had unopened mail dating back several months. She had bills that were unpaid. Her position at work was very tenuous because of her erratic performance. Her work was not consistently high quality, she was often late arriving to work, and she frequently didn't go to work at all. Typically she would wake up late, feel tired and/or depressed, and either not go to work or arrive late. When she awoke she would think either that she was sick (including PMS or having a heavy period) or have entitlement thoughts that she deserved to stay home and read. Her supervisor had become unsympathetic over time and her job was at risk.

In our first session we talked about the holiday that was near and what small things she could do to get into the spirit. She decided that getting some holiday candles that looked and smelled festive would help. We also discussed what she could initiate now that would make her life feel more under control and more pleasant. Cleaning her room was a natural choice. We discussed it in very specific detail. She could get boxes or bags and sort the paper materials into them. She could set up her computer, which she found very interesting. These small projects began our work in the learning of life skills and self-soothing behaviors.

The next week she came back and her mood was improved. She had cleaned her room and it did make her feel better. The candles seemed a nice touch. Thus began the path that Sophia and I would walk for the next two and one half years.

Developmental History

Her history began to unfold at the beginning of therapy. She was the oldest of three daughters. Her father was a physician and her mother was a housewife. Her father was foreign born, having come to the States from the Middle East as a young man. He came from a culture that was quite disparaging of women and he had expanded that sentiment considerably. He was an angry, hypercritical, negative man. He constantly belittled his wife, his daughters, and life in general. He seemed elitist in his attitudes, showing deference only to high-status medical personnel. He considered all other careers and people inferior and they received sarcastic and caustic remarks. He held 99 percent of the world in contempt and was very vocal about it. Sophia's mother was passive and avoidant in the face of this atmosphere. She would not challenge her husband's rude and hostile remarks directed toward her or her daughters.

The mother developed a sisterly relationship with Sophia. They would do activities together, such as going to movies. If they rented movies to watch at home, the mother and daughter would watch and the father would make disparaging remarks about the movies and the kinds of people who would watch them.

During Sophia's earlier years the father's remarks were also directed at Sophia for the way she looked. He ridiculed her in her teenage sexual development and commented negatively about her body. Despite the fact that Sophia is a pleasant-looking female, she became self-conscious about her body and developed a very negative body image. She is 10 pounds above typical weight and she has magnified the negativity of this.

The combination of the aggressive and emotionally abusive father and the passive mother left Sophia with schema of defectiveness/unlovability, incompetence, powerlessness, and mistrust. She took on the critical internal voice that was initiated with her father and the passive behavior of her mother. She began to mistrust others who in any way acted like her father, leaving her with compensatory strategies of avoidance and aggression toward herself and others. She responded to activation of the mistrust schema with aggressive outbursts. If someone at work or a friend would say something that made Sophia feel incompetent or unlovable, she would rage. Sometimes the rage reaction was verbal. At work she would get activated and yell, curse, or make extremely insulting remarks to co-workers who were seen as "crossing her." On other occasions she would act out with a behavioral version of this aggressive compensatory strategy. On one occasion she bought a gun in response to schema activation. She often had the impulse to buy a gun. When she felt powerless, a gun made her feel powerful. She would also buy alcohol and then drink and drive. She would get razor blades and have the urge to cut herself.

Compensatory Strategies

It is important as a first step in therapy to reduce the self-harming compensatory strategies. She agreed to tell me when she had an urge to cut or to get a gun. She kept that commitment and would call mid-week if she had razor blades. Each time she would agree to throw them away. In the beginning she would throw them away where she could retrieve them. She would then tell me she had retrieved them and we would work on how she could throw them away in such a way that she couldn't get them back. If she had an urge to get a gun, she would tell me. If she had purchased alcohol and had it in her car, she would tell me. She was always willing to pour out the alcohol. Once she came to a therapy session with the alcohol in the car. She poured it down the storm sewer before she drove home. We talked about things she could do when she was activated, such as call a friend. She had few pleasurable activities in her repertoire so we worked on this as well. She said she liked to be with a particular friend and the friend's child. So for homework she would have to spend time with them. She liked to ice skate but had given it up. So she was given homework to go skating with the friend and her child. This produced good results and she felt better when she had been skating.

Life Skills

Because her job was at risk, we very quickly intervened so that she wouldn't be fired. She told her boss she was working on the problem areas in therapy. We talked about what she could do to make sure she got to work each day. She wrote about the advantages of going to work rather than staying home. She had coping statements written on Post-it notes to help her remember her commitment to get to work. We also worked to make her daily habits more regular. She needed to get a lot of sleep, so the homework was to go to bed early and see what effect that would have on her morning routine. She loved to read and would often use reading as an escape. She decided that she could read all evening if she wanted and this would help satisfy her desire to read. She challenged the idea that staying home from work and reading would be a good decision. If she did stay home from work, she would check at the end of the day and see if she felt better by staying home. If she didn't want to go to work but did anyway, she again would check at the end of the day to see how she felt. Invariably, she felt better on the days that she went to work. She wrote in her therapy notebook about the consequences of staying home and of going to work.

Her performance on the job improved and her boss noticed her more consistent attendance. The boss as well as several co-workers commented on her performance, attendance, and clearly more pleasant mood. The stress from the threat of job loss was reduced.

Powerlessness Schema

We worked on her powerlessness by looking at what made her feel powerful. She said she felt powerful when she was riding a horse. So we started with homework of finding a place to ride a horse. She took up riding and it was a very functional way to feel powerful that didn't have the disadvantages of buying a gun. Next we added symbolic pieces. She would have a picture of a horse at her office and a plastic statue of a horse on her desk at work. If she became schema-activated, these images would help calm her down.

We added an item in another sense modality. Horses and the powerfulness they activated would be triggered by the smell of horses. This reaction could be triggered by the smell of sweaty leather. So she got a leather keyring and rubbed it on the palm of her hand until it took on this smell. She could deactivate a schema by smelling the sweaty leather.

So therapy began with reducing the self-harming, building life skills of coping and self-soothing, reducing the crisis of job threat, and identifying and challenging schema. The first six months of therapy focused mostly on these things.

MIDDLE STAGE OF THERAPY

Life Skills

Communication skills were needed. Sophia would get activated by something a friend or co-worker would do and she would lash out verbally. She had learned from her father how to be verbally caustic. She would use that "voice" only when she was schema-activated. Later she could begin to see that what she was experiencing was schema activation. We worked on identifying the similarities between the current activating situation and the emotional abuse she received as a child. We also examined in what ways the current situation was different from the abuse situation. This is called *separating then from now*. This would cause Sophia to calm down about what had happened and begin to see it differently. In the early stage of therapy she had no idea what she could do or say to rectify the situation. She didn't have communication skills or even the belief that it might be a good idea to go back and talk to the person she had verbally abused. This was not how they did things in her family. At home, vulnerability led to verbal attack by her father. So Sophia and I would discuss what she could say and then we would practice. It never occurred to her to say she was sorry. She would not know how to do it even if it had occurred to her. When the idea was first raised, she seemed quizzical as to how that might help. Then she quickly became defensive as it activated the belief that she was wrong and was being judged. This implied that she was defective. To reduce the schema activation, I continued to encourage her to distance herself from the internal critical voice who encouraged her to lash out at herself and others. I would say, "Who is it that's speaking? It's not you. You don't talk like that." When she would identify it as her father, I would ask, "Do you want your father inside your head, coming out of your mouth, verbally attacking your friends and co-workers? Tell him to leave." Then we would practice how to say "I'm sorry." After she would try out the new behavior, she would report back in therapy how she had done and what reaction she had received. We would summarize and draw conclusions and new rules. Often her friends and co-workers were kind, warm, and responsive to her apologies. She was very surprised that they seemed to like her more. This was unanticipated by Sophia. She also felt closer to them, which was a surprise too. This would be an opportunity to describe the overall conceptualization.

"When you were a child, your father would attack you and criticize you. He might say, 'You're stupid and ugly.' He would try to make himself feel better by making himself one-up and you one-down. You came to expect that people were hurters and that you shouldn't trust them. Of course you would. You were a child and your parents were the whole world to you. That makes sense to me. You tried to cope with the attack as best you could. But you were a child and didn't have a lot of resources. Sometimes you would fight back and sometimes you would get passive. You came to see yourself as defective and powerless because these strategies wouldn't always stop your father's attacks.

"So now, as an adult, when someone acts in a way that makes you feel as if your father is here again, you automatically go into the strategies you learned then. You believe that these current people are hurters and that you should fluff up all your fur and make growly noises to scare them away. You talk as your father talked. But these friends are not like your father. You don't have to attack them to keep yourself safe. If you are real with these friends, they won't hurt you. If some people do hurt you when you're vulnerable, you can decide if you want to have them in your life. You have power now that you didn't have when you were a child."

MISTRUST AND DEFECTIVENESS/UNLOVABILITY SCHEMA

Sophia's relationships with men were not healthy. Her ex-husband was a man with whom she had nothing in common. She would typically be drawn to men who were caustic, critical, and narcissistic. These men were like her father and felt familiar. One such man, Stan, was the office Lothario. He would pursue many females and make sexual remarks to them at work. He also made sexually degrading remarks about women in general or particular women at work. He began to pursue her and she liked the attention even though she knew there were things about Stan that she found very distasteful. He seemed familiar in his narcissism and hostility toward women, but she was attracted by his pursuing of her. She thought she would get it right this time. He wanted her to go away with him for a weekend and she considered going. She was concerned enough by his behavior that she put off the decision. He then relented and suggested they should go away with a group, which she thought would be safer.

To me, Stan seemed very threatening. He had invited her to

his apartment and had pushed for sexual contact, which Sophia didn't want. He left pornography around his apartment. He asked her to share her prescription medication with him, which she did. He had been sexually harassing women at work. I had the suspicion that if she went away with him, she would be the victim of some strong coercion or rape. I was very strong in my suggestion that she rethink her decision to go. The session went extra long until she agreed that she would call her friend and discuss the decision with her. We both knew that the friend was very much against Stan.

She decided not to go on that weekend, but later did go on a group weekend with Stan. She felt she was now armed and prepared to fend off his advances. She had some limited sexual contact with him on the weekend, however, which later upset her because it violated her principles. This wounded her self-esteem and we had to talk again about the lessons she had learned. She then decided not to have any more contact with him.

She had another relationship with Frank, a man who lived in another state whom she met when they were both hospitalized in Philadelphia. He seemed a somewhat better choice than Stan, sweet and shy but still quite depressed and dysfunctional. He could not get his life on track. They had some interests in common and he showed some interest in her but said he couldn't have a relationship right then because he was too depressed. On an impulse she went to spend a weekend with him. They had a good time and he was respectful of her boundaries. No unwanted sexual activity occurred. They shared pleasant experiences and spent time playing with his dog, which they both loved. During the weekend her purse was stolen and Frank was very helpful and calming, supportive and problem solving. She admired this in him and felt grateful for his kindness. Together they worked out a plan so that she could get money and get home. Despite these good qualities, Frank still suffered greatly from his psychological problems.

He was unable to work or go to school. His daily functioning was impaired and even basic household activities were beyond him. Even though he was not an ideal choice for Sophia, he was less like her father than Stan. Frank and Sophia stayed in phone and letter contact but did not pursue the relationship any further. This was good progress in the relationship area for the middle stage of therapy.

Her defectiveness/unlovability schema was also softened considerably by her love of animals and their love of her. She could respond to their unconditional affection and would love them back. She had to curb her impulsive behavior in this area as she would adopt and purchase dogs she could not care for or could not financially afford. However, there were tremendous advantages to playing with the dogs and birds she had and taking responsibility for their care. Walking them encouraged her exercising. Petting and cuddling them met some of her physical needs.

Incompetence Schema

Work was one area in which Sophia got information about her competence, but it was not the most significant area because she didn't see her work as a postal employee as meaningful to her self-image. In her second year of treatment she began to take college courses. She already had a college degree, but the courses she now chose were in linguistics, which she greatly enjoyed. She had a talent for language. The idea that course topics could be picked because they were a joy was new to Sophia. Despite her love of the work and her deep enjoyment of the class sessions, she had difficulty being persistent when things were tough. If she fell behind in her homework, reading, and so forth, she would avoid class and miss exams. The first course she took in linguistics showed this pattern and she didn't complete it. We discussed the possibility of talking to the professor and asking to make up the material. Her power-lessness schema, mistrust schema, and incompetence schema all came together to work against this plan. She thought that the plan would fail; that the teacher would be angry, judgmental, and critical; and that she was really too stupid and too out of control to produce a positive outcome from this talk with the professor. We talked about advantages and disadvantages and what the worst outcome would be. Did she have any evidence that the professor was really more kind than she was predicting? Whose image was she seeing in this professor? She decided to give the plan a try. The professor was very receptive and had been particularly struck by Sophia's love and enthusiasm for the material. They worked out a plan for Sophia to attend the final sessions of the course the next semester and to take the missed exams. The next semester Sophia did make up the work and finished the course with an A. She was very proud that she had persisted. We summarized the rules and lessons of this experience, looking at what beliefs and compensatory strategies she started with, where they came from, what she did differently, and what new rules and strategies she now had. The summary of the lessons learned was vital and was recorded in her therapy notebook.

Sophia later went on to take language courses in French, in which she did well because of her strong language skill. She also took courses in photography, in which she showed a tremendous artistic sense, a talent for line, form, color, and composition. She decided she would like to photograph dogs. The pleasure and enthusiasm she got from this was fanned by the positive feedback she got from the professor. She began to think of the possibility of an international career and/or a career as a photographer. Her self-esteem soared as did her optimism. The incompetence schema was being washed away by the experiences that challenged her old beliefs and strategies.

LATE STAGE OF THERAPY

Compensatory Strategies

During the second year of treatment a new self-harming behavior emerged: overspending. She had a problem with spending before, but this time it was considerably worse. She had worked to reduce her debt at the beginning of therapy to almost zero at the end of six months of treatment. Then she took a dream-of-a-lifetime trip to France with her sister, which caused her entitlement schema to be activated; she felt that she needed and deserved to have new luggage, top-level travel accommodations, and so forth. This set off a spending spree. If she thought that a particular purchase was good and psychologically healthy for her, then she deserved that purchase and ought to make it even if she didn't have the money. She charged books on tape, college courses, computer materials, and more. Many of these were to excess. She had ordered more books on tape than she could ever have time to listen to. "I'm entitled to pleasure so I can charge as many books on tape as I want even if I don't have time to listen to the ones that I have. Taking courses is a good thing so I am entitled to charge my tuition." This was also fueled by the charge card company's strategy of sending unsolicited cards. When she received a charge card in the mail, she considered it a compliment. She thought it meant that this company trusted her and felt she should have all the credit she wanted. She rationalized that the cards were protection for emergencies. She quickly accumulated six charge cards and in nine months had $13,000 of credit card debt—50 percent of what she earned in a year. This occurred despite the fact that she pays no rent or utilities to her parents for living at home and doesn't pay for her therapy. She resisted the suggestion to cut up the cards; learning to pay cash was a hard task.

Life Skills

Sophia continued to progress at work and her boss was pleasantly surprised by her consistency. During the second year of treatment we worked on her getting to work on time, which she was able to improve tremendously with a number of strategies. She would make a breakfast date with a friend to meet and eat in the cafeteria at work. She would listen to tapes on the way to work. We talked about the possible consequences of her speeding and erratic driving as she rushed to get to work. She created an image of having hit a child or a dog and how she would feel about that. She got positive feedback from her boss about her improved arrival time. She noted that she didn't start her day feeling frantic, which had a positive impact on her productivity. She also concluded that having gotten this long-standing problem under control was a sign of a positive personal attribute. All of these conclusions were written in her notebook to help reinforce them.

An important life skill for borderline patients to learn is boundary setting. Hypercritical parents engage in emotional boundary crossing. The hypercritical parent presents as emotionally intrusive and invalidating. The need to set limits on those who are hurtful is difficult but vital for continued improvement. As time went on, it became clear that Sophia needed to spend less time with her father. She reduced the contact and also began to refuse to accept his comments. He still had some ability to wound her, however, and her best strategy was to remove herself from the room if he started to make hostile comments. Not being around him at all was more insurance.

Defectiveness/Unlovability and Mistrust Schema

Sophia improved in the area of relationships by picking Peter, a man who is in every way different from her father. He is very honest, open, and tender. He loves animals and children. He is very responsible. Although he doesn't make a lot of money, he does work that he loves. He never seems to express his anger in caustic or critical ways, and seems a much better choice for Sophia. She has gotten farther away from her father with each relationship choice.

Unfortunately, the depth of feeling and intimacy of this healthy relationship activated her defectiveness/unlovability schema and sense of vulnerability. This activated the old compensatory strategies. If Peter acted in a way that made her feel rejected, Sophia would get activated. Once, talking to her on the phone, he received a call-waiting beep to which he responded. When he came back on the line he told Sophia that it was an old girlfriend who was upset about a death in the family, and that he would call Sophia back. He called in a reasonable length of time, but Sophia was highly schema-activated by that. She felt mistrust of Peter and unlovable because he had "chosen" his old girlfriend. She verbally trounced him. She called me in panic because she was sure she had ruined the relationship and thought maybe she should not ever be in a relationship.

We talked though the schema activation. What beliefs were triggered? Whose voice was speaking in the tongue-lashing she gave Peter? What could she do now? It was decided that she should call Peter, tell him what happened, and apologize. The relationship grew closer and more intimate. Later we discussed how intimacy is developed not by lack of conflict but by conflict resolution.

CONCLUSION

Sophia has currently been in treatment for two and a half years. She comes in once a month and we are about to move to a six-week schedule. Work and relationships are going well;

spending, drinking, gun purchasing, and cutting are under control. She spends little time with her father. She is considering marriage to Peter and may want to have a child. Her communication skills are much improved, though she will continue to work on these. Her problem-solving behavior is better, but work will continue in this area as well. She gets to work consistently and on time. Her self-soothing skills and her pleasure skills are much improved.

I never use the term *remission* when speaking of borderline patients. I believe that what we are working for is a patient who, if he or she presented for therapy now, would no longer be diagnosed as having borderline personality disorder. I believe that is true of Sophia. I suspect that in the future her functioning will be even better as the benefits continue to accrue.

REFERENCE

Layden, M. A., Newman, C., Freeman, A., and Morse, S. (1993). *Cognitive Therapy of Borderline Personality Disorder.* Needham, MA: Allyn & Bacon.

15

PSYCHOTIC DISORDERS

Rhonda S. Karg
Brad A. Alford

COGNITIVE THERAPY OF PSYCHOTIC DISORDERS

A substantive body of research has shown cognitive therapy to be an effective treatment for a broad scope of clinical disorders. This widespread applicability has led to studies investigating its possible adaptation to assessing and treating more chronic disorders, including delusions and schizophrenia (Alford and Correia 1994, Chadwick and Lowe 1990, Morrison 1994, Morrison et al. in press). The purpose of this chapter is to illustrate the application of selected principles of cognitive therapy to psychotic symptomatology and discuss a series of investigations into applying cognitive therapy and theory to psychotic symptoms, such as those found in schizophrenia. We conclude by exploring the implications of these findings and providing directions for future research.

PSYCHOTIC SYMPTOMATOLOGY

States of psychosis are typified by distortions of reality. The capacity to perceive, process, and respond to environment—internal and external—becomes so impaired that persons are rendered unable to function adaptively. Individuals may have hallucinations or delusions or may withdraw to the point where they are generally unaffected by external events. The delusions and hallucinations are often held with extraordinary conviction, have bizarre or impossible content, and are frequently thought to be impervious to counterargument or the impact of experience. Psychotic episodes may be psychopharmacologically induced (e.g., through abusing amphetamines, LSD, cocaine, alcohol, or other chemicals), or may result from brain injuries or disease. But most commonly, psychosis appears in the form of schizophrenia. In fact, one of every 100 people worldwide meets the *DSM* criteria for schizophrenia (Gottesman 1991). We will focus primarily, but not exclusively, on this specific psychotic disorder.

Assessment

Because of the severe level of impairment, clinical assessment of psychotic disorders should identify the individual's strengths in addition to problems or disabilities. Assessment should address all aspects of personal and social functioning, from molecular to molar levels of analysis. Standardized assessment measures (see Chatwick et al. 1996, Spaulding 1994) can provide important information regarding the nature of the symptoms, the accompanying emotional reactions, the antecedents, the consequences, and the effectiveness of cognitive or behavioral coping strategies.

One critical variable to be measured in psychotic patients is the degree to which they hold a specific delusional belief to be valid (Alford and Beck 1994). Also known as conviction ratings, this can be assessed using a subjective rating scale, ranging from zero to 100 percent. Interestingly, the interview in and of itself will, in many cases, reduce conviction ratings (see Hole et al. 1979).

During the first few sessions, an inventory of the patient's problems should be obtained with the focus on the assessment of areas of functioning, and on what the patient can realistically expect to achieve, rather than on symptoms. Whenever possible, symptoms are reformulated in terms of problems to be solved while attempting to increase the patient's awareness of the possible relationship between his or her symptomatology and problems in other areas of social functioning.

The following excerpt from an assessment interview (Perris 1992) illustrates the problem-focused nature of the evaluation and demonstrates the integration of cognitive and behavioral principles (as in Beck 1970). In this case example the therapist collects information both on the presenting problem (lack of a place to live) and on the reasons the patient is currently homeless (a paranoid attitude toward the neighbors). Also, the therapist can recognize the patient's lack of appropriate skills for renting an apartment.

TH: What is your major problem right now?
PT: I don't have any place to live in. I must get a flat or something.
TH: Have you ever lived on your own?
PT: Oh, yes! I have rented a flat on several occasions.
TH: Why is it that you don't have any right now?
PT: Well . . . It was every time the same problem . . . The other tenants in the houses where I lived were hostile.
TH: How did they manifest their hostility?
PT: They made noises to disturb me . . . You know . . . I'm sure that they were spying on me.
TH: Has it been a similar pattern in all the places where you have lived?

PT: It's become worse during the last few years . . . I've had to change apartments at least three times.

TH: Did you have any difficulty in changing apartments?

PT: Well . . . no . . . People at the social welfare have fixed it for me.

TH: Would you be able to get a new apartment by yourself?

PT: I don't know . . . I never tried.

TH: Well, let me summarize. It seems to me that you have voiced three different problems. The first is that you need a new flat to live in. Second, you experience hostility from the other tenants at the places where you live. And, third, you would have some difficulty in trying by yourself to rent a new flat. Right?

PT: It seems so.

TH: Would it help you if we worked together on all three of those problems?

PT: I don't know. . . . What I need is a new flat where nobody will disturb me.

TH: Okay. We will give the issue of getting a flat a top priority. On the other hand, how would you feel if this time everything went well and you did not get into further trouble with your neighbors?

PT: I would feel great.

TH: Do you think it would help if we looked together at what happened on the previous occasions?

PT: If you say so.

TH: It would be nice if we could look a little closer at your opinions about the behavior of your neighbors to see if there is any solution suitable for you. Also, you could devote part of your time while here at the center in training how to rent a flat when in need. That would make you even more independent in the future. [pp. 22–23]*

---

*Copyright © 1992 by Jossey-Bass and reprinted by permission.

The Clinical Picture of Schizophrenia

Among people who are diagnosed with schizophrenia, there is considerable variation in symptoms, course of the disorder, and responsiveness to treatment. In fact, schizophrenia is probably a group of many distinct brain disorders that share some common features. *DSM-IV* (1994), however, now classifies schizophrenia as a single disorder with numerous faces.

To illustrate the range and variety of forms schizophrenia may take, let us consider the following accounts by three people diagnosed as having it. These cases are taken from the files of E. Fuller Torrey, M.D., a prominent specialist on schizophrenia (1995).

"For about seven years—except during sleep—I have never had a single moment in which I did not hear voices. They accompany me to every place and at all times; they continue to sound even when I am in conversation with other people, they persist undeterred even when I concentrate on other things, for instance read a book or a newspaper, play the piano, etc.; only when I am talking aloud to other people or to myself are they of course drowned by the stronger sound of the spoken word and therefore inaudible to me." [p. 61]

"Sometimes I did not know clearly whether it was she or I who needed something. For instance if I asked for another cup of tea and Mamma answered teasingly, "But why do you want more tea; don't you see that I have just finished my cup and so you don't need any?" Then I replied, "Yes, that's true. I don't need any more," confusing her with myself. But at bottom I did desire a second cup of tea, and I said, "But I still want some more tea," and suddenly, in a flash, I realized the fact that Mamma's satiety did not make me satiated, too. And I was ashamed to let myself be thus trapped and to watch her laugh at my discomfort." [p. 64]

"It was evening and I was walking along the beach near my college in Florida. Suddenly my perceptions shifted. The inten-

sifying wind became an omen of something terrible. I could feel
it becoming stronger and stronger; I was sure it was going to
capture me and sweep me away with it. Nearby trees bent
threateningly toward me and tumbleweeds chased me. I became very frightened and began to run. However, though I knew
I was running, I was making no progress. I seemed suspended in
space and time." [p. 37]

Among these three individuals a range of psychotic symptoms is demonstrated: disturbance in content of thought, form
of thought, perception and attention, sense of self, relationship
to the outside world, and volition. As in the cases of these
patients, most patients with schizophrenia suffer with disturbances that are severe and chronic in nature. However, findings
have accumulated suggesting the possibility that cognitive
therapy may be a useful treatment for this population. In fact,
a number of studies have demonstrated positive outcomes in
the treatment of these relatively persistent conditions (e.g.,
Alford 1986, Chadwick and Lowe 1990, Harrow and Miller 1980,
Hole et al. 1979). In the ensuing pages we consider the current
application of clinical cognitive theory to these psychotic
disturbances.

Disturbances in Content of Thought

Disorders of content of thought—the most common of which
are delusions—are usually found in patients with schizophrenia. These abnormal beliefs have been defined as severe
maladaptive cognitive constructions of internal or external
phenomena that lead to negative (harmful) consequences
(Alford and Beck 1994). Delusions are typically held with
extraordinary conviction, have bizarre or impossible content,
and are resistant to counterargument or the impact of experience.

Several investigations have demonstrated the successful application of cognitive therapy to these disturbances in content of thought. Credited as the first to describe the use of reasoning techniques in the treatment of delusional thinking and beliefs (Kingdon and Turkington 1991), Beck's 1954 study involved a 28-year-old World War II veteran who presented with chief complaints that fifty men, many of whom had been in his outfit overseas, were currently being employed by the FBI to investigate him. To secretly observe his speech and behavior, he believed they had concealed an elaborate system of microphones that had the capability of recording all that he said, and perhaps even record his thoughts. They were trying to build up some case against him, the substance of which was unknown to him.

Treatment included thirty sessions over an eight-month period. Although the patient had suffered from this delusion for several years, he was eventually able to "distance" himself from his autistic productions (Beck 1954). Beck credited this success to the establishment of a therapeutic relationship and active listening to the patient's past experiences in which others had belittled and ridiculed him. In the early phases of treatment Beck employed a supportive, nondirective approach. As time progressed, however, the focus of therapy turned to the paranoid thoughts and their relation to external stress, emotions, and delusional beliefs.

Chadwick and Lowe (1990), likewise, tested the effectiveness of cognitive therapy with deluded patients. Using a multiple-baseline, across-subjects design, they studied six individuals diagnosed with chronic schizophrenia. The first phase of treatment included preliminary interviewing, which served the dual functions of establishing rapport and specifying the belief to be modified. During the second phase they gathered baseline data regarding the delusional beliefs. Measures included conviction ratings, preoccupation (frequency of delusional ideation), and anxiety associated with the delusional beliefs.

Ratings on these three measures were made by each patient for each belief at the close of each session through the study.

Two interventions were used: (1) a structured verbal challenge and (2) a reality test in which the belief was subjected to an empirical test. During the verbal challenge the experimenter suggested the delusional belief to be "only one possible interpretation of events." Rather than indicating the patient's beliefs to be incorrect, the experimenters simply asked the patients to consider critically (or compare) the interpretations proved by the experimenter and the interpretation originally held by the patient. In an apparent attempt to develop metacognitive skills, patients were told how initial beliefs determine future processing of evidence. When the verbal challenges were not persuasive, "reality testing" was conducted to test the patient's beliefs empirically. Of the six patients, two completely rejected their beliefs and three others had substantially reduced conviction ratings following the interventions. After a six-month follow-up, there was evidence that the cognitive interventions had enabled five of the six to effectively regulate their delusional thinking (Chadwick and Lowe 1990).

Disturbances in Form of Thought (Process)

In addition to thought content, disturbances in the production and organization of thought often accompanies schizophrenia. People who manifest process disturbances often experience intrusive thoughts—sudden and unintentional cognitions. Often these are accompanied by the delusional belief that the thoughts are being inserted into his or her mind by others.

Disorders in form are also manifested by speech pathology, such as pressured speech, tangential thought or looseness of associations, poverty of speech, mutism, neologism, echolalia, or perseverance. For example, the great Russian dancer Nijinsky wrote the following as he was developing schizophrenia, jumping from the round shape of a stage to his eye:

> "I am not artificial. I am life. The theatre is not life. I know the customs of the theatre. The theatre becomes a habit. Life does not. I do not like the theatre with a square stage. I like a round stage. I will build a theatre which will have a round shape, like an eye. I like to look closely in the mirror and I see only one eye in my forehead." [Cited in Torrey 1995, p. 45]

In psychopathological conditions such as anxiety disorders, depressive disorders, manic episodes, paranoid states, obsessive-compulsive neurosis, and others, a systematic bias is introduced into processing of information. In the case of schizophrenia, the dominant shift is typically toward indiscriminate attribution of abuse or interference; this is particularly the case with patients who suffer from paranoid beliefs and disorders (Beck and Weishaar 1989). Consider the following example:

> "After a fight with my lover I thought he might be sending his friends to harass me. Things were rearranged in my apartment. Pages were missing from my journal. I got very frightened and moved out. I believed some people around me were warlocks." [Margaret House, as cited in Shavelson 1986]

In traditional cognitive therapy the patient's maladaptive interpretations and conclusions are treated as testable hypotheses. In the most general terms, cognitive therapy explores basic beliefs that are tested for their accuracy through the processes of empirical investigation, reality testing, and problem solving between the therapist and patient. In the case of schizophrenia, delusional beliefs are explored and are tested for their accuracy and adaptiveness. Behavioral experiments are used to examine alternative interpretations and to generate contradictory evidence that supports more adaptive beliefs and in turn leads to therapeutic change.

Because *challenging* beliefs has been found to produce negative reactions in some patients (e.g., Greenwood 1983), the cognitive therapist instead works with the patient to *test* beliefs. Using a Socratic stance and collaboratively testing the beliefs, the cognitive therapist asks questions such as, "Do other people seem to agree with you regarding [delusion]?" If the patient responds, "No," then the therapist might ask: "How do we account for that?" This dialogue would lead nicely into considering the evidence upon which the belief is based (Alford and Beck 1994).

This technique is demonstrated in a case reported by Tarrier (1992) in which a patient, Tom, believed that he must shout back and argue with the hallucinated voices to avoid being physically assaulted. Tom and the therapist agreed that Tom would put this delusion to a test. After only three days of treatment, "Tom agreed that he had not been attacked and although his belief in the voices being real was still strong, he felt greatly relieved and much less concerned for his own safety" (p. 163).

Disturbances in Perception and Attention

Perceptual disturbances are faulty interpretations of sensory functioning. An illusion is a false interpretation of a real perception and appears to be inconsistent with the true meaning of the corresponding external stimuli. A patient may experience a picture in a magazine as moving, or see the image of the "devil" in the face of a friend. In a similar vein, patients may selectively attend to redundant stimuli, perceiving it as having special meaning. The sound of a person coughing, for example, may be attended to and interpreted as an alert to looming danger. This heightened awareness of irrelevant stimuli is expressed by this patient in his own words.

> "If I do something like going for a drink of water, I've got to go over each detail—find cup, walk over, turn cap, fill cup, turn off tap, drink it. I keep building the same picture. I have to change the picture each time. I've got to make the old picture move. I can't concentrate. I can't hold things. Something else comes in; various things. It's easier if I stay still." [Torrey 1995, p. 44]

Hallucinations are experiences of perception in the absence of the actual relevant stimuli. They may take the form of auditory, visual, olfactory, tactile, or gustatory sensations. Auditory hallucinations, however, are by far the most common and have been estimated in 50 to 75 percent of patients with schizophrenia (Cromwell and Snyder 1993). Although the exact origins of such symptoms is uncertain, Bentall (1990a,b) and Bentall and colleagues (1994) suggest that both hallucinations and delusions may be experienced because internal events are attributed to an external source. Based on his findings, Bentall (1994b) purports that patients with schizophrenia appear to make abnormal attributions "to protect them against negatively self-referent information" (p. 339). He further notes:

> [I]t seems likely that these attributional biases are associated with complex abnormalities in the processing of information related to the self-concept. These observations can be accounted for by a model in which it is hypothesized that, in deluded patients, explicit activation of self-ideal discrepancies by threat-related information triggers defensive explanatory biases, which have the function of reducing the self-ideal discrepancies but result in persecutory ideation. [p. 339]

In a case involving a 38-year-old patient with auditory hallucinations, Morrison's (1994) study was consistent with

Bentall's (1990a,b). As described by Morrison, "The vicious cycle between thoughts, misattribution as voices, subsequent appraisal and its affective, somatic, and behavioral consequences is consistent with the view that auditory hallucinations result from the attribution of internal events to an external source" (p. 262). These investigators (Bentall 1990b, Morrison 1994) have suggested that the decrease in discomfort following the misattribution of hostile or unacceptable thoughts may be responsible for the maintenance of this process. Thus it is possible that this may be annulled by education about the nature of intrusive thoughts. This could be accomplished by modifying the appraisal by making the thoughts more acceptable (see Morrison 1994).

Collaboration and the Self Concept

Closely allied with delusions and hallucinations is another cluster of symptoms characteristic of many patients with schizophrenia, namely, misconceptions and unclarities regarding the identity of the self. Alterations in their sense of self may range from somatic perceptual distortions (e.g., "I saw myself in different bodies") to, on the other end of the spectrum, confusion in distinguishing one's self from another person, as in the case previously mentioned in which the patient confused her desire for more tea with that of her mother. The altered sense of self may be further aggravated if hallucinations of touch or delusions about the body are also problems.

Typically, our sense of self is formed by a complex set of tactile and visual stimuli through which we can feel and see the limits of our own body and by which we differentiate it from the objects around us. It is likely that the same disease process that alters the senses and cognitive processes is also responsible for the altered sense of self. The disturbed sense of self typically found in schizophrenia results in special problems in developing a collaborative empirical approach to treatment. For example, in acknowledging the presence of psychotic symptoms there is the risk of lowering the patient's self-esteem. The case of Jack (presented below) shows how patients with schizophrenia typically experience great fear in becoming cognizant of the extent of their cognitive distortions of reality.

The overall strategies of cognitive therapy involve a collaborative enterprise between the patient and the therapist to explore dysfunctional interpretations and to modify them when they are unrealistic or unreasonable. This "collaborative empiricism" views the patient as a practical scientist who adapts by interpreting stimuli, but who has been temporarily thwarted by distortions in his or her own information-gathering and integrating apparatus. As presented in Alford and Beck (1994), the nature of psychotic symptoms creates special problems in developing this collaborative, working therapeutic relationship. Persons suffering from psychotic disorders typically experience severe interpersonal difficulties secondary to their extremely distorted view of themselves, the world, and other people.

Consider the following case of "Jack" (Alford and Beck 1994). During the initial session Jack described a long history of obviously paranoid beliefs that had created significant problems in his adjustment to both past and present environments. In reviewing this patient's history, it was discovered that he had dropped out of medical school largely because of a belief that professors were "talking about" him and were, in his words, "after me—trying to get something on me." When Jack sought treatment, similar cognitions were triggered, endangering his current employment. He was apparently convinced that these same people who had earlier been "after" him had now located him, even though he had intentionally moved hundreds of miles from his previous location. In his mind they were "monitoring my every move," and special federal agents were involved. In fact, he even personalized specific billboards that had recently been erected, thinking they were intended to communicate to him, "You have been found."

One central problem in attempting to establish a collaborative relationship was that initially Jack appeared completely convinced that these various agencies and persons were indeed plotting against him. (It was soon clear, however, that his convictions were not actually as high as originally reported.) When asked about his chief complaint during the initial consultation, Jack reported, "I need someone to help me cope with the stress caused by these people."

To pose an alternative, mutually agreeable agenda, the therapist suggested the goal of first evaluating the evidence that there was, in fact, such a threat. If such a threat was discovered, then the therapist and patient would collectively explore possible courses of action for those persons responsible for the alleged harassment. At that point the following conversation (Alford and Beck 1994) took place:

TH: How would you feel about adding that [an exploration of the beliefs] as an agenda item or goal for our collaborative efforts?

PT: I don't know. . . . I would not want to find that it was all me.

TH: What do you mean?

PT: I think that would be worse than finding out that there is a conspiracy.

TH: It would seem to me that you would not really want all those agencies and people after you. Wouldn't that be a bigger problem?

PT: Not really. I would not want to find out I've been the cause of all this.

TH: How would you feel if you did find that to be the case?

PT (*hesitating, tears in eyes*): I would be afraid.
TH: Of what?
PT: It would mean that I've *really* got a problem. [p. 374]

Metacognition and Resistance

Jack's recognition of the discrepancy between beliefs and reality indicates the emerging activation of metacognitive processing, or distancing from thoughts. However, such processing can, in specific circumstances, result in the increased likelihood of resistance or countercontrol. More specifically, the activation of metacognitive processing can threaten the self concept if the content of such processing incorporates negative meanings (or attributions) concerning the self.

Adding to the impact of such metacognitive awareness, paranoid schizophrenia is characterized by anger, argumentativeness, and delusions or persecution by others (*DSM-IV* 1994). Due to the nature of these and other manifestations of psychosis, minimizing reactance can often be a demanding feat when treating this clinical population. Factors influencing the magnitude of reactance include (1) the importance of the specific freedom being threatened (e.g., the "freedom" to own one's thoughts, despite the deluded content) and (2) the magnitude of the threat (e.g., having to give up delusional beliefs entirely, rather than only partially modifying them). Accordingly, to directly "challenge" such beliefs would generally be predicted to create high levels of reactance (Alford and Beck 1994).

Consistent with this, a number of studies have reported successful modification of psychotic symptoms (e.g., delusions) by intentionally keeping reactance to a minimum. Chadwick and Lowe (1990) emphasize how their "reality testing" procedure pays special attention to the collaborative nature of cognitive therapy: "In such cases, the client and researcher collaborated to devise a simple test of the belief [see Hole et al. 1979]. . . . An important principle behind the reality testing was that the client agreed in advance that the chosen task was a genuine test of the belief" (p. 227). Similarly, Watts and colleagues (1973) developed four guiding principles designed to minimize reactance. They suggested that (1) the modification begin with those beliefs that are the least strongly held; (2) clients be asked to consider only an alternative to their belief; (3) evidence for the belief be challenged, as opposed to the belief itself; and (4) the client be encouraged to voice the arguments against his or her belief.

Noting the large numbers of patients who drop out of psychotherapy after only one session, Anthony and colleagues (1980) identify attending, observing, listening, and responding skills as essential for engagement with this clinical population. They argue that the best way to increase involvement is to communicate attention and interest. Without this approach, attempts at rapport building, understanding, and explaining are bound to produce frustration (Wasylenski 1992). As noted by Alford and Beck (1994), the therapist must closely attend to the emotions associated with delusional thoughts and beliefs in order to facilitate collaboration and understanding of the patient's perspective. They note that, in some cases, knowing the patient's emotional state during activation of specific beliefs may assist in understanding the maintenance of such beliefs. But in other cases, successful treatment appears to hinge upon the therapist's ability to direct the patient to the more positive feelings associated with alternative explanations of events originally misinterpreted in delusional terms.

Perspective-Taking (Metacognitive) Techniques

Also known as "perspective taking," metacognitive processes can be construed as the act of viewing one's thoughts or beliefs as constructions of reality rather than reality itself. The term *metacognition* denotes those mental processes involved in knowledge of the cognitive enterprise itself, including both cognitive content and process activities (Alford and Correia 1994, Flavell 1979, Johnson and Raye 1981). Such processes are clearly important not only in introspection but also in the ability to direct and control his or her thinking (Flavell 1979). For example, Harrow and Miller (1980) found "impaired perspective taking" to be an important element in the thought pathology often found in cases of schizophrenia. They defined this metacognitive dysfunction as the inability to "recognize, in global fashion and in terms of broad consensual standards, which particular verbalizations and behavior are appropriate for a particular situation" (p. 717). According to their view, patients with impaired perspective often allow personal material to intermingle with their speech at inappropriate times or allow their speech to be guided by inappropriate personal themes (Harrow and Miller 1980). With a sample that consisted of thirty patients with schizophrenia and twenty-nine without schizophrenia, their data suggest that (1) loss of global perspective concerning the idiosyncrasies of one's own verbalizations is closely associated with a tendency toward disordered speech; (2) somewhat impaired perspective on what behavior is socially appropriate is common to all types of disturbed patients but is more severe in patients with schizophrenia; and (3) the impairment in schizophrenia is selective, involving difficulty in maintaining perspective on their own behavior, with better perspective when assessing others' behavior.

Some research in this area (Johnson and Raye 1981) suggests that the ability to discriminate between the "real" and the "imaginary" is an inferential skill. In other words, people do not automatically know whether a perceived event is self-generated (as in mental imagery) or generated by the external world, and must guess between these two possibilities based on the available evidence. According to this view, people hallucinate when they wrongly infer that internally generated cognitive events (e.g., verbal thoughts) are externally generated "real" stimuli (Bentall 1990b).

More recent studies also indicate that delusions are associated with a deficit in the ability to recognize the origins and causality of one's thoughts and beliefs (e.g., Bentall 1990a,b). Described by Bentall as "a deficit in reality discrimination," patients with schizophrenia appear to have underdeveloped metacognitive abilities. Rather than viewing their thoughts as perceptual creations, they are inclined to attribute their cognition to external causes, such as "voices," thought insertion, or other deluded explanations.

Using techniques to enhance perspective taking, Alford (1986) reported successful cognitive treatment of a 22-year-old inpatient with chronic paranoid schizophrenia. The patient had the delusional belief that a "haggy old witch" was stalking him in the hospital, and behavioral disturbances were directly attributed to these experiences. Treatment included two to three weekly sessions in which alternative interpretations were suggested. Reinterpretations of beliefs and hallucinatory experiences were developed collaboratively with the patient, who favored the alternative that his "imagination" was out of control. An A-B-A-B design was used, and placebo control sessions were conducted during baseline phases. In addition to a decrease in strength of delusional beliefs, independent ratings of nursing staff who were uninformed about the experimental phases showed marked reductions in their need for neuroleptic medications during active phases (Alford 1986). Follow-up investigations showed improvements had partially persisted three months after treatment, including maintenance of acquired metacognitive skills such as self-monitoring and critical evaluation of thoughts.

In another study focusing on the patients' introspective or metacognitive experience, Hole and colleagues (1979) employed a relatively nondirective, collaborative cognitive approach to delusions. Interviews were nonconfrontational and engaged the patient in a joint exploration of certain questions: "Did the belief rest on current experience? How did he process information inconsistent with the belief? If there was some change in any aspect of the belief, how did the patient account for the change?" (p. 314). Eight inpatients with delusions and schizophrenia were chosen randomly from the University of Pennsylvania psychiatric services. Regarding their delusions, subjects rated their conviction (certainty of the delusional idea, zero to 100 percent) and persuasiveness (time thinking about or seeking delusional goals). The outcome reported was mixed. Four of the patients showed no significant changes in persuasiveness or conviction ratings. One of the patients, however, was found to "accommodate" or alter their belief in response to data inconsistent with the belief. Two patients showed marked reductions in pervasiveness ratings but unchanged convictions. The two remaining patients were able to markedly reduce both pervasiveness and conviction ratings.

Because impaired perspective taking is a common symptom in cases of schizophrenia, one goal of the cognitive therapist is to help increase the awareness of subjective experiences. Toward this end the interrelated cognitive techniques of identifying, monitoring, and evaluating thoughts are applied directly to the treatment of clinical symptoms. The aim of these standard cognitive techniques is to facilitate "distancing" from thoughts, or the ability to view one's thoughts or beliefs as constructions of reality rather than reality itself (Alford and Correia 1994).

As noted previously, a most critical variable to measure in deluded patients is the degree to which they hold a specific delusional belief to be valid. Also known as conviction ratings, this can be assessed using a subjective rating scale, ranging from zero to 100 percent. Interestingly, we found that the interview in and of itself will in many cases reduce conviction ratings (see Hole et al. 1979). Based on these findings, we can surmise that the act of systematically obtaining conviction ratings activates metacognitive or "perspective taking" processes that in turn reduce the strength of conviction. This provides an example in which assessment and treatment activities are interdependent.

In one technique patients may be asked whether others seem to agree or disagree with their views regarding delusional material. Patients can be led through a guided discovery to recognize a discrepancy between their own perspective and those of others. The therapist then conducts a dialogue with the patient to discuss how best to account for the differences. Therapist and patient directly focus on evaluating the evidence upon which the belief is based (as in Alford 1986, Beck 1952, Kingdon and Turkington 1991, Tarrier 1992). By encouraging patients to temporarily take the perspective of other people, they are better able to distance themselves from abnormal beliefs. This is consistent with the finding by Harrow and Miller (1980) that "[perspective-taking impairment] in schizophrenia is selective, involving difficulty in maintaining perspective on their own behavior, with better perspective when assessing others' behavior" (p. 717).

CONCLUSIONS

The theoretical foundations of cognitive therapy suggest this approach to be a logical strategy in the treatment of schizophrenia and other psychotic disorders. A number of case studies and partially controlled experimental studies to date strongly suggest that there is considerable potential for directly modifying the cognitive impairments characteristic of schizophrenia. Ongoing research will continue investigating these areas in greater depth so that we may learn which forms of pathology respond to cognitive interventions and which do not.

The adaptation of cognitive therapy in the treatment of psychotic symptoms is guided by the basic theoretical axioms of clinical cognitive therapy. The following cognitive treatment components constitute the essence of cognitive therapy as applied to these disorders: conducting idiographic assessment, employing distancing or "perspective taking," treating cognitive content and cognitive processing, attending to the interpersonal context, focusing on emotions, reducing expressed emotion and interpersonal stress, and correcting the self concept (Alford and Beck, in press).

Finally, we believe it is important that cognitive therapy evolve *theoretically*, as well as in terms of its adaptation to the increasing range of clinical disorders for which its empirical validity has now been established. In contrast, categorizations of the techniques of cognitive therapy as "specific" versus "nonspecific" have been advanced (see John and Turkington 1996). The currently popular "integrative" conceptualizations (as in Castonguay and Goldfried 1994, John and Turkington 1996) could be counterproductive to the extent to which they result in theoretical incoherence. Advancing and testing *specific* scientific systems and theories of psychotherapy would appear more useful. (By definition, it is hard to test "nonspecific" factors.) Some of the specific research questions derived from cognitive theory are as follows (see Alford and Beck 1994, Alford and Correia 1994).

1. What are the limitations of developing metacognitive skills to distinguish disordered phenomenal experiences (delusions and hallucinations) from actual internal/ external physical events?
2. Does treatment of disordered cognitive processes (cognitive distortions) prevent or correct maladaptive content such as delusional beliefs?
3. Can the collaborative empirical framework of cognitive therapy facilitate generalization (ecological validity) of

cognitive remediation efforts? We hypothesize that cognitive processing errors are best eliminated in the environmental context in which they create problems in adaptive functioning (e.g., by means of homework assignments).

4. Sometimes an essential prerequisite for the application of psychological interventions is stabilization of the patient on appropriate neuroleptic medications (Grinspoon et al. 1972), yet a study by Blackwell (cited in Kendall and Lipman 1991) cites medication compliance rates of only 50 percent for filling a prescription. Once a prescription is filled, it is often not taken as directed. To what extent will cognitive approaches facilitate medication compliance with schizophrenic patients?

5. What is the effectiveness of cognitive therapy of stress (as in Beck 1993b) in reducing the psychotic symptoms of patients with schizophrenia? Can such an approach to stress reduction reduce relapse?

6. Of perhaps greatest interest, beliefs about hallucination experiences (such as "voices") theoretically determine responses and emotional reactions to such psychotic symptoms. An example is found in the study reported earlier by Alford (1986) in which the paranoid belief of the patient (persecution by a "haggly witch") related to visual hallucinations of the object of the belief (the "witch"). Could cognitive therapy focused on paranoid (danger) interpretations of hallucinated voices treat disordered interpretations of such experiences (e.g., apply cognitive therapy to eliminate the belief that voices are dangerous or that they represent persecuting identities)?

REFERENCES

Alford, B. A. (1986). Behavioral treatment of schizophrenic delusions: a single-case experimental analysis. *Behavior Therapy* 17:637–644.

Alford, B. A., and Beck, A. T. (1994). Cognitive therapy of delusional beliefs. *Behaviour Research and Therapy* 32:369–380.

——— (in press). *Cognitive therapy: An integration of contemporary theory and therapy.* New York: Guilford.

Alford, B. A., and Correia, C. J. (1994). Cognitive therapy of schizophrenia: theory and empirical status. *Behavior Therapy* 25:17–33.

Anthony, W. A., Pierce, R. M., Cohen, M. R., et al. (1980). *The Skills of Diagnostic Planning.* Baltimore: University Park Press.

Beck, A. T. (1952). Successful outpatient psychotherapy of a chronic schizophrenic with a delusion based on borrowed guilt. In *Psychoanalytic Psychiatry and Psychology*, ed. R. Knight. New York: International Universities Press.

——— (1970). Cognitive therapy: nature and relation to behavior therapy. *Behavior Therapy* 1:184–200.

——— (1993a). Cognitive therapy: past, present, and future. *Journal of Consulting and Clinical Psychology* 61:194–198.

——— (1993b). Cognitive approaches to stress. In *Principles and Practice of Stress Management*, ed. R. Woolfolk and P. Lehrer, 2nd ed. New York: Guilford.

Beck, A. T., and Weishaar, M. (1989). Cognitive therapy. In *Current Psychotherapies*, ed. R. J. Corsini and D. Wedding, 4th ed. Itasca, IL: Peacock.

Bentall, R. P. (1990a). The illusion of reality: a review and integration of psychological research on hallucinations. *Psychological Bulletin* 107:82–95.

——— (1990b). The syndromes and symptoms of psychosis: or why you can't play twenty questions with the concept of schizophrenia and hope to win. In *Reconstructing Schizophrenia*, ed. R. P. Bentall. London: Routledge.

Bentall, R. P., Haddock, G., and Slade, P. D. (1994a). Cognitive behaviour therapy for persistent auditory hallucinations: from theory to therapy. *Behavior Therapy* 25:51–66.

Bentall, R. P., Kinderman, P., and Kaney, S. (1994b). The self, attributional processes and abnormal beliefs: towards a model of persecutory delusions. *Behaviour Research and Therapy* 32:331–341.

Castonguay, L. G., and Goldfried, M. R. (1994). Psychotherapy integration: an idea whose time has come. *Applied and Prevention Psychology* 3:159–172.

Chadwick, P. D. J., Birchwood, M., and Trower, P. (1996). *Cognitive Therapy for Delusions, Voices, and Paranoia.* West Sussex, England: Wiley.

Chadwick, P. D. J., and Lowe, C. F. (1990). Measurement and modification of delusional beliefs. *Journal of Consulting and Clinical Psychology* 58:225–232.

Cromwell, R. L., and Snyder, C. R., eds. (1993). *Schizophrenia: Origins, Processes, Treatment, and Outcome.* New York: Oxford University Press.

Diagnostic and Statistical Manual of Mental Disorders (DSM-IV) (1994). 4th ed. Washington, DC: American Psychiatric Association.

Flavell, J. H. (1979). Metacognition and cognitive monitoring. *American Psychologist* 34:906–911.

Gottesman, I. I. (1991). *Schizophrenia Genesis: The Origins of Madness.* New York: Freeman.

Greenwood, V. B. (1983). Cognitive therapy with the young adult chronic patient. In *Cognitive Therapy with Couples and Groups*, ed. A. Freeman. New York: Plenum.

Grinspoon, L., Ewalt, J. R., and Shader, R. I. (1972). *Schizophrenia: Pharamacotherapy and Psychotherapy.* Baltimore, MD: Williams & Wilkins.

Harrow, M., and Miller, J. G. (1980). Schizophrenic thought disorders and impaired perspective. *Journal of Abnormal Psychology* 89:717–727.

Hole, R. W., Rush, A. J., and Beck, A. T. (1979). A cognitive investigation of schizophrenic delusions. *Psychiatry* 42:312–319.

John, C., and Turkington, D. (1996). A model-building approach in cognitive therapy with a woman with chronic schizophrenic hallucinations: Why did it work? *Clinical Psychology and Psychotherapy* 3:46–61.

Johnson, M. K., and Raye, C. I. (1981). Reality monitoring. *Psychological Review* 88:67–85.

Kendall, P. C., and Lipman, A. J. (1991). Psychological and pharmacological therapy: methods and modes for comparative research. *Journal of Consulting and Clinical Psychology* 59:78–87.

Kingdon, D. G., and Turkington, D. (1971). A role for cognitive-behavioral strategies in schizophrenia? *Social Psychiatry and Psychiatric Epidemiology* 26:101–103.

Morrison, A. P. (1994). Cognitive behavior therapy for auditory hallucinations without current medication: a single case. *Behavioral and Cognitive Psychotherapy* 22:259–264.

Morrison, A. P., Haddock, G., and Tarrier, N. (in press). Intrusive thoughts and auditory hallucinations: a cognitive approach. *Behavioral and Cognitive Psychotherapy*.

Perris, C. (1992). A cognitive-behavioral treatment program for patients with a schizophrenic disorder. In *Effective Psychiatric Rehabilitation*, ed. R. P. Liberman, pp. 22–23. San Francisco: Jossey-Bass.

Shavelson, L. (1986). *I'm Not Crazy, I Just Lost My Glasses*. Berkeley, CA: De Novo.

Spaulding, W. D., ed. (1994). *Cognitive Technology in Psychiatric Evaluation*. Lincoln, NE: University of Nebraska Press.

Tarrier, N. (1992). Management and modification of residual positive psychotic symptoms. In *Innovations in the Psychological Management of Schizophrenia*, ed. M. Birchwood and N. Tarrier. New York: Wiley.

Torrey, E. F. (1995). *Surviving Schizophrenia: A Manual for Families, Consumers, and Providers*, 3rd ed. New York: Harper Perennial.

Wasylenski, D. A. (1992). Psychotherapy of schizophrenia revisited. *Hospital and Community Psychiatry* 43:123–127.

Watts, F. N., Powell, G. E., and Austin, S. V. (1973). The modification of abnormal beliefs. *British Journal of Medical Psychology* 46:359–363.

16

HIV RISK BEHAVIOR*

Scott A. Cohen

As mental health professionals, psychotherapists are called upon to view their patients holistically, according to a biopsychosocial model. There is a consensus among professionals that dysfunctional behavior and emotional distress are seldom purely psychic in origin; therefore, standards of care dictate assessment of the social and biological conditions of patients as well as their psychological status (Freedman 1995). Yet the challenge of a holistic model of mental health goes beyond comprehensive assessment: just as psychopathology is multifactorial in origin, psychological difficulties can also be multidimensional in their effects. The problems therapists now treat, from addictions to personality and affective disorders, are complicated entities that may influence social adjustment,

*Special thanks to Robert Leahy, Ph.D., for his generous support and provocative discussions.

psychological well-being, and biological health. The challenge contemporary therapists face is to intervene effectively in each of these domains.

One example of the sort of cross-modal challenge that both patients and therapists face today is acquired immunodeficiency syndrome. To date, there have been more than 500,000 cases of fully diagnosed AIDS in the United States and an estimated 1,000,000 individuals infected with human immunodeficiency virus (HIV), the viral cause of AIDS. AIDS is life threatening, and usually fatal, but because individuals may not manifest symptoms for up to ten years from time of infection, most do not know they carry a transmissible virus, and continue activities that may put themselves and others at risk. As of this writing, AIDS is the leading cause of death among men and women between the ages of 25 and 44 in the United States (Centers for Disease Control and Prevention 1996). Most of these individuals were infected through sexual relations that involved the exchange of HIV-infected body fluids. Others have become exposed to HIV by sharing infected drug paraphernalia during injection drug use, as a result of receiving infected blood products, or through parenteral or perinatal transmission from parent to infant. The epidemiology of AIDS has reached pandemic proportions. As a global crisis, AIDS may affect the thoughts, feelings, and behavior of patients even though they may not allude to the disease directly.

Despite recent advances in the treatment of HIV and its associated infections, researchers and activists at the 11th Annual Conference on AIDS in Vancouver, British Columbia, have affirmed that prevention of primary infection remains a global priority. The care of HIV-infected individuals requires considerable expense of both energy and money, taxing government, social, familial, and affected individuals' resources to their limits. Despite the initially sluggish governmental response to AIDS, current realities confirm the credo that an ounce of prevention is worth a pound of cure.

Psychotherapy patients may be at greater risk for HIV exposure than others in the general population for several reasons: they are susceptible to the poor judgment and impulsive behavior that characterize many kinds of emotional distress; there are high rates of comorbidity between psychiatric disorders and substance abuse; and some distressed individuals allow themselves to be taken advantage of by others. The psychotherapist may be the only person in a patient's social milieu who is privileged to hear about drug use or sexual behavior. He or she may also be their only resource for accurate, nonjudgmental information that facilitates motivation toward behavior change. Whatever the therapist's clinical orientation, cognitive-behavioral techniques place a variety of potent tools at his or her disposal. Research and clinical experience have confirmed the power of cognitive-behavioral strategies to promote long-term change in HIV-related risk behavior (Kelly 1995). Not all patients (nor every therapist) welcomes such concrete intervention, yet the threat of diagnosis with a life-threatening condition reduces the impact of these objections.

HIV BASICS

Extensive knowledge of HIV is not required to help patients avoid behavior that puts them at risk. Nevertheless, some basic information is necessary to assure patient understanding and to answer questions.

Discovered in the early 1980s, HIV was found to be the cause of AIDS, a syndrome of immune suppression first identified in 1981 among gay men in New York and San Francisco. Since then, research on the virus has revealed that many individuals do not have any significant manifestations of infection for ten to twelve years, the mean interval between infection and the first AIDS-defining condition (Batchelor 1988, Volberding

1992). Although it was initially thought that the virus was "dormant" during this period, researchers at the Aaron Diamond Research Center in New York City have demonstrated that the virus is actively reproducing from the initial point of infection and that the host's immune system constantly mounts a strong, but incomplete, defense against it (Perelson et al. 1996). Over time, this immune response becomes less effective: viral reproduction rebounds, producing a cycle of escalating viral population and deteriorating immune function. As the immune system declines, persons with HIV become vulnerable to a host of opportunistic infections and ailments, such as Pneumocystis carinii pneumonia, a life-threatening infection of the lungs, or cytomegalovirus, a herpes virus that many individuals carry, but that seriously affects the retina of the eye, the small bowel, or the esophagus of people with AIDS.

Fifteen years of clinical experience with AIDS have led to many advances in the prophylaxis and treatment of these and other AIDS-related conditions. Increasingly, clinicians and researchers describe HIV as evolving into a chronic treatable condition (Ho 1995). This is important to keep in mind when discussing HIV risk behavior with patients who may already feel anxious about previous risky encounters. Conveying the hopeful message that an HIV diagnosis, while a serious medical condition, is neither hopeless nor untreatable can mitigate unproductive anxiety.

To become infected with HIV, the virus must move from the infected blood of one person into the bloodstream of another. In addition to blood, semen, vaginal secretions, and breast milk are known to contain blood components and virus in sufficient concentrations to make infection possible. Any activity, such as vaginal or anal intercourse or injection drug use, that exposes an individual to these body fluids may be considered a source of risk for HIV infection. Because the complications of HIV prevention with injection drug users are better addressed within the context of reducing substance use (which is beyond the scope of this chapter), I will concentrate here on initiating prevention through changes in patients' sexual behavior.

Not all sexual behavior has equal risk of HIV transmission. Overall, sexual behavior may be considered on a continuum of risk (Figure 16–1): from activities considered most risky, such as anal or vaginal intercourse without barrier protection (a latex condom); activities considered moderately risky, such as oral sex without barrier protection; lower-risk activities, such as oral sex with barrier protection; activities posing almost no risk of HIV transmission, such as internal manual sex with barrier protection (gloves or finger cots) or wet kissing; to no risk or "safe" activities, such as external manual sex or dry kissing.

The goal of integrating HIV risk prevention into ongoing psychotherapy is to help patients modify higher risk behaviors to those of lower risk. This is called *harm reduction*. As trusted helpers, psychotherapists can assist their patients to reduce harm by targeting their efforts to the patients' particular strengths and needs.

A BRIEF TRANSTHEORETICAL INTERLUDE

In their studies of addictive behaviors, James Prochaska and Carlo DiClemente (1982, 1983) describe what they have called a *transtheoretical* model of behavior change. Their model, consisting of six stages (Figure 16–2), is usually presented as a wheel to convey the fact that individuals may go through these stages repeatedly. (In their studies of smoking, most people repeated the last five stages an average of four times [Prochaska and DiClemente 1983].) Each stage is characterized by some patient attitude toward change and has been related to some therapeutic objective (Miller and Rollnick 1991).

Figure 16–1. Sample HIV Risk Behavior Continuum

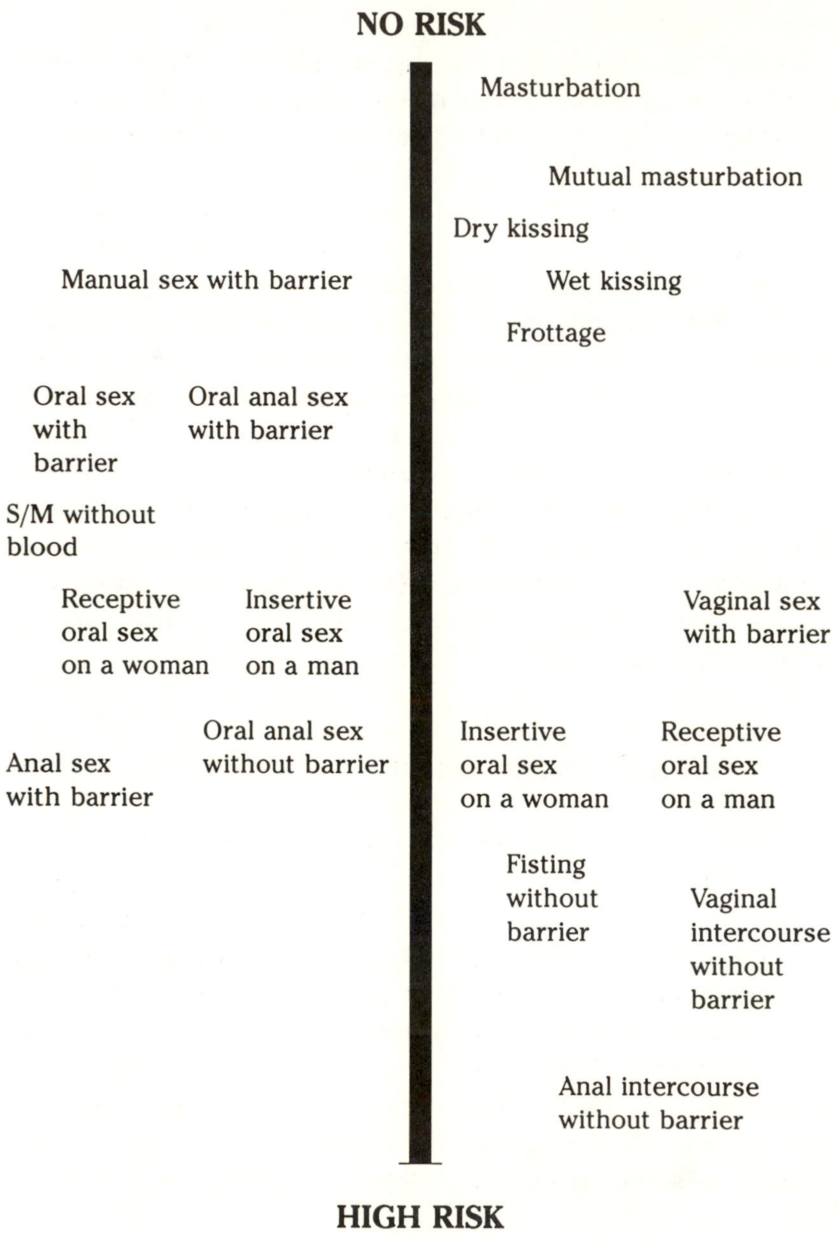

NO RISK

Masturbation

Mutual masturbation

Dry kissing

Manual sex with barrier   Wet kissing

Frottage

Oral sex   Oral anal sex
with   with barrier
barrier

S/M without
blood

Receptive   Insertive   Vaginal sex
oral sex   oral sex   with barrier
on a woman   on a man

Oral anal sex   Insertive   Receptive
Anal sex   without barrier   oral sex   oral sex
with barrier   on a woman   on a man

Fisting
without   Vaginal
barrier   intercourse
without
barrier

Anal intercourse
without barrier

HIGH RISK

In the first stage, *precontemplation*, the individual has not even considered the consequences of his actions. At this level the therapist must help the patient to recognize associations between the undesirable behavior and aversive consequences. For HIV prevention, the therapist might pose appropriate questions about the patient's behavior to facilitate examination of the relationship between unsafe sex and HIV transmission.

In the *contemplation* stage, patients are considering a change, but remain unsure about taking action. They alternate between (and sometimes simultaneously experience) worry and unconcern about, or justification of, their behavior: "Well, I know we should have safe sex, but this guy has never been with anyone else," or "We're safe most of the time, it won't matter if we don't use a condom once, will it?" Here the therapist must acknowledge and help resolve the patient's ambivalence. Not initiating prescriptive advice at this stage is important, as this may foreclose on the patient's ambivalence. It is more valuable to allow the patient to explore both sides of the conflict fully. The contemplation stage is often the most difficult stage for therapists as it arouses their impatience.

Contemplation is followed by a *determination* stage, where, for a time, most of the ideas and statements about changing behavior are positive: "If she won't talk about safer sex with me, then we just won't have sex." The therapist's task during this stage is to ensure that the patient's newfound motivation proceeds into action.

The particular actions that the patient selects characterize the fourth or *action* stage of change. By helping the patient individualize action steps to his or her particular strengths and deficits, the therapist ensures that motivation can be maintained.

In the *maintenance* stage the patient must sustain behavioral change, such as safer sex, while remaining wary of relapse. A thorough assessment helps prevent relapse by showing patients the steps or cues that precede undesirable actions.

Because most individuals attempting long-term behavior change at some point experience *relapse*, Prochaska and DiClemente (1982, 1983) included it as the sixth stage in their model. Patients in this stage often feel defeated, and it is the therapist's task to help motivate them to resume the change process. Examining and helping a patient to restructure cognitive distortions at this stage can often facilitate this goal.

The stages-of-change model can be extremely useful in helping psychotherapists target their interventions to a patient's specific needs. Some therapists teach it to their patients, but this can be cumbersome and a bit pat. One subtle implication of the model is that it is easier to motivate patients for change in the context of novel information; laying out for

Figure 16–2. Stages of Change Model

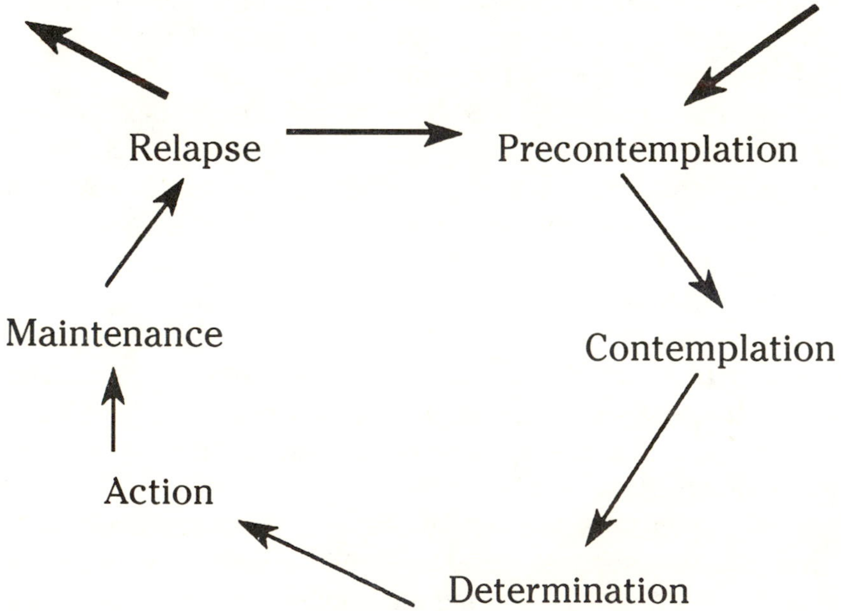

patients what one expects them to experience may provoke resistance. Nevertheless, the model, which is patient-focused, is an important complement to the therapist-based approach toward HIV prevention presented in this chapter.

PREVENTION STRATEGY

Most therapists would prefer an approach to psychotherapy that focuses on the patient's distress, not lessons in HIV prevention. A good therapeutic guideline is to minimize goals ancillary to patient concerns. Nevertheless, this reluctance to disrupt the therapeutic process needs to be balanced against the realistic danger of a patient's becoming infected with a life-threatening disease. This chapter presents a model that seeks to balance traditional therapeutic concerns about intrusion with interventions to motivate concrete health behavior change.

One of the critical areas of disagreement between therapeutic paradigms is on the nature of motivation for change. Broadly speaking, psychodynamic psychology attributes motivation to unconscious impulses or wishes (the content of these wishes varies considerably within psychodynamic schools); hence the goal of therapy is to bring these impulses into awareness so that they do not interfere with or disrupt consciously desirable behavior. Third-force or organismic theorists believe that individuals are naturally directed toward growth, that provided with a nurturing psychological environment people will take actions that maintain and enhance health. Contemporary behavior therapists believe that motivation derives from the results of actions: thus, if I enjoy the benefits of writing papers, I will continue to do so; however, if paper writing feels so onerous to me that I derive no rewards from it, I am less likely to write in the future.

Growing out of behavioral principles, cognitive psychologists noted that individuals seem to have their own notions of reward and punishment and that access to these ideas can be gained by articulating their conscious and preconscious thoughts. Some individuals might find an evening with friends a satisfying reward after a good day's work, but for a social phobic the dread associated with the evening's activities may preclude work altogether. While it is not the purpose of this chapter to debate the accuracy or scientific merit of these motivational schemes, within the context of AIDS prevention the cognitive framework provides a useful method for achieving what may be considered minimally intrusive, yet vitally important, behavior change.

A general model of cognitive-behavioral intervention strategy involves five phases: (1) assessment, (2) education, (3) decision making, (4) skills acquisition, and (5) ongoing assessment and booster sessions. While not every specific technique described below will be suited to a particular patient, if any phase in this process is neglected, relapse into risky sexual behavior is the likely result. (The word *phase*, rather than *stage* is used here advisedly. The five phases described need not be completed in order, nor is any one irrevocably concluded.)

ASSESSMENT

Unlike some other forms of psychotherapeutic practice, cognitive-behavioral assessment is active and specific. The goal is to find out what the patient is doing, where, when, with whom, and what it means to him. As one moves into decision making, it also becomes necessary to understand what the patient thinks and how he feels or reacts to the behavior and its associated settings or cues.

Ideally, therapists would have access to a thorough biopsychosocial assessment including sexual history from the inception of the therapeutic relationship; this is rarely the case, however. Although helpful, a complete sexual history is not required for successful reduction of HIV risk behavior *in the future*. Within the context of the therapeutic relationship, patients frequently mention that they are dating or having sexual relations with an ongoing partner. Most individuals are socialized to gloss over specific details of this behavior; however, in a therapeutic setting, especially when one goal of the therapy is HIV risk reduction, details will need to be specified. It is necessary for the therapist to inquire about the patient's sexual activity in a nonjudgmental spirit of concern and relative neutrality. It is also important not to overemphasize sexual behavior so that it becomes the primary focus of therapy or so that the patient comes to impute ulterior motives to the therapist. Try to be matter of fact, as if one were asking for detail about any interpersonal relationship.

Chris, a 33-year-old gay male stockbroker, has just ended a four-year relationship in which he had been monogamous and engaged exclusively in safer sex. Shortly after breaking up, he met a man to whom he felt very attracted. Feeling rather vulnerable, Chris had sexual relations that he initially considered safe but that upon retrospect he decided might have placed him at risk.

Chris: So I'm really scared about this guy, I mean he's really attractive and all, but how can I tell if he's telling the truth about his sero-status?

Therapist: I'm not clear on why that matters . . .

C: Well, if he's infected. It's just that it's the first time since I broke up with Thomas and I'm worried.

T: I can see that you are worried, but it isn't clear what you're worried about, what you actually did. Suppose we back up a bit and you tell me what happened at his apartment.

C: We had a few drinks and then we began kissing and holding each other. He began kissing my neck and before I knew what was happening we were undressing each other. It felt so good to be held again and I must have had three or four glasses of wine between dinner and his place. It was so comfortable with him. He was this sexy guy, real dark and handsome, very masculine, just the type I'm attracted to. So I asked if he had a condom. He said yes, but it didn't matter because he was negative anyway. But now I wonder if he could have been lying, I mean I hardly know the guy.

T: You asked about a condom before you had any sexual contact with him?

C: No, he had gone down on me for a few minutes and I wanted him to fuck me, but he said that he liked my mouth so I just went down on him.

T: Without a condom?

C: Yes, without and that's the problem. I think he may have come in my mouth . . .

Notice how the therapist attempts to incorporate assessment into the therapeutic dialogue as naturally as possible without interrupting the patient's flow. He has acquired a great deal of information about the conditions and settings in which unsafe behavior has taken place and has a basis for continuing assessment. With patients as knowledgeable and comfortable as Chris, this is a relatively easy task, but many patients are more guarded.

Danielle, a 23-year-old graduate student, had come to therapy for assistance in completing work in school. It soon became apparent, however, that she had difficulty asserting herself with advisors and colleagues; she would then become overwhelmed and unable to complete her work. Some five months into therapy she began to describe a friendship that was growing increasingly sexual.

Danielle: I like Mark, he's very attractive, but I can't see myself spending the rest of my life with him. He's too pushy, like we talked about before, he doesn't listen to me. If I don't want to have sex right now he thinks it's because I'm a prude, but I'm really worried about getting pregnant . . .

Therapist: Have you had intercourse with Mark?

D: Sure, we made love once about a week ago. I told you about it; the night we were housesitting for friends. He was very gentle and loving that night.

T: When you say "made love" I'm not sure whether you mean vaginal intercourse, oral intercourse, or touching each other.

D: Oh, I see what you mean—only it's kind of embarrassing.

T: Yes, I know it is, but it's important for me to know what you and Mark did if I am to help you. It isn't just pregnancy but also sexually transmitted diseases such as HIV that are important to protect yourself from.

D: You mean AIDS? I never thought of that. Mark's a jock, but I bet he's been with hundreds of girls. He didn't have a condom, so we decided not to go all the way. He pulled out before anything happened.

T: He pulled out of your vagina before he ejaculated?

D: Yes.

Notice that this therapist suggests sexual vocabulary to her patient. This "permission giving" may be necessary for particularly reticent individuals. It represents the behavior therapy technique of vicarious learning or modeling, and has been demonstrated to enhance self-efficacy and motivation for action (Bandura 1988). The therapist normalizes sexual talk for the patient through her demonstrated comfort with discussing sexual behavior using appropriate terminology.

There are two goals of the assessment process in HIV prevention: first, the patient must recognize situations that place him or her at risk of HIV infection; second, he or she needs to identify specific environmental triggers or cues that increase the likelihood of higher risk behavior. Because sexual behavior is such an emotionally loaded topic, patients often focus on the former while ignoring the latter. Assessment of situational or internal (emotional, cognitive) cues, however, provides patients with a focus for action and a hope-inducing first step toward behavior change.

Some patients will already be familiar with HIV and need little education about their vulnerability to it; others will be relatively naive about HIV; still others will have employed a variety of cognitive distortions to reduce their anxiety about the presence of a sexually communicable, life-threatening disease. The education phase of the intervention process can facilitate assessment by helping some patients recognize the link between their sexual behavior and risk of infection, increasing motivation for behavior change toward self-protection.

EDUCATION

Imparting information plays a role in almost every therapeutic process, whether it takes the form of the psychoanalyst's illustrating the significance of early childhood experience to his or her patient or the humanistic therapist's demonstrating how thought may have been used to foreclose upon authentic feeling. The cognitive-behaviorist differs from other therapists in his or her comfort with direct instruction as a curative factor in therapy. This willingness to acknowledge the role of education in therapy has freed cognitive therapists to be creative in their integration of learning into the therapeutic relationship. A number of cognitive-behavioral educative strategies exist, from bibliotherapy (assigning patients to read essays or book chapters) and role-playing (in which patients have the opportunity to practice newly acquired skills) to brief writing assignments (in which patients describe what they have learned from some experience or event). Some therapists unfamiliar with cognitive-behavioral models misunderstand education as a unidirectional process in which the therapist imparts information to the patient as he or she patiently (and passively) listens. This is seldom the case; in fact, most education in the context of cognitive therapy is active and dialectical. Aaron Beck, one of the principal originators of cognitive-behavioral methods, advocates a Socratic approach in which the therapist poses questions that elucidate gaps in the patient's knowledge or logic (Beck et al. 1979). This technique can work very well as a mode of HIV education, with the caveat that one must be careful not to embarrass or shame the patient for what he may not know.

> David, a highly educated professional bisexual man, had a brother who was recently diagnosed with HIV. He did not believe that he could contract HIV from insertive vaginal sex.

David: We were safe, or rather I was. I feel guilty for not telling her about my other relationships, though, but I did hardly know her, after all, and she was the one who hit on me.

Therapist: And what did you do?

D: We fooled around for a while, then we sixty-nined, and then she got on top of me.

T: Did you have an orgasm inside her?

D: Yes, I know I shouldn't have, but she was so hot and she said that she was on the pill, so there's no danger of pregnancy at least.

T: Are there other dangers that concern you?

D: Well yeah, ever since Sam's diagnosis, I've been freaked out about HIV. But he was screwing around with guys and this was a woman. Besides I put it into her.

T: That does seem to reassure you, but I wonder if you can tell me how you believe HIV is transmitted?

D: Through blood and body secretions . . .

T: And did you come in contact with those?

D: Yes, but only a little—I made sure that there were no cuts on my penis and she wasn't bleeding or anything.

T: What made you check to make sure she wasn't bleeding?

D: I just figured if she wasn't bleeding then I was okay. I mean blood's a lot more dangerous than cum, isn't it?

T: Yes, blood probably carries more HIV than semen or vaginal secretions, but they carry enough that people who have not protected themselves have become infected. You seem to have taken some cautious steps but not the one—using a condom—that would have assured protection for both of you.

D: I just figured if there were no cuts then I was okay.

T: Well, let's think about that. Have you ever had a sexually transmitted disease?

D: Not really, just a urinary tract infection that I caught from Nina.

T: And did you have a cut then?

D: Not that I noticed.

T: So it must be possible for some infections to get into your body without your noticing a break in your skin.

D: I guess so. So you're saying that I should have used a condom even though she was on the pill?

T: What do you think?

D: If I want to avoid AIDS or any sexually transmitted disease, I guess I'd better think about using a condom when I have sex.

The advantage to using the dialectical approach with someone like David is that it opens a window into his thinking process. David minimizes the risk to himself, focusing instead (somewhat ambivalently) upon the risk to others. Although a psychodynamic therapist may wish to explore David's motives in maintaining this defense, it is still necessary that he recognize

and correct the misinformation for appropriate HIV prevention. What then is the minimum a patient needs to know?

In order for patients to make effective safer-sex decisions,
they must know:

- HIV stands for human immunodeficiency virus, the virus
  that is believed to cause AIDS.
- AIDS is a life-threatening disease that weakens the immune system, making it difficult for the body to fight off
  infections.
- People can carry and transmit HIV without looking sick or
  manifesting any overt symptoms for many years.
- HIV does not discriminate based upon the groups (e.g.,
  ethnic minorities, gay men, drug users) to which one
  belongs; behavior, not identity, determines risk of HIV
  infection.[1]
- HIV is not transmitted through casual contact such as
  talking, coughing, sneezing, sharing eating utensils or
  toilets, hugging, dry kissing, or insect bites.
- HIV is transmitted through a limited number of body
  fluids (blood, semen, vaginal secretions, breast milk).
- Behaviors such as sex and injection drug use that place
  one in contact (usually internal contact) with these fluids
  are considered HIV risk behaviors.
- There is a continuum of HIV risk behavior from the least
  to most risky (see Figure 16–1).
- It is not necessary to engage in activities that place one at
  risk. However, if one chooses to engage in these activities
  (and when it comes to sex, most people do), it is possible

---

1. Although there is increasing evidence that constitutional factors
may indeed contribute to who becomes infected with HIV, until tests are
widely available, behavior change remains the most viable prevention
option.

to take precautions, like changing to less risky behaviors or using barrier protection to minimize risk.

- Reducing the risk of HIV transmission for yourself reduces the risk of transmission to others.
- AIDS is not a death sentence. People are living longer, fuller lives with both HIV and AIDS, thanks to new information and treatments.

While most of these points may be integrated as natural discussion within the therapy, some lend themselves to active learning techniques. One creative therapist, for example, likes to have her patients develop their own safer sex continuum and compare it to those she has gleaned from various educational resources.

It is critical to emphasize that HIV prevention does not end with education. Numerous HIV prevention studies dramatically illustrate the point that being well informed does not always result in effective behavior change. Educators thus conclude that motivational factors are paramount; information is a necessary, but insufficient, prerequisite to effective HIV prevention (Kelly 1995, Rotheram-Borus et al. 1991).

FACILITATING DECISION MAKING

Few patients purposely wish to place themselves in harm's way by exposing themselves to HIV, yet they may do so because they have other objectives that conflict with their desire to protect themselves. Within a cognitive model, behavior and mood are mediated by *automatic thoughts*, constantly occurring cognitions that are available to awareness but that are not produced by logic or intentional reasoning. After helping the patient recognize these automatic, preconscious thoughts, the cognitive therapist encourages him or her to examine the logic and consistency of these thoughts within the context of his or her other goals and intentions. Finally, the patient is encouraged to weigh the costs and benefits of his or her current behavior against those of alternative actions. While not a component of traditional practice, this third step provides critical help to confused patients trying to negotiate HIV prevention behavior consistent with the amount of risk they are prepared to tolerate.

Steve, a 36-year-old single gay copywriter living in New York City, believes that infection with HIV is an inevitable aspect of being a sexually active urban gay man and therefore applies HIV prevention behaviors inconsistently.

Toni, a 28-year-old black attorney, is reluctant to bring up condom use to her boyfriend of several months because she fears that it might offend him.

Carla, a self-possessed 40-year-old Latina mother of two, feels uncomfortable talking about sex. She becomes flustered and predicts that her boyfriend of six years will retaliate against her if she discusses safer sex with him.

John, a 54-year-old depressed heterosexual, thinks that condoms rob sex of intimacy. He is also afraid that they may inhibit his ability to sustain an erection.

Each of these individuals was concerned about HIV and wished to protect him- or herself from transmission, but other expectations, desires, and intentions interfered with the consistent application of safer-sex principles. Both psychodynamic and cognitive-behavioral therapists could call attention to these inconsistencies with relative fidelity to their models; however, their approaches would differ considerably. For the psychodynamic thinker, articulating the conflict and interpreting its motivational origins is construed as sufficient intervention. The cognitive therapist would not assume that each of the conflicting motives of his or her patient is of equal merit; the patient's thoughts must be subjected to tests of logic and consistency with his or her other intentions. Carla may have direct evidence of threatening behavior on the part of her boyfriend, but does Toni *know* that her boyfriend would be offended, or has she merely *assumed* so to avoid an unpleasant confrontation?

In therapy, Toni's reluctance to discuss condom use with her boyfriend was found to be based on several distortions in logic. For example, underlying the assumption that her boyfriend would object to condom use was Toni's belief that she had an accurate window into her boyfriend's emotional responses. While often this may have been true (sometimes she could accurately predict her boyfriend's behavior), it was not always true. Toni was applying the cognitive distortion of overgeneralization. The cognitive therapist would assist her to examine evidence about her assumptions by devising, collaboratively, an experiment in which she could explore her boyfriend's feelings about condom use in a mutually safe situation. Perhaps Toni is less concerned about her health than the quality of her relationship. While most therapists would point out Toni's inconsistency (attributing motivation to a variety of possibly relevant phenomena), cognitive therapists insist that knowing why something is happening is not enough: true understanding must result in changed behavior. To facilitate this change, Toni and her therapist might then examine the decisional balance (costs and benefits) of maintaining her assumption that her boyfriend will be offended and compare this to the possible consequences of continued unsafe sexual relations. Finally, it would be useful to examine what Toni really fears if her boyfriend were to become offended: Does she believe that he will leave her or punish her, and what about her capacity to adapt to these possibilities? Such explorations of "feared fantasy" have a venerable place both in psychodynamic and cognitive-behavioral practice, where they serve as invaluable tools for examining impediments to practical action.

Steve's reasons for inconsistent application of safer-sex guidelines are different from Toni's, but the general principles of intervention remain the same: *articulation* of the automatic thought—in this case that no matter what he does he'll get HIV; *recognition* of the underlying distorted assumption—that his future is inevitable regardless of his behavior; and the *acknowledgment* of alternative interpretations, or design of experiments to obtain more information. Steve eventually recognized that not everyone in New York City had HIV (even though a number of his peers were infected) and that his personal risk of becoming infected was entirely dependent on his behavior. He also noticed that he frequently responded to anxiety-provoking situations with similarly passive nihilistic thoughts, which he began to question and alter.

Carla had reasonable fears that her boyfriend might act violently if provoked, so together with her therapist she developed a strategy that would allow her to avoid being hurt (by discussing safer sex in a public place, like a restaurant or park). Later, through assertiveness exercises and role-playing, she developed the confidence to deal with her partner from a position of strength. Although this might seem like a pyrrhic victory, given the threat of violence in Carla's household, she was unwilling to leave her children's father, but was ultimately able, by taking a stand toward safer sex, to insist that her boyfriend get help for his abusiveness.

A complete physical examination determined that John's anxiety about erectile dysfunction had no physiological basis. His therapist therefore concentrated on John's feared fantasies and especially his cognitive distortions around erectile problems. John believed that one incident of erectile difficulty would cause women to reject him and that he would spend the remainder of his life alone. What he discovered was that most women appreciated his concern for their health as well as his own and that they were quite generous in helping him remain aroused during the process of putting on a condom.

SKILL BUILDING

Skill building is an essential phase of cognitive-behavioral HIV prevention, yet because it is difficult to assess patients' skills in the therapy setting, psychotherapists may be tempted to overlook it. Not all patients have equal need to practice and review concrete behaviors such as putting on a condom or using the female condom, but most will have some skills deficits. Of the four cases mentioned above, John and Carla required the most skill building and practice, while Toni and Steve still needed to practice their cognitive restructuring in social contexts. There are three areas of skill development especially relevant to HIV transmission:

- Negotiation of sexual practices
- Assertiveness and problem solving
- Specific skills using barrier protection (condoms)

Skill building begins with assessment of deficits. Ideally this would include observed modeling and feedback in specially designed practice sessions. However, it is possible to use patients' self-reports with some additional probing of the frequency and efficacy of their behavior in various situations. This will enable the therapist to gain an adequate sense of the areas that require additional attention.

The skills involved in negotiating safer-sexual practices are basic communication proficiencies, such as stating one's intentions clearly, listening to and acknowledging partners' concerns, and offering alternatives; yet because sex is such a loaded topic for many individuals, they may have difficulty transferring otherwise adequate skills into the bedroom. For some patients anticipating difficulties can be helpful in itself, but others will need additional encouragement or concrete practice with feedback in order to apply the necessary skills in naturalistic settings. Role-playing can serve as an extremely useful skill assessment and development technique in therapeutic settings. Toni's therapist used a list of "challenging situations" that she had developed as the basis for relevant topics to role-play. Carla, who became flustered just talking about sex, needed to use covert relaxation techniques such as paced breathing in order to complete a role play in which she declined unsafe sex. The capacity to successfully apply skills in the safety of a therapeutic environment does not guarantee that they will be utilized outside of therapy, so ongoing monitoring and assessment is one of the more crucial aspects of skill building.

Assertiveness and other problem-solving skills are more specialized aspects of effective communication. The capacity to refuse unsafe sex may require a range of abilities from appropriate use of eye contact to prearranged plans should sexual coercion arise. Because of the threat of violence from her partner, Carla and her therapist developed a specific plan she could follow if her partner became coercive or violent. Her capacity to apply the plan consistently, which included agreement with a relative that she could spend nights with her, was one of the catalysts for her partner's seeking treatment.

Building skills emerges out of the behavioral tradition; therapists from other orientations may thus be most uncomfortable attempting to integrate it into their work. Despite this caveat, a number of talented clinicians and theoreticians from other schools have demonstrated how behavioral techniques can promote self-exploration and insight (Goldfried 1982, Wachtel 1977, 1987). Learning how to use a condom properly is one of the most important skill-building techniques. Studies show that most condom breakage results from improper use:

people either don't put them on (or, in the case of female condoms, in) correctly, they use nonwater-based lubricants that weaken the integrity of latex, or they use insufficient quantities of lubricant. Nevertheless, many therapists will feel uncomfortable grabbing a penis model in the middle of a session to show a patient how to unfurl a latex condom over it.

There are alternatives. They can retain a referral list of educators at agencies or community-based organizations who will demonstrate technical aspects of HIV prevention. Alternatively, they can provide patients with literature and encourage them to practice on their own. This is what John's therapist did. After assisting the patient in altering cognitions around condom use, the therapist had John practice using condoms at home and attempt to break one to learn just how much handling it could tolerate. This practice had the additional benefit of teaching John that using condoms need not necessarily undermine his sexual arousal. Role plays also need not be done in sessions if they are perceived as too intrusive. Patients can practice problem solving or refusal statements in a mirror, on video, or with significant others. What is most critical is the capacity to learn from the exercise, so a feedback period should be built into each skill-enhancement technique. Then adjustment in response to feedback must be practiced and reinforced.

MAINTENANCE AND ONGOING ASSESSMENT

In Prochaska and DiClemente's transtheoretical model of how individuals change, relapse is an integral part of the change process (Prochaska and DiClemente 1984). Relapse does not necessarily mean that the individual returns to a precontemplative state, yet the very fact of some reversal or movement toward unsafe sex suggests that there is more to be learned about the patient's personal change process. Most psychotherapists don't need to be reminded about the fragility and impermanence of change; however, it's prudent not to allow our wishes for therapeutic omnipotence interfere with continuous assessment of actual patient practice.

After a period in which Steve had successfully negotiated safer sex with an ongoing partner, his therapist was surprised to discover how quickly he relapsed into unsafe sexual practices after the relationship ended. Steve had not lost the skills gained in ongoing therapy; he could still recognize his automatic thoughts and respond appropriately to them, but he excused himself from this in the wake of his painful breakup.

Steve: I know that I should be reminding myself that it's not inevitable, but I just don't seem to care as much anymore. I guess when Bob and I broke up, I didn't really care what happened to me.

Therapist: Are you feeling that way now?

S: Sort of, but I know what you'll say, I'm "catastrophizing"; one breakup does not consign me to a lifetime of abandonment and loneliness.

T: Does having unsafe sex make it more or less likely that you'll feel lonely in the future?

S: Well, if I get AIDS, I'll feel lonely, because it will probably be harder for me to find a lover, but maybe I'll also have more support. The gay community in New York's pretty good about taking care of PWAs [persons with AIDS].

T: You assume that becoming HIV positive will enable you to get more support, but I wonder if you are using all the support available to you now. It seems like the amount of support is not the problem. Your friends have expressed a great deal of concern and really reached out to you since your breakup with Bob, yet you consistently reject their advances.

S: It's not fun, I don't like myself right now.

T: What makes you think that you will utilize support that is available if you become HIV positive? Do you imagine you would like yourself any more then?

S: Definitely not! I'd be incredibly ashamed. I see your point. I guess I'm not really thinking this through, am I?

Steve's therapist was able to use his patient's insight to point out logical inconsistencies that interfered with behavior change. Other patients may not be so easy to redirect back toward contemplation and behavior change.

John stopped using condoms after he had difficulty maintaining an erection during a sexual encounter with a prostitute.

John: I tell you, Doc, it was the most embarrassing moment of my life. There was this hot chick laying there and here I was fumbling around with this Trojan and trying to get hard and she's probably thinking, "God, what a loser, this joker can't even get it up . . ."

Therapist: So you imagined her laughing at you. Was there any evidence that she was getting impatient?

J: Not really. She kept saying—aww, I'm embarrassed.

T: She said . . . ?

J: She kept saying, "Hey, big boy, you're pretty hot stuff . . ." and stuff like that (*grins*).

T: So you can pretty much see that the notion that she was disappointed in you was an automatic thought. And were there any silent assumptions?

J: Naw, just the usual thought that I'd better get it up or else.

John's emotional response to being with a prostitute has disrupted his capacity to identify irrational assumptions. His therapist therefore tried a vertical descent, a method of establishing what was really frightening John. In this technique the therapist asks what the patient thinks would happen if his assumptions were true.

T: Or else?

J: Or else she might walk out, leave me high and dry.

T: And if she did leave, what would you think then?

J: That I deserved it.

T: Deserved it how?

J: Because I let her down.

T: Let's say you had let this woman down. How would you feel?

J: Like I was no kind of man, you know, shamed.

T: John, you'd feel ashamed for letting down this woman?

J: Maybe that's too strong a word, embarrassed like.

T: You'd feel embarrassed for not getting an erection with a woman you hardly knew.

J: Kinda stupid, huh? And besides, I didn't know what to expect. This chick could have been packing a knife or whatnot. She coulda robbed me.

T: So was it the condom, or your fear of this woman, that kept you from getting aroused?

J: You know, you're right! My not getting hard mighta had nothing to do with the Trojan.

John recognized that he was exaggerating the consequences of this one incident and had misattributed it to condom use rather than sex with a stranger of whom he was somewhat frightened. Vertical descent is a valuable tool for helping overwhelmed patients clarify their real fears and regain perspective.

Within cognitive-behavioral therapy, once skills or actions have been mastered they must be reinforced, yet reward or reinforcement is an uncomfortable issue for many psychotherapists. Some gestalt and systems-oriented therapists have no difficulty reinforcing their patients after a particularly nice analysis of their underlying assumptions or issues. Often this will involve direct praise or calling attention to the effort. Objections to reinforcement come from two quarters: client-centered theory and psychodynamic theory. Client-centered or Rogerian therapists see reinforcement as overly directive and undermining of the patient's organismic freedom. Psychodynamic therapists set reinforcement under the rubric of "indulging the patient's transference wishes." Yet this objection of principle must be weighed against the facts of dynamic practice. How different is the therapist's comment "nice work," or inquiring how a patient managed to accomplish a particularly difficult task, from acknowledging a profound insight, noting the relationship between dream structure and affect, or pointing out the connection between conscious awareness of one's wishes and the ability to initiate effective behavior, things dynamic therapists do all the time?

Rogerians have a much stronger point: if an action is truly satisfying, it will not need artificial reinforcement. Yet maintaining successful HIV prevention behavior is neither easy nor immediately satisfying. It has many long-term advantages, but patients may need help in recognizing the benefits of behavior that is inconvenient, uncomfortable, and often experienced as depriving.

A FINAL THOUGHT
ABOUT PSYCHOTHERAPY INTEGRATION

Recently a respected colleague commented that he did not believe it was possible to integrate cognitive-behavioral techniques into other forms of psychotherapy without also accepting the assumptions of cognitive-behavioral theory. While his argument seems logical—"pure" psychotherapies are generally *assumed* to be more effective—this chapter attempts to make the opposite point: effective psychotherapy involves a combination of techniques, rigorously learned and sensitively applied.

Psychotherapists show notorious inconsistencies between what they say they're doing and what they actually do in the consulting room. No matter what their theoretical orientation or professional affiliations, the majority of clinicians actually practice something akin to eclectic psychotherapy (Jensen et al. 1990). Rather than denigrate this, we should applaud their efforts. Contemporary practice is richer for its open-mindedness.

This does not mean that theory has no place in the therapeutic milieu. On the contrary, psychological theory provides valuable guidelines for clinical endeavor: at difficult decision points it tells us what to do next; it enables the therapist to maintain relative consistency over time, which may in itself serve as a curative factor; and it guides new modes of scientific and clinical inquiry. But to the degree that theory becomes rigid or hegemonic, it also becomes obstructive and endangers creativity. If we are to treat patients holistically, indeed effectively, we cannot allow fidelity to theory to constrain therapeutic alternatives.

HIV prevention should be integrated into psychotherapy because it is *pragmatic*—meaning it is effective and prudent—to do so: within the context of therapy, HIV prevention techniques can be individualized to the patient's unique needs and skills, they can engender greater trust between patient and therapist, and they show recognition that the patient is a whole person with diverse problems and circumstances. Furthermore, it may be unethical not to do it: If a patient in three-day-a-week psychotherapy were to set the couch on fire with a lit cigarette, should the analyst interpret the meaning of the cigarette or get the patient away from the flames? This somewhat obvious analogy applies to HIV prevention: If we know our patients are endangering themselves yet do not help them to change their behavior, what is the use of therapy?

The value of psychotherapy ultimately rests on pragmatic innovation rather than on fidelity to any parochial theoretical stance. Yet therapists of all stripes continue to betray misguided dogmatism. This is all the more ironic as evidence increasingly shows that therapy in most of its forms can work most of the time, and that no one approach is necessarily better than another (Seligman 1995). Contemporary therapists are therefore free to adopt a pragmatic approach, doing what works. A century of psychotherapeutic practice has given us a considerable repertoire of techniques that work to improve the quality (and quantity) of patient experience. Good therapists will have a variety of these skills at their disposal. The challenge for the contemporary clinician is to appreciate and employ the diverse options of psychotherapeutic practice.

REFERENCES

Bandura, A. (1988). Perceived self-efficacy in the exercise of control over AIDS infection. In *Primary Prevention of AIDS: Psychological Approaches*, ed. V. M. Mays, G. W. Albee, and S. F. Schneider, pp. 128–141. Newbury Park, CA: Sage.

Batchelor, W. (1988). AIDS 1988: science and the limits of science. *American Psychologist* 43:853–858.

Beck, A. T., Rush, J. A., Shaw, B. F., and Emery, G. (1979). *Cognitive Treatment of Depression*. New York: Guilford.

Centers for Disease Control and Prevention (1996). *HIV/AIDS Surveillance Report* 8(1). Atlanta, GA: U. S. Department of Health and Human Services.

Freedman, A. M. (1995). The biopsychosocial paradigm and the future of psychiatry. *Comprehensive Psychiatry* 36(6):396–406.

Goldfried, M. R., ed. (1982). *Converging Themes in Psychotherapy*. New York: Springer.

Ho, D. D. (1995). Time to hit HIV, early and hard. *New England Journal of Medicine* 333:450–451.

Jensen, J. P., Bergen, A. E., and Greaves, D. W. (1990). The meaning of electicism: a new survey and analysis of components. *Professional Psychology: Research and Practice* 21:124–130.

Kelly, J. A. (1995). *Changing HIV Risk Behavior: Practical Strategies.* New York: Guilford.

Miller, W. R., and Rollnick, S., eds. (1991). *Motivational Interviewing: Preparing People to Change Addictive Behavior.* New York: Guilford.

Perelson, A. S., Neuman, A. U., Markowitz, M., et al. (1996). HIV-1 dynamics in vivo: virion clearance rate infected cell lifespan, and viral generation time. *Science* 271:1582–1586.

Prochaska, J. O., and DiClemente, C. C. (1982). Transtheoretical therapy: toward a more integrative model of change. *Psychotherapy: Theory, Research, and Practice* 19:276–288.

——— (1983). Stages and processes of self-change of smoking: toward an integrative model of change. *Journal of Consulting and Clinical Psychology* 51:390–395.

——— (1984). *The Transtheoretical Approach: Crossing Traditional Boundaries of Therapy.* Homewood, IL: Dow Jones/Irwin.

Rotheram-Borus, M. J., Koopman, C., and Haignere, C. (1991). Reducing HIV sexual risk behavior among runaway adolescents. *Journal of the American Medical Association* 266:1237–1241.

Seligman, M. E. P. (1995). The effectiveness of psychotherapy: the Consumer Reports study. *American Psychologist* 50:965–974.

Volberding, P. A. (1992). Clinical spectrum of HIV disease. In *AIDS: Etiology, Treatment, and Prevention*, ed. V. T. DeVita, Jr., S. Hellman, and S. A. Rosenberg, pp. 123–140. Philadelphia: Lippincott.

Wachtel, P. L. (1977). *Psychoanalysis and Behavior Therapy: Toward an Integration.* New York: Basic Books.

——— (1987). *Action and Insight.* New York: Guilford.

17

PHYSICAL DISABILITY

Cynthia L. Radnitz
Dennis D. Tirch

In treating those with disabilities, the role of a cognitive behavioral therapist is to help patients as they face the unavoidable challenges and psychological sequelae that accompany a disabling condition. In addressing the psychological aftermath of a disability, limitations imposed by such a condition may indicate cognitive-behavioral therapy as a treatment of choice (Sweetland 1990). This is due to its emphasis on promoting change on a cognitive level, an area that is not limited by the effects of most disabling conditions. In addressing dysfunctional thought patterns, patients can move toward an experience of mastery and adequacy that they may be denied in their physical interaction with the environment.

Behavioral change may also be pursued through more direct methods. For example, a common goal of cognitive-behavioral therapy for those with disabilities is the scheduling of pleasurable activities. The therapist attempts to assist the patient in realizing the range of available behaviors that can provide fulfilling experiences regardless of the presence of a disability.

Other behavioral techniques that may be employed include assertiveness training and time management instruction.

The psychological difficulties faced by a person with a disability may be understood primarily as a process of adjustment and integration. Thus a synthesis of stage models of adjustment with cognitive-behavioral theory has been put forward (Calabro 1990). Calabro divides the adjustment process into three phases: the preencounter phase, the postencounter phase, and the rational reencounter phase. The preencounter stage takes place after the onset of a disability, yet before the reality of becoming disabled has been accepted. Calabro hypothesizes the use of shock and denial as ways of avoiding acknowledging the ramifications of the disability. During the postencounter phase a person with a disability uses higher-order irrational cognitions to distance in order to avoid addressing the psychological issues that accompany a disabling condition. For example, a person may "bargain" with God for full rehabilitation, or may experience cognitive distortions regarding his or her personal worth and relationship to his or her environment. During the rational reencounter phase, distress has diminished to a point at which a therapist may intervene using cognitive-behavioral techniques.

While Calabro's model emphasizes cognitive changes that occur during different stages of adjustment, the model we propose focuses instead on how various factors interact to create cognitive distortions in persons with disabilities and how these distortions give rise to feelings and behaviors.

COGNITIVE-BEHAVIORAL MODEL

Description of the Model

Before describing our model, we feel it is important to address the issue of its applicability to different disabilities. Depending on the nature and severity of the disability, cognitive-behavioral therapists should adopt different approaches. Disabling conditions are quite diverse, so a unitary approach will prove inadequate in some cases. For example, the techniques described by Swendson and Carmody (1994) for conducting cognitive-behavioral therapy with memory-impaired patients would not be appropriate for persons without memory impairment who have another disabling condition, such as a newly acquired spinal cord injury or congenital blindness. Hence, the model we propose should not be considered universally applicable to all persons with disabilities. Rather, we hope it will prove to be a useful heuristic for understanding what contributes to the psychological impact of acquiring a disability or realizing that one has become disabled. The model should not be applied to many persons with disabilities, especially those with substantial cognitive impairment who may not have the capacity to understand what it means to have a disability. It may be helpful, however, for those who do have this capacity, and who experience some of the negative consequences of having a disabling condition.

From a cognitive-behavioral perspective, the way people interpret their experience will determine feelings and behaviors. Persons with disabilities often present with irrational cognitions concerning their future, their environment, and themselves. This set of maladaptive thoughts corresponds to the "cognitive triad" of dysfunctional assumptions that Beck and colleagues (1979) have used to construe the cognitive schemata of depressive patients.

Key distortions in this cognitive triad may stem from a number of sources, and may lead to various problems. In applying such a perspective to persons with disabilities, an interactional relationship between preexisting factors, environmental factors, and the consequences of suffering a disabling condition is apparent (see Figure 17–1). Accordingly, the therapist must emphasize a careful formulation, viewing

Figure 17–1. Cognitive-Behavioral Model

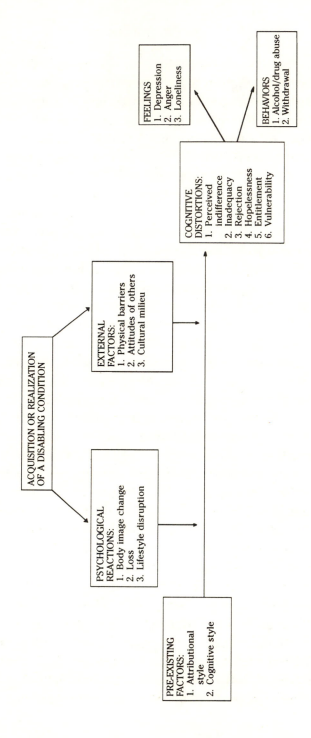

the client's narrative history with attention to events or other circumstances that may have led to the development of maladaptive cognitions. Our model is based primarily on clinical experience with persons with spinal cord injury, and accordingly it is more focused on the needs of individuals with acquired disabilities. Nevertheless, as Calabro's (1990) model suggests, the activating event in the development of a cognitive distortion is not necessarily the acquisition of a disability, but an apprehension of the nature of the disabling condition itself. The model can therefore be applied to persons who have been disabled since birth.

In the model, preexisting factors can influence the content of cognitive distortions. Among such factors, preinjury cognitive and attributional styles will determine the nature of irrational and distressing cognitions for persons with acquired disabilities. For example, after acquiring a disability and having to ask others for help, a self-reliant person may develop a greater sense of inadequacy than would someone who depended on others for help in solving problems preinjury. In the case of individuals with lifelong disabilities, internal factors include the processing style that emerged prior to the mature development of the cognitive representation of the condition.

Along similar lines, attributional style will also contribute to the character of cognitive distortions. For example, persons who make global, stable attributions for negative life events are more likely than others to report negative cognitions and to experience depression (Abramson et al. 1978). They may have increased difficulty adjusting to the presence of a disability. These individuals come to view the world as a perpetually threatening place or a source of constant suffering. Obviously, they will most likely present with cognitive distortions different from persons with other attributional styles.

These preexisting factors will influence the processing of external events. Life circumstances and environmental factors may also play a large role in deciding the character of maladaptive cognitions and assumptions. The therapist should never lose sight of the impact of external elements on the phenomenology of a person with a disability. Adaptation to the physical barriers challenging the daily life of a person with a physical disability is an environmental condition that may be addressed in cognitive-behavioral therapy. For example, an individual with a physical disability may be forced to ask others for help to negotiate places that are not appropriately accessible. Shyness, embarrassment, prejudice, or social awkwardness may interact with the need to handle an actual obstacle. Thus a physical barrier may call for behaviors that the individual may not feel comfortable engaging in, or may not have sufficient skills to manage. Consequently, an interactional relationship that can engender cognitive distortions can develop between preexisting factors and external barriers.

Social as well as physical barriers clearly impact upon the thoughts of a person with a disability. We all define ourselves in relation to others on some level. Often, biases against individuals with disabilities may extend far beyond their immediate social support network. Portrayal of those with disabilities in the media and culture is not always reality-based or free from prejudice. It is easy to recall commonly employed cultural images of a sickly handicapped shut-in or a drunken, despondent, and disabled veteran. Insensitive and inaccurate media depiction of those with disabilities can enhance an individual's feelings of stigmatization. Perceived cultural biases may lead to a person's thinking of him- or herself as an "oppressed minority" (Hepner et al. 1980–1981).

Interacting with preexisting factors and external events is the individual's psychological reaction to becoming disabled or realizing that he or she is disabled. For those with acquired disabilities, the psychological impact often includes loss, body image change, and life-style disruption. The losses that occur as a result of acquiring a disability, although variable, are often substantial. They can include loss of ability, loss of body parts, (amputation), loss of significant others, loss of job/profession, loss of health, and loss of independence. A change in body image may occur after an injury that results in amputation or requires placement in a wheelchair. Even becoming hearing impaired may result in body image change if the individual is required to wear a hearing aid. Finally, life-style disruption is often part of the psychological impact of acquiring a disability. The interruption of plans and ongoing projects and being unable to meet responsibilities certainly can influence the content of thought, especially soon after the acquisition of the disability. For those with nonacquired disabilities, the impact of realizing that one has a disability often centers around the apprehension that one is different from or inferior to others. This recognition of differences may take the form of noticing differences in appearance and/or abilities. Whether the psychological reaction is to acquiring a disability or realizing that one exists, the reaction will nonetheless influence the character of subsequent cognitions.

Cognitive distortions may arise from the interaction between preexisting factors, external factors, and the psychological impact of a disabling condition. These cognitive distortions can lead to the subjective experience of sadness, anger, frustration, and fear. By addressing the dysfunctional assumptions that lead to such feelings, the cognitive-behavioral therapist seeks to disrupt the maintaining cognitive infrastructure that causes psychological distress. Accordingly, interventions focusing on the restructuring of such maladaptive cognitions have shown clinical utility. Cognitive-behavioral therapy does not pursue the fundamental reorganization of the patient's personality. Rather, the cognitive behavioral therapist seeks to promote behavioral circumstances to ease the process of adaptation that a person with disability endures, interacting with the limitations and challenges present in his or her environment.

Beyond initiating cognitive distortions, a disability imposes limitatations that may lead the individual to withdraw and avoid behaviors that could result in pleasure or mastery. For instance, a physical disability may impair the ability to engage in leisure activities, such as playing sports or attending nonaccessible events. Alternatively, persons with disabilities may misuse alcohol or other drugs as a way to cope or fill their time. A common goal of cognitive-behavioral therapy with persons with disability is the scheduling of pleasurable activities. In this way the therapist attempts to help the patient to discover behaviors that can be fulfilling despite their disability and to avoid the risks of engaging in maladaptive coping behaviors. Assertiveness training can also be employed with persons with disabilities to remove the barriers of shyness or social stigma from their interactions with others. Thus they will be more likely to feel comfortable asking for help when it is needed, or simply to engage in conversation more readily.

Types of Cognitive Distortions

We have identified six categories of cognitive distortions that seem particularly relevant to those with disabilities (see Figure 17–1). The first category revolves around the belief that the world is an indifferent place that will never go out of its way to accommodate those who deviate from the norm. Those with disabilities may come to believe that people they encounter in their daily lives are insensitive and indifferent toward them. In essence, they believe that the world is geared toward others. While biases against persons who deviate from a perceived norm do exist in our culture, they are not as pervasive or generally as overtly mean-spirited as those who present with this cognitive distortion believe. Accordingly, behavior based on such beliefs may reduce the likelihood that they will experience positive social interactions with others and thus validate the distortions by negative experience.

A second cluster of cognitive distortions centers around feelings of inadequacy. As the individual must increasingly rely upon others, he or she may come to believe in their own fundamental worthlessness due to a perceived lack of ability. In making comparisons between themselves and others, those with disabilities may persist in seeing themselves as deficient.

Such a negative appraisal of self-worth can lead directly into the third group of maladaptive cognitions, those of rejection. Persons with a disability may expect that others will reject them based on their disability. They may anticipate rejection during social situations, job interviews, and/or interactions with co-workers. Their lack of capacity comes to represent an absence of personal worth to them, and they imagine that others will share this view. Such persons may believe others are treating them with contempt rather than compassion, and condescension rather than respect and concern. Consequently, those who present with this distortion expect rejection and failure when interacting with others.

The fourth cognitive distortion exhibited by those with disabilities is that of hopelessness. Faced with considerable concrete obstacles, they begin to expect consistent failure. They believe there is no hope that they will be happy or meet reasonable personal, social, or occupational goals. Such cognitive distortions can lead to feelings of despair, depression, and anxiety. In coping with the negative affect resulting from these distortions, many individuals with disabilities may withdraw from others or engage in alcohol or other drug abuse. This behavior in turn can hamper their developing faith in their own capacities as well as a sense of hopefulness.

Distortions focused on a sense of personal entitlement constitute the fifth group of maladaptive cognitions. Persons who have such cognitions believe that, as they have been dealt an unfair hand by life, others should consistently go out of their way to take care of and provide for them. In an attempt to reframe positively and summarily avoid accepting the limitations imposed by a disability, some individuals will draw excessive pleasure from being catered to in a hospital setting or by a caring family. They may come to draw their pleasure exclusively from being the center of attention of caregivers. Such behavior can lead to hostility from others who may come to resent their dependency.

An overemphasis on the vulnerability that accompanies a disability constitutes the sixth cognitive distortion. For example, a person who is blind may have some early experience of physical accidents that they may perceive as embarrassing, catastrophic, or foreboding. As a result, they may overestimate the risks present in simply going from place to place in a safe manner. Admittedly, we live in a dangerous society. Moreover, persons with disabilities who live in low socioeconomic status, high-crime neighborhoods may be constantly reminded of the dangers of violent crime and their potential vulnerability as victims. However, individuals who present with cognitive distortions centering on vulnerability tend to overestimate risks of accident and victimization. They experience fear of their environment and may endure a great deal of resulting anxiety. This may lead to isolation and withdrawal from pleasurable activities.

CASE STUDY

Through the application of cognitive-behavioral techniques such as role-playing, visualization, thought-stopping, and rational reframing of cognitive distortions, the clinician seeks to lead the client toward behavior informed by rational, reality-based thoughts. From such a point, the clinician can guide the client in the application of adaptive coping methods to adjust to life with a disability. To illustrate how this may be done, we have provided the following case example.

Background

D. L. was a 40-year-old white divorced male admitted to a specialized unit for treating substance abuse in veterans with spinal cord injury. He sought treatment in order to stop using drugs, to become less depressed, and to find a meaningful career path. His primary substance of abuse was marijuana, which he first used in 1987. Upon admission, he reported smoking twenty "joints" per day so that he would remain high throughout the day; he also reported intermittent cocaine use (two or three times per month). He had completed one previous inpatient program for drug use, after which he remained clean for one year. During that year he lived in a small city in Washington state where wheelchair-accessible housing and public transportation were scarce.

He described many frustrating episodes in which, because of the disability, he encountered obstacles. Often he would have to wait over an hour for a bus with a functioning wheelchair lift. When seeking support in overcoming drug abuse, he would sometimes have to wait for someone to carry him into an AA meeting, since accessible meetings were held only once each week. He also reported difficulty living within his income of only $500/month. His eventual relapse to both drug use and drug selling he attributed to his persistent frustration in having to negotiate barriers and having to live on a small income.

His psychiatric history was remarkable for both depression and suicidality. He described being depressed intermittently since his spinal cord injury in April 1985 when the jealous ex-boyfriend of one of his girlfriends (he was separated from his wife at the time) stabbed him in the spine. He was diagnosed with C5–6 quadriplegia, incomplete. Since his injury he has made two suicide attempts, one in 1988 and one in 1992. In both cases he reported taking too many diazepam pills, and in both cases he was hospitalized for a few days and then released. He reported no previous outpatient psycho-therapy, although follow-up visits had been scheduled after each of his hospitalizations. A mental status examination revealed no evidence of psychosis or gross cognitive impairment. However, the patient did appear depressed.

D. L. was the fourth of eight siblings, and the third boy. His father was his mother's second husband. During most of D. L.'s young life his father was absent from the family, serving in the Navy aboard a submarine. His parents divorced when the patient was 10 years old, after which his mother began living with the man who fathered her youngest two children. This man remained living with the patient's mother until two years ago, when he died. While D. L. was growing up, his stepfather had a job delivering beer. According to D. L., his stepfather frequently drank on the job and came home drunk. Although he never beat them, the stepfather was often intoxicated in the presence of the patient and his siblings.

D. L. described his childhood as difficult. His older brothers would beat him daily, and he described one instance when his oldest brother tried to drown him. He began leaving school after lunch to avoid them, and ran away repeatedly from age 7 to 14. At that time he was sent to reform school for stealing a car. While there, he received training in the Job Corps, having at the time completed only the sixth grade. With the exception of a two-year tour of duty in the military from age 18 to 20, he worked as a truck driver "off the books" until his injury in 1985. D. L. has been married once, and has two children by his ex-wife, a daughter age 22 and a son age 18. His daughter has one son, age 3. The patient married his wife two years after his daughter was born. They separated in 1990 and divorced in 1992. At the time of admission, the patient was not on good terms with his ex-wife, and had not spoken with his children in three months. He did not think they had a telephone at home, and his children had not responded to two letters he had written.

Treatment Plan

In discussions of the treatment plan with the interdisciplinary team (psychiatrist, psychologist, social worker, and clinical nurse specialist) and the patient, it was agreed that in individual therapy a cognitive-behavioral approach would be adopted. Individual treatment would focus on treating depressive symptomatology, assertiveness, and time management. Issues related to substance abuse would be addressed in group therapy.

Intervention and Outcome

Individual therapy was conducted once per week for six months. Upon admission, the patient's Beck Depression Inventory (BDI) (Beck et al. 1961) score was 35. The rationale for cognitive behavioral therapy was explained to him. To address his maladaptive cognitive distortions he was introduced to self-monitoring. He did not seem enthusiastic about self-monitoring, but agreed to do it. During the first few sessions the patient repeatedly reported having neglected to complete his self-monitoring homework. The importance of complying in this respect was reinforced, yet still he would not complete this assignment. Although initial investigation failed to reveal the reason for his noncompliance, it was soon discovered that he was ashamed of his penmanship and spelling. The patient possessed a sixth-grade education, yet his handwriting was slow and primitive, and his spelling abilities were also less advanced (testing showed him to be at a third-grade level). The patient admitted, however, that he self-monitored without writing anything down, and in this way was able to reframe his thoughts effectively. As he became proficient in cognitive restructuring techniques, his BDI score decreased to 12. Patient and therapist agreed that instead of the written self-monitoring, the patient would self-monitor cognitively, and thoughts would be reviewed in session. The patient was also taught to identify distortions and to substitute rational responses for the maladaptive cognitions. Core cognitions centered on issues of rejection, inadequacy, and hopelessness.

Periodic assessment of depression using the BDI revealed a consistent decline in scores to the point where, at discharge, the patient was asymptomatic. He attributed this improvement to learning to change his thinking pattern.

Other interventions included problem-solving, how to renew contact with his children. The therapist modeled how to obtain directory assistance long distance. The patient was able to call his children's schools and talk to his children at school. He discovered that they had moved and had not received his letters. D. L. gave his children his telephone number and has remained in frequent contact with them ever since. On his own, he initiated a reconciliation with his ex-wife, who was planning to remarry. They reconciled their differences in the interest of their children. The patient seemed confident that he would maintain contact with his children.

The patient was also taught assertiveness skills to better enable him to cope with environmental obstacles. Typically, persons with disabilities need to be more assertive than others, since they often need assistance from the environment to meet their needs. After the rationale for assertiveness skills was presented, the patient described several situations in which assertive responses were required. Initially, the therapist [CLR] modeled assertive behavior. Then the patient practiced these responses in role-play situations with the therapist, where she would give him feedback to help him improve his skills. The final step involved having D. L. practice his new skills in situations which occurred in his daily life. In this way he learned how to cope with a variety of situations frequently encountered by individuals in wheelchairs. These included others pushing him without being requested to do so, asking someone to carry him over the door threshold into inaccessible AA meetings, and so forth. By the time treatment ended, the patient showed substantial improvement in assertiveness, as demonstrated by his taking an active role in planning his discharge.

One final intervention involved teaching D. L. to schedule his time so that he would avoid boredom and better meet his obligations. In the past he reported boredom as a frequent precursor to using drugs. Persons with disabilities who do not work often report being bored a great deal of the time, not only because they lack employment but also because their disabilities in some ways limit the activities in which they can participate. D. L. learned to better schedule his time (although there was room for improvement) and discovered that he liked to read more than he thought.

With respect to his substance abuse problem, toxicological tests confirmed that he was abstinent from drugs and alcohol during his entire stay; upon discharge he was confident that he could remain abstinent.

Discussion

In many ways D. L. is illustrative of the issues presented by persons with disabilities. We can easily apply our model to his case. Before he was injured, he was at risk for developing depression and a substance abuse problem, having suffered severe abuse during childhood and having as his primary male role model an alcohol abuser. We can hypothesize that the occurrence of his spinal cord injury reinforced cognitions centering on the themes of inadequacy, hopelessness, and rejection. Moreover, living in a city not easily accessible and lacking the skills to assert himself in order to acquire what he needed served only to reinforce his belief that his environment was indifferent. He also reported negative cognitions stemming from having lost contact with his children. These negative cognitions, in turn, led to feelings of deep depression. Also contributing to his depression was his inability to organize his time, to regularly schedule pleasant events and find structured activities that would give him a sense of purpose. It is likely that his drug use was an attempt to medicate his depression. He reported engaging in it to forget how miserable reality was. However, although drug use afforded temporary relief, in the long run it only worsened his despondency.

CONCLUSION

The choice of how to approach a person with a disability from a cognitive-behavioral perspective depends upon the nature and severity of the disability. Persons with diverse disabilities present different issues in the therapeutic setting so that a "one size fits all" approach may at times meet with failure. However, in trying to capture how the experience of acquiring a disability or realizing that one is disabled affects an individual, we have presented a model that we hope may serve as a heuristic for the clinician attempting to treat a patient with a disability. In this model, preexisting factors are hypothesized to interact with the psychological fallout of the onset of a disability or the realization that one is disabled. Also contributing to the mix are external factors such as physical and attitudinal barriers and the cultural milieu. As a result, the individual may develop a set of cognitive distortions centering around themes of indifference, inadequacy, rejection, hopelessness, entitlement, and vulnerability. Consequences of these cognitions may include negative emotions such as depression, anger, anxiety, and frustration and/or behaviors such as substance abuse, withdrawal, and inactivity. To address the psychological sequelae of a disability, we have suggested several cognitive-behavioral techniques, and we have provided as an example a description of a clinical case treated from a cognitive-behavioral perspective.

REFERENCES

Abramson, L. Y., Seligman, M. E. P., and Teasdale, J. D. (1978). Learned helplessness in humans: critique and reformulation. *Journal of Abnormal Psychology* 87:49–74.

Beck, A. T., Shaw, B. F., and Emery, G. (1979). *Cognitive Therapy of Depression.* New York: Guilford.

Beck, A. T., Ward, C. H., Mendelson, M., et al. (1961). An inventory for measuring depression. *Archives of General Psychiatry* 4:561–571.

Calabro, L. E. (1990). Adjustment to disability: a cognitive-behavioral model for analysis and clinical management. *Journal of Rational-Emotive and Cognitive Behavior Therapy* 8(2):79–102.

Hepner, R., Kirshbaum, H., and Landes, D. (1980/1981). Counseling substance abusers with additional disabilities: The Center for Independent Living. *Alcohol Health and Research World* 5:11–15.

Sweetland, J. D. (1990). Cognitive-behavior therapy and physical disability. *Journal of Rational-Emotive and Cognitive-Behavior Therapy* 8(2):71–78.

Swendson, J., and Carmody, T. P. (1994). Cognitive behavioral therapy for memory-impaired patients. *The Behavior Therapist* 17(8):187–189.

18

INTEGRATIVE COGNITIVE THERAPY

Stephen J. Holland

Cognitive therapy is now widely recognized as one of the treatments of choice for major depression. Numerous studies have found it to be as effective as medication for most patients, and superior to medication in preventing relapse (Hollon et al. 1991). Nonetheless, not all depressed patients respond to cognitive therapy. Patients with personality disorders, in particular, are known to have poorer response to all forms of treatment, including medication and cognitive therapy. These patients often appear to cling to dysfunctional behaviors and beliefs even when the costs of such behaviors are clear to them. They also frequently fail to comply with the requirements of treatment, such as regularly attending sessions and completing homework.

This chapter describes a form of cognitive therapy that integrates aspects of theory and technique from psychodynamic therapy. After describing the theoretical model, I discuss some of the technical implications and potential advantages for dealing with patients with personality disorders. A case example illustrates the application of the model to a case of treatment-resistant depression.

INTEGRATIVE COGNITIVE THERAPY

The psychodynamic aspects of the model of integrative cognitive therapy to be described here derive largely from the short-term dynamic work of Malan (1979), Davenloo (1980), and Alpert (1992). At the core of all of these approaches is Malan's concept of the two triangles—The Triangle of Defense and the Triangle of Person—which are shown in Figure 18–1.

The central idea of Malan's model is that patients' difficulties are caused by defensive maneuvers that are initiated in

Figure 18–1. The Two Triangles*

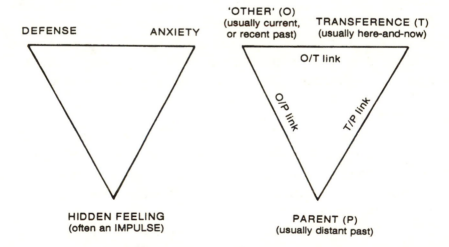

*From Malan 1979, p. 80. Copyright © 1979 by Butterworth-Heinemann and reprinted by permission.

response to anxieties they feel about experiencing or expressing certain impulses or feelings. The chief therapeutic technique is to make interpretations linking the defense, the
anxiety, and the hidden feeling. Interpretations also link the
patient's experience of these patterns with significant figures
in their past and current life, and with their behavior with the
therapist.

Careful consideration of this model indicates much that is
compatible with cognitive-behavioral theory. The Triangle of
Person is easily reconceptualized as the Triangle of Generalization. What is learned from one's parents is generalized to
other people, including the therapist, and what is learned in
therapy must also be generalized to other figures in the
patient's life.

Similarly, if the Triangle of Defense is examined carefully, it
becomes clear that cognition, in one form or another, plays a
central role. First, the anxiety that triggers the defense is
always caused by some belief, conscious or otherwise, about
what will happen if the impulse or feeling is experienced or
expressed. For example, expressing a certain emotion, such as
anger, may be seen as leading to loss of love, retaliation, or
some other painful consequence. In addition, defenses, almost
by definition, result in some compromise in reality testing. In
other words, they lead to cognitive distortions. Thus cognitions may be seen as forming the sides of the Triangle of
Defense.

When the role of cognition in the Triangle of Defense is made
explicit, one gets a model that looks like Figure 18–2. Defenses
involve distortions in reality testing, which result in unrealistic
automatic thoughts and/or behavior that is triggered by those
thoughts. The anxiety that initiates the defense is caused by
schemas or assumptions about the dangerousness of certain
impulses or feelings. The beliefs that produce the anxiety can
be seen as primary, while the defensive beliefs are secondary.

There is no theoretical reason to assume that conscious

Figure 18–2. Role of Cognition in the Triangle of Defense*

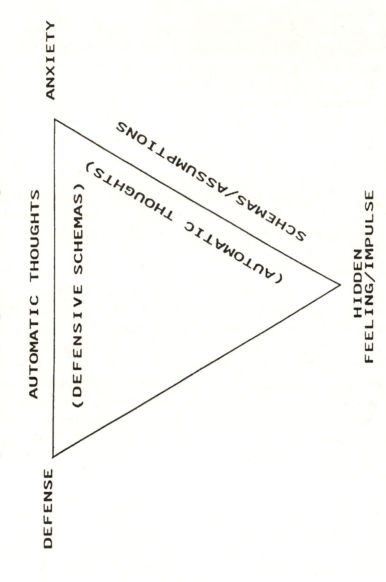

*From Holland 1996.

automatic thoughts occur only on the defensive side of the triangle or that schemas occur only on the anxiety side. In fact, schemas can be defensively activated or elaborated outside of conscious awareness. Similarly, the primary fears associated with experiencing certain impulses may manifest directly as conscious automatic thoughts.

Theoretical Implications

Integrating Malan's (1979) model with cognitive therapy has two important theoretical implications. First, it brings to cognitive therapy a theory of defense. Second, it suggests that special attention must be paid to patients' fears about experiencing certain basic emotions and impulses.

A theory of defense is crucial in understanding resistance. In this model, resistance to therapy, such as failing to do homework or set an agenda, rather than being viewed as evidence of lack of motivation or a character flaw, is seen as a defensive reaction to some anxiety. Inquiring about the anxiety that triggers such behavior (or nonbehavior) will often provide important information about patients' primary fears.

A theory of defense is also important in case conceptualization, particularly with patients with personality disorders. This model suggests that the tenacity with which such patients cling to their dysfunctional beliefs and behaviors is related to the strength of their primary fears. It also suggests that, for therapy to be successful, those primary fears must be accessed and modified.

Technical Implications

Using the Triangle of Defense as a guide in conducting cognitive therapy also has several technical implications. The first is that it is not always necessary to know where on the triangle one is when beginning to challenge a patient's automatic thoughts. A common fear for dynamically trained clinicians is that using cognitive techniques to address a patient's conscious thoughts will reinforce the patient's defenses. In fact, if the belief is defensive, challenging it effectively will often lead to the primary fear.

For example, a patient came into session one day and reported that he was very angry at a female co-worker. His presenting problem was that he spent several hours a day masturbating while having angry thoughts about women. From his description it sounded as if the woman had simply been acting friendly. However, the patient's automatic thought was, "She's a manipulative bitch." Socratic dialogue was initiated and the patient was asked whether he would think a man was manipulative if he engaged in the same behavior. After some minutes of cognitive challenge, the patient suddenly blurted out, "OK, you're right. It's just that I'm afraid that I'll like her too much." His fear was that he would be attracted to the woman and she would then reject him. Thus "She's a manipulative bitch" turned out to be a defensive cognition that was triggered by the anxiety produced by his underlying belief that he would be rejected by any woman he found attractive.

A second technical implication of this model is that while it is not always necessary to know where one is on the triangle, it can often be very useful. Ultimately one wants to be targeting primary schemas. This means that rather than spending time refuting a secondary belief, it will sometimes be more fruitful to point out its defensive function and focus instead on the primary belief. For example, I was working with a patient who presented with writer's block but was also dysthymic. After about ten sessions she was writing well and gave a very successful reading of new work. The next week she reported that she had had many thoughts berating herself for past mistakes. In standard cognitive therapy we would have done rational responding to those thoughts. Instead, I suggested that we look at why she needed to berate herself after a success. We quickly uncovered a primary fear: "If I get too excited about something, it will be taken away from me." It was only after we addressed this fear that she began to allow herself to really enjoy life and her dysthymia lifted.

Another implication of this model is that, while one can often bypass defensive beliefs, there are times when the defense is so deeply ingrained that it will require considerable attention. Some defensive patterns are self-perpetuating in ways that are best described in behavioral terms. Two classic examples of this are obsessive-compulsive disorder and substance abuse. In such cases it is usually necessary to first break the self-reinforcing cycle of defensive behavior, often using behavioral techniques. Only then can primary schemas be accessed and modified.

A final technical implication is that a wide range of techniques from various schools of therapy may be used to accomplish the ultimate goal of accessing and modifying primary schemas. This last point deserves more attention. In this model schema is defined broadly to include not only symbolic representation—what is commonly meant by thought or belief—but also emotions, physiological responses, behavior patterns, memories, and motivational states. Activating any one of these components makes it more likely that the others will also be activated. Since it is necessary to access a schema in order to modify it, this means that any technique that leads to any one of these components can be useful in therapy.

For example, techniques for accessing emotion have traditionally been the strong suit of psychodynamic and gestalt approaches. Reflection and accurate empathy can help patients focus on their emotions. Confronting defenses against feeling can help access emotions that are normally warded off. Gestalt techniques such as focusing on bodily sensations, guided imagery, and empty chair exercises can also be useful.

For accessing symbolic representation, cognitive techniques are obviously important. Daily Thought Records and cognitive descents can help identify typical automatic thoughts and underlying schemas. Examining the advantages and disadvantages of a belief may reveal defensive functions and hint at primary fears. Cognitive challenges to defensive beliefs will often lead directly to more primary beliefs. However, it is also important to recognize the strong cognitive component of psychodynamic technique. Interpretation is a cognitive tool. If you assume that not all schemas are fully accessible to consciousness, then it will often be very useful to point out to patients patterns in their thinking, emotions, or behavior and suggest tacit assumptions or beliefs that could explain these patterns. Also, careful listening to patients' associations— including unusual word choices, slips, and transitions from one thought to the next—can reveal a great deal about the content of their schemas.

Accessing schemas through behavior is of course the strong suit of behavioral approaches. Exposure is the best example of this. Putting a patient in contact with a feared object or situation will almost always activate schematic fears. For this reason exposure is often a good way of circumventing defenses against emotion.

In this regard, transference can be considered a special case of exposure. Most of our patients' dysfunctional beliefs were formed in and relate to interpersonal situations. The therapeutic relationship, therefore, provides a ready-made exposure situation that is bound to evoke primary fears. Not the least of the reasons why transference is so important is that being in therapy is likely to activate certain motivational states, such as a desire to be cared for and loved.

If transference is important for accessing schemas, then so too is countertransference. Our own emotional reactions to patients can provide important clues to the roles they see us as filling in their interpersonal schemas.

Finally, exploring memories that are linked to thoughts or emotions can provide information about the beliefs and rules that have guided patients' lives.

Accessing schemas is, of course, only the preliminary step. The ultimate goal is to modify the schemas, and it is here that an integrated approach can be particularly useful. If schemas consist of multiple components, it follows that using a variety of techniques to target as many aspects of the schemas as possible can enhance the speed and efficacy of therapy. It is often not enough to point out to patients that they are acting as if people in the present will treat them as they were treated by people in their past. It is generally more helpful to actively arrange a variety of experiences that help patients modify the cognitive, emotional, and behavioral components of dysfunctional schemas that may have been formed during their early life.

Cognitive techniques can be tremendously useful here. For example, examining the evidence for a primary belief across a patient's life can be a very powerful intervention. Often this will result in the patient's seeing that he or she has failed to attend to repeated contradictory evidence. It will also often help the patient see how events that he or she regarded as evidence for the fear are in fact the resultant behavior on their part that created a self-fulfilling prophecy. It can also be helpful to have patients consider whether their fears hold true for other people. Behavioral experiments as well can be important in changing beliefs.

Working with childhood memories, while not always necessary, can be an important part of this process. Obviously, the content of the memory cannot be changed, but the meaning attached to it can. Usually this takes the form of pointing out to patients that their original childhood interpretation of the event was wrong in some way or, if it was correct, that it no longer applies to their adult life. Role-playing formative events in such a way that patients can bring an adult perspective to the experience is often helpful in this regard.

The primary technique for modifying the emotional component of schemas is exposure. It is one thing for patients to believe logically that a feared catastrophe will not occur— though this is no small feat. It is another for them to believe it in their gut. The best way for that change to occur is for patients to repeatedly experience their feared situations, without the feared consequences occurring, until their anxiety is reduced. Adding response prevention to the exposure helps to change the behavioral pattern associated with the schemas by blocking avoidance behaviors.

Again, transference can be considered a special case of exposure. After all, what is the corrective emotional experience we want patients to have in therapy if not the opportunity to risk being vulnerable in spite of their anxiety, and to discover that we will not attack them, belittle them, abandon them, seduce them, or whatever their primary fear is. What is crucial for dynamically trained clinicians to recognize is that this kind of exposure work does not always have to happen in therapy. By doing formal exposure work, particularly involving interpersonal situations, one can achieve many of the same goals. At the same time, cognitive and behaviorally trained clinicians need to recognize that the transference does provide an especially potent form of exposure if properly utilized.

One final technique for changing schemas is skills building. Dynamically trained therapists often assume that if patients can resolve their intrapsychic conflict, adaptive behavior will emerge spontaneously. This is sometimes the case. However, if the conflict existed for so long that the patient never had the opportunity to learn adaptive behaviors, it will be necessary to teach them. In addition, patients often have to learn adaptive ways of coping before they feel confident enough to give up maladaptive ones.

In summary, integrating Malan's model with cognitive therapy allows greater flexibility in conceptualizing issues such as defense and resistance. It also provides a unified framework for bringing to bear a number of techniques from various schools of therapy with the ultimate goal of modifying patients' dysfunctional schemas. The following section describes the application of this model to a case of treatment- resistant depression.

CASE EXAMPLE

Susan was a 48-year-old Caucasian woman. She was married and worked as a lawyer in a small firm doing highly specialized work that was consistent with her political beliefs. She was referred by her psychiatrist because she had been depressed for over two years and had been unable to tolerate the side effects of several antidepressants. She was taking Wellbutrin at the time of intake and remained on it during treatment. She had previously been in psychotherapy with the same therapist for over ten years.

When I first saw Susan, she was having great difficulty concentrating at work. She found her work rewarding, but felt overwhelmed by the amount she had to do. However, she did not seem capable of refusing requests from either her superiors or her clients. She was also very dissatisfied with her marriage and complained that her husband was overly dependent on her and did not support her in working the long hours she felt were required by the responsibilities of her job. She frequently thought about divorce, but had not discussed this with her husband. She was so distressed by her ambivalent feelings about him, which she experienced as being like having two different voices in her head, that she was worried she was going crazy. In addition, she was troubled by recurring images of the death from cancer of a close friend approximately a year earlier. Susan met criteria for recurrent major depression. She also evidenced obsessive-compulsive personality features.

We initiated standard cognitive therapy for depression, including scheduling pleasurable activities and identifying and rationally responding to her negative automatic thoughts. Not surprisingly, we quickly ran into resistance. Susan had difficulty setting aside time for activities she enjoyed because she could not say no, either at work or at home. She appeared to believe that she had to meet all requests by anyone in her life, including her husband, her mother, her colleagues, and her clients.

In discussing this we uncovered an assumption: "I always have to help others because I am the strong one." It turned out that Susan had been given this message explicitly growing up and had actually taken care of her depressed mother and her siblings during her teenage years. We used cognitive techniques to begin to challenge this belief, with some success. Still, while it was clear how the assumption had formed, I wondered why Susan had never rebelled against it.

Since Susan was reporting ongoing conflict with her husband, I recommended couples therapy. However, Susan said she was too afraid to broach the subject with her husband. Among other things, she was afraid he would become angry and she wouldn't be able to handle his reaction. There was no history of violence in the relationship. In lieu of couples therapy, we began to look at the ways Susan reinforced her husband's dependent behaviors and failed to express her wishes to him. As she changed these behaviors she reported favorable changes by her husband, including more communication.

Susan's depression reduced somewhat, and she began to actively consider whether she wanted to stay married. After a few sessions of talking about this, however, she became unbearably anxious and requested that we change our focus to the intrusive images of her friend's death. It was apparent that we were hitting resistance again, but it was not yet clear what the resistance was about, so I agreed to the shift.

Susan had been friends with Sam for a number of years. Sam was gay, and although he had a longtime partner, Susan was a primary caregiver during the final gruesome months of Sam's death from cancer. The recurring images came from this period. She attempted to avoid the images by thinking of times when Sam had been healthy, but this tactic was not very successful. We approached the problem as if we were dealing with post-traumatic stress disorder. I first taught Susan anxiety management skills, including relaxation, thought stopping, and distraction. We then initiated imaginal exposure to the intrusive images, first in session and then as homework. Susan again became very anxious. In fact, she began to report that she was unable to remember portions of the sessions or what had been assigned for homework. She also called me a couple of times between sessions because she was afraid of how upset she had become while doing exposure work at home.

What began to be clear at this point was that Susan was very afraid—phobic, really—of any strong emotion. This was reflected in her fear of her husband's anger, in her fear that her ambivalent feelings about her marriage meant she was going insane, and in her difficulty tolerating her feelings about Sam's death.

I pointed out this pattern to Susan; as we began to discuss it, she reported the thought, "I am stable, responsible, reliable, capable, and all those other able words." The implied assumption was that any strong emotion she might experience could not be part of her and was therefore dangerous. We used cognitive techniques to explore whether it was possible to experience strong emotion and still be stable and capable, and whether, in fact, being able to tolerate rather than avoid strong emotion might not make her more stable. At this point she reported another spontaneous thought: "If I don't feel, you can't hurt me."

This thought sounded more primitive and probably more important. I asked who "you" was and Susan replied, "I don't know." So I asked her to look at an empty chair and repeat the thought out loud ten times. Susan balked. She became highly anxious and demanded to know why I was asking her to do such a thing. When I backed off from the request, she told me that "you" was her mother. This led to a discussion of part of her developmental history we had not yet explored.

It turned out that when Susan had been a young child she lived in what she described as an almost constant state of conflict with her mother. Their disputes often started with Susan asking to have some age-appropriate need met. When her mother refused, Susan would become angry. Her mother would respond by becoming enraged and abusive. For example, Susan would be forced to kneel on the floor for long periods of time and repeat Catholic prayers over and over. She experienced this as physically painful and emotionally overwhelming. Susan's way of coping was to try not to feel any need or emotion. As her mother was highly emotional and religious, she would become rational and nonreligious. She felt this was the only way she could triumph over her mother.

At this point we had a clearer picture of what was going on with Susan. Her belief that she was strong and stable and nonemotional and her pattern of always meeting other people's needs, while they had some origins in her developmental experience, also served a defensive function. They kept her from recognizing that she too had needs and from the anxiety associated with expressing those needs. The anxiety, in turn, was triggered by her largely unconscious fear that her needs would be denied, and that if she felt anger about this she would be humiliated and overwhelmed. Her fear of her own anger generalized to fear and avoidance of any strong emotion. Figure 18–3 shows how this conceptualization fits on the Triangle of Defense.

Having identified Susan's primary fears, we needed to modify

Figure 18–3. Case Conceptualization*

BELIEFS: I have to take care of others
                    because I am the strong one
                 I am stable, responsible, reliable,
                    capable, etc.

BEHAVIORS: Take care of others' needs
                    Do not express own needs

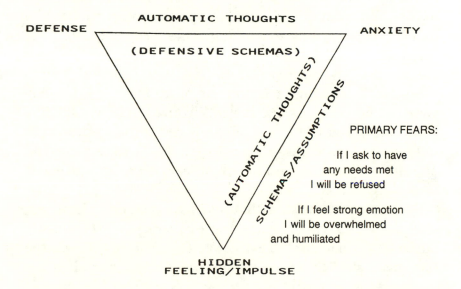

*From Holland 1996.

them. We used some cognitive techniques, but I felt that exposure would be crucial in bringing about emotional change. Susan repeatedly had to allow herself to experience strong emotion and discover that she would be all right. We therefore reinitiated the exposure to the intrusive images of Sam's death. Within a few weeks Susan reported that she was no longer bothered by the images and she could now remember happier times with Sam.

Unfortunately, we soon had another opportunity to do exposure work around these primary fears. Shortly after the sessions described above, I had to inform Susan that I was moving out of state and we would need to terminate. She initially responded by expressing some disappointment, but said that of course she understood, and wished me the best. We discussed arrangements to have her continue with a colleague. I also suggested that she might find herself feeling some other emotions about my leaving, possibly including some anger, and if so we should talk about them. Although I did not say this to Susan, I suspected that my leaving would activate emotions related to her primary fear that her needs would not be met.

Susan initially insisted that she was not angry. However, after a few sessions she came in with a remarkable document. Susan kept a diary, which we had come to understand was the one place she felt safe to write about and experience her emotions. She brought in a series of pages from the diary. In them she wrote with great intensity about how angry she was at me for leaving, and about how irrational and out of control she felt. She likened it to throwing a temper tantrum. She wrote that she realized that she felt just as she had as a child when she was angry at her mother. She then wrote quite lucidly about how she had avoided these feelings all her life, but now realized that she could tolerate them. She began to discuss how she had failed to express her needs in her marriage and had pushed her husband away. She closed with a line asking for his forgiveness.

From the point of view of exposure, Susan had moved up her hierarchy. Rather than facing anger in the past, she was now allowing herself to feel it in the present. Of course, by writing rather than speaking about it, she was still avoiding expressing the anger directly to me. However, by bringing the diary pages into the session, she ensured that we would talk about her feelings.

As Susan began to feel freer to discuss her emotions about my leaving—including not only anger but sorrow, gratitude, and pride at her accomplishments—two things happened. First, her depression lifted further. She actually began to look happy, smiling and laughing in sessions for the first time since I had known her. Second, she began to seriously explore the question of whether she wished to stay married.

This is where things stood at our termination. Susan continued therapy with a colleague. I had occasion to speak to her several months later and she reported that she felt happier than she had in years and had initiated a separation from her husband.

DISCUSSION

Susan presented with major depression and therapy was initiated using standard cognitive treatment for this disorder. We quickly encountered resistance, however, which manifested first in her difficulty with taking time for herself, and then in her inability to tolerate imaginal exposure to the images of her friend's death. Exploration of the resistance eventually led to primary schemas involving fears of expressing her needs and not having them met and being overwhelmed and humiliated by strong emotion. These fears were addressed using a variety of techniques, including cognitive restructuring, exposure, and transference work. This resulted in a lifting of the depression Susan had been suffering for several years and in her being able to face the difficult task of making a decision about the future of her marriage.

REFERENCES

Alpert, M. C. (1992). Accelerated empathic therapy: a new short-term dynamic psychotherapy. *International Journal of Short-Term Psychotherapy* 7:133–156.

Davenloo, H. (1980). *Short-term dynamic psychotherapy.* New York: Jason Aronson.

Holland, S. (1996). *Integrating short-term dynamic and cognitive-behavioral therapies: a working model.* Paper presented at the meeting of the Society for the Exploration of Psychotherapy Integration, Berkeley, CA, April.

Hollon, S. D., Shelton, R. C., and Loosen, P. T. (1991). Cognitive therapy and pharmacotherapy for depression. *Journal of Consulting and Clinical Psychology* 59(1):88–89.

Malan, D. H. (1979). *Individual Psychotherapy and the Science of Psychodynamics.* London: Butterworth.

19

FAMILY THERAPY

Frank M. Dattilio

Cognitive therapy, as it applies to families in general, developed as an extension of its application to couples in conflict in the early 1980s (Epstein 1982). While Ellis (1977) has stated that he adapted his model of rational emotive therapy (RET) to work with couples as early as the late 1950s, little appears in the literature on this topic prior to 1980 (Ellis 1977, 1978, 1986). The later studies developed as an offshoot of the behavioral approach, which first described interventions with couples and families in the late 1960s and early 1970s.

Principles of behavior modification were applied to interactional patterns of family members only subsequent to their successful application to couples in distress (Bandura 1977, Patterson and Hops 1972, Stuart 1969, 1976). This work with couples was followed by several single-case studies involving the use of family interventions in treating children's behavior, and for the first time family members were recognized by behaviorists as being highly influential components of the child's natural environment and were subsequently included directly in the treatment process (Faloon 1991).

Several years later a more refined and comprehensive style of intervention with the family unit was described in detail by Patterson and colleagues (1967) and Patterson (1971). Since that time, applications of behavior therapy to family systems have become more prominent in the professional literature, with a strong emphasis on contingency contracting and negotiation strategies (Gordon and Davidson 1981, Jacobson and Margolin 1979, Liberman 1970, Patterson 1982, 1985). The application of behavior therapy to this day remains oriented toward families with children who are diagnosed with specific behavioral problems (Sanders and Dadds 1993).

Since its introduction almost thirty years ago, behavioral family therapy has received only minimal attention among practitioners of marriage and family therapy for a number of reasons: for one, due to the overwhelming popularity of the strategic and structural approaches to family therapy, many practitioners have been influenced primarily by such noted theorists as Minuchin (1974), Bowen (1978), Satir (1967), and Madanes (1981) to the exclusion of more empirically tested interventions. In addition, the behavioral approach may be perceived in some circles as too rigid and rigorous in methodology to apply to families and as failing to capture some of the commonly occurring dynamics of a family's interaction (Dattilio 1994). Last, there is some question about the true effectiveness of this approach based on the outcome studies conducted (Jacobson and Christensen 1996).

In fact, it does appear that the behavior therapies' strength lies more in addressing specific behavioral problems—such as poor communication or acting-out behavioral problems with children and adolescents—as opposed to understanding the comprehensive system of family dynamics (Goldenberg and Goldenberg 1991, Sanders and Dadds 1993). Specifically, the behavior therapies focus on observable behavior (symptoms) rather than on efforts to establish any intrapsychic or inter- personal causality. Certain targeted behaviors are directly manipulated through external means of reinforcement. Fami- lies are also trained to monitor these reinforcements and make modifications where necessary. In addition, an ongoing assess- ment of observable behavior is made in the interest of empiri- cally evaluating the effects of the therapeutic interventions. This is clearly highlighted in an article by Jacobson and Addis (1993) that reviews the outcome studies available in the litera- ture. A cognitive component to behavioral marital therapy received attention earlier as providing a supplement to behavior- oriented couples and family therapy (Margolin et al. 1975). In addition to the work of Ellis (1977), an important study by Margolin and Weiss (1978), which suggested the effective- ness of a cognitive component to behavioral marital therapy, sparked further study of the use of cognitive techniques with dysfunctional couples (Baucom and Epstein 1990, Baucom and Lester 1986, Beck 1988, Dattilio 1989, 1990, 1993, Dattilio and Padesky 1990, Doherty 1981, Ellis et al. 1989, Epstein 1992, Fincham et al. 1990, Schindler and Vollmer 1984, Weiss 1984). This interest in behavioral approaches to couples has also led to the recognition by behavioral family therapists that cogni- tion plays a significant role in the events that mediate family interactions as well (Alexander and Parsons 1982). The impor- tant role of cognitive factors, not only in determining relation- ship distress but also in mediating behavioral change, has become a topic of increasing interest (Alexander 1988, Dattilio 1993, 1994, in press, Epstein et al. 1988).

While marital and family therapists began to realize decades ago that cognitive factors were very important in the allevia- tion of relationship dysfunction (Dicks 1953), it took some time before cognition was formally included as a primary compo- nent of treatment (Munson 1993). As research continues on the significance of cognition in couples therapy, so it is hoped will its integration with other modalities (Baucom and Lester 1986, Dattilio 1993, 1994, in press).

COGNITIVE-BEHAVIORAL APPROACH
TO FAMILY THERAPY

As mentioned previously, cognitive couples therapy grew out of the behavioral approach, first as a supplemental component and then as a more comprehensive system of intervention. The same progression holds true to some degree for cognitive family therapy. Munson (1993) notes that there are at least eighteen different subtypes of cognitive therapy used by various practitioners, with the result that it would be impossible to discuss cognitive family therapy broadly in a single chapter. Consequently, the focus of this discussion will be limited to those approaches proposed by the rational emotive-behavioral theories (REBT) (DiGiuseppe and Zeeve 1985, Ellis 1982, 1978, Ellis et al. 1989) and the cognitive-behavioral theories (Beck 1988, Dattilio 1993, 1994, Epstein et al. 1988, Teichman 1984, 1992, Wright and Beck 1993).

The rational-emotive approach to family therapy, as proposed by Ellis (1978), places emphasis on each individual's perception and interpretation of the events that occur in the family environment. The underlying theory assumes that "family members largely create their own world by the phenomenological view they take of what happens to them" (p. 310). The focus of the therapy is on how particular problems of the family members affect their well-being as a unit. During the process of treatment, family members are treated as individuals, each of whom subscribes to his or her own particular set of beliefs and expectations (Huber and Baruth 1989, Russell and Morrill 1989). The family therapist helps members come to the realization that illogical beliefs and distortions serve as the foundation for their emotional distress.

The use of the A-B-C theory is introduced, in which family members blame their problems (C) on certain activating events in the family environment (A) and are taught to probe for irrational beliefs (B) which are then to be logically challenged by each family member and finally debated and disputed (D). The goal is to modify the beliefs and expectations to fit a more rational basis (Ellis 1978). The role of the therapist, then, is to teach the family unit in an active and directive manner that the causes of emotional problems lie in irrational beliefs. By changing these self-defeating ideas, they may improve the overall quality of the family relationship (Ellis 1978, 1982). Little of the rational-emotive philosophy is directed toward uncovering core schemata that are held by the family members and that contribute to family dysfunction. Rational-emotive-behavior therapists appear to focus more on addressing only the more immediate content of family members' thoughts, with less emphasis placed on underlying schemata or the need to blend the techniques with other modalities of family therapy treatment.

The cognitive-behavioral approach, which balances the emphasis on cognition and behavior, takes a more expansive and inclusive approach by focusing in greater depth on family interaction patterns and by remaining consistent with elements derived from a systems perspective (Dattilio in press, Epstein et al. 1988, Leslie 1988). Within this framework, family relationships, cognitions, emotions, and behavior are viewed as exerting a mutual influence upon one another, so that a cognitive inference can evoke emotion and behavior, and emotion and behavior can likewise influence cognition. Teichman (1992) describes in detail the reciprocal model of family interaction, proposing that cognitions, feelings, behaviors, and environmental feedback are in constant reciprocal process among themselves and sometimes serve to maintain the dysfunction of the family unit.

Consistent and compatible with systems theory, the cognitive-behavioral approach to families includes the premise that members of a family simultaneously influence and are influenced by each other. Consequently, a behavior of one family member leads to behaviors, cognitions, and emotions in other members, which in turn elicit cognitions, behaviors, and emotions in response to the former member (Epstein and Schlesinger 1995). As this process continues to cycle, the volatility of the family dynamics escalates, rendering them vulnerable to a negative spiral of conflict. As the number of family members involved increases, so does the complexity of the dynamics, adding more fuel to the escalation process. Epstein and Schlesinger (1991, 1995) cite four factors in the process of family members' cognitions, behaviors, and emotions interacting and building to a volatile climax:

1. The individual's own cognitions, behaviors, and emotions regarding family interaction (e.g., the person who notices himself or herself withdrawing from the rest of the family).
2. The actions of individual family members toward him or her.
3. The combined (and not always consistent) reactions that several members have toward him or her.
4. The characteristics of the relationships among other family members (e.g., noticing that two other family members usually are supportive of each other's opinion).

The above all serve as stimuli or combinations of stimuli during family interactions that often become ingrained in family patterns and permanent styles of interaction.

Cognitive therapy, as set forth by Beck (1976), places a heavy emphasis on schema or what has otherwise been defined as core beliefs (Beck et al. 1979, DeRubeis and Beck 1988). As this concept is applied to family treatment, the therapeutic intervention focuses on the assumptions that family members make in interpreting and evaluating one another and the emotions and behaviors that are generated in response to these cognitions. While cognitive-behavioral theory does not suggest that cognitive processes cause all family behavior, it does stress that cognitive appraisal plays a significant part in the interrelationships existing among events, cognitions, emotions and behaviors (Epstein et al. 1988, Wright and Beck 1993). In the cognitive therapy process, restructuring distorted beliefs has a pivotal impact on changing dysfunctional behaviors.

The notion of schema is also very important in the application of cognitive-behavior therapy with families. Just as individuals maintain their own basic schema about themselves, their world, and their future, they maintain a schema about their family. This author believes that heavier emphasis should be placed on examining cognitions among individual family members as well as on what may be termed the "family schemata" (Dattilio 1993, 1996): jointly held beliefs of the family that have formed as a result of years of integrated interaction among members of the family unit. I suggest that individuals basically maintain two separate sets of schemata about families: family schemata related to the parents' family of origin and schemata related to families in general or what Schwebel and Fine (1994) refer to as personal theory (PT) of family life. It is the experiences and perceptions from the family of origin that shape the schema about both the immediate family and families in general. These schemata have a major impact on how the individual thinks, feels, and behaves within the family setting. Epstein and colleagues (1988) propose that these schemata are "the longstanding and relatively stable basic assumption that he or she holds about how the world works and his or her place in it" (p. 13). Schwebel and Fine (1992) elaborate on the term *family schemata* as used in their family model.

Elsewhere (1994) I have suggested that the family of origin

of each partner in a relationship plays a crucial role in the shaping of immediate family schema. Beliefs funneled down from the family of origin may be both conscious and unconscious and contribute to a joint or blended schema that leads to the development of the current family schema.

This family schema is then disseminated and applied in the rearing of the children, and, when mixed with their individual thoughts and perceptions of their environment and life experiences, contributes to the further development of the family schema. The family schema is subject to modification as major events occur during the course of family life (e.g., death, divorce), and it also continues to evolve over the course of ordinary, day-to-day experience.

CASE EXAMPLE

It is not unusual for practitioners of marriage and family therapy to encounter couples who are contemplating divorce. After all, this is much of what their business entails—dealing with troubled relationships. But for a therapist to receive a request from two teenage children who want a divorce from their parents, now this is an altogether different and unusual dilemma.

This was the request of Rollie and Janice Steigerwalt, ages 15 and 17 respectively, who entered the initial family session with their parents in a united front. "We're sick of them telling us what to do and we would just as soon live somewhere else—divorced from them!" "Ouch," I stated—"That's an unusual request." The parents, who sat inquisitively silent, gave me the distinct impression, through their quiescence, that this was clearly not the first time that this song had been sung in the Steigerwalt household.

The Steigerwalts were an interesting family who had moved about the United States quite a bit during the course of their nineteen-year marriage. Robert, a 44-year-old draftsman, was a rather conservative gentleman who demonstrated little imagination or affection with his family. He was a mediocre employee for a large national automation firm, but managed to secure a stable position over the years. His wife, Carole, age 43, was an administrator at a nursing home and actually displayed characteristics similar to those of her husband, except for being more outgoing and flexible. In a sense then, Carole struck an emotional balance between the two.

Mr. and Mrs. Steigerwalt had experienced a rather tumultuous marriage until approximately three years before, when they sought intense marital therapy. Since that time, the atmosphere in the marriage had improved significantly, except for the issues around spending money and Bob's occasional verbal abusive toward the family, an ongoing conflict between him and Carole at the time they presented for family therapy.

A detailed history revealed that the problems leading up to the children's request appeared to begin at about the time that Bob and Carole started "getting our act together" with the marriage, as Carole colloquially described it. Both parents assumed a rather matter-of-fact posture as the two children proceeded to intrigue me with the rationale for their wish to divorce their parents.

Session 1

Rollie: You see, Doctor, we've been taking a lot of crap from our parents for a long time and we're tired of it—we don't think that we deserve this type of treatment—we're good kids and it's just not fair. They treat us like scum!

Mother (interjecting emotionally): What crap, Rollie? What on earth are you talking about, son?

Father: Yeah, Rollie, I really don't understand. Why do you feel that we give you crap and treat you like scum?

Rollie: Can I finish, please? You're always telling me not to butt in while you are talking! As I was saying, doctor, we don't deserve the crap we get, like being told that we can go somewhere for the weekend and then they go back on their word and say, "Well, you can only go if you do this or if you do that."

Janice: Yeah! That's really unfair and selfish as far as I am concerned.

Dr. D.: Okay . . . I am just a little bit confused here and need to back up. Did this just come about out of the blue or have these tensions been mounting over time?

Father: They've been building, Doctor—I mean, talk about crap, we've been hearing this for the last several years, over and over, like a broken record. Carole and I just think that these kids have gotten out of hand and have become ridiculous with their demands. I am beginning to think that we're the ones who are treated like scum.

Mother: Oh my God, yes. . . . If we would ever have spoken like this to our parents or even demanded one-eighth of what they demand from us, . . . we would have . . . well, that's another story—I don't want to get into that right now.

Dr. D.: All right, I need to try to understand where we are missing each other here. It sounds as though you are operating under two separate assumptions of how things should work in the family and I am wondering how this has come to be the case. Help me understand the picture here. Think of it like a movie and I just entered halfway through the film. Bring me up to date.

Mother: I don't know. . . . We are kind of at a loss as to how to explain this ourselves. Bob and I have, er, *had*[1] a rather

---

1. Normally, my inclination here would have been to address this slip of the tongue ("have" instead of "had"); however, it was much too early in the game, plus this family was in somewhat of a state of semicrisis. A similar slip

stormy marriage for quite a few years and we eventually sought help—which resulted in a significant improvement in our relationship, I must say! This is not to infer that we still don't have our problems, but they are much more manageable than they were. I just almost get the impression that these kids resent this or something . . . I don't know . . . something's just not right here.

Dr. D.: Well, Carole, you just said something that caught my attention. I think your statement about the kids "resenting something . . ."

Mother: Oh, resenting Bob and me reconciling our differences. Yes, I've wondered about that—if perhaps they've come to resent our new unity in some way.

Dr. D.: Tell me how things have become different since the two of you reconciled and became more unified in your relationship.

Mother: In my opinion?

Dr. D.: Well, I'd like to hear everyone's impression, actually, but we can start with your and your husband's impressions first, if you like.

Father: OK. Well, I guess Carole and I sort of grew apart shortly after the kids were born and we began relocating quite a bit with my job. We've lived in about six different states throughout the U.S. in the last fifteen years and some of the locations haven't been all that great. I think that this contributed significantly to the alienation between Carole and myself.

Mother: A big part of the problem was that I resented all of the moving around for what has resulted in very little remuneration or promotional reward with Bob's job. Albeit Bob has changed companies in order to better himself, but I always felt that he could have done much better for all that we

---

is made by Mr. Steigerwalt later in therapy and the issue of ongoing marital tensions is addressed at that point quite appropriately.

sacrificed over the years—and then, on top of it all, we had to take his verbal abusiveness . . .

Dr. D.: I'd like to come back to this issue of "verbal abusiveness," but for now let's go on with your rendition of the sacrifices.

Father: Yes. So anyway, this really drew a wedge between us and I guess we became somewhat remiss with things in the marriage and also with the kids. This is what we learned during the course of our marital therapy anyway.

Dr. D.: So, the kids were affected then in what way?

Mother: Well, I guess they were kind of left to do their own thing. We sort of didn't parent together and I don't know—maybe you could say we were both very lax with them regarding discipline and other things.

Dr. D.: Is lax really the word that describes it?

Parents (together): What do you mean?

Dr. D.: Well, I'm wondering if there isn't more here than just a matter of being lax.

Mother: I am sorry, I don't follow you.

Father: Yeah, me either.

Rollie: I am not, I think that he means that . . . well, go ahead, you can explain it better—I'm not even sure what I want to say (*everyone chuckles*).

Dr. D.: OK. Well, I'm just wondering whether or not the children were somehow inadvertently used in your discontent with each other—you know—in a spiteful or subtly retaliatory way.

Mother: I am still lost, I am sorry.

Father: Oh, OK, I think what he means is that, maybe we would go against each other by telling the kids opposite things or letting them do something that one of us said they were not permitted to do. Is that what you are talking about, Doctor?

Dr. D.: Yes—to some extent.

Mother: Oh, I don't know about that.

Rollie: Yes, Mom—it's true—you and Dad would never agree and now all of a sudden you agree about everything and are both real strict and our lives really suck!

Janice: Yeah, we never get to do anything anymore—I hate this freakin' house.

Dr. D.: It sounds to me that there has been a major shift in the family's disposition about rules and how things are conducted in the household.

Rollie: What rules? There are no rules. They just make things up as they go along. This is what really pisses me off . . .

Father: Hey, Rollie—watch the mouth, OK son? You're not out with your friends. We're in a doctor's office here.

Mother: That's another thing, the language . . .

Dr. D.: Well, OK. We can come back to that later when we address the verbal abusiveness, but I want to get back to this issue of rules, particularly those that are written and, more important, what we might refer to as the "unspoken or unwritten" rules. So, who sets the standards in your household? Who makes up the rules?

Mother: Well, I guess Rollie is correct, no one in particular, they're just understood. I mean, we talk about them to some degree, but at some point they always seem to fall apart somewhere along the line.

Father: You know, I think that Carole and I kind of hope that things will just come together automatically—but I guess they don't.

Dr. D.: Where does this type of thinking come from? I mean, you both strike me as intelligent people and fairly conscientious in many ways. What were your experiences like growing up? How were the rules devised in your respective families?

Early during the assessment phase of family therapy I attempt to develop an understanding of the parents' families of origin, in the presence of the entire family. The main intention is to help the family to see how schema from the family of origin has trickled down to the immediate family system.

Father: Are you talking to me or Carole?

Dr. D.: Both of you.

Father: Oh, well, my father was sort of strict, without really having to say too much. We never really stepped out of line very often, but he sort of set the rules. My mother just followed along. Dad would shoot us the evil eye if we got out of line and that would say it all—you straightened up real fast.

Dr. D.: So rules were never really clearly established in your family, you just sort of winged it?

Father: Yeah, so to speak, but my father was clearly the disciplinarian when we needed it. I guess it's safe to say that he made up the rules and my mother followed along and everything just fell into place.

Dr. D.: Carole, what about you?

Mother: Well, my parents were the opposite. They were both extremely controlling. They had an equal hand in the rules and very strongly enforced them—to the point that I could hardly stand it.

Dr. D.: So, would it be fair to say that you possibly rebelled against using that type of system during the process of raising your own children?

Mother: You know, it's really funny. I was very stern with our kids early on, more like my folks were during my upbringing, but then I softened about the time that they became preteens for some reason.

Dr. D.: Well, perhaps that was when you yourself began to really resent your own parents' firmness—during your preteen years?

Mother: I really never thought about it that way. I guess I just didn't want to be like my parents since I despised them so much—so maybe I did do that, I don't know!

Dr. D.: Yes, but you see, this must have been somewhat confusing to your children, even though it may have made some type of sense to you.

Rollie: Confused is not the word—every day is a different story in our house.

Dr. D.: Well, let's try and see if we can make some sense out of it all. The role of our experiences in what we call the "family of origin" is extremely important in understanding how our belief systems develop about ourselves and how our respective families function. The different experiences and philosophies affect what trickles down into any new family system and how it's governed.[2]

Mother: OK, so help us make sense of our family here. I mean, how does all of this relate to us?

Dr. D.: All right, let's look at it in writing. (*I began to map out a diagram on a chalkboard to delineate Bob and Carole's schemas from their respective family of origin and then attempted to demonstrate how the melding or integration of these two schemas have contributed to a joint schema. [See Figure 19–1.]*)

Father: That pretty much sums up the philosophy that we adhered to in raising our kids!

Mother: Yeah! I guess when you put it like that, that is the way we operated—and it seemed to work OK for a while—but then Bob and I started arguing and becoming distant from each other and then, in a way, we sort of formed two separate camps—we became divided and things just grew more tense between the two of us.

---

2. Here I would normally go into much more detail about the philosophy and theory of the cognitive-behavioral approach as the educational component of treatment. It may be considered a process of orienting the family to the model of treatment.

Figure 19–1.
Cognitive-Behavioral Approach to Family Therapy

<u>Family of Origin</u>

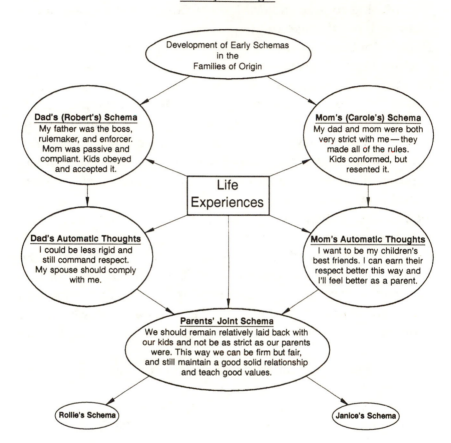

Dr. D.: So how did this affect the kids?

Mother: Well, I guess I sort of bonded with them, Rollie especially, particularly since Bob started traveling with his job a great deal and he seemed to be the hardest on Rollie.

Janice: Yeah, we were sort of a threesome and Dad became like a stranger in the house—that's when he became nasty to us and picked on me and became verbally abusive with every-body (*starts to become teary-eyed*).

Father: Now wait a minute here—it wasn't all me!

Mother: Yes it was, Bob, a lot of it was with you becoming verbally abusive to all of us. You were really ugly sometimes.

Father: Talk about verbally abusive! What about the things that the kids say to me? Call me a "bull fucker" and choice statements like that.

Dr. D.: Who called you that?

Janice: I did—because he called me his "fat little tomato" (*begins to cry. Dad and Rollie begin to snicker*).

Mother: This goes on frequently—Bob always picks on Janice's weight and it only makes her worse. She's gained a tremen-dous amount of weight over the past year and a half, and personally, I think that she's eating out of anger, like I sometimes do.

Dr. D.: I am surprised at the exchange between family mem-bers—particularly the foul language. Do you as parents permit this?

Mother: Well, I think that Bob set the precedent with his use of foul language in the house over the years and I guess it's sort of been tolerated. We all do it—it's terrible.

Rollie: Yeah—we talk like that to them because they talk to us the same way.

Dr. D.: It seems like there has been a total breakdown in respect for one another, not to mention the boundaries. I am trying to understand how things deteriorated to this point.

Father: I don't know—that bothers me a lot since I really don't like seeing things this way. I wasn't raised like that.

Mother: Neither was I, but you know, I think that Bob and I need to really face the fact that we've failed as parents (*begins to tear*).

Dr. D.: All right, let's go back to the idea of the schemas and see if we can't make some additional sense of the dynamics here and maybe gain a better understanding of what happened. . . . Mom and Dad, we saw how both of you came to the point where you adopted the schema, or belief system, that you didn't want to maintain the same type of child-rearing style that your respective parents maintained during your upbringing. Therefore, I am wondering whether or not you gravitated too much in the opposite direction. Is this a possibility?

Mother: Yes, definitely.

Dr. D.: OK. So what is important for us to understand here is that this has certainly had an impact on the entire family, most particularly the children, who we may view as acting out the conflict that existed between the two of you. This is not to say that they should be left off the hook for their own behaviors, but that it has set the groundwork for them to do what most kids would normally do in this type of situation— take advantage of the turmoil. What is important to understand is that their belief system or schema about how things are run in the family has developed as a result of their exposure to this atmosphere. In addition, this is garnished with their own needs and desires to gain autonomy and power in the family. For example, if we question both of the kids about how they have come to perceive the dynamics in the family, you may develop a better understanding of why they think and do the things that they do.

Father: Well, we really don't know what they think because every time we attempt to investigate, things end up in a verbal brawl and nothing is accomplished.

Dr. D.: This might be due to maladaptive patterns of miscommunication that have developed—something that we will certainly address later. For now, however, I think that I need to inquire more into their individual schemas. (*To Rollie and Janice*) Help us understand how you each view things there.

Rollie: Well, I used to see my parents as friends really—I viewed them as peers—and there was nothing wrong with the way that it was. It was kind of cool!

Dr. D.: So, you mean that you were left to use your own judgment with things.

Rollie: Yes, definitely.

Dr. D.: And what role do you view your parents as playing in your life?

Rollie: I'm not sure—as a peer, as someone to guide us, but . . . well, I don't know.

Dr. D.: You're confused! See, I believe that you came to operate under some distortions that may have been formed by erroneous information. I am wondering whether Janice sees it the same way . . .

Janice: Yeah, sort of—I think that they should just let us do what we want and if we have a problem, we'll let them know. Right now, though, Mom is still somewhat of a friend to me and Rollie. It's Dad who's the big pain—and now Mom's starting to be the same way. It's sickening. We're supposed to change everything overnight and give up our comfort zone.

Dr. D.: Comfort zone?

Janice: Yeah, you know, at least we knew where we stood. Now everything's a mess.

Dr. D.: OK. Well, let's take a look at all of this from a new perspective. As you may recall, earlier we discussed how sometimes individuals may tend to engage in what are called "cognitive distortions." These distortions are something that everyone may engage in at one time or the other in their lifetime. They are based on misinformation and contribute frequently to conflict within families.

At this point I began to educate the family to the cognitive distortions described below and began to show them how these distortions apply to their particular family situation by using examples.

COGNITIVE DISTORTION

1. *Arbitrary inference:* A conclusion is made by family members in the absence of supporting substantiating evidence. For example, one of the children who returns home half an hour after his/her curfew is judged by the family as having been "up to no good."
2. *Selective abstraction:* Information is taken out of context; certain details are highlighted and other important information is ignored. Example: Dad fails to answer Rollie's greeting the first thing in the morning, and Rollie concludes, "Dad must be angry at me again."
3. *Overgeneralization:* An isolated incident or two is allowed to serve as a representation of similar situations everywhere, related or unrelated. Example: Because Bob and the kids have left food out from time to time, Carole develops the belief that her family is wasteful and takes everything, including her, for granted.
4. *Magnification and minimization:* A case or circumstance is perceived in greater or lesser light than is appropriate. Example: Bob demands that the children wash their hands before eating, but he fails to do so himself. When confronted by the children, he minimizes it by saying, "Well, I don't miss very often—so I'm excused."
5. *Personalization:* External events are attributed to oneself when insufficient evidence exists to render a conclusion. Example: Carole blames herself for her children's repeated arguments, saying, "Maybe I should have never been a mother."
6. *Dichotomous thinking:* Experiences are codified in all-or-nothing terms—a complete success or a total failure. Example: After repeated incidences in which Rollie becomes involved in trouble at school, Bob and Carole conclude, "We failed as parents."
7. *Labeling and mislabeling:* Imperfections and mistakes

made in the past are allowed to serve as a stereotype for all future behaviors. Example: Bob and Carole failed to follow through on their word on one occasion and are consequently regarded by the children as being unreliable.

8. *Tunnel vision:* Family members sometimes see only what they want to see or what fits their current state of mind. Example: Bob holds on to the rigid belief that the man is the "head of the household," because this is the way he perceived a father to be when he was growing up.

9. *Biased explanations:* This is a polarized manner of thinking that family members develop during times of distress; they assume that another member has an ulterior motive. Example: Rollie and Janice distrust their parents because they are reluctant to disclose to them what they had been discussing in their marital therapy.

10. *Mind reading:* A family member has the magical gift of being able to know what others are thinking without the aid of verbal communication. Example: Carole anticipates that the family views her as a failure because she is unable to stand up for herself and demand what she wants.

These distortions become key targets to identify in family therapy. Family members are oriented to the cognitive-behavioral model and are taught to identify such distortions in their own thinking as well as in the thinking of other family members. Much of the intervention in therapy involves helping members to identify such distortions and then gather evidence to aid in reconstructing their thinking. It may also include practicing alternative patterns of behavioral interaction and dealing with their negative attributions.

Dr. D.: For example, let's use Rollie's perception of his relationship with Mom. Now Rollie stated a while ago that Mom was basically a friend, someone whom he could confide in and relate to—isn't that correct, Rollie?

Rollie: Oh yeah, definitely.

Dr. D.: But yet, at the point that she would then attempt to instill discipline, or collaborate with Dad on a disciplinary issue, this would then evoke a feeling of . . .

Rollie: Betrayal!

Dr. D.: OK. That's a descriptive term—betrayal. So, in essence, according to Rollie, Mom could never function in both roles, as friend and as disciplinarian. It had to be either/or for him. According to our list of cognitive distortions, how might we categorize that?

Rollie (laughs): All-or-nothing thinking? Uh-oh, I am sinking quick here! (*everyone laughs*)

Dr. D.: Correct, Rollie, but don't yell "Mayday" yet. You are engaging in a dichotomous thought pattern that Mom had something to do with reinforcing—I would guess by accommodating you over the years.

Mother: True, I'll admit to that.

Dr. D.: OK. But the important thing to recognize here is that it is a distorted, or more accurately "rigid," way of thinking since it allows no room for flexibility in your roles and has certainly caused some conflict among the family members. As you remember, earlier we discussed that we sometimes tend to engage in cognitive distortions and that these distortions are something that develop as a result of a faulty informational processing that develops during our upbringing. These distortions occur as a result of our schemas or belief systems about the way things should be. Let's go back and use Rollie's all-or-nothing thinking as an example. You recall how we uncovered Mom and Dad's schemas from their own families of origins, right?

Rollie: Yeah.

Dr. D.: OK, and Mom's schemas caused some conflict for her once she began having children and raising them, particularly in light of the problems that she experienced with your father's ideas and beliefs. So, in a sense, she was torn between maintaining a friendship type of relationship with you and Janice and how to simultaneously remain firm and institute discipline. She vacillated between two roles, which created confusion for you and caused you to view things in black or white terms. Naturally, as a kid, you're going to be attracted to the more permissive role and attempt to extract that from Mom rather than the role of disciplinarian. Consequently, when she and Dad began to team up and present more of a supportive and united front with their relationship, you resented it and tended to view it in dichotomous terms—"all or nothing." Is this clear to everyone?

Mother: Well, I am feeling particularly guilty about that because I think that I've done this with both children.

Dr. D.: OK, but do you think that it is fair to place the blame totally on yourself? It's actually more of a problem with our entire family system. Each one of us must accept the fact that we all have our individual schemas about the way the family works along with our own needs and demands. These are full of cognitive distortions simply because we are human and this is what humans sometimes do. We also have what I have come to term a *family schema*, which is something in addition to our individual schemas. It involves our joint understanding of how things work in our system and contains our understanding of the written as well as unwritten rules.

Father: Wow, I guess there's a lot of stuff going on here.

Dr. D.: Yes. Families tend to be rather complex units, but it is important for us to make an attempt to understand this so that we can begin to develop some strategies for modifying the system and help it to run more smoothly. I realize that this is a lot to digest and we will go over it more specifically as we work together.

Janice: So how is this going to change anything? I don't get it. What are we supposed to do?

Dr. D.: Well, Janice, by making some alterations in the way that we think and behave toward one another, change will hopefully occur. But we're still in the learning stage right now and I would like to ask you to just hang on a bit until we gather more information and then hopefully things will begin to come together. Can we all agree to return for another session?

Father: Well, I certainly want to come back. I am sort of interested in all of this.

Mother: Yeah, me, too. And plus we've got to get things straightened out here—because things are just not good.

Dr. D.: You mean before you all get divorced? (*everyone laughs. To Rollie and Janice*): Will you guys come back?

Rollie and Janice: Yeah, I guess (*both smirk a bit as they look at each other*).

Dr. D.: How about if we meet in a week or ten days? But in the meantime I would like you all to think a little bit about this idea of distortions and how it pertains to each one of you on an individual basis. I would prefer that you don't discuss this openly with one another yet. Just think about it to yourselves.

Mother: OK, but what about the tensions that exist in the household? Things are terrible. Is there anything that we can do right now?

Dr. D.: Well, I don't know. What could we all agree on temporarily? Can we all agree on making a short-term effort to call a truce, at least until the next time we meet? Just put a hold on lashing out at each other? (*Bob and Carole nod affirmatively; Rollie and Janice shrug*).

Dr. D.: OK. Let's see what we can do. I'll see you all next time.

This was a very busy first session, which lasted approximately ninety minutes. More information was covered than usual, but this seemed to be a rather bright family that had great potential. I also wanted to obtain a good feeling for how this family operated and wanted to grab as much as I could while they were all verbalizing openly to me. The initial session may vary, of course, depending on the level of sophistication of the family.

I deliberately did not provide them with a more structured homework assignment because I wanted to see what they could accomplish on their own with minimal instruction. I do realize that I risked somewhat of a catastrophe here, but sometimes this is diagnostic in and of itself. My agenda for the next session was to move into the identification of cognitive distortions and strategies for weighing evidence and considering alternative self-statements. Simultaneously, it was my hope to learn more about this family's dynamics and why these children have been left to assume so much power and control.

Not to my surprise, an incident occurred that required immediate attention in the subsequent session.

Session 2

Dr. D.: Well, I am glad to see that all of you agreed to return. Before we get started, I'm wondering if anything eventful transpired during the past week or so since our last meeting?

Mother: We had a terrible week. I think the tension in the family is at an all-time high. It's so depressing.

Dr. D.: Oh, really—what happened?

Mother: Well, it started with Bob being verbally abusive to all of us last Friday night and . . .

Father (interrupting abruptly): Now wait a goddamn minute! Right off the bat you're all over my case—*I* am responsible for the lousy week—it's *my* fault!

Janice: Well, you started, Dad, with the stupid pizza.

Dr. D.: Hold it! What does "stupid pizza" have to do with it? Help me, I'm lost again here. (*kids begin to snicker*).

Father: Friday night I brought home pizza, like I usually do on weekends. I called Carole from the office and we agreed that neither of us felt like cooking, so I picked up a pizza.

Dr. D.: OK, sounds good to me.

Father: Yeah, well, I come in the door, lay the pizza on the kitchen table, and go into the hallway to hang up my coat in the closet. Well, the three of them swoop down like vultures, each grabbing two pieces of pizza and scurry off. They leave two thin little pieces for me with hardly any cheese on them. So this really ticked me off and I lost my temper and called them all gluttons. I said that they were ingrates—and I guess a few other choice words. . . . I don't know. I don't remember.

Mother: Well, I remember! You called Rollie an asshole and Janice and I pigs. (*Rollie and Dad start snickering*).

Dr. D.: OK. I get the picture. So let's get right into it and pick up where we left off last time. Dad, let's go back to Friday night when you brought the pizza home. Do you remember what you were feeling?

Father: Uh, I don't know. I guess I was tired, hungry, just like everybody else.

Dr. D.: So you brought this pizza home and set it down on the kitchen table to share with everyone. First let me ask you, what did you anticipate would happen? What were your expectations?

Father: Ah . . . I don't know, I didn't think about it. I guess that everyone would just sort of sit down and we'd eat the pizza normally. You know, like you're supposed to. Like human beings do! (*glaring at Rollie and Janice*).

Dr. D.: So, when everyone kind of just dove in, this troubled you.

Mother: Well, wait a minute! Bob set the pizza down and yells,

"Pizza's here," and then goes in to hang up his coat and he must have done something else because he didn't come right back to the kitchen immediately. The kids were watching a TV program and they ran in and grabbed their pizza—again which they normally do—and took it and sat in front of the television to eat it.

Dr. D.: So, Dad, this violated your expectations of what you thought should be?

Father: Yeah! I guess so.

Dr. D.: All right, and that no doubt aggravated you to some degree?

Father: Yes. Then when I came in and saw the two slices of pizza with hardly any cheese left on them, I flipped.

Dr. D.: All right, stop right there! What thoughts went through your mind at that moment?

Father (stops and thinks for a minute): Ah, I don't know. I don't remember.

Dr. D.: Let's try this—close your eyes for a minute and try to visually recall yourself back in that situation.

Rollie: No, don't tell him to do that, he'll fall asleep.

Dr. D.: No he won't—I won't let him. So close your eyes and try to imagine this scene. Let me know when you have it in your head.

Father: OK—I'm there (*grinning with his eyes closed*).

Dr. D.: Good. Now think about what you were wearing, where you were standing, and the surrounding atmosphere—smells, et cetera.

Father: Yes—OK.

Dr. D.: Can you remember what your thoughts were upon seeing those two measly, pathetic pieces of pizza laying in the box—just staring at you?

Father: Yeah. I thought, "What gluttons—this is just typical."

Dr. D.: What's typical?

Father: You know, this selfishness, this disregard for me. I bring the damn pizza home and no one sits with me. They aren't even considerate enough to see that I get a decent piece of pizza. They just don't care.

Dr. D.: So what is the schema attached to this?

Father: I'm not sure what you mean.

Dr. D.: Well, your automatic thought is, "They aren't considerate of me." That means what?

Father: Well, that means that they don't care. They're just using me. I'm just a meal ticket.

Mother: Aw, come on, Bob!

Dr. D.: No, wait, Carole. Let him finish!

Father: That's all I am—they don't give a shit about me.

Dr. D.: So your schema, or core belief, is that no one in the family really cares about you, and your worth to them is symbolized by the lean pieces of pizza that they left for you, after you went through all of the trouble to pick it up, pay for it, et cetera. Correct?

Father: Yep, that's it in a nutshell.

Dr. D.: All right now, here's the important question. What evidence, other than the pizza incident, do you have that truly substantiates the blanket statement "They don't give a shit about me—I am just a meal ticket"?

Father: Uh—well, it's happened before.

Dr. D.: When?

Father: I don't know, there have been times.

Dr. D.: A lot? Enough to substantiate such a strong statement?

Father: Uh—well, no, not a lot, but it's happened.

Dr. D.: So, you don't have a lot of evidence, just a few incidences.

Father: Yeah, maybe one other time.

Dr. D.: So, could there possibly be some cognitive distortions at work here?

Father: Well, yeah, maybe, but still, I don't think that it was unreasonable to be irritated by this. It was very selfish of them.

Dr. D.: No, I am not disputing that issue with you. I am sure that you were looking forward to your cheese pizza too. So to end up with two slices of "sauce-covered bread" is a big letdown, I'm sure—especially when you're hungry (*kids begin to snicker*). But to say that this equates to them not caring at all—I just don't see where this is an accurate assumption. Do you?

Father: Well, I guess not, but it's frustrating.

Dr. D.: Sure, but the emotion attached to what you tell yourself about your value and worth makes a significant difference in how you react emotionally and behaviorally. You can see this clearly if we plot it out on the Daily Dysfunction Thought Sheet (DDT). Let's map it out.

I begin to write this out on a chalkboard so that the entire family can view it.

Situation	Automatic Thought	Emotion	Cognitive Distortion
Everyone helps themselves to the best pieces of pizza, leaving the lean pieces for Dad.	They just don't give a shit about me! I am just a meal ticket.	Agitated/Angry Devalued	1. Arbitrary inference 2. Maximization 3. Dichotomous thinking

Dr. D.: All right. So when we break it down like this, it is easy to see the distortions that are occurring and how the statements that you are making to yourself are erroneously based.

Father: Yeah. I guess I can see that.

Dr. D. So the emotions and behavior that follow are what set the stage for your reactions and what this evokes in the other members of the family.

Father: So I am the one who is wrong.

Dr. D.: No, not entirely. Let's look at the thoughts that occurred to everyone else. Carole, what happened when Bob reacted the way he did?

Mother: Well, I thought that he clearly jumped the gun. I mean, I would have been angry also, but he could have said to the rest of us, "Come on, guys, how about leaving me some pieces with more cheese on them." I mean, they were still left. The kids hadn't eaten them all yet. They could have put some of them back.

Dr. D.: But how did this affect the rest of you?

Rollie: Well, I wasn't even sure what happened, and the next thing you know, Dad's yelling and he's calling me an ungrateful asshole. So I got mad.

Dr. D.: Janice? What about you?

Janice: I don't know—I just kept eating my pizza (*everyone laughs*).

Dr. D.: But something must have gone through your mind.

Janice: Well, I thought, "Here he goes again. He's always making everyone miserable."

Dr. D.: So it caused a lot of disruption. If Dad had come to you with a little less fury and said that he wanted his share of the decent slices of pizza, how would you have responded?

Rollie: No problem—I would have given him the other piece. I don't want to be unfair.

Dr. D.: So it wasn't your deliberate intention to cheat your father or leave him with the scraps—you're not really gluttons, are you?

Rollie and Janice (laughing): No, it's just that he's slower than we are and we were starving.

Dr. D.: All right, but can you understand how your father felt?

Rollie and Janice: Yeah, I guess.

Dr. D.: And Dad, you are aware now that the conclusion you arrived at was a bit exaggerated?

Father: Yeah, I exaggerated, I guess.

Dr. D.: Mom, what are you thinking—you're awfully quiet.

Mother: Well, I am just thinking about how typical this is of our family. I mean this stuff just goes on all the time and I think that you have made a very good point here tonight—that we jump the gun a lot with our thinking—sometimes to the point that it really gets us all in serious trouble.

Dr. D.: Well, yes—I can see that.

As can be seen with this scenario, I have encouraged the entire family to begin to think about the dynamics that are occurring with their thought processes and how easily they can distort things. More important, they have begun to make a connection with their thoughts and how they are linked to their emotions and how this specifically leads to conflicts in their relationships with one another.

I have deliberately chosen father to use as a role model since I believe that in many ways he sets the main tone for the family. Mother, who has a special strength and control of her own, watches quietly as I make these maneuvers with her husband. My thoughts are that the restructuring process might have had less of an impact had I chosen her as a role model. Also, I wanted to silently disarm her power by shifting the focus away from her and on to father. This would clearly be less threatening to this family at this point in the treatment process.

Dr. D.: So, what about the rest of the family—do you all recognize how you may have had similar experiences where your own automatic thoughts have affected how you responded emotionally?

Rollie: Well, yeah, I do—but sometimes I just get so upset about things, I can't stop and think straight. I mean, for me to slow things down is real hard. Also, I don't see why I have to do this if no one else does.

Dr. D.: Well, that's sort of the point, Rollie. You see, everyone will need to begin to examine the way in which they cognitively process things here and learn to challenge thoughts and distortions that cause conflict. One of the ways in which we can begin to do this is by asking ourselves the following questions when we catch ourselves engaging in distorted thinking. We call this "questioning your interpretations."

1. What is the evidence in favor of my interpretation?
2. What evidence is there contrary to my interpretation?
3. Does it logically follow from my family member's actions that he (or she) has the motive that I assign to him (or her)?
4. Is there an alternative explanation for his or her behavior?

Take an example in which one of the members of your family spoke harshly or in some other way that upset or annoyed you. Ask yourself these questions:

- Does it follow that because they spoke sharply that he or she was angry at me?
- Are there alternative explanations for their tone of voice (for example, he or she could have a cold or be strained or bothered by something else).
- Even if they are angry, does it follow that:
    - A They don't care about me or are devaluing me in some way?
    - B Or that they are always this way?
    - C Does it necessarily mean that they will make life miserable for me?
    - D That I have done something wrong?

(To the entire family): Do you see how this might be helpful?

Mother: Yes, I do. Now we just need to learn how to slow things down in our family and remember to do this without being so darn emotional.

Dr. D.: Well, yes—that's the tough part. Families are interesting but complicated systems that operate on principles or assumptions. These assumptions can significantly affect our emotions and behaviors. (*I went on to explain to the Steigerwalts in a simplified fashion some of the assumptions that were posited by Schwebel and Fine [1994].*)

• *Assumption 1:* All members of a family seek to maintain their environment in order to fulfill their needs and wants. They attempt to understand their environment and how they can function most effectively in it, even if it sometimes means testing the boundaries. (For example, Rollie may exceed his curfew by one half hour.) As family members gather data about how the family operates, they use this information to guide their behaviors and to aid in building and refining family-related cognitions. This leads to the development of an individual's construct of family life and family relationships. So, in Rollie's case, he may begin to develop the concept that he can stretch the limits and not be chastised, thus inferring that rules may be broken with little consequence.

• *Assumption 2:* Individual members' cognitions affect virtually every aspect of family life. Five categories are identified as cognitive variables that determine these cognitions: (1) selective attention (Bob and Carole's focus on the children's negative behaviors), (2) attributions (Bob's explanations for why the children act up), (3) expectations (Bob's expectation that Carole and the children will do as he asks without questions), (4) assumptions (Janice's view that life is not fair), and (5) standards (Rollie's thoughts about how the world should be).

• *Assumption 3:* Certain "obstacles" to satisfaction lie within individual family members' cognitions (for example, Carole's belief that she needs to always be her children's best friend).

• *Assumption 4:* Unless family members become more aware of their family-related cognitions and how these cognitions affect them in certain situations, they will not be able to identify areas that cause distress and replace them with healthy interaction.

These assumptions are usually unspoken within a family structure and simply exist and are maintained on an unconscious level. In a sense they occur automatically and often form the rules by which our family operates.

Rollie: But it seems as though our rules or assumptions are all screwed up. I mean, that's what gets us crazy about the family, that half the time we don't know what's what. The rules are always changing.

Dr. D.: I am not clear on what you are saying, Rollie—could you be more specific?

Janice (interrupting): I think that what he is trying to say is that my parents shift things around a lot—they confuse us. They do what they think is right at the time.

Mother: All right, I'll buy that, I think that's fair to say. But you guys (*pointing to Rollie and Janice*) then take it and run with it and manipulate the hell out of your father and me.

Janice: Well, yeah, we're kids, what do you expect?

Dr. D.: You know, it just struck me that perhaps Rollie and Janice are waiting for you to come down on them more firmly, but until you do, they act out or give you a hard time.

Mother: But that's what they are complaining about, the we're too hard on them or "give them crap," in Rollie's words.

Dr. D.: No, that's not what I'm hearing. You (*to Rollie and Janice*) can correct me if I'm wrong, but what I am hearing is that it's the inconsistency they are reacting to. In fact, I believe that this has been the issue all along.

Father: You mean the inconsistency?

Dr. D.: Sure. My guess is that they feel as though they are in somewhat of a double bind and it's disruptive to them.

Mother: Well—again, I think that I am the one who is guilty of that, because I would flip-flop so much. I usually struggle with playing the role of the tough guy and also trying to be their best friend at the same time.

Dr. D.: And it's my impression that Bob would react to that by assuming a more rigid posture, thus polarizing the two of you. When this occurs, it gives the kids a lot of room to do what they want, causing conflict in the family.

Mother: God, what a mess—do you think that you can help us straighten all of this out?

Dr. D.: I am sure going to try—as long as everybody gives me their best effort.

At this point I reaffirmed the family's commitment to working with me in treatment. This was very important since the volatility and vying for power among these family members was such that the cohesion could quickly deteriorate, depending on what I did.

In the subsequent five visits, the majority of my focus centered around addressing family schemas about rules and regulations and, more important, how family members truly felt about one another.

Following is an excerpt from the sixth session.

Dr. D.: Janice, a moment ago you mentioned something about your parents' not really being concerned about what you are going through right now. I'd like to hear more about your thoughts.

Janice: Well, I am sick of my parents getting on me about my weight. I know I am fat and I can't help it—and they talk to me like it's so easy to just stop eating and lose weight.

Dr. D.: So, what are the specific thoughts that go through your mind when you hear another family member make a remark about your weight?

Janice: I feel hurt and frustrated.

Dr. D.: OK, that's what you feel, but what about the thought that precedes your feelings?

Janice (takes a moment to think): Well, that they don't care about how it might hurt me. That they are not thinking that I can't help it.

Dr. D.: Good! Now how do you think that this affects how you react to them, how you behave?

Janice: Well, for one, it makes me want to eat more.

Mother: Ah, that's interesting, I never knew that.

Dr. D.: You mean you actually experience anger and engage in overeating?

Janice: Yes. All the time.

Dr. D.: It also sounds retaliatory. Like you then try to get back at them for being insensitive toward you.

Janice: Right.

Dr. D.: It's sort of like insulation, your eating.

Father: Yeah, literally! (*Rollie and Father snicker. Janice begins to cry*)

Mother: Ah, you see, Bob? That's what I mean. It's wisecracks like that, that are really destructive.

Father: All right, I'm sorry (*still snickering*); I just couldn't help myself.

Dr. D.: I can't help but notice that laughing seems to serve a very special purpose in this family.

Mother: How is that?

Dr. D.: Well, every time someone expresses their feelings or really shows their vulnerability, family members either lash out or they laugh. What do you think that means?

Rollie: We're screwed up?

Dr. D.: Well, but something more than that . . . it's almost like you have trouble handling intimacy. You as a family almost avoid it, either by arguing or making fun of each other.

Mother: Oh, I couldn't agree more.

Dr. D.: What could we say about the family schema regarding intimacy? What form does intimacy take in your family?

Father: Well, it kind of is expressed in jest. Like when I call Janice my little tomato queen—I really mean it affectionately.

Dr D.: So why can't this just be said to each other as opposed to being disguised in a joke or negative statement?

Father: I don't know. That's a really good question.

The majority of my work with this family focused on the restructuring of their individual and family schemas by helping them to identify cognitive distortions and correct their faulty thinking. One of these distortions had to do with exposing their individual vulnerabilities to one another while expressing their emotions.

Therapy continued for an additional fifteen sessions over the subsequent six months. All family members reported improvement in their relationship with a marked reduction in the tension at home. Rollie and Janice decided not to file for divorce.

DISCUSSION

In the foregoing case it was decided to target the father since he was perceived by the therapist as being the center of the conflict in this particular crisis. It was thought that attempting to restructure his thoughts first might have a significant impact on the rest of the family members. In subsequent sessions the focus was directed toward having each member restructure his or her thoughts as well as trying some alternative behaviors as a specific therapeutic exercise.

It is important to note that cognitive-behavioral therapy works best with families when it is used within a systems approach as in this case example. It differs from a strict traditional systems approach in that when using a cognitive-behavioral modality, more emphasis is placed on targeting cognitions, particularly belief systems.

Most important, one of the strengths of the cognitive-behavioral modality of family therapy is that it is readily integrated with other therapeutic modalities and is very likely to be utilized more actively in the future, particularly in crisis settings (Dattilio in press).

REFERENCES

Alexander, J., and Parsons, B. V. (1982). *Functional Family Therapy.* Pacific Grove, CA: Brooks/Cole.

Alexander, P. (1988). The therapeutic implications of family cognitions and constructs. *Journal of Cognitive Psychotherapy* 2(4):219–236.

Bandura, A. (1977). *Social Learning Therapy.* Englewood Cliffs, NJ: Prentice-Hall.

Baucom, D. H., and Epstein, N. (1990). *Cognitive-Behavioral Marital Therapy.* New York: Brunner/Mazel.

Baucom, D. H., and Lester, G. W. (1986). The usefulness of cognitive restructuring as an adjunct to behavioral marital therapy. *Behavior Therapy* 17:385–403.

Beck, A. T. (1976). *Cognitive Therapy and the Emotional Disorders.* New York: International Universities Press.

––––––– (1988). *Love Is Never Enough.* New York: Harper & Row.

Beck, A. T., Rush, J. A., Shaw, B. F., and Emery, G. (1979). *Cognitive Therapy of Depression.* New York: Guilford.

Bowen, M. (1978). *Family Therapy in Clinical Practice.* New York: Jason Aronson.

Dattilio, F. M. (1989). A guide to cognitive marital therapy. In *Innovations in Clinical Practice: A Source Book,* vol. 8, ed. P. A. Keller and S. R. Heyman, pp. 27–42. Sarasota, FL: Professional Resource Exchange.

——— (1990). Cognitive marital therapy: a case study. *Journal of Family Psychotherapy* 1(1):15–31.

——— (1993). Cognitive techniques with couples and families. *The Family Journal* 1(1):51–65.

——— (1994). Families in crisis. In *Cognitive-Behavioral Strategies in Crisis Intervention*, ed. F. M. Dattilio and A. Freeman, pp. 278–301. New York: Guilford.

——— (1995). A cognitive-behavioral approach to family therapy with Ruth. In *Case Approach to Counseling and Psychotherapy*, ed. G. Corey, pp. 282–298. Pacific Grove, CA: Brooks/Cole.

——— (in press). *Integrative Cases in Couples and Family Therapy: A Cognitive-Behavioral Perspective*. New York: Guilford.

Dattilio, F. M., and Padesky, C. A. (1990). *Cognitive Therapy with Couples*. Sarasota, FL: Professional Resource Exchange.

DeRubeis, R. J., and Beck, A. T. (1988). Cognitive therapy. In *Handbook of Cognitive Behavioral Therapies*, ed. K. S. Dobson, pp. 273–306. New York: Guilford.

Dicks, H. (1953). Experiences with marital tensions seen in the psychological clinic. In Clinical studies in marriage and the family: a symposium on methods. *British Journal of Medical Psychology* 26:181–196.

DiGiuseppe, R., and Zeeve, C. (1985). Marriage: rational-emotive couples counseling. In *Clinical Applications of Rational-Emotive Therapy*, ed. A. Ellis and M. Bernard, pp. 72–95. New York: Springer.

Doherty, W. J. (1981). Cognitive processes in intimate conflict: 1. Extending attribution theory. *American Journal of Family Therapy* 9:5–13.

Ellis, A. (1977). The nature of disturbed marital interactions. In *Handbook of Rational-Emotive Therapy*, ed. A. Ellis and R. Greiger, pp. 77–92. New York: Springer.

——— (1978). Family therapy: A phenomenological and active-directive approach. *Journal of Marriage and Family Counseling* 4(2):43–50.

——— (1982). Rational-emotive family therapy. In *Counseling and Therapy*, ed. A. M. Horne and M. M. Ohlsen, pp. 302–328. Itasca, IL: Peacock.

—————— (1986). Rational-emotive therapy applied to relationship therapy. *Journal of Rational-Emotive Therapy* 4–21.

Ellis, A., Sichel, J. L., Yeager, R. J., et al. (1989). *Rational Emotive Couples Therapy.* Needham Heights, MA: Allyn & Bacon.

Epstein, N. (1982). Cognitive therapy with couples. *American Journal of Family Therapy* 10(1):5–16.

—————— (1992). Marital therapy. In *Comprehensive Casebook of Cognitive Therapy*, ed. A. Freeman and F. M. Dattilio, pp. 267–275. New York: Plenum.

Epstein, N., and Schlesinger, S. E. (1991). Marital and family problems. In *Adult Clinical Problems: A Cognitive-Behavioral Approach*, ed. W. Dryden and R. Rentoul, pp. 288–317. London: Routledge & Kegan Paul.

—————— (1995). Cognitive-behavioral treatment of family problems. In *Cognitive Therapy with Children and Adolescents: A Casebook for Clinical Practice*, ed. M. Reinecke, F. M. Dattilio, and A. Freeman, pp. 299–326. New York: Guilford.

Epstein, N., Schlesinger, S., and Dryden, W. (1988). Concepts and methods of cognitive-behavioral family treatment. In *Cognitive-Behavior Therapy with Families*, ed. N. Epstein, S. Schlesinger, and W. Dryden, pp. 5–48. New York: Brunner/Mazel.

Faloon, I. R. H. (1991). Behavioral family therapy. In *Handbook of Family Therapy*, ed. A. S. Gurman and D. P. Kniskern, pp. 65–95. New York: Brunner/Mazel.

Fincham, F. D., Bradbury, T. N., and Beach, S. R. H. (1990). To arrive where we began: a reappraisal of cognition in marriage and in marital therapy. *Journal of Family Psychology* 4(2):167–184.

Goldenberg, I., and Goldenberg, H. (1991). *Family Therapy: An Overview.* Pacific Grove, CA: Brooks/Cole.

Gordon, S. B., and Davidson, N. (1981). Behavioral parenting training. In *Handbook of Family Therapy*, ed. A. S. Gurman and D. P. Kniskern, pp. 517–577. New York: Brunner/Mazel.

Huber, C. H., and Baruth, L. G. (1989). *Rational-Emotive Family Therapy: A Systems Perspective.* New York: Springer.

Jacobson, N. S., and Addis, M. E. (1993). Research on couples and couples therapy: what do we know? Where are we going? *Journal of Consulting and Clinical Psychology* 61(1):85–93.

Jacobson, N. S., and Christensen, A. (1996). *Integrative Couple Therapy.* New York: Norton.

Jacobson, N. S., and Margolin, G. (1979). *Marital Therapy: Strategies Based on Social Learning and Behavior Exchange Principles.* New York: Brunner/Mazel.

Leslie, L. A. (1988). Cognitive-behavioral and systems models of family therapy: how compatible are they? In *Cognitive-Behavioral Therapy with Families*, ed. N. Epstein, S. E. Schlesinger, and W. Dryden, pp. 49–83. New York: Brunner/Mazel.

Liberman, R. P. (1970). Behavioral approaches to couple and family therapy. *American Journal of Orthopsychiatry* 40:106–118.

Madanes, C. (1981). *Strategic Family Therapy.* San Francisco: Jossey-Bass.

Margolin, G., Christensen, A., and Weiss, R. L. (1975). Contracts, cognition and change: a behavioral approach to marriage therapy. *Counseling Psychologist* 5:15–25.

Margolin, G., and Weiss, R. L. (1978). Comparative evaluation of therapeutic components associated with behavioral marital treatments. *Journal of Consulting and Clinical Psychology* 46:1476–1486.

Minuchin, S. (1974). *Families and Family Therapy.* Cambridge, MA: Harvard University Press.

Munson, C. E. (1993). Cognitive family therapy. In *Cognitive and Behavioral Treatment: Methods and Applications*, ed. D. K. Granvold, pp. 202–221. Pacific Grove, CA: Brooks/Cole.

Patterson, G. R. (1971). *Families: Applications of Social Learning to life.* Champaign, IL: Research Press.

—— (1982). *Coercive Family Processes: A Social Learning Approach*, vol 3. Eugene, OR: Castalia.

—— (1985). Beyond technology: the next stage in developing an empirical base for parent training. In *Handbook of Family Psychology and Therapy*, vol. 2, ed. L. L'Abate, pp. 36–52. Homewood, IL: Dorsey.

Patterson, G. R., and Hops, H. (1972). Coercion, a game for two: intervention techniques for marital conflict. In *The Experimental Analysis of Social Behavior*, ed. R. E. Urich and P. Mounjoy, pp. 424–440. New York: Appleton.

Patterson, G. R., McNeal, S., Hawkins, N., and Phelps, R. (1967).

Reprogramming the social environment. *Journal of Child Psychology and Psychiatry* 8:181–195.

Russell, T., and Morrill, C. M. (1989). Adding a systematic touch to rational-emotive therapy for families. *Journal of Mental Health Counseling* 11(2):184–192.

Sanders, M. R., and Dadds, M. R. (1993). *Behavioral Family Intervention*. Needham Heights, MA: Allyn & Bacon.

Satir, V. (1967). *Conjoint Family Therapy*. Palo Alto, CA: Science and Behavioral Books.

Schindler, L., and Vollmer, M. (1984). Cognitive perspectives in behavioral marital therapy: some proposals for bridging theory, research and practice. In *Marital Interaction: Analysis and Modification*, ed. K. Hahlwag and N. S. Jacobson, pp. 146–162. New York: Guilford.

Schwebel, A. I., and Fine, M. A. (1992). Cognitive-behavior family therapy. *Journal of Family Psychotherapy* 3:73–91.

—— (1994). *Understanding and Helping Families: A Cognitive-Behavioral Approach*. Hillsdale, NJ: Erlbaum.

Stuart, R. B. (1969). Operant-interpersonal treatment of marital discord. *Journal of Consulting and Clinical Psychology* 33:675–682.

—— (1976). Operant interpersonal treatment for marital discord. In *Treating Relationships*, ed. D. H. L. Olsen, pp. 675–682. Lake Mills, IA: Graphic.

Teichman, Y. (1984). Cognitive family therapy. *British Journal of Cognitive Psychotherapy* 2(1):1–10.

—— (1992). Family treatment with an acting-out adolescent. In *Comprehensive Casebook of Cognitive Therapy*, ed. A. Freeman and F. M. Dattilio, pp. 331–346. New York: Plenum.

Weiss, R. L. (1984). Cognitive and strategic interventions in behavioral marital therapy. In *Marital Interaction: Analysis and Modification*, ed. K. Hahlwag and N. S. Jacobson, pp. 337–355. New York: Guilford.

Wright, J. H., and Beck, A. T. (1993). Family cognitive therapy with inpatients: part II. In *Cognitive Therapy with Inpatients: Developing a Cognitive Milieu*, ed. J. H. Wright, M. E. Thase, A. T. Beck, and J. W. Ludgate, pp. 176–190. New York: Guilford.

20

REFLECTIONS ON COGNITIVE THERAPY

Robert L. Leahy

VARIETIES OF COGNITIVE THERAPY

As the reader of this volume may recognize, there are a variety of approaches to conducting cognitive therapy. Because cognitive therapy is an empirically derived therapeutic model, there is no requirement that clinicians working within this framework need to comply with "standard techniques." There are seven dimensions along which therapists vary in their application of cognitive therapy. Where an individual therapist is placed along these dimensions may reflect the particular problem areas they address, the length of therapy anticipated, the personal style and psychological theories of the clinician, and the interest in integrating cognitive therapy with other approaches. Since most clinicians, in fact, describe themselves as "eclectic," it might be helpful to examine how "eclectic" cognitive therapy is in its applications.

The seven dimensions of variation in approaching cases that I discuss in this chapter are the following:

- Emphasis on techniques
- Examination of levels of cognition
- Use of developmental material
- Consideration of resistance
- Focus on transferential issues
- Use of case conceptualization
- Integration of other approaches

EMPHASIS ON TECHNIQUES

Although cognitive therapy involves specific techniques directed toward eliciting, examining, testing, and modifying dysfunctional thinking, there is considerable variation in which techniques and how many techniques the individual therapist will use. Some novices, untrained in cognitive therapy, may believe that this modality is reducible to simply asking the patient what he or she is thinking. However, cognitive therapy is far from simplistic. There is some empirical evidence that adherence to certain elements of the cognitive therapy "protocol" (as exemplified in Beck et al. 1979) results in better improvement in the patient (De Rubeis et al. 1990, DeRubeis and Feeley 1990).

Beginning therapists are wise to master a set of cognitive therapy techniques that they may draw upon readily. For example, when presented with a depressed patient, the beginning therapist would be well advised to turn to Beck and colleagues' (1979) treatment manual and adapt it as a guide until the therapist feels he or she is comfortable with using these techniques on his or her own. Vague philosophical discussions with patients about the meaning of life, or empty exhortations to the patient that he or she is irrational and must change, will fall on deaf ears and lead to premature termination.

Complete reliance on techniques, however, may lead both patient and therapist to feel that the therapy is too pat and superficial, and that the therapist can be replaced by a mass-market paperback book on cognitive therapy. The patient needs to believe that the therapy is tailored to his or her specific needs and life history. In the pages to follow, I illustrate the variety and importance of individualizing treatment for the patient.

EXAMINATION OF LEVELS OF COGNITION

The cognitive approach proposes that there are three levels of cognition—automatic thoughts, maladaptive assumptions, and underlying schemas. In addition to the three levels, the individual experiences the world in terms of images, primitive emotionalized schemas, and unconscious or dissociated memories. Therapists differ in their consideration of these cognitive and emotional phenomena.

In the initial phase of treatment the clinician focuses on the immediately available behavioral repertoire and automatic thoughts. It is relatively easy to see that the patient is inactive, that his or her moods vary with the activities that he or she pursues, and that he or she feels worse when articulating dysfunctional thoughts, such as "I'm a failure," or "I'll always be alone." Indeed, many patients report improvement in their mood by virtue of modifications in the behavioral level and in recognizing the irrationality of their automatic thoughts. Many "treatment packages" for cognitive therapy will give primary focus to behavioral interventions (e.g., behavioral activation, exposure to feared stimuli, social skills training) and the identification and modification of automatic thoughts.

However, patients with chronic or recurring problems, or

diffuse complaints, or multiple diagnoses, may be better served by "deepening" the therapy to consideration of maladaptive assumptions and schemas. (I believe all patients can benefit from this "deeper" approach, but reality often necessitates the "quick and easier" five-session therapy because of the patient's self-imposed constraints or because of limitations of coverage.) Indeed, patients whose underlying assumptions (that is, "shoulds" and "if-then" rules) are modified are more likely to maintain their gains in therapy (Persons 1989, Persons and Miranda 1992).

As is evident in the chapters of this volume, many cognitive therapists emphasize the maladaptive personal schemas of the patient. Because most individuals seldom use the metacognitive skill of examining their own biases, it is a revolutionary experience for many patients to realize that they have been focused on any and all evidence consistent with their personal schemas of abandonment, helplessness, or control. The more the therapist works with patients presenting with personality disorders or resistance, the greater the emphasis on schematic analysis (see Dowd, Greenberg, Holland, Layden, Leahy, Smucker, and Tompkins in this volume).

Therapists also differ as to their examination and use of imagery, primitive processes (such as dissociation), and fragmented or even repressed memories. Generally, the greater the emphasis on intense anxiety (for example, post-traumatic stress disorder, dissociative disorders) or the more profound the personality disorder (e.g., borderline personality), the greater the emphasis on imagery, primary process cognition, and fragmented memories. Here, similar to the psychodynamic ego psychologist, the cognitive therapist views "defense mechanism" as a cognitive-control mechanism that protects the individual from excessive flooding of anxiety. The discussions of cognitive hypnotherapy by Dowd, integrative cognitive therapy by Holland, and the treatment of post-traumatic stress disorder by Smucker illustrate the importance of addressing the defensive and primitive nature of these cognitive (or "precognitive") phenomena. Indeed, the therapist may find it useful to integrate a "defense-dynamic" conceptualization to evaluate how the patient uses emotion, primitive processing, or acting out to avoid, escape from, or numb thinking and experience. Emotive and experiential techniques—such as those advocated by Dowd and Smucker or by Safran and Segal (1990) or Young (1990)—help elicit "deeper" cognitive schemata that are often obscured by the patient's defenses.

USE OF DEVELOPMENTAL MATERIAL

Although cognitive therapy is often described as "ahistorical"—with no emphasis on the effects of earlier experience—the readers of this volume can readily see that clinicians differ as to their incorporation of developmental material. Generally, clinicians will focus almost exclusively on the present with patients in shorter-term (e.g., fifteen session) cognitive therapy. However, patients presenting with chronic, recurrent, and complicated clinical features, or patients whose personality disorder impedes progress, are good candidates for developmental cognitive therapy.

Perhaps a shortcoming of the cognitive model is the lack of a clear developmental model of psychopathology. In my work (Leahy 1992a, 1993, 1995, 1996), I have drawn upon the work of Bowlby (1969, 1980) and Piaget (1970), as Guidano and Liotti (1983) have. However, because there is no clear developmental model, it is difficult to assess "normal development" or "developmental fixation and regression." The lack of a clear stage-theory, the absence of a model of developmental sequences and rates of development, and the lack of a description of transitional mechanisms of change in development may limit the utility of developmental approaches in cognitive theory (see Leahy 1992b, 1995). The attempt to "integrate" philosophically incompatible theories—such as Beck's structural model with hydraulic models—will inevitably lead to conceptual confusion. I believe that the cognitive model is consistent with models that emphasize *cognitive structure* (e.g., schema, object concept, categorical thinking, systemic processes, self-organizing principles), *biological adaptation* (e.g., evolutionary processes accounting for fixed behavioral patterns, preparedness), and the *management of threat* (e.g., signal systems, fixed modes of response, ego defense).

Many therapists find it useful to draw upon historical antecedents to explain current functioning. However, clinicians should be aware that life events (such as "abandonment") may mean different things to individuals at different ages (or stages of development). The cognitive model that Beck has advanced suggests that these earlier schemata may lie dormant until provocative life events activate them in current functioning. Guidano and Liotti (1983) and Mahoney (1991) have proposed that defensive barriers to recognition of these schemas help "protect" the individual—perhaps from the overwhelming flood of earlier memories. For example, Smucker (this volume) draws parallels with Freud's model of primary and secondary process thinking—that is, between affect-laden primitive thinking on the one hand and more logical, language-based thinking on the other. The questions that arise about historical antecedents are: (1) are there certain life events that are essentially formative? (2) what was the level of affect at the time of the earlier life event? (3) what was the level of cognitive and emotional processing of that earlier life event? and (4) how easily does the adult patient see or experience parallels with these earlier life events? We might also ask a fifth question—perhaps about resilience: Why is that other life events are not as disturbing to the individual?

Consider the following illustration of these points. An adult female patient, experiencing a sexual anesthesia (that is, no sensation in any sexual area and complete numbing at penetration), reported that she had been physically abused by her mother and sexually abused by father. The physical and sexual abuse were recurrent and uncontrollable and occurred between the ages of 5 and 12. Certainly this would qualify as formative experience. The level of affect initially at the time of abuse was one of terror and intense physical pain. The level of cognitive and emotional processing was primitive—soon after experiencing the abuse, she dissociated, eventually forming an alter personality. As an adult she experienced as "similar" sexual relations with men—especially at the point of penetration, which she experienced as a "switch turning off." Her recollections of earlier abuse were often accompanied by dissociation and splitting in sessions, but her recollection of being raped, at the age of 12, by an older adolescent, was not characterized by any dissociation. The reason for this difference, she observed, was that she recalled that she consciously attempted not to dissociate during the rape, lest she be murdered. Consequently, her earlier processing matched her current processing of the rape event—full awareness—whereas her processing and experience of the parental abuse was and remained dissociated.

The importance of assessing the level of processing and defensiveness of the earlier memory is that memories are not just about content—they are about *meaning and coping*. The meaning that the patient attaches to an event may be quite idiosyncratic—it cannot be derived from the therapist's meaning for the event. The patient's style of coping—and the patient's belief in the ability to cope—will determine the impact of events later in life. The patient who is raped by a teenage neighbor, but who believes that she can cope by remaining aware of the experience, may be less emotionally disabled than the patient who experiences the abuse as overwhelming and recurring. It is this latter condition—that is, of overwhelming, ongoing abuse marked by dissociation—that leads the therapist to incorporate "developmentally appropriate" techniques that allow the access of the primitive processing of the experience. One needs to delay the use of logical-rational discussion until after the more primitive-experiential material has been elicited and addressed through imagery rescripting, exposure, age regression, or other interventions.

Clinicians will often begin with the focus on the "treatment package" in cognitive therapy, limiting interventions to the current symptomatology and cognitive content. However, some patients presenting with resistance to the process of change may require a developmental phase in their therapy. For example, Holland (this volume) demonstrates how a developmental schema-based approach is useful in treating a chronically obsessive-compulsive patient. Emphasis on developmental material in treatment is indicated in my description of the treatment of a resistant patient and in Smucker's (this volume) developmental-imagery interventions in the treatment of post-traumatic stress disorder.

How does the clinician know when to apply developmental interventions? I would propose the following criteria: (1) the patient has recurring, powerful recollection of earlier events that continue to cause discomfort; (2) the patient's developmental history is characterized by events that plausibly might continue to affect him or her—even if the patient denies the effect of these events; (3) the patient's life history is characterized by recurrent, self-defeating patterns in relationships and in work; (4) the patient does not respond to standard cognitive therapy interventions or to medication; (5) the transference or countertransference is intense or powerful and seems to undermine therapeutic goals; (6) there is a complicated and primitive personality organization—for example, borderline personality—or reliance on primitive coping mechanisms—for example, dissociative disorder. (See McGinn and Young 1996, for a description of criteria for schematic analysis in therapy.)

CONSIDERATION OF RESISTANCE

For some, it may seem odd that a cognitive-behavioral therapist would speak of resistance. After all, this has always been the intellectual territory of the psychoanalysts. Some cognitive therapists avoid the use of the term *resistance* and would rather view the patient's lack of progress as a lack of motivation, biological limitations, or the irrelevance of the therapeutic approach. My approach to resistance is multifaceted: I view resistance as the interaction of schematic processes of compensation and avoidance, self-handicapping, face-saving, and "investment strategies" to limit loss (Leahy 1993, 1996, and this volume). Many view resistance as the management of threat—for example, the activation of defensive or avoidant cognitive strategies—as evidenced in behavioral avoidance, dissociative states, or the detachment of affect from percept (see Dowd, Holland, Leahy, Smucker, this volume; Guidano and Liotti 1983, Young 1990).

Cognitive therapists may confront resistance directly by examining the underlying assumptions and schemas activated in therapy and submitting them to cognitive evaluation—for example, the costs and benefits of the thoughts, vertical descent, examining logical errors and thought distortions, arguing back at the thoughts, or acting against the thought. However, clinicians may differ on the next level of strategic intervention. For example, Dowd and Smucker emphasize emotive and experiential interventions, including hypnosis, age regression, and imagery restructuring. Others, like myself (Leahy 1991, 1996) and Young (1990), may also examine how resistant schemas and scripts have continued to maintain themselves by the choices that the patient has made over his or her lifetime.

In this volume I presented a case in which resistance—for a major phase of the treatment—was the major focus of treatment. Others may see resistance as a peripheral or unnecessary issue: "If the patient isn't committed, why bother?" I think that the contributors to this volume have made a strong case for a strategic approach to resistance for the difficult patients for whom it is necessary.

FOCUS ON TRANSFERENTIAL ISSUES

It is quite common for critics of cognitive therapy to claim that we do not deal with the transference. These criticisms are both accurate and inaccurate. Many people conducting cognitive therapy avoid any discussion of transference, and indeed might look at me with a jaundiced eye if I were to raise the topic. Other therapists—most, if not all, of the contributors to this volume—utilize transference to the benefit of the patient. Indeed, transference, in learning theory terms, is simply another word for *stimulus–response generalization*.

The ability of the therapist to use information about the transference is partly related to the ability of the therapist to *accept* the transference. This is an ability that comes with experience, supervision, and self-discovery—perhaps self-discoveries that are not always flattering to one's ego. Safran and Segal (1990) have emphasized the importance of the therapeutic relationship in facilitating change, yet cognitive therapists have not articulated a model of transference that allows us to utilize this important source of information. Although some researchers have emphasized the importance of the patient's perception of empathy on the part of the therapist (Burns and Auerbach 1996, and Burns and Nolen-Hoeksema 1992), there is little beyond this dimension that has gained the attention of researchers and clinicians. Attempts to describe transference phenomena have been made by Leahy (1996) and Young (1990), but these attempts are only the beginning of what needs to be done. There is no developed model of transference yet articulated in cognitive therapy.

The irony, of course, is that most experienced clinicians use the transference material, to benefit the patient, it is hoped. I believe that an adequate model of transference must include recognition of the following: the history of significant object relations disturbances on the part of the patient, a topography of the patient's schemas, the interpersonal agendas of the patient, the therapeutic style and schemas of the therapist, and the ability and willingness of patient and therapist to resolve conflicts. Perhaps this area of therapy may prove to be the most meaningful and may provide the strongest generalization to significant object relations outside of therapy. As of now, it is unchartered, undiscovered, and promising.

Unfortunately, however, the emphasis on managed care and shortened therapy, while ultimately "good" for cognitive therapy, may prevent therapists from deepening the therapy by examining and developing the transference. We all want quick, even miraculous, results. Perhaps many therapists— perhaps many cognitive therapists—are uncomfortable with that murky, messy, but meaningful territory of the transference. Perhaps some of us like to hide behind our techniques, omniscient, "effective," aloof, and emotionally insulated from the relationship. If so, I would ask, "Who are we kidding?" The transference is there, as they say, "for better or for worse." My comment to therapists is, "If you don't deal with the transference, the transference will deal with you." Patients will see the therapy as too glib, too easily replicated by a self-help book, too devoid of human impact.

USE OF CASE CONCEPTUALIZATION

Although I am a great believer in the power of techniques, the contributors to this volume all draw upon case conceptualization. Cognitive therapy is *both* techniques and conceptualization. Beck (1976) had cautioned against a shotgun approach to therapy, and Jacqueline Persons (1989) has convincingly argued for case conceptualization in the treatment of patients. But how are cases conceptualized?

Tompkins indicates how a conceptualization of the patient's developmental history and schemas guide him in the selection and timing of interventions. Similarly, Layden's discussion of the treatment of borderline personality focuses on the multiple schemas of the patient and the stages of change in therapy. My discussion of resistance as a strategy of risk management is entirely based on case conceptualization. In this volume you will see how varied cognitive therapists are in their use of case conceptualization—some drawing on schema theory, others describing the level of processing, others referring to the developmental history of the patient.

Clearly, there is no agreed-upon model of conceptualizing the case. Therefore, let me take this opportunity to join Tompkins and Persons in advocating a model that, I suggest, should include the following:

- *Psychiatric evaluation:* A comprehensive assessment of current and past symptoms, diagnoses, and history, including evaluation of medical conditions
- *Cognitive assessment:* A comprehensive description of the patient's automatic thoughts, assumptions, and schemas of self and others
- *Behavioral assessment:* A description of behavioral deficits and excesses, especially as related to access to rewards, exposure to punishment, problem-solving ability, and social skills
- *Developmental history:* A developmental history describing significant life events related to sociotropy (relationships) and autonomous (independent-competence) issues
- *Life-events:* A description of current or recent life events, including daily hassles

- *Decision making:* A model of the patient's decision-making processes (e.g., risk aversion, myopia, hedging)
- *Emotional processing:* A description of the patient's level of processing, including the use of cognitive avoidance, dissociation, numbing, emotional integration, ability to gain distance or decenter, and logical-rational processing
- *Schema-coping:* A description of schema compensation and avoidance
- *Resilience:* A description of the patient's resilience and positive coping skills
- *Goals:* The patient's explicit goals in therapy

INTEGRATION OF OTHER APPROACHES

In addition to the foregoing recommendations, a case conceptualization should entail an implicit theory of human functioning. Unfortunately, this is not always apparent from the therapist's conceptualizations and, of course, there is no one theory of human functioning guiding cognitive therapists. Individuals (as cases) are conceptualized by referring to the work of Bowlby, Piaget, Masterson, Kernberg, and others, with little attempt to offer a comprehensive single theory. This style of eclectic conceptualization is typical of cognitive therapy today—and is very different from stricter behavioral models of the past.

I view this eclecticism as both a potential strength of the model and a potential weakness. Its strength derives from the fact that we can draw upon the work of a variety of models, borrowing their strength and using any technique that allows us to elicit thoughts and emotions and modify them. Indeed, why reinvent the wheel? Why not use what is useful in object relations theory or in cognitive-developmental theory?

The cautionary note, however, is that eclecticism may lead to the eradication of theory. After all, cognitive therapy, based on a clear, testable model of how cognition affects depression and anxiety, has advanced because it has been a fairly clear, empirically verifiable theory that has some internal consistency and face validity. But what is the "grand integrated theory" that is to be advanced by "eclecticism"? As Alford and Beck (1997) cogently indicate, there are no empirical data demonstrating the efficacy of "eclectically oriented" therapies, nor is there any obvious way that one can even adequately describe what a single eclectically oriented therapy would be. If it can integrate anything into itself, then what is the therapy that arises? How do we know what to integrate, what to discard? How do we test out the hypotheses that are derived from the "eclectic theory?" In fact, is it even possible to derive hypotheses from eclectic theories? If the hypothesis that is derived is falsified, then does the eclecticist simply develop an ad hoc hypothesis to handle the exception? Would we say that science is advanced by the development of theories (paradigms) or is it developed by ad hoc explanations and wholesale integration of ideas from a variety of apparently conflicting models?

Quite frankly, I see the value in both schools—that is, the more "traditional" theory building, internally consistent cognitive model and the model(s) derived from eclecticism. The attraction of "integrating" clinical approaches is that we all know (but are reluctant to admit) that none of us has a monopoly on the truth. All of us are looking for new ideas, new techniques, perhaps an added edge in the pursuit of better therapy and understanding. I have found it useful to go to the work of Bowlby on attachment or the writings of microeconomic theorists to understand the process of resistance. The authors of the current volume, comfortable with their established knowledge in cognitive theory, have found it important to draw on the intriguing and creative work of other clinical models. Like a pendulum that helps us keep better time by encompassing a wider range, but maintaining a center, our progress is marked by our ability to move beyond where we are while being able to return to who we are.

Some may read these chapters and decide that cognitive therapy is the way to go—many more others will find something useful to integrate into their repertoire of skills and knowledge. We, as cognitive therapists, can mark our own progress by recognizing that we have much to learn from those whom we teach.

REFERENCES

Alford, B. A., and Beck, A. T. (1997). *Cognitive Therapy: An Integration of Current Theory and Therapy*. New York: Guilford.

Beck, A. T. (1976). *Cognitive Therapy and the Emotional Disorders*. New York: International Universities Press.

Beck, A. T., Rush, A. J., Shaw, B. F., and Emery, G. (1979). *Cognitive Therapy of Depression*. New York: Guilford.

Bowlby, J. (1969). *Attachment and Loss*, vol. I, *Attachment*. New York: Basic Books.

—— (1980). *Attachment and Loss*, vol. III, *Loss: Sadness and Depression*. London: Hogarth.

Burns, D. D., and Auerbach, A. (1996). Therapeutic empathy in cognitive-behavioral therapy: does it really make a difference? *Frontiers of Cognitive Therapy*, ed. P. Salkovskis, pp. 135–164. New York: Guilford.

Burns, D. D., and Nolen-Hoeksema, S. (1992) Therapeutic empathy and recovery from depression in cognitive-behavioral therapy: a structural equation model. *Journal of Consulting and Clinical Psychology* 57:414–419.

De Rubeis, R. J., Evans, M. D., Hollon, S. D., et al. (1990). How does cognitive therapy work? Cognitive change and symptom change in cognitive therapy and pharmacotherapy for depression. *Journal of Consulting and Clinical Psychology* 58:862–869.

De Rubeis, R. J., and Feeley, M. (1990). Determinants of change in cognitive therapy for depression. *Cognitive Therapy and Research* 14:469–482.

Guidano, V., and Liotti, G. (1983). *Cognitive Processes and the Emotional Disorders*. New York: Guilford.

Leahy, R. L. (1991). Scripts in cognitive therapy: the systemic perspective. *Journal of Cognitive Psychotherapy: An International Quarterly* 5:291–304.

—— (1992a). Cognitive therapy on Wall Street: schemas and scripts of invulnerability. *Journal of Cognitive Psychotherapy: An International Quarterly* 6:1–14.

—— (1992b). *Development and emotion in cognitive therapy*. Paper presented at meeting of the Association for Advancement of Behavior Therapy, Boston, November.

—— (1993). *Strategies of resistance in cognitive therapy*. Paper presented at meeting of the Association for the Advancement of Behavior Therapy, Atlanta, November.

—— (1995). Cognitive development and cognitive therapy. *Journal of Cognitive Psychotherapy: An International Quarterly* 9:173–184.

—— (1996). *Cognitive Therapy: Basic Principles and Applications*. Northvale, NJ: Jason Aronson.

Mahoney, M. (1991). *Human Change Processes*. New York: Basic Books.

McGinn, L. K., and Young, J. E. (1996). Schema-focused therapy. In *Frontiers of Cognitive Therapy*, ed P. Salkoviskis, pp. 182–207. New York: Guilford.

Persons, J. (1989). *Cognitive Therapy in Practice: A Case Formulation Approach*. New York: Norton.

Persons, J., and Miranda, J. (1992). Cognitive theories of vulnerability to depression: reconciling negative evidence. *Cognitive Therapy and Research* 16:485–502.

Piaget, J. (1970). *Genetic Epistemology*. New York: Norton.

Safran, J., and Segal, Z. (1990). *Interpersonal Process in Cognitive Therapy*. New York: Guilford.

Young, J. E. (1990). *Cognitive Therapy for Personality Disorders: A Schema-Focused Approach*. Sarasota, FL: Professional Resource Exchange.

INDEX

Abrams, D. B., 221

Abramson, L. Y., 3, 377

Activating situations, case formulation model, 41

Adaptation, depression as, resistance, 62–64

Addis, M. E., 411

Age regression, modification of core cognitive schemata, 30–31

Alcoholics Anonymous (AA), 221

Alexander, J., 411

Alford, B. A., 5, 18, 315, 317, 320, 324, 327, 328, 329, 330, 331, 332, 333, 334, 335, 336, 464

Alpert, M. C., 392

Anthony, W. A., 330

Anxiety, generalized anxiety disorder. *See* Generalized anxiety disorder

Arntz, A., 151, 153

Arousal, post-traumatic stress disorder, 210–212

Assumptions, schemas and automatic thoughts related, 10

Attachment theory, post-traumatic stress disorder and, 198–199

Auerbach, A., 460

Automatic thoughts
depression, 99–101
schemas and assumptions related, 10

Ball, W. A., 132

Bandura, A., 353, 409

Barlow, D. H., 42, 108, 109, 110, 124, 125, 152, 184

Barsky, A. J., 171, 189

Baruth, L. G., 412

Batchelor, W., 343
Baucom, D. H., 250, 252, 253, 254,
     255, 256, 257, 269, 411, 412
Baur, S., 170
Beach, S. R. H., 249, 259
Beck, A. T., 3, 4, 5, 17, 18, 21, 38,
     40, 88, 89, 90, 94, 100, 110,
     126, 127, 128, 129, 181, 221,
     237, 317, 320, 321, 323, 324,
     327, 328, 329, 330, 334, 335,
     336, 355, 375, 385, 411, 412,
     414, 452, 456, 461, 464
Beck, J. S., 45, 269
Becker, G. S., 64
Behavioral techniques, cognitive
     techniques compared,
     10–16
Bentall, R. P., 325, 326, 332
Berne, E., 282
Bienvenu, M. J., 254
Biology
   developmental factors, cogni-
        tive therapy, 455–458
   looming vulnerability model,
        generalized anxiety dis-
        order, 130–132
   panic disorder, 109–110
Bishop, D. R., 230
Blowers, C., 125
Booth, R. G., 125, 130
Borderline personality disorder,
     295–314
   described, 297–299
   overview, 295–297
   treatment, 299–313
     early stage, 300–305
     goals of, 299–300

late stage, 310–313
middle stage, 305–310
Borkovec, T. D., 124, 125, 126, 130
Bowen, M., 410
Bowlby, J., 63, 198, 455
Bradbury, T. N., 257
Bretherton, I., 198, 199
Burns, D. D., 100, 234, 237, 460
Butler, G., 125, 128, 130, 131

Calabro, L. E., 374, 377
Carmody, T. P., 375
Case formulation, 37–59
   model of, 38–43
     core and conditional beliefs,
          40–41
     obstacles, 43
     origins, 41–42
     precipitants and activating
          situations, 41
     problem list, 39–40
     treatment plan, 42–43
     working hypothesis, 42
   overview, 37–38, 57–58
   role of, 38
   use of (case example), 43–57
     collaboration, 44–46
     compliance, 50–52
     homework assignments,
          49–50
     intervention point selection,
          46–47
     intervention strategy selec-
          tion, 47–49
     summary table, 52–57
Cashdan, S., 199
Castonguay, L. G., 335

Cautela, J. R., 33
Centers for Disease Control and Prevention, 342
Cerny, A. C., 184
Chadwick, P. D. J., 315, 316, 320, 321, 322, 329
Chambless, D. L., 249
Christensen, A., 254, 410
Clark, D. M., 110, 113, 115, 116
Cognitive-behavioral therapy, case formulation in, 37–59. *See also* Case formulation
Cognitive-developmental theory, hypnosis and, 21–36. *See also* Hypnosis
Cognitive distortions, summary table of, 7–9
Cognitive rehearsal, modification of core cognitive schemata, 28–29
Cognitive restructuring, marital conflict, 269–270
Cognitive therapy, 3–20
  cognition levels, 453–455
  conceptualization use, 461–463
  of depression, 88–90. *See also* Depression
  developmental material, 455–458
  development of, 3–5
  expanded applications of, xi–xii
  integrative, 391–408, 463–465. *See also* Integrative cognitive therapy
  principles of, 5–19

resistance and, 61–84, 459–460. *See also* Resistance
  techniques, 452–453
  transferential issues, 460–461
  varieties of, 451–452
Collaboration, case formulation model, 44–46
Communication skill training, marital conflict, 268
Conditional beliefs, case formulation model, 40–41
Conditioning, hypnotic, modification of core cognitive schemata, 33–34
Coping imagery, modification of core cognitive schemata, 27–28
Core beliefs
  case formulation model, 40–41
  identification of, depression, 98–99
Core cognitive schemata
  identification of, 25–27
  modification of, 27–28
Correia, C. J., 315, 331, 333, 335
(Counter)conditioning, hypnotic, modification of core cognitive schemata, 33–34
Courchaine, K. E., 22, 23
Cowey, A., 132
Craske, M. G., 249
Cromwell, R. L., 325
Cuk, M., 132

Dadds, M. R., 410
Dattilio, F. M., 410, 411, 412, 413, 415

Davenloo, H., 392
Davey, G. C., 128
Davidson, N., 410
Deffenbacher, J. L., 259
Denial
    confrontation of, substance
        abuse, 236–243
    substance abuse, 230–232
Depression, 87–106
    as adaptation, resistance,
        62–64
    case example, 91–104
        automatic thoughts and
            behaviors, 99–101
        continuation, 95–98
        core beliefs identification,
            98–99
        initiation, 93–95
        presentation, 91–93
        strategy refinement,
            102–104
    cognitive therapy and, 3–4
    cognitive therapy of
        described, 88–90
        effectiveness of, 104–105
    double depression, 90–91
Depressive portfolios, resis-
    tance, 64–65
Depressive risk management,
    resistance, 65–66
DeRubeis, R. J., 414, 452
Desensitization, modification of
    core cognitive schemata, 28
Developmental factors
    borderline personality dis-
        order, 301–303
    cognitive therapy, 455–458

*Diagnostic and Statistical Manual
    of Mental Disorders (DSM-III)*
    generalized anxiety disorder,
        123, 124
    panic disorder, 108, 112
*Diagnostic and Statistical Manual
    of Mental Disorders
    (DSM-III-R)*
    generalized anxiety disorder,
        124
    panic disorder, 108
*Diagnostic and Statistical Manual
    of Mental Disorders (DSM-IV)*
    borderline personality dis-
        order, 295–297
    depression, 90, 91
    generalized anxiety disorder,
        123, 124
    hypochondriasis, 170, 171
    marital conflict, 251, 254
    obsessive-compulsive dis-
        order, 152
    panic disorder, 108–109, 113
    post-traumatic stress disorder,
        193
    psychotic disorders, 319, 329
    sexual dysfunction, 280
DiClemente, C., 345, 348, 364
DiGiuseppe, R., 412
Dill, L. M., 132
Disability. *See* Physical disability
Disattribution, self-handicapping
    strategies, resistance, 67
Dissociation, post-traumatic
    stress disorder, 212–214
Divorce, rates of, 249
Dobson, K. S., 4

Doherty, W. J., 411
Double depression, 90–91
Dowd, E. T., 22, 23, 24, 25, 31
Durham, R. C., 125

Eckerman, C. O., 132, 133
Eifert, G. H., 58
Ellis, A., 21, 22, 278, 409, 411,
     412, 413
Emery, G., 126, 129, 221
Emotional catharsis, modifica-
     tion of core cognitive
     schemata, 30
Emotional numbing, generalized,
     post-traumatic stress dis-
     order, 214–215
Engagement, hypochondriasis,
     178–183
Epstein, E. E., 17, 249
Epstein, 1?., 252, 253, 254, 255,
     256, 257, 269, 409, 411, 412,
     413, 414, 415
Evans, C. S., 132
Exposure, hypochondriasis,
     187–189

Fallon, B. A., 173, 189
Faloon, I. R. H., 410
Family therapy, 409–450. See
     also Marital conflict
  case example, 416–445
     initial session, 416–427
  cognitive-behavioral approach,
     412–416
  cognitive distortion, case
     example, 428–445
  overview, 409–412

Feeley, M., 452
Fetzler, W. D., 34
Fincham, F. D., 257, 411
Fine, B. D., 201
Fine, M. A., 415, 441
Flavell, J. H., 331
Fleming, K., 32
Flooding, modification of core
     cognitive schemata, 28
Foa, E. B., 156, 195, 196
Folkman, S., 126
Freedman, A. M., 341
Freeman, A., 4, 17
Freud, S., 201, 277
Friedberg, F., 26
Friedman, A., 17
Friedman, J. M., 278

Garfield, Z. H., 278
Generalized anxiety disorder,
     123–149
  case example, 137–145
     anxious thoughts, 140–141
     automatic thoughts, 139
     behaviors, 141
     conceptualization, 142
     goals, 143
     history, 138–139
     outcome, 145
     presentation, 137–138
     treatment plan, 143–145
     underlying beliefs, 141
  clinical model, 128–130
  cognitive model, 126–128
  looming vulnerability model,
     130–132
  outcome studies, 124–126

Generalized anxiety disorder
   (*continued*)
   overview, 123–124
   research review, 132–135
   treatment implications,
      135–137
Generalized emotional numbing
   case example, 216–218
   post-traumatic stress disorder,
      214–215
Glasser, W., 221
Golden, W. L., 26
Goldenberg, H., 410
Goldenberg, I., 410
Goldfried, M. R., 335, 363
Goldstein, A. J., 249
Gordon, S. B., 410
Gottesman, I. I., 316
Gottman, J. M., 255
Greenberg, M. S., 17, 128
Greenberg, R. L., 5
Greenwood, V. B., 324
Grinspoon, L., 336
Guerney, B. G., Jr., 256, 268
Guidano, V. F., 23, 154, 455, 456,
      459

Hahlweg, K., 255
Harrow, M., 320, 331, 334
Hayes, S. C., 38
Heiman, J. R., 249, 281
Hekmat, H., 132
Henry, W. P., 199
Hepner, R., 378
Heyman, R. E., 253, 255
HIV risk behavior, 341–371
   assessment, 350–354

   basic facts, 343–345
   decision making, 358–362
   education, 354–358
   maintenance and ongoing
      assessment, 364–368
   overview, 341–343
   prevention strategy, 349–350
   psychotherapy and, 368–370
   skill building, 362–364
   transtheoretical perspective,
      345–349
Ho, D. D., 344
Hof, L., 249
Hole, R. W., 317, 320, 330, 332,
      333
Hollander, E., 175
Hollon, S. D., 4, 104, 105, 391
Holtzworth-Munroe, A., 256
Homework
   case formulation model, 49–50
   post-traumatic stress disorder,
      209–210
Hops, H., 409
Horowitz, M. J., 195, 196
Huber, C. H., 412
Hypnosis, 21–36
   identification of core cognitive
      schemata, 25–27
   modification of core cognitive
      schemata, 27–34
      age regression and memory
         review, 30–31
      cognitive rehearsal, 28–29
      desensitization and flooding
         imagery, 28
      emotional catharsis, 30

hypnotic (counter)conditioning, 33–34
imaginary dialogue creation, 29–30
memory modification, 32–33
replacement and coping imagery, 27–28
overview, 21–25
Hypnotic (counter)conditioning, modification of core cognitive schemata, 33–34
Hypochondriasis, 169–191
case examples, 173–177
conceptualization, 172–173
criteria, 171–172
overview, 169–171, 189–190
treatment, 177–189
engagement and assessment, 178–183
exposure and maintenance, 187–189
skill building and restructuring, 183–187

Ideation, partial intrusive, post-traumatic stress disorder, 215
Ierulli, K., 64
Imagery, post-traumatic stress disorder, 200–201, 205–209
Imaginary dialogue, modification of core cognitive schemata, 29–30
Integrative cognitive therapy, 391–408
case example, 401–407
described, 392–395

overview, 391–392
technical implications, 395–401
theoretical implications, 395
utility of, 463–465
Intervention
resistance, 71–72
selection of, case formulation model, 47–49
Intervention point selection, case formulation model, 46–47
Introjects, post-traumatic stress disorder and, 199

Jacobson, E., 184
Jacobson, N. S., 250, 256, 410, 411
Jaffe, J. H., 221
Jensen, J. P., 369
John, X., 335
Johnson, M. K., 331
Johnson, V. E., 278

Kaplan, H. S., 278
Karg, R. S., 5
Karno, M., 151
Kaslow, F. W., 251
Kelley, H. H., 253
Kelly, J. A., 343, 358
Kendall, P. C., 336
King, S. M., 132
Kingdon, D. G., 321, 334
Klein, D. F., 109, 114
Kosten, T. R., 221
Kozak, M. J., 195, 196
Kroger, W. S., 34
Krokoff, L. J., 255

Lang, P. J., 132
Layden, M. A., 297
Lazarus, A. A., 278
Lazarus, R. S., 126
Leahy, R. L., 5, 17, 64, 455, 459, 460
Leslie, L. A., 413
Lester, G. W., 411, 412
Levy, M., 230
Liberman, R. P., 317, 410
Liebowitz, M. R., 109
Linehan, M. M., 50
Liotti, G., 154, 455, 456, 459
Lipman, A. J., 336
Looming vulnerability model, generalized anxiety disorder, 130–132
LoPiccolo, J., 278, 281
Lowe, C. F., 315, 320, 321, 322, 329

MacLeod, C., 128
Madanes, C., 410
Maddux, J., 132
Mahoney, M., 456
Maisto, S. A., 37
Malan, D. H., 392, 395
Margolin, G., 256, 410, 411
Marital conflict, 249–275. See also Family therapy
  affective factors, 258–259
  assessment, 251–252
  behavioral factors, 253–257
  case example, 259–267
  cognitive factors, 257–258
  outcomes, 271
  overview, 249–251, 271–272
  treatment, 267–270

cognitive restructuring, 269–270
communication skill training, 268
problem-solving skill training, 269
Markman, H. J., 255, 256
Marks, I. M., 63
Marlatt, G. A., 229
Marton, K. I., 190
Masters, W. H., 278
Mastery imagery, post-traumatic stress disorder, 206–208
Mathews, A., 125, 128, 131
Mavissakalian, M., 177
McCrady, B. S., 249
McGinn, L. K., 458
McMullin, R. E., 184
Meichenbaum, D. A., 21, 22, 178, 194
Memory
  modification of, modification of core cognitive schemata, 32–33
  post-traumatic stress disorder, 196–197
  review of, modification of core cognitive schemata, 30–31
Mercier, M. A., 5
Miller, J. G., 320, 331, 334
Miller, W. R., 345
Minuchin, S., 410
Miranda, J., 454
Moore, B. E., 201
Morrill, C. M., 412
Morrison, A. P., 315, 325, 326
Munson, C. E., 411, 412

Nelson, R. O., 38
Nesse, R. N., 62
Newman, C. F., 230
Niaura, R. S., 221
Niederee, J. L., 197, 205, 208
Nolen-Hoeksema, S., 460
Norcross, J. C., 18
North, C. S., 194
Notarius, C. I., 255

Object relations theory, post-
    traumatic stress disorder
    and, 199
Obsessive-compulsive disorder,
    151–168
  behavioral model of, 152–153
  case example, 154–166
    exposure and response
      prevention phase,
      157–159
    history, 154–156
    preparation phase, 156–157
    schema-focused therapy
      phase, 159–166
  clinical presentation, 152
  cognitive models of, 153–154
  overview, 151–152, 166–167
Obstacles, case formulation
    model, 43
O'Leary, K. D., 256
Onken, L. S., 222
Origins, case formulation model,
    41–42
Outcomes
  depression, cognitive therapy
    of, 104–105

generalized anxiety disorder,
    124–126, 145
  marital conflict, 271
  physical disability, 385–387
  substance abuse, 243–244

Pace, T. M., 23
Padesky, C. A., 411
Panic disorder, 107–122
  case example, 110–121
    assessment, 112–114
    history, 111–112
    presentation, 110–111
    treatment course, 114–121
    treatment selection, 114
  described, 107–109
  treatment approaches,
    109–110
Parsons, B. V., 411
Partial intrusive ideation, post-
    traumatic stress disorder,
    215
Patterson, G. R., 409, 410
Perelson, A. S., 344
Persons, J. B., 17, 37, 38, 57,
    454, 462
Physical disability, 373–389
  case example, 382–388
    history, 383–384
    intervention and outcome,
      385–387
    treatment plan, 385
  cognitive-behavioral model,
    374–380
  cognitive distortions, 380–382
  overview, 373–374
Piaget, J., 23, 195, 455

Pilowsky, I., 172
Portfolio theory
  depressive portfolios, 64–65
  resistance, 75–79
Post-traumatic stress disorder,
    193–220
  attachment theory and,
    198–199
  cognitive conceptualization,
    194–198
  cognitive processing, primary
    and secondary, 201–202
  imagery, 200–201
  object relations theory and,
    199
  symptomatology, 193–194
  treatment, 202–218
    goals, 203–204
    homework, 209–210
    imaginal exposure, 205–206
    initial interview, 202–203
    mastery imagery, 206–208
    of peripheral symptoms,
      210–215
    processing and debriefing,
      209
    rationale presentation,
      204–205
    self-nurturing imagery,
      208–209
    subjective units of distress
      (SUDs), 205
  Type I versus Type II events,
    194
Power, K. G., 125
Precipitants, case formulation
  model, 41

Pretzer, J. L., 257
Primary cognitive processing,
  post-traumatic stress disorder, 201–202
Problem list, case formulation
  model, 39–40
Problem-solving skill training,
  marital conflict, 269
Prochaska, J. O., 230, 345, 348,
  364
Psychotic disorders, 315–339
  assessment, 316–318
  clinical picture, 319–320
  cognitive therapy for, 315
  collaboration and self concept,
    326–329
  metacognition and resistance,
    329–330
  overview, 334–336
  perception and attention dis-
    turbances, 324–326
  perspective-taking, 330–334
  thought content disturbances,
    320–322
  thought process disturbances,
    322–324

Rachman, S. J., 132, 195
Rapee, R. M., 108, 113
Raye, C. I., 331
Reingold, H., 132, 133
Relapse
  HIV risk behavior, 364–368
  substance abuse, 235–236
Replacement, modification of
  core cognitive schemata,
  27–28

Resistance, 61–84
  to change, 73–75
  cognitive therapy, 459–460
  depression as adaptation,
    62–64
  depressive portfolios, 64–65
  depressive risk management,
    65–66
  interventions, 71–72
  overview, 61–62, 81–83
  portfolio theory, 75–79
  self-handicapping overcome,
    79–81
  self-handicapping strategies,
    67–71
Restructuring, hypochondriasis,
  183–187
Revenstorf, D., 255
Rholes, W. S., 127
Riskind, J. H., 124, 127, 131, 132,
  134, 135, 136
Rollnick, S., 345
Rosen, H., 23
Rotheram-Borus, M. J., 358
Russell, M. C., 176
Russell, T., 412

Safran, J., 455, 460
Salkovskis, P. M., 116, 151, 153
Sanders, M. R., 410
Sanderson, W. C., 124
Satir, V., 410
Schemas, assumptions and
  automatic thoughts
  related, 10
Schiff, W., 132
Schindler, L., 411

Schizophrenia. See Psychotic
  disorders
Schlesinger, S. E., 414
Schweber, A. I., 415, 441
Secondary cognitive processing,
  post-traumatic stress dis-
  order, 201–202
Segal, Z., 455, 460
Self-handicapping
  overcoming of, 79–81
  resistance, 67–71
Self-limitation. See Resistance
Self-nurturing imagery, post-
  traumatic stress disorder,
  208–209
Seligman, M. E. P., 370
Sexual dysfunction, 277–294
  case example, 283–293
  overview, 277–280
  treatment issues, 280–283
Shapiro, D. A., 104
Shea, M. T., 90
Skill building, hypochondriasis,
  183–187
Smith, W. H., 31
Smucker, M. R., 195, 197, 205, 208
Snyder, C. R., 325
Snyder, D. K., 251
Sobell, L. C., 221
Spaulding, W. D., 316
Stamm, B., 203
Steiner, C. M., 282
Steketee, G. S., 151, 152, 153, 154
Stuart, R. B., 256, 409
Subjective units of distress
  (SUDs), post-traumatic
  stress disorder, 205

Substance abuse, 221–245
  case example, 232–244
    background and diagnosis,
      232–233
    denial confrontation,
      236–243
    initial sessions, 233–235
    outcome, 243–244
    relapse signs, 235–236
  cognitive model, 224–229
  cognitive therapy, 222–223
  denial, 230–232
  diagnostic issues, 223–224
  overview, 221–222
Sweetland, J. D., 373
Swendson, J., 375

Tarrier, N., 324, 334
Teasdale, J. D., 176
Teichman, Y., 412, 413
Terr, L. C., 194
Therapy-interfering behavior,
  case formulation model,
  50–51
Thibaut, J. W., 253
Tomassi, M., 64
Tompkins, M. A., 38
Torrey, E. F., 319, 323
Transferential issues, cognitive
  therapy, 460–461
Trause, M. A., 133
Treatment plan, case formulation
  model, 42–43
Turkat, I. D., 37
Turkewitz, H., 256

Turkington, D., 321, 334, 335
Turvey, A. A., 125

van der Hart, O., 196, 200
van der Kolk, B. A., 196, 200
van Oppen, P., 151, 153
Vardi, D. J., 197
Volberding, P. A., 343
Vollmer, M., 411
Vurploot, E., 132

Wachtel, P. L., 363
Wahl, O., 132, 135
Wasylenski, D. A., 330
Waters, E., 198, 199
Watts, F. N., 330
Weerts, T. C., 132
Wegner, D. M., 153
Weishaar, M., 323
Weiss, R. L., 253, 258, 411
Wenegrat, B., 63
Westby, G. W. M., 132
Williams, G. C., 62
Wilson, R., 156
Wolpe, J., 277
Woody, G. E., 224
Working hypothesis, case
  formulation model, 42
Wright, J. H., 412, 415

Young, J. E., 25, 26, 29, 90, 100,
  455, 458, 459, 460

Zeeve, C., 412
Zilbergeld, B., 281
Zoellner, L. A., 249